Currier's Price Guide To AMERICAN ARTISTS 1645-1945 AT AUCTION

Current Price Ranges On

Of Over Nearly 7000 American Artists At Auction

1988 Edition

Revised and Updated With Over 500 Additional Artists

Written and Compiled by William T. Currier

Foreword by Robert W. Holmes, Jr., Esq.

CURRIER PUBLICATIONS

BROCKTON, MA 02403

ISBN 0-935277-05-6 Softcover
Library of Congress
Catalog Card Number 88-70305

Printed in the United States of America

COVER PHOTO:

Frosty Morning, Jamaica, Vermont, **Aldro Hibbard**, Oil on Canvas, 28" x 36", Courtesy of Vose Gallaries of Boston, Inc.

Additional copies of this book may be obtained from bookstores and selected antique dealers. To order directly from the publisher, remit $14.95 per copy, plus $2.75 shipping(book rate),or $3.75(first class). Massachusetts addresses add 5% sales tax. For bulk order discounts (5 or more copies) please write, or call, for details to:

TO:
CURRIER PUBLICATIONS
P.O. Box 2098S
Brockton, MA 02403
(617) 588-4509

[Make check or money order payable to CURRIER PUBLICATIONS]

ACKNOWLEDGEMENTS

Many thanks for assistance with this 1988 Edition go out to:

Cynthia Tukis, for her expertise and valuable assistance in preparation of the final copy.

Vose Galleries of Boston, Inc. for providing many of the photographs in this book, and to Terri Vose in particular,a special thanks, for his warm reception into the Gallery, and his enthusiastic willingness to help me select appropriate photographs for the book. It is refreshing to have gallery personnel who make you feel at home.

Judy Goffman American Paintings, New York, for taking, from her hectic schedule, the time to edit the list of over 300 illustrators that I submitted to her, and for providing photographs for the content of the book.

The additional galleries or auction houses who contributed photos for the content of the book:

Richard A. Bourne Co., Inc., auction gallery, Hyannis, Massachusetts

Philip C. Shute, Inc.,auction gallery, West Bridgewater, Massachusetts

Henry B. Holt, American 19th and 20th Century Paintings, Montville, New Jersey

Each and every one of the hundreds of individuals who took time during the past year to send in corrections and additions of which we would, otherwise, have never been aware. Their contributions helped to make this *Guide* more accurate and ultimately more useful.

Frank Miele of *Hirschl and Adler Folk*, New York, and Jay Johnson of *America's Folk Heritage Gallery*, New York, for contributing their special talents to my *Guide* by editing the prices of artists in their specialty area, American folk art.

Robert W. Holmes, Jr., attorney for *Powers and Hall*, Boston, for his foreword, which is an invaluable contribution to the content of this *Guide*.

My parents, Lillian and William, for their encouragement and support - as always.

My sister Sandra for her inspirational words and her unerring faith in me.

Mike and Linda Joy for their invaluable assistance in keeping my projects accurate and on schedule.

My wife, Donna, her mother, Lorraine, and my daughter,Danielle, who from the beginning, all supported me, encouraged me, and showed, most of all, understanding. They sacrificed so much every day, every evening, every weekend, month after month, to make each new edition possible. I thank you especially, with love.

William T. Currier

To Mom, Dad, and Lorraine

About The Author, Contributors, and Consultants

William T. Currier

William T. Currier, a graduate of Boston University, has been an educator with the Boston Public Schools for over fifteen years. Although his knowledge of art history was not acquired through a "formal" education in art history, he spent thousands of hours during the past twenty years in intense independent study of both art history and the art market. Mr.Currier has been a guest speaker at adult education classes, lecturing on identifying original prints and paintings, and has attended many lectures and professional seminars on art history and art investment. He is presently president of *Currier Publications*, a division of Currier's Fine Art, a member of The New England Appraisers Association, and also works privately as an agent, market liaison, consultant, and dealer.

Robert W. Holmes, Jr., Esq

The *foreword* was contributed by Robert W. Holmes, Jr., an attorney with *Powers & Hall, Professional Corporation* in Boston. A graduate of Harvard College and Boston University Law School, Mr. Holmes has been practicing law since 1970 and has dealt extensively in cases involving fine art transactions. He is general counsel for the *Artists Foundation* of Massachusetts, has lectured at various seminars and meetings on the legal aspects of fine art transactions, and is a legal consultant to many art dealers, galleries, collectors, and artists.

Karl Gabosh

Since the 1970's, Karl Gabosh, from Princeton, Massachusetts, has been a specialist in American paintings (American marine paintings, the White Mountain School, still life, and expatriate painters). His particular interest has been in the research and authentication of unsigned and previously unknown works in those areas.

Mr. Gabosh has recently published *The Collectors Blacklight Guide*

- a structured introduction to long wave ultra-voilet (blacklight) examination, and is awaiting the publication of an article, in the *Magazine Antiques*, on New Hampshire painter, William P. Phelps.

Frank Miele and Jay Johnson

Because of the great number of Americana sales around the country each year, the prices realized for fine examples of American folk art (i.e., 18th, 19th, and 20th century works) are the hardest to compile. Very qualified to quote the prices realized at these numerous sales are the folk art experts, Frank Miele (18th and 19th century folk artists), and Jay Johnson (20th century folk artists).

Frank Miele has had over 25 years experience as a folk art collector and dealer. He is presently beginning his second successful year as director of the prestigious New York City gallery of *Hirschl and Adler Folk.* Mr. Miele is considered an authority on the work of 18th and 19th century American folk artists.

Jay Johnson, owner of *America's Folk Heritage Gallery* in New York City, is recognized as the leading American dealer and authority in the field of twentieth-century American folk art. He has written and lectured extensively on folk art and is personally acquainted with most of the major figures.

Judy Goffman

Judy Goffman, owner of Judy Goffman Fine Art of New York, N.Y., specializes in the sale and exhibition of fine paintings by leading American illustrators. Ms. Goffman's experience dates back over fifteen years. She began her career with a Bachelor of Arts, then a Masters degree, from the University of Pennsylvania. She has always maintained an active interest in the work of the finest American illustrators. She frequently loans work by well known American Illustrators to such prestigious institutions as the Brandywine Museum, The Society of Illustrators, and most recently, the Musee des Arts Decoratifs, Louvre, Paris.

Ms. Goffman is responsible for showcasing Norman Rockwell's work in two important exhibits over the past several years. During 1986 she organized a wonderful exhibit and sale of Norman Rockwell's work in an exhibit entitled *Norman Rockwell:An American Tradition.*

This year, Ms. Goffman was guest curator of the Mississippi Museum of Art's exhibition, *Norman Rockwell: The Great American Storyteller*. She was also invaluable in both arranging loans for this exhibit and writing the catalogue which accompanies the exhibition.

In the Kiva
by Frank E. Schoonover, oil on canvas, 29" x 38"
(Courtesy of Judy Goffman Fine Art, New York, NY)

Sharecroppers' Cabin
by William Aiken Walker, oil on canvas, 6" x 12"
(Courtesy of Henry B. Holt, Montville, NJ)

TABLE OF CONTENTS

Chapter Two: Using This Guide

American Artists At Auction

Record Prices

Appendix

FOREWORD

The author of this *Guide*, William Currier, has asked me to point out some legal concerns relating to art transactions. With heightened interest in American paintings, price increases have been unprecedented. Market conditions have spawned a variety of legal complications.

Many dealers, collectors, and fiduciaries seem to be unaware of formalities that apply generally to large commercial transactions. Others may be aware but, for some reason, feel that they do not apply to fine art. There is a tendency in the trade to rely upon informal practices, which may have been workable in the past when less was at risk, but which are inappropriate in today's market. Fine art transactions often take place with little or no documentation. Amazingly, it is commonplace that no attention whatsoever is given to basic legal considerations which would not be overlooked in routine matters of equivalent value, such as buying a house or taking out a bank loan.

Collectors and dealers often allow valuable pieces to go out on approval without obtaining anything in writing. Then they close the sale by accepting a down payment and the buyer's oral agreement to pay the balance over a period of time. Such a transaction is a loan and should be supported at least by a bill of sale and promissory note. Both the seller and the buyer need to document the purchase price, payment terms and rate of interest so that later misunderstandings will be avoided and enforceable rights will be created. In instances where buyers default, sellers usually seek to recover their property. This can be difficult, at best, unless the seller has a perfected security interest, which means even more documentation. If the buyer is insolvent, an unsecured seller probably will have to wait in line with other general creditors, such as utilities and credit card companies, and may recover only a fraction of the debt owed.

Liens and title problems are a major source of concern in fine art transactions. Other than the *Uniform Commercial Code* (which covers certain secured liens) there is generally no public recording system in which to search title such as there is for real estate. The best one can do is to review whatever documentation the seller may have relating to the background of the piece. This can be a fruitless endeavor, because, as previously stated, pieces frequently change hands without any documentation whatsoever. If possible, try to obtain confirmation of title from prior owners. In addition, a check should be made for *Uniform Commercial Code* fillings, federal tax liens and bankruptcy petitions. If the sale is by a partner or by a fiduciary (such as, an executor or trustee), check for their authority to act in the transaction. If the sale is by a corporation, it may be necessary to obtain other documentation, such as, an attested copy of a director's or shareholders' vote of the corporation authorizing the sale. If the sale involves several pieces, perhaps all of the corporation's assets, other serious corporate, tax and bulk sales considerations arise.

Aside from the technical problems briefly highlighted above, stolen works are offered for sale frequently enough to warrant extreme caution. Particularly affected are paintings that do not receive extensive publicity. Prints, maps and other antique graphics also have been stolen in massive quantities from museums and libraries. Items even disappear from grandmother's attic. Generally, an unauthorized conversion of property cannot result in clear title. The buyer must beware. Title insurance, such as for real estate, is generally not available for art. Again, checking out the background of a piece can save you a lot of heartache.

Forgery is another real problem that should not be underestimated. Materials for signature forgery (unfinished works, studies, student copies) are available at large in many areas. In addition, complete and well executed forgeries are in circulation. Reputable dealers evaluate the authenticity of paintings and offer them for sale accordingly. Be alert to other sellers who market pieces of dubious authenticity for lack of training, judgement or ethical standards. If possible, get a piece evaluated in advance of the purchase and obtain some written warranty or certificate of authenticity. Often this will not be possible. The next best thing is to get the piece evaluated as soon as possible after purchase. You may have certain rights under the *Uniform Commercial Code* and other laws which will be lost if you do not act promptly. Obviously, the safest course is not to buy from unknown sources at all. Deal with reputable people who have been in the business and who have assets and character to back up their mistakes.

Finally, consignments of fine art pose a variety of difficulties. Placing a valuable piece in the hands of a consignee/dealer creates serious risks and should not be taken lightly. In many cases, dealers are free to convey title to good faith purchasers, notwithstanding the fact that they may be violating their consignor's instructions as to price, credit terms and the like. This is yet another reason to deal only with reputable firms. Always know who has your piece and where it is. When in doubt, retain possession of a work or demand its return.

The foregoing is intended only as a superficial and selective discussion of complicated issues. As a rule of thumb, maintain a high level of vigilance and do not take a risk that is unacceptable in view of a potential loss. Certain laws are available to protect some of your rights but only if you adhere to their requirements. Other areas of law are not so clear. You do not want to be the test case. Attention to details and proper documentation will help to avoid these pitfalls.

Boston, Massachusetts, 1988
Robert W. Holmes, Jr., Esq.
Powers & Hall
Professional Corporation

New York, Winter
by Guy Wiggins, oil on canvas, 25" x 30"
(Courtesy of Vose Galleries of Boston, Inc., Boston, MA)

The Sentinels
by Paul Sample, oil on board, 24" x 36"
(Courtesy of Vose Galleries of Boston, Inc., Boston, MA)

PREFACE

Until the publication of our *Guide* there was no other practical reference available in an inexpensive, compact, concise and portable format that could help quickly assess the probable worth of fine examples of American art from the 18th , 19th, and 20th centuries. It is invaluable to: antique dealers, auctioneers, art collectors, estate lawyers, bank trust officers, art consultants, appraisers, and art dealers. *Currier's Price Guide to American Artists 1645-1945 at Auction* may well be the most profitable investment that anyone, who has occasion to buy and sell American art, could ever make.

You will find that you have purchased the most practical price guide to 300 years of American art [artists born 1645-1945] available today. The compilation of data here will be useful to even the most seasoned veteran of the American art marketplace:

- Accurate spellings of artists' names.
- Accurate birth and death dates not easily found elsewhere.
- A "mnemonic" (meaning to assist the memory) list of subject matter typical for each artist "value prioritized" - the most sought-after subjects for each artist are listed first.
- Current, accurate price ranges (compiled from thousands of auction results over the past eighteen years) for America's most sought-after artists.

As accurate as the 1987 Edition was, and as well received as it was, this 1988 Edition has many exciting improvements:

- An important foreword written by Boston attorney Robert W. Holmes, Jr. stating his views on legal pitfalls inherent in some art transactions.

- To continually assure the greatest accuracy, nationally known dealers have agreed to edit the price ranges of those artists sold at auction in their specialty area:

    - **Frank Miele**, the American folk artists of the 18th and 19th century.
    - **Jay Johnson**, the American folk artists of the 20th century.
    - **Karl Gabosh**, the American marine artists.
    - **Judy Goffman**, the American illustrators.

- Over 1000 changes were made in this 1988 Edition. The updated price ranges reflect sales results from over 200 auction houses thru January 1988.

- During the 1987 auction season, there was unprecedented movement upward in the prices realized for hundreds of American artists, especially American contemporary artists. Some have risen dramatically from the hundreds to the thousands of dollars. Users of this *Guide* will certainly want to be aware of those changes.

- We have added over 500 additional American artists.

- We corrected some misspelled names, added birth and death dates where there were none, and added, or made changes to, the *typical subjects* of numerous artists.

- We expanded the *Record Prices* section from 233 artists to over 290 artists.

- There is a revised *Appendix* which reflects changes to information found in the 1987 Edition, and includes new information.

- There are new and additional illustrations.

Since the publication of our first edition, we have received hundreds of calls and letters from people from all parts of the country. Without exception, all comments regarding the book's usefulness have been positive ones. With the 1987 Edition, each trade review that we received was a positive one. Art collectors, art dealers, appraisers, and many others found our *Guide* continually useful for *quickly* checking the auction record of the many American artists they encountered every month.

Many auctioneers would use the price ranges to help establish a starting bid on works of artists with whom they were unfamiliar, or help screen items for possible consignment.

Art collectors found the *Guide* extremely interesting and especially helpful when hunting for artists whose work falls only within certain price ranges (e.g., 500-7500) and/or who specialize in certain subjects (e.g., marines, landscapes, still life etc.). Many collectors reported that they would keep a copy with them as they frequented yard sales, flea markets, thrift shops, or country auctions. Not infrequently, many "sleepers" were uncovered.

Appraisers used the *Guide* to quickly find what the highest price realized at auction had been on a particular artist's work. They used this information as a starting point, then proceeded to do further research of the actual auction results. For appraisers, knowing the highest price realized at auction for the work of a particular artist will help avoid the chance of being penalized by the IRS for overvaluation.

Estate lawyers working with appraisers find it beneficial to know the *least* amount certain works by a particular artist have sold for, so they can justify a low valuation for estate tax purposes.

Because of information gleaned from our *Guide*, many estate executors have pursued a professional appraisal on certain works of art. It would not be unusual for someone running an estate "tag sale" to price something **well** below its true market value.

Antique dealers, who have occasion to buy and sell American art, but who have very little knowledge of the art market have found our *Guide* to be one of the most important references books in their library. The *Guide* helps many dealers to avoid the problem of buying too high or selling too low. And helps them to *quickly* assess the *potential* value of American artwork in many situations: house calls, estate sales, etc. Dealers can quickly determine if a recent purchase needs more research before pricing it for resale. Obviously, if a dealer purchased a large landscape, signed David Johnson, at a yard sale for $100, and he found in our *Guide* that the highest price realized for the artist's work exceeds $35,000, he'd want to have it examined by an "expert"(more on that in Chapter One.)

One financial consultant for a major Boston firm forwarded a letter stating that our *Guide* would "prove to be very helpful in my efforts to help my clients fulfill their financial goals" and added, "a person could have a fortune in artwork and not even realize it. A quick look in your guide and one can tell if there is a need for further investigation."

Recently, one important dealer in American paintings,Henry B. Holt, forwarded to us the following letter which sums up quite well the *Guide's* purpose and usefulness.

> *I recently realized how very valuable I have found "Currier's Guide" and felt compelled to write to you. I keep a copy in each of my offices and ordinarily carry one in my car. This weekend, I was called out to look at some paintings and found that I didn't have my "Currier's" with me. Because a few of the artists were somewhat obscure, the Guide really would have come in handy. I have found "Currier's Guide"to be indispensable in such cases. Compact, concise, accurate, dependable! I can't imagine any collector, appraiser, or dealer's library would be complete without "Currier's Guide", since it provides a valuable insight on the price range based on auction records of so many artists, as well as many other useful and informative sidelights. My compliments on a job well done.*

Add to the list, the many thrift shop owners, pickers, museum personnel, art framers, and yard sale and flea market fanatics who find our *Guide* useful; and you can only agree that *Currier's Price Guide to American Artists 1645-1945 at Auction* is the ***first*** place to look for values on American artists.

One final note: You are welcome and encouraged to comment, make note of errors, and feel free to suggest changes or additions which will improve this guide. Please write or call:

CURRIER PUBLICATIONS
William T. Currier
P.O. Box 2098-A
Brockton, MA 02403

(617) 588-4509
TELEX: 4941988 (CURRIER)

DISCLAIMER

Although every attempt, within reason, has been made to keep the price ranges herein as accurate as possible, there may be mistakes, both typographical and in content. Therefore, this guide should be used only as a general guide, not as the final, or ultimate, source of the only prices which may be realized at auction by any particular artist.

Special care must be exercised when examining the prices of contemporary artists. Because of the "dynamic" nature of the market as a whole, prices can rise and fall quickly. With living artists, it is best to check with those galleries that represent them for the "final" word on current values. Prices charged in the galleries for the works of living artists can be many times those realized at auction.

Also, the compilation of recommended conservators, auction houses and private galleries in the *Appendix* is only a representative sampling of the hundreds of other conservators, auction houses and private galleries which I am sure may be of equal distinction.

The author and *Currier Publications* shall have neither liability nor responsibility to any person with respect to any loss or damage caused or alleged to be caused directly or indirectly by the information contained in this book.

CHAPTER ONE

Determining Value

Please Note: **Two assumptions are made throughout this Guide: that you are a novice in the art marketplace, and that we will always be talking about prices at fair market value (i.e., auction results).**

Until your work of art is sold, it has no real value (unlike stocks); only a subjective value based on many factors. No one can guarantee that your piece will bring a specified dollar amount at some future date. Factors influencing the price of a work of art may vary and, for that reason, you can expect a different price at each new auction. Let's look briefly at some of the direct factors and outside influences which, the author feels, most dramatically affect price.

Seven Important Factors

ARTIST The most important factor. When we can prove who the artist is, whether or not the piece is signed, it will most directly influence the price realized. Almost without exception, the first question you will get from any major auction house, or dealer, when you call them to look for price information, will be: "Who is the artist?" Once the name is known, everything else follows: "What's the subject matter?", "What's the condition?", etc.

If you buy a piece which is unsigned, but you have been told by the seller that it was painted by a well-known artist, obtaining a letter from an authority, which states without question that it is the particular artist the seller said it was, will help immensely in increasing its desirability and value.

Most would consider the signature to be exceedingly important. The truth is that it is of the very least value, until it can be proved without question that it is indeed the signature of the artist who painted the particular work.

Signatures can be added to an oil painting by anyone feeling it will increase its value. If you have a magnifying glass of at least 10-30x, examine the signature to be sure that "old" cracks running through the signature do indeed run through - that they are not filled with paint from a "recent" signature. If you suspect a forged signature, another way to check is to rub the signature gently with a little turpentine on a soft cloth - it will usually wash out a recent signature.

An authentic signature with a date is more desirable than one without.

MEDIUM There are many good books available which explain the peculiarities of the various mediums. The novice to the art market should endeavor to familiarize him/herself with several.

The most popular medium overall today is still oils. It should be mentioned that, in the case of many contemporary artists, mixed media is extremely popular - much to the chagrin of today's conservator. Also, with contemporary artists, it is their mixed media work which often brings the highest prices.

Try to remember, that the price ranges in this *Guide* which begin with an asterisk (*) denote: mixed media, watercolors, gouaches, pastels, and/or pencil and ink drawings. With such a variety of mediums, you can expect a price range often to start in the hundreds (for drawings) and end in the hundreds of thousands of dollars (for contemporary mixed media.) Don't be mislead, though, in thinking all drawings will be of least value - *there are exceptions.* A drawing which is a preparatory study for a painting, which today is historically important, can have great value. For example, an ink and watercolor drawing by Benjamin West, a study for the painting, *The Death of General Wolfe*, sold at Sotheby's (5/84) for $165,000.

QUALITY Without question, the most exceptional pieces, regarding quality, in any medium, by any artist, will bring exceptionally high prices. Every dealer will tell you that he has no problem quickly moving the pieces of the highest quality.

The work of a much sought-after artist will only bring a meager price, if it is of meager quality. Artists are human, of course, and have their good and bad days.

During an artist's lifetime, his/her work could have evolved through several style changes, and within each style change works of varying quality can be found. The months or years which represent a particular style change are called "periods." It may happen that a small work of great quality, from a much sought-after earlier,or later period, will be of more value than a much larger work from some other "period" which is not highly sought after.

At the end of the alphabetical listings in this *Guide*, is a separate section entitled: *Record Prices*. Those prices represent values realized for works which were considered of exceptional quality. They had to be isolated, because the prices were well above the high end of all other works by that artist, and to include them would have distorted a "true" picture of the normal price range of that artist's work.

There are many factors which the novice can consider in determining a "probable" value of a fine painting, but judging quality, style, and period is best left up to the "expert": university scholar, museum curator, art dealer, certain art consultants, qualified appraiser, or some independent author or connoisseur.

SUBJECT In a broad sense, this is the main theme of a work of art. In a narrower vein, it is the "subject matter" within the subject that can affect value. As an example, the subject of a painting might be a still life, but its "subject matter" might be dead game birds. The subject of another painting might be marine, and the "subject matter," a coastal harbor scene.

Most artists have one or two subjects for which they are best known. These particular subjects are the ones most sought after and bring the highest prices (see the section on Typical Subjects in Chapter 2 for a list with an explanation.) Robert Spear Dunning is best known for his still life; John George Brown is best known as a painter of genre, etc. Knowing the subject(s) most sought after for any particular artist is very important for you in determining the *potential* value of a piece. I have done most of that work for you in this *Guide* - more on that in Chapter 2.

After attending a number of art auctions, you will begin to

note which subjects and subject matter are most and least desirable. In general, collectors today want bright colorful, non-offensive pieces for their walls. Let's look more closely at our subjects:

Figures: Studio portraits, with the exception of early folk portraits (see Primitives below), and historical figures, hold very little interest among collectors, unless done by a well- known artist. The most desirable figure paintings are those in a non-studio setting, e.g., groups of people in an interior or outdoor setting. Collectors often prefer women and children over men in both portraits and figure studies. Religious figures are not very popular, unless they are old master paintings. To certain collectors, the nude figure is desirable. Western figures are presently very popular, as are many Arabian, and Orientalist figure paintings.

Genre: Themes which can be considered genre probably number in the thousands. Some of the more popular themes might be: a public fete, a friendly conversation, the comedies of the household, or the little dramas of private life.

Illustrations: Because of the scope of this subject and the endless variety of both subject matter and mediums, it is very difficult to point out a most and least popular subject matter. If you have any questions about American illustrators it is best to talk to someone who specializes in American illustration. I would recommend contacting Judy Goffman who is a leading authority on American illustration. Her address can be found in the *Appendix*.

Landscapes: Collectors today prefer bright,colorful landscapes with identifiable landmarks - especially if the landmarks have local interest. Of the four seasons, winter scenes seem to draw the most attention. Landscapes with a "luminous" quality are popular. American scenes are usually more desirable than European scenes by the same artist.

Marines:

Collectors of marine subjects can be very particular about their ship portraits. The rigging, the position of the sails, the flags that are being flown, and many other details can affect the desirability of a marine painting. American vessels, flying American flags, are always more desirable than foreign. From my own observations, the old sidewheelers and clipper ships under full sail enjoy considerable popularity. As with landscapes, collectors prefer coastal scenes in which there is an identifiable landmark - such as, a familiar lighthouse. Again, local interest increases value.

Primitives:

Very little of the early folk art is undesirable; nearly all examples are eagerly collected. However, pieces in very poor condition, or poorly restored are an exception and attract little interest. With primitives, it is best to sell them "as is," rather them having them restored. Collectors usually have their own conservator to whom they entrust their new acquisitions, and prefer no previous restoration.

Still Life:

All types of still life are collected, from our earliest primitives to today's paintings of photographic realism. Floral pieces today are enjoying popularity, as are elaborate fruit and vegetable compositions. The "grander" the composition, the greater the value. When objects which are not essential to it are introduced into a composition, they are known as accessories and can often add interest and value to a still life.

Wildlife:

Scenes with an abundance of blood will be least desirable and farm yard fowl don't enjoy much popularity. Of all the animals around the farm, horses are the most popular with collectors. Deer are always popular, if not shown being shot, and most hunting and fishing scenes will attract buyers, if there is no blood and gore.

STYLE Sir Joshua Reynolds (1723-1792) said,"In painting, style is the same as in writing: some are grand, others plain; some florid and others simple." Styles can be peculiar to a "school," or a master, in design, composition, coloring, expression, and execution, but not necessarily peculiar to the artist. In many instances, artists have changed their personal styles several times during their lifetime. As stated earlier, each new style change is considered a new period. Some periods, or styles, are more sought after than others because of a greater appeal. Leading the list would be the work of the American Impressionists.

When you're assessing the "probable" value of a painting, it may be necessary to let an "expert" determine the style of the work (see "Quality" above.)

CONDITION Although "condition" seems a long way down on our list of "factors determining value," it is really the one variable to which we must pay the most attention. No matter who the artist is, a painting in very poor condition, or one that has been heavily restored, will have very little value - at best, a fraction of the worth of a similar painting in pristine condition.

Before you buy a painting on canvas in need of conservation, consider the following:

- After you spend anywhere from $100-$1500 for the cost of restoration, will you be able to realize a profit?

- Are you willing to tie that painting up for what may take as long as six months?

- If there is paint loss, is any of it in critical areas which will affect value? For instance, you do not want the paint to be falling away from the faces and bodies of people in a figure painting.

- Is the overall paint loss greater than 25% ? If so, unless the painting is extremely valuable, pass on it!

- Besides restoration, will the painting need an appropriate frame to make it saleable - another expense?

- Is the painting covered with a very dark layer of dirt and varnish? Only a professional conservator will be able to ascertain if that painting will "clean up." If she/he says definitely not, you may never see a profit.

- Has the painting already had any "bad" restoration?

- The cost of restoration can be very high if the conservator has to do a relining and extensive "inpainting" in addition to a cleaning. Relinings are often necessary when the canvas is extremely wrinkled, torn, abraded, or too loose and floppy. Inpainting is an expensive and involved process of repainting damaged areas to their original condition.

Remember: Though cleaning may be useful to restore the original brilliance of an old painting - though relining is sometimes needed to save it from imminent destruction - to let it be attempted by a non-professional is a sacrilege. ***Always make sure that the conservator has an impeccable reputation for quality work***. Also, *never* use water to clean a painting - leave it alone until an expert can look at it.

To assist you in finding a conservator, I have compiled a representative list from around the country and abroad and have included it in the *Appendix* of this *Guide*. Your best source for a reputable conservator is the recommendation of an art museum or prestigious art gallery. Some of the latter are also listed in the *Appendix* - see if there is one near you.

For those of you who are only vaguely familiar with the use of a blacklight for assistance in finding previous restorations, added signatures, etc., and wish to become more "expert" in its use, there is information available. This past year, Karl Gabosh, who edited the price ranges of our American marine painters, assembled a guide, complete with samples and text, entitled: *The Collector's Blacklight Guide*. It is an important tool for the serious art dealer, collector, and others.

To obtain more information on the *The Collector's Blacklight Guide*, or to order directly please remit (Massachusetts addresses add a 5% sales tax) $35.00 per copy to:

Karl Gabosh
P.O. Box 142
Princeton, MA 01541

• *Please mention us when you write!* •

SIZE All it will take is one afternoon at an art auction to see that there is a definite correlation between size and price. This relation holds true only among paintings by the same artist, and among paintings that are similar in subject matter, quality, and style.

You may never hear of a painting that is too small to be desirable, but you will likely hear of a painting being too big to be desirable. When a painting is larger than sofa size, you will find that your buying audience has shrunk considerably. Of course, there could be exceptions to this, in cases where the artist is an eminent American master.

Outside Influences On Value

As discussed above, when you purchase a painting for resale, there are inherent factors (e.g., artist, size, medium, condition, quality, subject, style) which can be quickly ascertained for determining an approximate value. There are other outside influences (e.g., historical importance, provenance, time and location of sale, competitive bidding, publicity and fads) which can have a positive or negative affect on value. Let's take a brief look at each.

HISTORICAL IMPORTANCE All preparatory studies (drawings, watercolors, oil sketches, etc.) for any major historical American painting can be valuable. If you find, while researching your artist, that he/she painted many historically important paintings, check your piece or have an "expert" check your piece, to determine if it could be an important preparatory study. The likelihood of finding an actual canvas which is a major historical painting is slim. Most are either in museums, historical societies, or private corporate collections. Don't expect to find one in someone's attic next month.

PROVENANCE Provenance is simply a list of previous owners, analogous to a pedigree. It can be important to some collectors;

not so important to others. Provenance works in reverse, for example, the present owner is listed first, the previous owner is listed second, and so on, until we are back, ideally, to the artist himself. This line of ownership can make the piece very desirable, particularly if the list has some important names on it. But there can be a problem since we sometimes have no way of checking the authenticity of a particular document. Most of the people on the list may be deceased, and therefore, not available to vouch for their prior ownership of the piece in question.

A provenance is not at all necessary to transact a sale, but if you have supportable evidence that the provenance is unquestionably genuine, then it can be even more important than the signature on the piece.

Sometimes, you will find that names have been filled in to complete a gap in its provenance. Be careful. Always try to judge the piece first on its own merit as a fine work of art. If it turns out later that all the documentation included with it is authentic, then the value of the piece will increase immeasurably.

The topic of Provenance is closely related to a discussion of authentication. If you feel you have just bought an "important" painting and would like to have it properly authenticated, see the *Appendix* under "Appraisal Organizations" for a list of authentication services.

SELLING: TIME AND LOCATION OF SALE Some auction houses do better than others, selling the works of certain artists. It is valuable information to know at which auction house an artist continually commands the highest prices. Information of this type is not easily obtainable, unless you have been closely following the market all over the country. If you have a "potentially" valuable painting, I might suggest that you contact some art consultants in your area, to see if they provide that service. If they do not, the author can help you. Please call or write to William Currier, *Currier Publications* (the address is included in the front of this book.)

The worst months of the year to sell at auction are in July and August. The best months to sell are April, May, June, October, November, December.

If you plan to send your art to auction at one of the major auction houses (a list can be found in the *Appendix*), and if you are in a hurry to see your money, then keep two things in mind:

1. From the day you send your piece to auction

until the day of the actual sale, two to five months may pass. Auction officials need that time to research all the paintings, determine estimates, do the presale advertising, and photograph most of the paintings in the sale for placement in a catalog, which goes out (at a price) to the patrons of the sale.

2.Many of the major auction houses do not send you your money (less commission) until 35-40 days after the sale.They wait for buyers' checks to clear. [*Please Note*: Some auction houses, such as Sotheby's, will advance you up to 100% of the low estimate on very important works of art. This *loan*, plus interest, will be subtracted from the net proceeds of the sale of your painting. When you are consigning your piece, inquire into the options available to you.]

Be aware that the work of certain artists may only sell at a high price if there is a large concentration of collectors in the close geographical area of that artist. One name which readily comes to mind is Ralph Cahoon (d.1982), who always does well at the Richard Bournes Auction Gallery, Hyannis, Massachusetts.

Many of the artists who sell in the $500-10,000 range will fare better at auctions in regions where they spent most of their lives painting. The "home-town artist" will do best near his home-town; the big name artist will sell everywhere.

Before you ship your piece to auction, check the offers of dealers who specialize in work by your artist - you may get an offer you can't refuse.

COMPETITIVE BIDDING At almost every major auction there is a number of fine paintings which sell well above the estimates - much to the delight of the consignor. Competitive bidding can drive the price up well above estimate. All that is needed is two or more people who want that piece desperately enough, that it seems money is no object. In June of 1981, a Charles Sprague Pearce painting sold (with a pre-sale estimate of $10-15,000) for $247,500. Can you imagine how happy that consignor was!

PUBLICITY AND FADS The resale value of your work of

art will leap, if it has appeared as an illustration in one or more pieces of literature. If the work of art also has a well-documented exhibition record, that will increase its desirability.

Someone once said, "As New York goes,so goes the country." It often seems that what starts out popular and fashionable in New York, catches on elsewhere. If you get a chance to follow the market more closely each year, you'll be able to stay on top of what is currently "fashionable."

Thin Ice, Vermont
1987 Record Price for artist: $1320
by Jacob Greenleaf, oil on canvas, 20" x 24"
(Courtesy of Philip C. Shute, Inc. Auction Gallery, West Bridgewater, MA)

CHAPTER TWO

Using This Guide

An Overview

In the process of compiling the over 6000 names of artists, it was found that in many instances, the spelling of names was incorrect, or incomplete, with only initials and a surname, as they appeared in many of the auction house catalogs nationally. This was due in part, understandably, to the haste with which many of these artists were researched and then recorded in the catalog in time for the pre-sale promotion. The full and correct spelling of names was determined as accurately as possible by checking more than one dictionary of artists for each name. If no dates were available, the century during which that artist is known to have worked was placed next to the name.

The birth and death dates, when available, were researched for accuracy and recorded next to the name. In many instances, birth and death dates which could not be easily found elsewhere were recorded.

Price ranges and typical subject(s), "value prioritized" and listed, using mnemonic letters, were established by studying the sales record of each individual artist. Vast amounts of biographical data, from my own reference library and sources outside, were carefully reviewed, in an attempt to establish those subjects most typical for each artist in question. From that point, we ascertained as accurately as possible which subject(s) consistently brought the highest prices - the most sought-after subjects by the collectors. After carefully recording all of the auction prices for each artist over an eighteen year period, it was possible then to record a price range which reflected the "practical" low and high for that particular artist. Any dollar amount which was well above the average high end, and which did not obviously fit into the typical price range for that artist, was recorded alphabetically on a separate list entitled, *Record Prices* - found on page ???.

Let's Keep It Simple

The names and dates need no more explanation than presented above. It will be the "price ranges" and the "typical subjects" that need clarification.

PRICE RANGES: You have to remember four things:

1. Most of the price ranges are simply low and high dollar amounts, indicating the range within which you would expect the artist's oils, acrylics, and/or tempera paintings to sell.

Example:

ARTIST	PRICES	SUBJECT
CAPP, AL (20TH C)	2500-18000	A

2. A small number of the price ranges will be preceded by an asterisk (*), indicating a price range for that artist's drawings, watercolors, gouaches, pastels, and/or mixed media. If an artist's name was listed twice, he/she was prolific enough in all mediums to have two separate price ranges. When a name is listed twice, the "typical subject" follows the second price range and the birth and death dates also follow the second listing of the name.

Example:

ARTIST	PRICES	SUBJECT
STEVENS, WILLIAM L.	*150-1500	
STEVENS, WILLIAM L.(1888-1969)	600-7000+	L,M,S

3. You're probably already asking, "What's that plus "+" sign doing on the previous example?" The plus "+" simply indicates that that artist has a *record price* which you will find in the section entitled *Record Prices*, found on page 275. In the above example, the record selling price for a painting by W. L. Stevens is $12,100. Obviously, to have said that Stevens' price range is $600-$12,000 would have distorted the true range within which 99% of his work falls. In all instances where one price was *well* above all others realized at auction, it was included in the *Record Prices* section.

4. A few of the price ranges will not show any prices at all - only four question marks (????). They identify an artist who was considered one of America's important artists, but who has had very few paintings, if any, appear at auction in the past 15 years. If his or her work does appear, it could sell at prices running into the hundreds of thousands of dollars or much higher.

Typical Subjects: "Mnemonic" Letters

"Mnemonic" (pronounced "ni-monic") means *assisting or designed to assist the memory.* In that respect, you will find after each artist, if the information was available, single letters corresponding to the subjects most typical for the artist, arranged "value prioritized" (see below.) Each letter matches the following subjects:

A	Avant-Garde
F	Figures
G	Genre
I	Illustrations
L	Landscapes
M	Marines
P	Primitives
S	Still Life
W	Wildlife
X	Unknown

In the section which follows, for the benefit of the novice, we will briefly explain, with photo examples, each of the subject areas.

"Value Prioritized" simply means that you will find the subjects arranged in descending order according to value. Those subjects by a particular artist, which *generally* bring the highest prices, are listed first, and so on. Please keep in mind that no such list can be compiled with the certainty of "death and taxes" - the author has made a sincere effort to keep the list as accurate as possible. If you are aware of an error and can substantiate it, please bring it to my attention. I will make the correction in the 1989 Edition, for the benefit of everyone.

Let's take a closer look at each subject area, with examples:

TYPICAL SUBJECTS

AVANT-GARDE

For our purposes,"Avant-Garde" will refer to all the art works which do not easily fit into any of the other categories herein because of their unconventional styles. Such works might typically include the "experimental" works or "fads" of the 20th century - such as, Cubism, Dadaism, Surrealism, Abstract Expressionism, Minimal Art, Photorealism, and Pop Art.

Please Note: It is important to repeat here a statement made earlier in the "Disclaimer." When examining the prices of Contemporary artists (over 300 in this *Guide*),care must be exercised. Because of the "dynamic" nature of the contemporary market as a whole, prices rise and fall quickly. With regard to living artists,it is *always* best to check with those galleries that represent them for the "final" word on current values.

The best reference for finding those Galleries which represent many of the artists listed here is Paul Cumming's book, *Dictionary of Contemporary American Artists*, St. Martin's Press, New York (ISBN 0-312-20097-8, $50.00). There are no prices, but it contains plenty of biographical material covering over 900 contemporary artists.

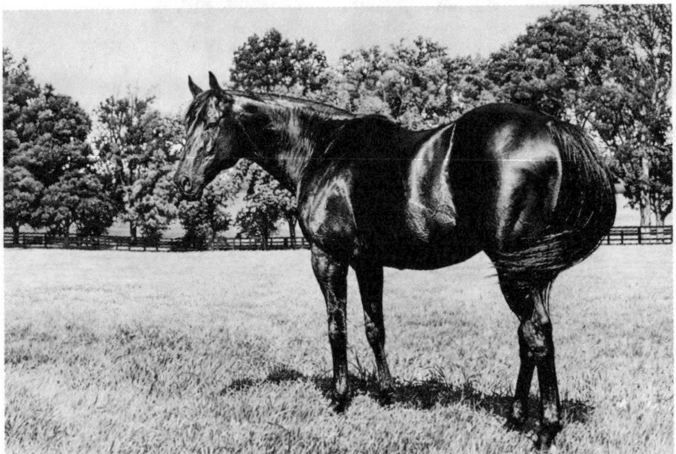

Seattle Slew (Photorealism)
by Richard McLean, oil on canvas, 42" x 60"
(Courtesy of OK Harris Works Of Art, New York, NY)

Kafka's Village At Dawn
by Joan Perreira, oil on canvas, 40" x 30"
(Courtesy of Richard A. Bourne Co. Inc., Hyannisport, MA)

Trail Mark
by Carl Sprinchorn, oil on canvas, 30" x 25"
(Courtesy of Richard A. Bourne Co. Inc., Hyannisport, MA)

FIGURES

Most typically under this category are works which depict adults and/or children in various studio and non-studio settings. These figure studies may include: portraits (single and/or group), miniatures, historical figures, and people from all walks of life in settings typical of the period and location. Many "experts" will argue, with good reason , that many non-studio figure paintings are genre.

In figure painting, the artist usually is more interested in depicting the character of the individual, not so much the human situation, as in genre (see next topic.)

Religious, historical, and allegorical subjects will also be included in this category for our purposes.

Apple Blossoms, the Artist's Daughter
by Hamilton Hamilton, oil on canvas, 25" x 30"
(Courtesy of Henry B. Holt, Montville, NJ)

By The Seashore
by Abbott Fuller Graves, oil on canvas
(Courtesy of Henry B. Holt, Montville, NJ)

Gineo Scott
by Eastman Johnson, oil on canvas, 40" x 50"
(Courtesy of Vose Galleries of Boston, Inc., Boston, MA)

GENRE

Genre refers to people of all ages engaged in everyday activities typical for the period and location. Genre differs from figure studies in that usually the activity in the composition is the main theme. Typical compositions might include: western, sporting, city, country, seafaring, or domestic subjects.

Of particular note are the genre, or American scene paintings of the late 1920's, 30's, and 40's. The scenes were generally a preoccupation with the political and social realities of the day: contemporary morals and manners, the "beauty" found in the drabness and decay of our cities, studies of the poor and underprivileged, studies of the blue-collar worker of the farm and mine - a literal protest against the "pretty" pictures of the 19th century.

Sharecroppers' Cabin
by William Aiken Walker, oil on canvas, 9" x 12"
(Courtesy of Henry B. Holt, Montville, NJ)

Painting the Little House
by Norman Rockwell, oil on canvas, 28" x 24"
(Courtesy of Henry B. Holt, Montville, NJ)

Blowing Bubbles, the Artist's Daughters
by Hamilton Hamilton, oil on canvas, 30" x 36"
(Courtesy of Henry B. Holt, Montville, NJ)

ILLUSTRATIONS

This is a broad category which typically involves works which were executed for the purpose of reinforcing an idea or theme of a publication and/or advertisement. In this category, you will find the greatest variety of mediums and subject matter.

King Arthur Receiving Ecalibur
by N. C. Wyeth, oil on canvas, 40" x 32"
(Courtesy of Vose Galleries of Boston, Inc., Boston, MA)

Jack and the Giant
by Maxfield Parrish, oil on panel, 22" x 16"
Reproduced: *Collier's Weekly* cover, July 30, 1910
(Courtesy of Judy Goffman Fine Art, New York, NY)

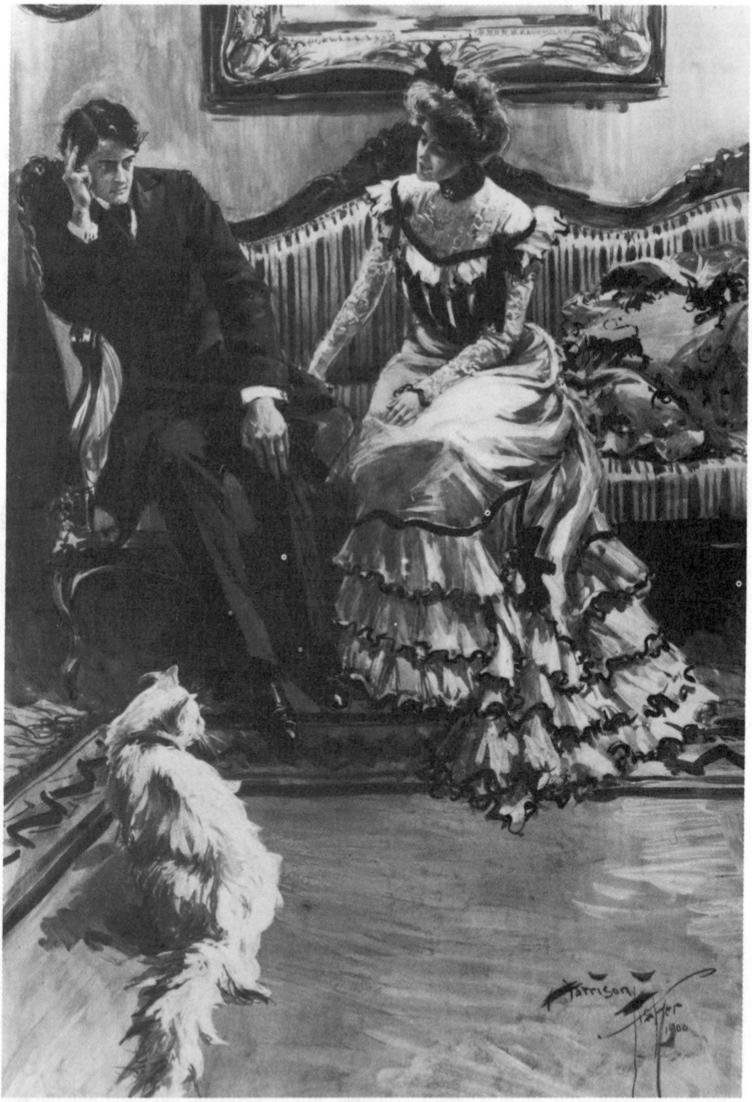

Greater Higher Love
by Harrison Fisher, Ink wash and gouache on board, 31" x 22"
Reproduced: *Life Magazine*, January 17, 1901, p.55
(Courtesy of Judy Goffman Fine Art, New York, NY)

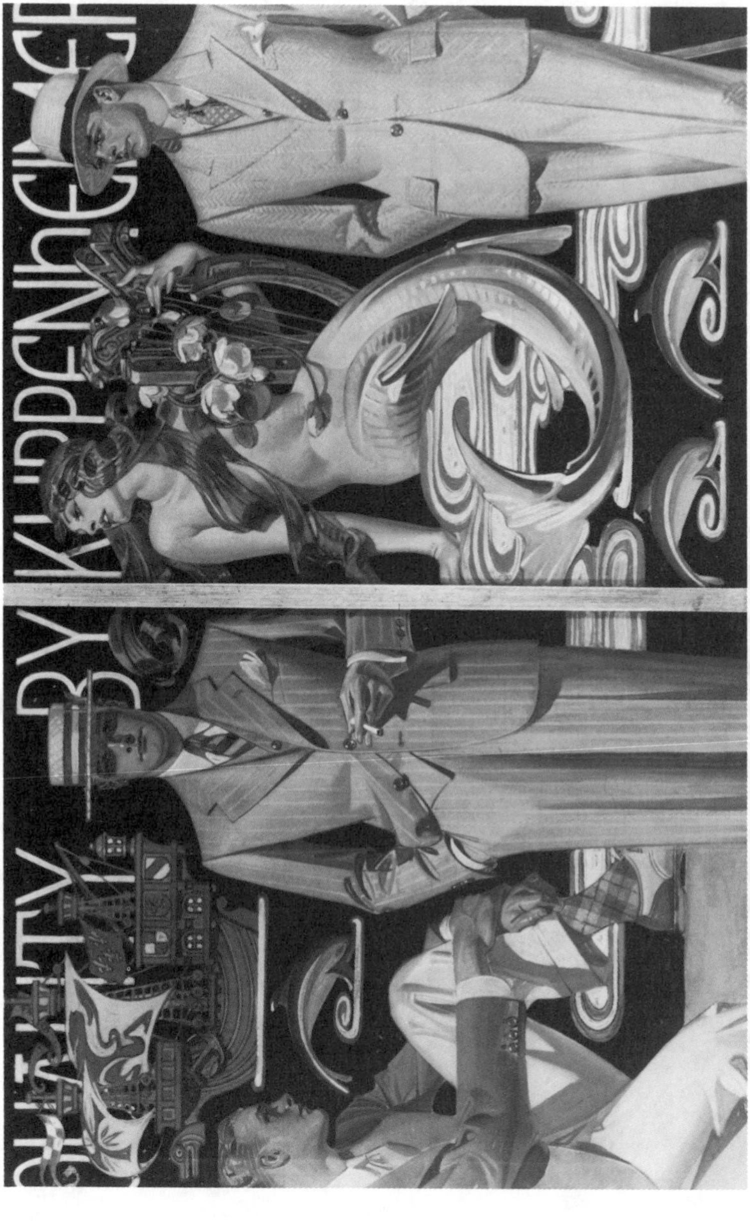

Quality by Kupenheimer
by Joseph C. Leyendecker, 2 oils on canvas, 25" x 19" each
(Courtesy of Judy Goffman Fine Art, New York, NY)

September Afternoon
by N.C. Wyeth, oil on canvas, 42" x 48"
Reproduced: Douglas Allen, *N.C. Wyeth*, Crown Pub., N.Y., 1972, p. 173
(Courtesy of Judy Goffman Fine Art, New York, NY)

Grandpa Listening in on the Wireless
by Norman Rockwell, oil on canvas, 22" x 19"
Reproduced: *Literary Digest* cover, Feb. 21, 1920
(Courtesy of Judy Goffman Fine Art, New York, NY)

LANDSCAPES

In this category, you may find compositions which depict natural scenery, and which may or may not include figures and/or man-made objects. All seasons and all times of the day may be depicted, and views might include any of the following: scenes west or east of the Mississippi, seascapes (shoreline views), and scenes outside the United States. *Genre* may often be combined into a landscape composition.

Springtime in the Village
by Daniel Garber, oil on canvas, 30" x 28"
(Courtesy of Henry B. Holt, Montville, NJ)

Winter Landscape
by Walter Koeniger, oil on canvas, 41" x 45"
(Courtesy of Henry B. Holt, Montville, NJ)

An Old Homestead
by Henry P. Smith, oil on canvas, 20" x 28"
(Courtesy of Henry B. Holt, Montville, NJ)

A Pond in Sudbury
by George H. Smillie, watercolor
(Courtesy of Henry B. Holt, Montville, NJ)

Cotuit, Massachusetts, 1899
by George H. Smillie, watercolor, 9" x 13"
(Courtesy of Henry B. Holt, Montville, NJ)

MARINES

This category will be used in instances where the artist's major output was nautical compositions, such as, drawings and/or paintings of vessels of all descriptions and sizes, sea scenes, and coastal or harbor scenes.

If you need assistance in researching a marine painting or painter, please consider getting in touch with Karl Gabosh. He specializes in works either unsigned or by obscure artists. His address and telephone number can be found in the Appendix.

Schooners at Dock
by William E. Norton, watercolor, 10" x 14"
(Courtesy of Henry B. Holt, Montville, NJ)

Narragansett, Rhode Island, 1890
by Edmund Darch Lewis, watercolor, 10" x 21"
(Courtesy of Henry B. Holt, Montville, NJ)

Sailing Off Nassau
by John Whorf, watercolor, 21" x 29"
(Courtesy of Henry B. Holt, Montville, NJ)

Thomas Hunt and the Schooner America
by James Bard, oil on canvas, 35" x 65"
(Courtesy of Henry B. Holt, Montville, NJ)

Came Ashore in the Night
by Alfred T. Bricher, oil on canvas, 25" x 50"
(Courtesy of Henry B. Holt, Montville, NJ)

PRIMITIVES

The term "primitive" may be used interchangeably with two other terms: "folk art" and "naive art." For our purposes here,"primitive" will refer to all those compositions done by "non- professional" artists - typically referred to as "limners."

Primitive compositions may depict subjects from any of the other categories listed herein (e.g., portraits, landscapes, genre, etc.). Typically, a primitive painting may appear two-dimensional, lack a source of light, and be characterized by an undeveloped spatial sense.

The price ranges of the American folk artists found in this *Guide* were edited by Frank Miele and Jay Johnson. They have helped countless collectors with questions concerning Folk Art. Whether buying, selling, or researching American folk art, you may want to get in touch with one, or both, of them. Mr. Miele is considered an expert in 18th and 19th century folk art and Mr. Johnson is an expert in the folk artists of the 20th century. The address and telephone of their respective galleries can be found in the *Appendix*.

Henry C. Hulbert
by Eratus Salisbury Field, oil on canvas, 35" x 28"
(Courtesy of Henry B. Holt, Montville, NJ)

Captain James Perkins, Jr.
by John Brewster, Jr., oil on canvas, 30" x 25"
(Courtesy of Vose Galleries of Boston, Inc., Boston, MA)

STILL LIFE

These are most often paintings of inanimate objects characterized by their beauty of color, line, or arrangement. During the 19th and 20th centuries these compositions were almost always set indoors and most typically depicted the following: fruit and/or vegetables, flowers, or objects found around the home or farm.

When objects are introduced into a composition to add interest and color, they are usually called accessories.

Still Life of Box of Havana Cigars, etc.
by William M. Harnett, oil on canvas, 29" x 36"
(Courtesy of Henry B. Holt, Montville, NJ)

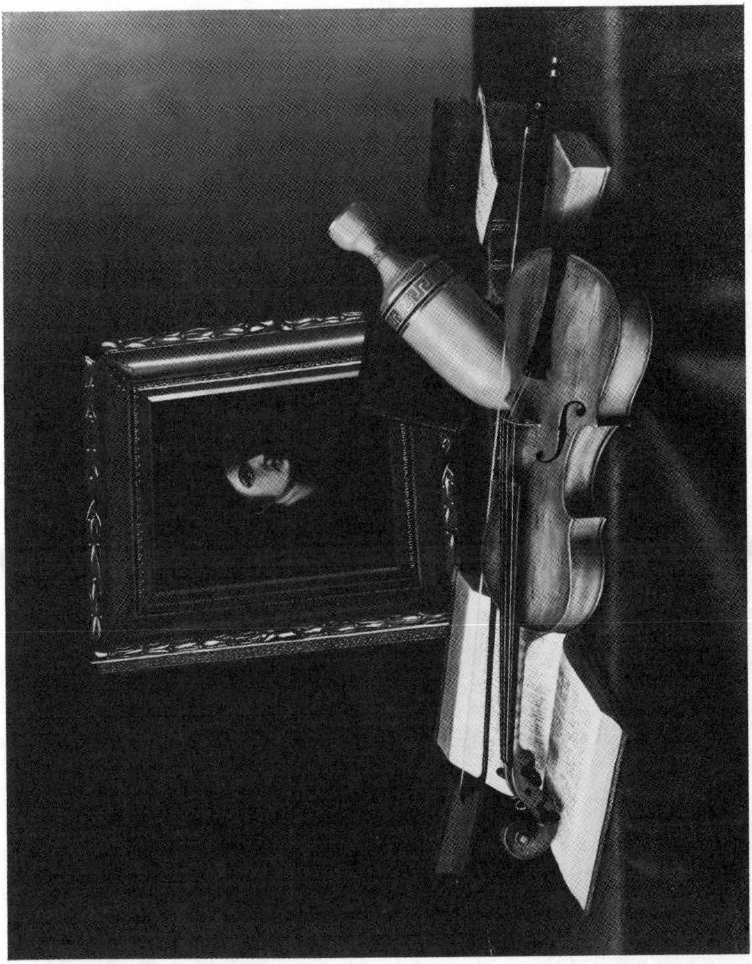

Still Life with Violin, etc.
by William M. Harnett, oil on canvas, 28" x 34"
(Courtesy of Henry B. Holt, Montville, NJ)

Spilt Peaches
by William Mason Brown, oil on canvas, 20" x 15"
(Courtesy of Henry B. Holt, Montville, NJ)

Wheelbarrow of Chrysanthemums
by Emil Carlsen, oil on canvas, 51" x 65"
(Courtesy of Vose Galleries of Boston, Inc., Boston, MA)

WILDLIFE

Many artists made a career of drawing and painting wildlife subjects (animals, fish, and/or birds) set in their natural habitat. These subjects will be included in this category along with animal subjects in a domestic or farm setting - such as, horse portraits, family pets, farmyard animals and fowl.

Exploring
by Ben Austrian, oil on canvas, 11" x 10"
(Courtesy of Henry B. Holt, Montville, NJ)

Anticipation
by Howard Hill, oil on canvas, 10" x 16"
(Courtesy of Henry B. Holt, Montville, NJ)

Farmyard Fowl
by August Laux, oil on canvas, 16" x 24"
(Courtesy of Henry B. Holt, Montville, NJ)

Ducks Alighting
by Frank W. Benson, watercolor, 18" x 24"
(Courtesy of Vose Galleries of Boston, Inc., Boston, MA)

Unknown

An "X" was used when sufficient data were not available at the time, to determine the type of subject matter "most" typical for this artist. If the "X" is followed by any of the letters "A" thru "W" in parentheses, then that artist is known to have executed *some* works in that particular category. If you have verifiable information regarding prices or subject matter for any artists listed here with an "X", please send it along to the address at the front of this *Guide*.

Expert or Sleuth?

Now that you are familiar with the use of this *Guide*, what next? When you want to quickly estimate the *potential* value of a certain work of art, you'll want to use this *Guide* first. After determining that you may have a very valuable painting, and before you sell (privately, to a dealer, on consignment, through advertisement, or in your shop, etc.), you will want to determine more accurately what the painting may be worth (i.e., fair market value). You have two choices. Either you consult with an "expert" (e.g., art appraiser, qualified auctioneer, art dealer, art consultant), or you try to research it yourself. Whichever route you decide on, you will find help in the Appendix of this *Guide* under "Resources For Pricing", and "Appraisal Organizations".

One last comment. If you are a complete novice to the art market, I would recommend seeking the help of an expert. Only an expert will have the trained eye and the references on hand to make the most accurate estimate of the value of your piece. It is also helpful, and may eliminate later heartache, to keep in mind that you should consult with more than one expert if you feel your piece is very important!

AMERICAN ARTISTS AT AUCTION

ARTIST	PRICES	SUBJECT
AARON, MABEL (19TH C)	100-700	X (L)
ABARE, CONSTANCE (20TH C)	100-400	X (L)
ABASCAL, MARY (20TH C)	100-800	X (F)
ABBETT, BOB K. (1926 -)	100-1200	G,F
ABBEY, EDWIN AUSTIN	*350-14000	
ABBEY, EDWIN AUSTIN (1852 - 1911)	2000-28000	I,G,F
ABBOTT, ELENORE PLAISTED (1875 - 1935)	100-1000	X (F,L)
ABBOTT, HAZEL NEWHAM (1894 -)	*100-500	L
ABBOTT, JACOB B. (- 1950)	*100-750	I
ABBOTT, LENA H. (20TH C)	200-2000	L
ABBOTT, SAMUEL NELSON	*100-1000	
ABBOTT, SAMUEL NELSON (1874 - 1955)	300-3500	I
ABBOTT, YARNALL (1870 - 1938)	200-1500	M,G,F
ABBRECIA, JOE (20TH C)	100-800	G
ABDY, ROWENA MEEKS (1887 - 1945)	*150-1200	L,G,I
ABEEL, ETHEL M. (- 1969)	100-900	X
ABEL, KEVIN (20TH C)	150-500	F
ABEL, MYER (1904 - 1948)	100-750	F,G
ABERCROMBIE, GERTRUDE (1909-)	200-1500	L,S
ABERNATHY, JOHN (20TH C)	*100-400	X(M)
ABRAHAM, CAROL SCHMIDT (20TH C)	100-900	X
ABRAMOFSKY, ISRAEL (1888-)	100-1800	L,F
ABRAMOVITZ, ALBERT (1879 - 1963)	400-2500	L,F
ACEVES, JOSE (1909-)	200-1800	L
ACHEFF, WILLIAM (20TH C)	2000-65000	G,F
ACHERT, FRED (20TH C)	200-800	X (L)
ACHESON, GEORGINA ELLIOT (19TH - 20TH C)	*300-600	X (F)
ACKERMANN, FRANK EDWARD (1933 -)	*100-750	L,I
ADAM, JOHN (19TH - 20TH C)	100-800	G,L
ADAM, RICHARD B. (20TH C)	200-600	X (G)

* Denotes watercolors, pastels, drawings, and/or mixed media

ADAM, WILBUR G. (1898-)	250-2000	L
ADAM, WILLIAM (1846-1931)	200-1200	L,M
ADAMS, CATHERINE LONGHORNE (20TH C)	600-3000	L
ADAMS, CHARLES PARTRIDGE	*350-3000	
ADAMS, CHARLES PARTRIDGE (1858 - 1942)	500-5000	L
ADAMS, CHRISTOPHER (19TH C)	200-1000	F
ADAMS, F.W. (20TH C)	100-750	L
ADAMS, GEORGE E. (1814-1885)	300-3500	L,F
ADAMS, HERBERT (1858 - 1945)	200-1200	X (F)
ADAMS, J. HOWARD (19TH C)	100-800	X
ADAMS, JOANNE (20TH C?)	*100-600	X (I,F)
ADAMS, JOHN OTTIS (1851 - 1927)	600-8000	L
ADAMS, JOSEPH ALEXANDER (1803 - 1880)	300-1000	X (L)
ADAMS, M.B.(early 19TH C)	300-1000	F
ADAMS, PHILIP (1881-)	100-650	L,F
ADAMS, WAYMAN (1883 - 1959)	400-4000	W,F,L
ADAMS, WILLIAM ALTHROPE (1797-1878)	200-2400	L,F
ADAMS, WILLIS SEAVER (1842 - 1921)	300-1200	L
ADDY, ALFRED (19TH - 20TH C)	100-800	L
ADELA, ELIZABETH (20TH C)	*100-600	X (I,F)
ADLER, OSCAR F. (20C)	100-1000	L
ADOLPHE, ALBERT JEAN (1865 - 1940)	150-3500	L,F,G,S
ADOLPHE, VIRGINIA (1880 -)	100-900	X (S)
ADOMEIT, GEORGE G. (1879 - 1967)	100-950	L,M
ADRIANCE, M. HORTON (- 1941)	150-1500	L
AGATE, ALFRED THOMAS (1812 - 1846)	200-2500	M,F,W
AGATE, MISS H. (19TH C)	200-1200	L
AGOSTINI, TONY (1916 -)	300-3200	A
AHL, HENRY CURTIS (1905-)	100-400	M,L,S
AHL, HENRY HAMMOND (1869 - 1953)	150-2500	L,I
AHLBORN, EMIL (early 20TH C)	100-500	X (L)
AHLROTH, ARTHUR (20TH C)	100-800	X (F)
AIKEN, CHARLES AVERY	*100-850	I
AIKEN, CHARLES AVERY (1872 - 1965)	200-1800	I,S
AIKEN, CHARLES G. (20TH C)	100-350	X

* Denotes watercolors, pastels, drawings, and/or mixed media

AINSLEY, DENNIS (20TH C)	100-900	X (L)
AITKEN, HARRY G. (19TH - 20TH C)	100-300	L
AITKEN, JAMES (early 19TH C)	200-3500	X (F)
AKELEY, CARL E. (1864 - 1926)	1000-18000	W
AKERS, VIVIAN MILNER (1886-)	400-4500	L,F
AKIN, LOUIS B. (1868 - 1913)	350-4500	L,G,I
ALAJALOV, CONSTANTIN (1900 -)	*200-1000	I
ALBEE, PERCY F. (1883 - 1959)	*100-750	G,F
ALBERS, JOSEF (1888 - 1976)	2500-85000	A
ALBERT, ERNEST (1857 - 1946)	800-18000	L
ALBRECHT, KURT (20TH C)	100-10000	L
ALBRICH, W. (early 20th c)	100-200	X (L)
ALBRIGHT, ADAM EMORY (1862 - 1957)	800-8500+	G
ALBRIGHT, DANIEL K. (19TH C)	200-2000	L
ALBRIGHT, HENRY JAMES (1887 - 1815)	200-2000	L,F
ALBRIGHT, IVAN LE LORRAINE	*800-4800	
ALBRIGHT, IVAN LE LORRAINE (1897 -)	1500-20000	A,F,S
ALDEN, REBECCA B. (early 19TH C)	*100-400	X (S)
ALDERMAN, GEORGE P.B. (1862 - 1942)	*200-850	I
ALDRICH, GEORGE AMES (1872 - 1941)	500-8000	L,F
ALEX, KOSTA (1925 -)	400-2500	F
ALEXANDER, CLIFFORD GREAR (1870 -)	100-900	L,I
ALEXANDER, ESTHER FRANCES (19TH C)	*200-800	X (F)
ALEXANDER, FRANCIS	*200-900	
ALEXANDER, FRANCIS (1800 - 1880)	400-8000	F
ALEXANDER, GEORGIA (20TH C)	100-900	F
ALEXANDER, HELEN DOUGLAS (1897 - 1984)	*200-900	X (I)
ALEXANDER, HENRY (1860 - 1895)	1000-7000	X (F,G)
ALEXANDER, JOHN WHITE (1856 - 1915)	1000-28000	F,I
ALEXANDER, MICHAEL (19TH C)	100-900	F
ALF, MARTHA (1930 -)	1000-3000	X
ALLEN, CHARLES CURTIS (1886 - 1950)	300-3500	L
ALLEN, COURTNEY (1896 -)	200-850	I
ALLEN, DOUGLAS (20TH C)	500-5000	W
ALLEN, F.B. (early 20TH C)	*100-200	X (L)

* Denotes watercolors, pastels, drawings, and/or mixed media

ALLEN, HOWARD (19TH - 20TH C)	100-850	X (G)
ALLEN, J.D. (1851 - 1947)	400-3000	X (G)
ALLEN, JOEL KNOTT (1755-1825)	300-3000	F
ALLEN, JOHN WILLIAM (19TH C)	*100-600	L,W
ALLEN, JUNIUS (1896 - 1962)	300-3500	L,G
ALLEN, MARION BOYD (1862 - 1941)	200-8500	F,L
ALLEN, PEARL WRIGHT (1880 -)	250-1800	X (L)
ALLEN, THOMAS (1849 - 1924)	300-7500	L,G
ALLIS, C. HARRY (1876 - 1938)	200-2400	L
ALLISON, J. S. (20TH C)	200-900	X
ALLSTON, WASHINGTON (1779 - 1843)	5000-????+	F,G,L,M
ALTEN, MATHAIS JOSEPH	*100-400	
ALTEN, MATHIAS JOSEPH (1871 - 1938)	400-2800	F,L
ALTOON, JOHN (1925 - 1969)	*500-2500	A
ALVERSON, MARGARET BLAKE (20TH C)	100-850	X(S)
AMANS, JACQUES (1801 - 1888)	500-8500	F
AMES, DANIEL F. (active 1840-55)	800-3500	F
AMES, EZRA (1768 - 1836)	1000-50000+	F,L
AMESDEN, WILLIAM KING (20TH C)	100-1000	X (L)
AMICK, ROBERT WESLEY	*400-2500	
AMICK, ROBERT WESLEY (1879 - 1969)	2500-18000	G,I
ANDERSON, ALEXANDER (1775 - 1870)	600-3000	F,G
ANDERSON, CLARENCE WILLIAM (20TH C)	*100-900	I
ANDERSON, DOROTHY VISYU (20TH C)	100-1200	L
ANDERSON, FRED (early 20TH C)	100-300	X (G)
ANDERSON, FREDERIC A. (19TH - 20TH C)	500-1200	X (G)
ANDERSON, HAROLD EDGERLY (1899 -)	100-400	X (G)
ANDERSON, HAROLD N.(1894 -)	500-4000	I
ANDERSON, HARRY (1906 -)	*200-1500	I
ANDERSON, J.B. (20TH C)	100-1200	X(F)
ANDERSON, KARL (1874 - 1956)	500-6500	F,G,I
ANDERSON, LENNART (1928 -)	500-1500	X (L)
ANDERSON, M.J.(19TH - 20TH C)	100-300	X (F,S)
ANDERSON, MARTINUS (1878-)	200-1600	L
ANDERSON, OSCAR (1873-)	200-3500	X(M)

* **Denotes watercolors, pastels, drawings, and/or mixed media**

ANDERSON, PETER (19TH C)	*200-1800	M,L
ANDERSON, RONALD	*200-400	
ANDERSON, RONALD (1886 - 1926)	300- 2000	X (F,S)
ANDERSON, RUTH A.(1884 - 1939)	150-2000	F,L
ANDERSON, VICTOR C. (1882 - 1937)	200-1800	I
ANDERSON, VICTOR COLEMAN	*100-850	
ANDERSON, VICTOR COLEMAN (1882 - 1931)	300-4200	G,L,I
ANDRADE, MARY FRATZ (early 20TH C)	200-1000	X (L,G)
ANDREW, INEZ LANGDEN (late 19TH C)	100-400	L
ANDREW, RICHARD (1867 -)	200-4000	L,F,M
ANDREWS, AMBROSE (active 1825-60)	300-5000	L,F
ANDREWS, BENNY (1930 -)	100-4500	X
ANDREWS, JAMES (?)	*200-1000	S
ANDY, JOHN BABTIST (19TH C)	200-1500	F
ANGAROLA, ANTHONY (1893 - 1929)	400-3500	X
ANGEL, RIFKA (1899 -)	100-850	X (G)
ANGELL, LOUISE M. 19TH - 20TH C)	100-600	X (L)
ANGULO, CHAPPIE (1928 -)	150-1000	I
ANISFELD, BORIS (1879 - 1973)	400-2000	X (F,I)
ANNAN, ABEL H. (20TH C)	*100-900	X (F)
ANNES, HECTOR L. (20TH C)	100-250	L
ANNOT, JACOBI (1894 -)	300-3000	X (I,G)
ANSHUTZ, THOMAS POLLACK	*250-25000+	
ANSHUTZ, THOMAS POLLOCK (1851 -1912)	5000-125000	F,L,G,M
ANSON, WILLIAM (19TH C)	200-1600	F
ANTHONY, CAROL (1943-)	*300-4000	A
ANTHONY, RENEST EDWIN (1894 -)	100-800	X (L)
ANUSZKIEWICZ, RICHARD (1930 -)	3000-20000	A
APPEL, CHARLES P. (1857 -)	500-5000+	L
APT, CHARLES (1933 -)	500-3000	X
ARCANGELO, ALLAN D'(1930 -)	500-5000	A
ARCENZA, NICOLA D' (19TH C)	*100-300	X (L)
ARDLEY, A.A.(19TH C)	100-300	X (S)
ARENTZ, JOSEF M. (1903 - 1969)	300-1500	X (G,L)
ARIOLA, FORTUNATO (1827 - 1872)	800-10000	L,M

* Denotes watercolors, pastels, drawings, and/or mixed media

ARKWRIGHT, R.V. (20TH C)	*100-900	X(M)
ARMER, LAURA ADAMS (1874-1963)	300-9000	F,L,I
ARMOR, CHARLES (1844 -)	100-1000	L,G
ARMS, JESSIE (1883 -)	100-450	X (F,G)
ARMSRONG, ROLF (1881 - 1960)	*200-6000	I
ARMSTRONG, DAVID MAITLAND (1836 - 1918)	400-4500	G,F,M
ARMSTRONG, WILLIAM G. (1823 - 1890)	800-4800	L
ARMSTRONG, WILLIAM W. (1822 - 1914)	400-2500	L
ARNAUTOFF, VICTOR MIKHAIL (1896-1979)	200-2500	M
ARNDT, PAUL WESLEY (1881-)	150-950	L
ARNO, PETER (1904 - 1968)	*100-1000	I
ARNOLD, CLARA MAXFIELD (1879-1959)	100-1000	S
ARNOLD, JAMES (20TH C)	100-850	X
ARNOLD, JAY (19TH - 20TH C)	200-850	M
ARONSON, BORIS (1900 -)	*300-2500	X (I)
ARONSON, DAVID (1923 -)	*300-2500	F
ARSTE, KARL (1899 - 1942)	200-1200	L
ARTER, J. CHARLES (- 1923)	150-850	F
ARTHURS, G. (20TH C)	100-900	L
ARTHURS, STANLEY MASSEY (1877 - 1950)	300-8000	I
ARTIGES, EMILE (20TH C)	100-1000	L
ARTSCHWAGER, RICHARD (1924 -)	5000-50000	A
ARY, HENRY (1802 - 1859)	1000-6500	L
ASCENZO, NICOLA D'(1869 -)	*200-800	I,L
ASHBROOK, PAUL (1867 -)	200-1500	X (F)
ASHE, EDMUND M.(20TH)	*250-900	X (F,I)
ASHLEY, ANITA (19TH - 20TH C)	*200-1500	F
ASHLEY, CLIFFORD WARREN (1881 - 1947)	800-8500	L,M,I
ASHLEY, FRANK N.	*150-1500	
ASHLEY, FRANK N. (1920-)	300-1500	G,F
ASHTON, THOMAS B. (19TH C)	350-4500	G,L
ASPLYND, TARE (20TH C)	100-300	X (G)
ATCKISON, JOSEPH ANTHONY (1895 -)	*100-300	X (M,L)
ATHERTON, JOHN C. (1900 - 1952)	200-1200	L,I
ATKEN, JAMES (19TH C)	500-3000	G,L

 * Denotes watercolors, pastels, drawings, and/or mixed media

ATKINSON, LEO F. (1896-)	200-1800	L
ATWOOD, HELEN (1878-)	100-800	X(W)
ATWOOD, WILLIAM E. (19TH-20TH C)	250-2000	L
AUBRY, EARL (20TH C)	300-3500	X (L)
AUDUBON, JOHN JAMES (1785 - 1851)	*2500-275000	W
AUDUBON, VICTOR GIFFORD (1809 - 1862)	1000-5000	L
AUERBACH-LEVY, WILLIAM (1889 -)	200-900	F
AULISIO, JOSEPH (1910 - 1974)	2000-25000	P,L
AULMANN, THEODORA (1882 -)	100-300	L
AULT, GEORGE C.	*300-6500	
AULT, GEORGE C. (1891 - 1948)	500-30000	A,L
AUREL, BERNATH (19TH C)	*150-800	X (L)
AUSTEN, EDWARD J. (1850 - 1930)	100-750	L
AUSTIN, ARTHUR E.JR. (20TH C)	1500-8000	A
AUSTIN, CHARLES PERCY (1883 - 1929)	500-1200	X (G,L)
AUSTIN, DARREL	*100-900	
AUSTIN, DARREL (1907 -)	500-4800	F
AUSTIN, EDWARD C.(20TH C)	*100-300	X (M)
AUSTRIAN, BEN (1870 - 1921)	400-7500	L,W
AVEDISIAN, EDWARD (1936 -)	500-6500	A
AVERY, ADDISON E. (19TH C)	*100-300	S
AVERY, MILTON	*500-65000	
AVERY, MILTON (1893 - 1965)	600-125000	A
AVINOFF, ANDRE (1884 - 1949)	*200-850	X (L)
AVISON, GEORGE (1885-)	300-3500	I
AYARS, MARGARET T. (19TH - 20TH C)	100-800	L
AYERS, H. MERVIN (1902 - 1975)	*100-300	X (F)
AYLWARD, WILLIAM JAMES (1875 - 1956)	400-1500	G,M,I
AZADIGIAN, MUNUEL (19TH-20TH C)	200-1200	X(S)

B

ARTIST	PRICE	SUBJECT
BABBIDGE, JAMES GARDNER (1844 - 1919)	2000-6500	M
BABCOCK, WILLIAM P.(1826 - 1899)	300-4500	S,G,L
BABER, ALICE (1928 -)	800-6500	A
BACH, BERTA (19TH C)	400-3500	X(S)
BACH, ESTHER E.(20TH)	*150-350	X (W)
BACH, FLORENCE JULIA (1887 -)	100-1200	X
BACHELDER, JOHN B. (1825 - 1894)	200-1200	L
BACHER, OTTO HENRY (1856 - 1909)	1500-50000	L,S,I,M
BACK, JOE W. (1899 -)	*100-400	X (W)
BACON, C.E. (19TH C)	100-600	L
BACON, CHARLES ROSWELL (1868 - 1913)	400-5000	L
BACON, FRANCIS (1909 -)	20000-1500000+	A
BACON, FRANK A. (1803 - 1887)	500-3000	L
BACON, HENRY	*300-2500	
BACON, HENRY (1839 - 1912)	1500-18000	F,G,L
BACON, I.L.(late 19TH C)	100-1500	X (S)
BACON, IRVING R. (1875 - 1962)	*150-800	L,G
BACON, PEGGY B.	*100-2000	
BACON, PEGGY B.(1895 - 1987)	500-4500	F,G,I
BADGER, FRANCIS (19TH - 20TH C)	500-1500	X (G)
BADGER, JAMES W. (19TH C)	200-1000	F
BADGER, JOHN C. (1822 -)	*200-1000	F
BADGER, JOSEPH (1708 - 1765)	1500-6000	P
BADGER, S.F.M.(19TH C)	1000-10000+	M
BADGER, THOMAS (1792 - 1868)	250-850	F
BAEDER, JOHN (1938 -)	3500-35000	A
BAER, JO (1929 -)	3000-12000	A
BAER, MARTIN (1894 - 1961)	200-2500	A
BAER, NORMAN (20TH C)	*100-900	I
BAER, WILLIAM JACOB (1860 - 1941)	400-3500	F,G,S
BAILEY, JAMES G. (1870 -)	200-850	I,L
BAILEY, S.S. (19TH C)	*100-350	L
BAILEY, S.T. (LATE 19TH C)	300-3000	X(S)
BAILEY, T.(19TH - 20TH C)	100-1000	M,L

 * Denotes watercolors, pastels, drawings, and/or mixed media

BAILEY, VERNON HOWE (20TH C)	*100-700	I
BAILEY, WALTER ALEXANDER (1894-)	200-2500	L
BAILEY, WILLIAM H.	*1000-6000	
BAILEY, WILLIAM H. (1930 -)	5000-45000	A
BAIRD, WILLIAM BABTISTE (1847 -)	500-8500	L,W,M
BAKER, A.Z.(19TH-20TH C)	100-900	X(I)
BAKER, CHARLES (1844 - 1906)	*100-800	L,M
BAKER, ELISHA TAYLOR (1827 - 1890)	2000-12000	M
BAKER, ELIZABETH GOWDY (1860 - 1927)	*100-900	F
BAKER, ELLEN KENDALL (- 1912)	200-1500	X(F)
BAKER, ERNEST (19TH C)	300-1200	M
BAKER, G.A. (19TH - 20TH C)	800-9000	M
BAKER, GEORGE A. (1821 - 1880)	200-2000	F
BAKER, J. ELDER (19TH C)	*300-3500	G,S
BAKER, O.F. (19TH C)	300-1000	M
BAKER, SAMUEL BURTIS (1882 - 1967)	100-900	L,F
BAKER, T.E. (19TH - 20TH C)	1000-6500	M
BAKER, W.C. (19TH C)	100-700	L
BAKER, WILLIAM BLISS (1859 - 1886)	500-6500	M,L
BAKER, WILLIAM H. (1824-1875)	350-4000	L
BALAGH, BELA (20TH C)	200-1500	X (S)
BALCOM, LOWELL L. (1887 - 1938)	400-3500	X (F,I)
BALDWIN, ALBERTUS H.(1865 -)	*100-350	X (M)
BALDWIN, CLIFFORD PARK (1889-1961)	300-2500	L,I
BALDWIN, G.B. (19TH C)	300-1500	F
BALINK, HENRY C.(1882 - 1963)	3000-20000	L,F
BALL, ALICE WORTHINGTON (- 1929)	200-1200	M,S
BALL, L. CLARENCE	*200-750	
BALL, L. CLARENCE (1858 - 1915)	300-3000	L,W,S
BALL, STANLEY CRITTENDEN (1885 -)	200-1800	L
BALLAINE, JERROLD (20TH C)	250-1500	X (F)
BALLIN, HUGO (1879 - 1956)	300-2000	F
BALLINGER, HARRY (1892 -)	200-2500	I
BALLOU, ADDIE L. (1837 - 1916)	200-1800	F
BAMA, JAMES ELLIOTT	*4000-20000	

* Denotes watercolors, pastels, drawings, and/or mixed media

BAMA, JAMES ELLIOTT (1926 -)	8000-25000	G,F,S
BAND, MAX (1900-)	300-3000	A,F
BANKS, RICHARD (1929 -)	500-3500	X (F)
BANKSON, GLEN (1890-)	100-900	L
BANNARD, (WALTER) DARBY (1934 -)	1000-20000	A
BANNISTER, EDWARD MITCHELL (1828 - 1901)	1000-20000	L,F
BANNISTER, J. (1821 - 1901)	500-2000	M,S
BANTA, WEART (19TH C)	100-1800	L,F
BARBER, JOHN (1898 - 1965)	500-6000	G,L
BARBER, JOHN WARNER (1798 - 1885)	*150-400	I
BARBER, JOSEPH (1915 -)	*100-300	M
BARCHUS, ELIZA R. (1857 - 1959)	200-3800	L
BARCLAY, MCCLELLAND	*100-400	
BARCLAY, MCCLELLAND (1891 - 1943)	400-3500	I,G,S
BARD, JAMES (and JOHN) (1815 - 1897)	35000-125000	M
BARDAZZI, PETER (1943 -)	500-3000	A
BARFUSS, INA (20TH C)	*300-2500	X (L)
BARILE, XAVIER J. (1891 - 1981)	200-2000	X (A,L)
BARKER, ALBERT W. (1874 - 1947)	*100-800	X (I,L)
BARKER, GEORGE (1882 - 1965)	100-1000	L
BARLOW, JOHN NOBLE (1861 - 1917)	500-6500	L
BARLOW, MYRON (1873 - 1938)	800-12000	G,F
BARNARD, EDWARD HERBERT (1855 - 1909)	500-2800	S,L
BARNES, ERNEST HARRISON (1873 -)	300-3000	L
BARNES, GERTRUDE (1865 -)	300-4200	L
BARNES, JOHN PIERCE (1893 -)	400-4800	L
BARNES, PENELOPE BIRCH (early 19TH C)	*300-800	S
BARNES, WILL R. (20TH C)	*100-750	X (L)
BARNET, WILL (1911 -)	1000-20000	F,A
BARNETT, BJORN (JR) (1887 -)	300-1200	L
BARNETT, HERBERT (1910 - 1978)	500-3000	A,L
BARNETT, RITA WOLPE (20TH C)	150-400	X (L,S)
BARNETT, THOMAS P.(1870 - 1929)	100-2000	L,M
BARNETT, WILLIAM (20TH C)	100-800	A
BARNEY, FRANK A. (1862-)	100-3000	L

 * Denotes watercolors, pastels, drawings, and/or mixed media

BARNITZ, A.M. (19TH C)	150-400	X (L)
BARONE, ANTONIO (1889 -)	500-25000	F
BARR, WILLIAM (1867 - 1933)	300-1500	L,G
BARRATT, GEORGE W. (20TH C)	200-2000	I
BARRAUD, ALFRED T. (1849 - 1925)	*100-500	L
BARRETT, ELIZABETH HUNT (1863 -)	100-1200	L
BARRETT, MARY E. (19TH C)	*500-3000	L
BARRETT, OLIVER GLEN (20TH C)	100-600	L
BARRETT, WILLIAM S. (1854 - 1927)	400-3000	L,M
BARRON, ROS (1933 -)	300-900	X (A)
BARROW, JOHN DOBSON (1827 - 1907)	400-2000	L
BARRY, CHARLES A. (1830 - 1892)	300-4500	X (G)
BARRY, EDITH CLEAVES (early 20TH C)	150-500	L
BARSE, GEORGE RANDOLPH (JR) (1861 - 1938)	500-8000	L
BARSTON, S.M. (19TH C)	500-3500	L
BARTH, CARL E. (1896 - 1976)	300-3000	X(F,S)
BARTHOLOMEW, TRUMAN (19TH C)	300-3500	L
BARTHOLOMEW, WILLIAM N.(1856 - 1919)	*100-500	L
BARTLETT, DANA (1882 - 1957)	400-3000	L
BARTLETT, FREDERICK EUGENE (1852 - 1911)	*100-200	X (M,L)
BARTLETT, GRAY (1885 - 1951)	500-7000	L
BARTLETT, JONATHAN ADAMS (1817 - 1902)	3000-10000	P
BARTLETT, PAUL WAYLAND (1881 - 1925)	400-2000	L
BARTOLL, WILLIAM THOMPSON (1817 - 1859)	250-2500	P
BARTON, LOREN R.	*300-800	
BARTON, LOREN R. (1893 - 1975)	500-2000	L,G,M
BARTON, MATTHEW (18TH-19TH C)	*150-850	L
BARTON, MINETTE (1889 - 1976)	600-6000	X (G)
BARTON, RALPH (1891 - 1931)	*200-800	S,I
BARTOO, CATHERINE R. (1876 - 1949)	100-300	X
BASCOM, RUTH HENSHAW (1772 - 1848)	*3000-18000+	P
BASHFIELD, EDWIN HOWLAND (1848 - 1936)	800-4800	F
BASING, CHARLES (1865 - 1933)	500-3000	X (L)
BASKERVILLE, CHARLES (1896 -)	450-3000	X (F,G)
BASKIN, LEONARD (1922 -)	*400-4800	A

BASSFORD, FRANKLYN (19TH C)	2000-25000	M
BASSFORD, WALLACE (1900-)	200-3000	M
BATCHELLER, FREDERICK S.(1837 - 1889)	600-6500	S,L
BATES, BERTHA CORSON DAY (1875 -)	100-1200	L
BATTY, ROLAND W. (20TH C)	300-4500	X (F)
BAUCHMANN, C.(late 19TH C)	100-500	L
BAUER, WILLIAM (1888 -)	200-1000	L
BAUM, CARL (CHARLES ?)(19TH C)	500-8000	S,L
BAUM, CHARLES (1812 - 1877)	800-10000+	S,L
BAUM, WALTER EMERSON (1884 - 1956)	300-15000	L,I
BAUMAN, KARL HERMAN (1911 - 1984)	100-750	L,I
BAUMANN, GUSTAVE (1881 - 1971)	200-800	L
BAUMGARTEN, WILLIAM (19TH - 20TH C)	*500-3500	I
BAUMGARTNER, WARREN W.(1894-1963)	*150-3200	X(M)
BAUMGRAS, PETER (1827 - 1904)	500-3500	L,S,F
BAUMHOFER, WALTER M. (1904 -)	200-1000	I
BAXTER, ELIJAH (JR) (1849 - 1939)	300-1000	L,S
BAYARD, CLIFFORD ADAMS (1892 - 1934)	400-3000	L
BAYER, HERBERT	*200-900	
BAYER, HERBERT (1900 -)	1000-6000	X (A)
BAYHA, EDWIN F. (20TH C)	500-38000	G,F
BAYLES, ? (19TH C)	100-400	X (L)
BAYLINSON, A.S. (1882 - 1950)	200-900	X (S)
BAZIOTES, WILLIAM A.	*4000-75000	
BAZIOTES, WILLIAM A. (1912 - 1963)	5000-275000	A
BEAL, GIFFORD	*100-3000	
BEAL, GIFFORD (1879 - 1956)	1000-42000+	L,G
BEAL, JACK (1931 -)	1500-20000	X (A)
BEAL, REYNOLDS	*400-6000	
BEAL, REYNOLDS (1867 - 1951)	1000-20000+	L,G,M
BEALL, CECIL CALVERT (1892 -)	*100-750	I
BEAMAN, GAMALIEL WALDO (1852 - 1937)	400-1800	L
BEAMAN, WILLIAM (19TH C)	100-400	L
BEAME, W. (19TH C)	150-800	L
BEAN, CAROLINE VAN HOOK (1880 - 1970)	150-1000	X (G)

 * Denotes watercolors, pastels, drawings, and/or mixed media

BEAN, HANNAH (early 19TH C)	*250-800	P
BEAR, JESSIE DREW (20TH C)	100-400	X
BEARD, ADELIA BELLE (- 1920)	400-2500	L,F,I
BEARD, ALICE (19TH - 20TH C)	300-2500	X (G)
BEARD, DANIEL CARTER (1850 - 1941)	*400-2500	I
BEARD, FRANK (1842-1905)	400-3500	X (L)
BEARD, HARRY (19TH C)	250-1200	X (W,S)
BEARD, JAMES CARTER (1837-1913)	*200-1200	X(F)
BEARD, JAMES HENRY (1812 - 1893)	1500-25000	F,G,L,W
BEARD, WILLIAM HOLBROOK (1824 - 1900)	1500-25000	F,G,L,W
BEARDEN, ROMARE (1914 -)	*1000-30000	A
BEARS, ORLANDO HAND (1811-1851)	3000-35000	P(F)
BEATON, CECIL (1904 - 1980)	*300-1500	X (I,S)
BEATTIE, ALEXANDER (20TH C)	100-400	X
BEATTY, FRANK T. (1899 -)	*400-3600	M
BEATTY, JOHN WILLIAM (1851 - 1924)	400-5500	L
BEAUCHAMP, ROBERT (1923 -)	300-4000	A
BEAUFORT, JOHN (19TH C)	800-9500	L
BEAUMONT, ARTHUR EDWAINE (1879 - 1956)	150-1500	M,L,F
BEAUMONT, LILIAN ADELE (1880-1922)	150-3500	G,F
BEAUREGARD, C.G.(19TH C)	250-1500	X (G)
BEAUX, CECILIA	*500-5000	
BEAUX, CECILIA (1861 - 1942)	1000-30000	F,L
BEBIE, HENRY (1824 - 1888)	800-3500	L,F
BECHER, ARTHUR ERNST (1877 - 1960)	300-4000	I,W,L,G
BECHTLE, ROBERT (1932 -)	5000-35000	A
BECK, AUGUSTUS (19TH C)	200-1800	X (F)
BECK, BERNARD (20TH C)	400-3000	A
BECK, FREIDRICH (1873 - 1921)	200-2000	L
BECKER, FREDERICK W. (1888 - 1953)	300-2500	L
BECKER, J. (19TH C)	500-30000	S
BECKETT, CHARLES E. (active 1840-50)	100-850	L,M
BECKHOFF, HARRY (1901 - 1979)	*100-2500	I
BECKINGHAM, ARTHUR (19TH C)	300-1200	G,F
BECKMANN, MAX	*500-75000	

* Denotes watercolors, pastels, drawings, and/or mixed media

BECKMANN, MAX (1884 - 1950)	3500-300000	A
BECKWITH, ARTHUR (1860 - 1930)	250-1500	L,M
BECKWITH, JAMES CARROLL (1852 - 1617)	400-60000	F,G
BEELER, JOE	*1500-15000	
BEELER, JOE (1931 -)	5000-35000	L,G
BEERS, JULIE HART (1835 - 1913)	800-3000	L
BEEST, ALBERTUS VAN (1820 - 1860)	800-7500+	M
BEET, CORNELIUS DE (1772-1840)	900-8500	S
BEHRE, FREDERIC JOHN (19TH - 20TH C)	400-2000	X (S)
BELARSKI, RUDOLPH (20TH C)	100-600	X
BELKNAP, ZEDEKIAH (1781 - 1858)	650-35000+	P
BELL, CECIL C. (1906 - 1970)	500-6000	L,F
BELL, CHARLES (1874 - 1935)	1000-50000	A
BELL, EDWARD AUGUSTE (1862 - 1953)	800-7000+	F
BELL, GEORGE (19TH - 20TH C)	100-800	X (L)
BELL, LARRY (1939 -)	500-3500	A
BELLINGER, MARGARET T. (1899-)	100-900	X(L)
BELLOWS, ALBERT F.	*400-7500	
BELLOWS, ALBERT F.(1829 - 1883)	800-8500	L,G
BELLOWS, GEORGE W.	*500-24000	
BELLOWS, GEORGE W.(1882 - 1925)	6000-125000	G,F,L
BEMELMANS, LUDWIG (1898 - 1962)	*150-4000	I
BEMISH, R. HILLS (19TH - 20TH C)	*100-300	L
BEN-ZION, (1897 -)	250-1500	A
BENBRIDGE, HENRY (1743 - 1812)	2000-12000	F
BENDA, WLADYSLAW T. (1873 - 1948)	*150-500	I
BENDER, BILL (1920 -)	300-3000	X (A)
BENDLE, ROBERT (1867 -)	150-900	X (L)
BENEDICT, A.C.(19TH - 20TH C)	800-3500	L
BENEDICT, ENELLA (20TH C)	100-900	L
BENEDUCE, ANTIMO (1900 -)	*100-800	L,S
BENEKER, GERRIT ALBERTUS (1882 - 1934)	500-5000	I,G,F
BENGSTON, BILLY AL (1934 -)	500-10000	A
BENJAMIN, KARL (1925 -)	500-3000	A
BENJAMIN, NORA (1899 -)	*100-900	X(I)

 * Denotes watercolors, pastels, drawings, and/or mixed media

BENJAMIN, SAMUEL G.W. (1837 - 1914)	350-2000	M
BENN, BEN (1884 - 1983)	300-4500	F,S
BENNETT, EMILY (19TH-20TH C)	100-500	X(S)
BENNETT, LYLE HATCHER (1903-)	400-3000	A
BENNETT, RAINEY (1904 -)	*100-400	L
BENNETT, WILLIAM JAMES (1787-1844)	*900-42000	L
BENSELL, GEORGE FREDERICK (1837 - 1879)	500-8000	F,G
BENSON, EUGENE (1839 - 1908)	500-9000+	F,L
BENSON, FRANK WESTON	*500-20000	
BENSON, FRANK WESTON (1862 - 1951)	1000-100000	F,W,L,S
BENSON, JOHN P.(1865 - 1947)	200-3500	M
BENSON, LESLIE LANGILLE (1885 -)	200-1500	G,I
BENTLEY, JOHN W.(1880 -)	300-2500	L
BENTLEY, LESTER W. (1908 -)	400-2500	X(M,L)
BENTON, DWIGHT (1834 -)	250-2500	L
BENTON, THOMAS HART	*450-90000	
BENTON, THOMAS HART (1889 - 1975)	3000-375000	G,F,L,I
BERDANIER, PAUL F. (1879-)	650-6500	L,I
BERKE, ERNEST (1921 -)	800-18000	F,L
BERMAN, EUGENE	*100-3500	
BERMAN, EUGENE (1899 - 1972)	300-10000	I,F
BERMAN, HARRY G. (20TH C)	400-6000	L
BERMAN, SAUL (1899 -)	800-3500	X (G)
BERMAN, WALLACE (1926 - 1976)	400-3500	A
BERNEKER, LOUIS FREDERICK (1876 - 1937)	300-3200	F,L
BERNINGER, JOHN E. (20TH C)	100-600	X(S)
BERNINGHAUS, J. CHARLES (1905 -)	250-1800	L
BERNINGHAUS, OSCAR E.(1874 - 1952)	3500-225000	G,L,I
BERNSTEIN, RICHARD (1930 -)	400-3200	X
BERNSTEIN, THERESA (1890 -)	900-20000	F,L,S
BERRY, CARROLL THAYER (1886 - 1978)	100-1500	M,L
BERRY, PATRICK VINCENT (1852 - 1922)	350-3000	L,W
BERS, JULIE HART (1835 - 1913)	500-3000	L
BERTHELSEN, JOHANN	*350-1500	
BERTHELSEN, JOHANN (1883 - 1969)	400-8000	L,M

* Denotes watercolors, pastels, drawings, and/or mixed media

BERTHOT, JAKE	*300-2500	
BERTHOT, JAKE (1939 -)	1000-18000	A
BERTRAM, H.C. (19TH C)	*100-400	G
BESS, FORREST CLEMENGER (1911 - 1977)	1500-20000	A
BESSIRE, DALE PHILLIP (1893-1974)	250-3000	L
BEST, ALICE (19TH C)	100-1500	L
BEST, ARTHUR WILLIAM (1865 - 1919)	100-2500	L,M,F
BEST, HARRY CASSIE (1863 - 1936)	250-2000	L,F
BETTINGER, HOYLAND B. (1890 - 1934)	300-2500	L
BETTS, ANNA WHELAN (19TH-20TH C)	500-6000	F
BETTS, HAROLD HARRINGTON (1881 -)	300-4500	F,L
BETTS, LOUIS (1873 - 1961)	400-30000	F,G,S
BETTS, VIRGINIA BATTLE (20TH C)	150-500	X (S)
BEWICK, WILLIAM (1795 - 1866)	600-1200	X (G)
BEWLEY, MURRAY PERCIVAL (1884 - 1964)	400-3500	F
BEYER, M.O. (19TH C)	100-900	X(S)
BEYER, WILLIAM E. (1929 -)	*200-800	L,M
BIANCHI, A. (20TH C)	100-350	X (S)
BICKERSTAFF, GEORGE (20TH C)	100-1000	L
BICKFORD, SID (1862 - 1947)	400-5000	W
BICKNELL, ALBION HARRIS (1837 - 1915)	350-8000	F,G,S
BICKNELL, E. (19TH - 20TH C)	*150-400	X (L)
BICKNELL, EVELYN M. (19TH C)	300-2800	X(F)
BICKNELL, FRANK ALFRED (1866 - 1943)	400-5000	L
BICKNELL, WILLIAM H.W. (1860 -)	400-1200	X (G)
BIDDLE, GEORGE (1885 - 1973)	500-7500	G,I,L
BIDWELL, A.(19TH C)	100-400	X (G)
BIEDERMANN, H.(19TH-20TH C)	*400-4500	L
BIEL, JOSEPH (1891 - 1943)	200-1800	X (L,G)
BIERSTADT, ALBERT (1830 - 1902)	2500-575000+	L,M
BIGELOW, CHARLES C. (1891 -)	100-250	F
BIGELOW, DANIEL FOLGER (1823 - 1910)	300-2500	L,S
BIGELOW, THOMAS (1849 - 1924)	600-3000	L
BIGGS, GEOFFREY (1908 -)	*100-800	I
BIGGS, ROBERT OLDHAM (1920 -)	500-1800	L,G

 * Denotes watercolors, pastels, drawings, and/or mixed media

BIGGS, WALTER (1886 - 1968)	*100-3000	I
BIGGS, WALTER (1886 -)	300-3200	X
BILLING, FREDERICK W. (1835 - 1914)	250-2500	X (G)
BILLINGS, EDWIN T. (1824-1893)	300-1500	X(F)
BILLINGS, HENRY (1901 -)	*800-4500	I
BILLMEYER, JAMES IRWIN (1897 -)	*100-900	I
BINFORD, JULIEN (1908 -)	400-4500	X (G,F)
BINGHAM, GEORGE CALEB (1811 - 1879)	5000-????	G,F,L
BINKS, WARD (20TH C)	400-3000	W
BINNEY, H.N. (19TH C)	*250-800	X (M)
BINTONI, ROLLIN (19TH C)	100-350	L
BIRCH, REGINALD B. (1856 - 1943)	*100-900	I
BIRCH, THOMAS (1779 - 1851)	3500-180000	L,M,F
BIRCH, WILLIAM (1755 - 1834)	*500-8000	L,G
BIRCHALL, WILLIAM MINSHAL (1884 -)	*100-1800	M
BIRDSALL JR, AMOS (1865 - 1938)	400-6000	M
BIRMELIN, ROBERT (1933 -)	200-800	A,M
BIRNEY, WILLIAM VIERPLANCK (1858 - 1909)	800-12000+	F,G
BIRREN, JOSEPH P. (1864 - 1933)	350-3500	L
BISBING, HENRY SINGLEWOOD (1849 - 1919)	600-3000	L,W
BISCHOFF, FRANZ ALBERT (1864 - 1929)	500-18000	L,M
BISHOP, ALBERT F. (1855 -)	800-5000	L,M
BISHOP, ISABEL	*200-2500	
BISHOP, ISABEL (1902 -)	1000-4800	G,F
BISHOP, RICHARD E. (20TH C)	150-1500	X(W)
BISPHAM, HENRY COLLINS (1841 - 1882)	250-6800	L,W
BISSELL, EDGAR JULIAN (1856 -)	100-1000	L
BISSELL, KATE (19TH C?)	400-4500	X (S)
BISTTRAM, EMIL J.(1895 - 1976)	500-8500+	A,F,L
BIXBEE, WILLIAM JOHNSON	*200-1200	
BIXBEE, WILLIAM JOHNSON (1850 - 1921)	250-3000	L
BLACK, LAVERNE NELSON	*500-9500	
BLACK, LAVERNE NELSON (1887 - 1938)	1000-60000	F,G
BLACK, MARY C. W. (- 1943)	200-1200	X (S)
BLACK, OLIVE PARKER (1868 - 1948)	500-4800	L

BLACKBURN, JOSEPH (1700 -)	800-45000	P
BLACKMAN, WALTER (1847 - 1928)	400-8000	G,L,F
BLACKWELL, TOM (1938 -)	3000-25000	A
BLAIKLEY, ALEXANDER (19TH C)	*800-8500	G,L
BLAINE, NELL (1922-)	100-900	X(S)
BLAIR, STREETER (1888 - 1966)	400-12000	L
BLAKE, LEO B. (1887-1976)	250-2500	L
BLAKELOCK, MARION (1880 -)	200-1800	L
BLAKELOCK, RALPH A.(1847 - 1919)	500-35000	L
BLANCH, ARNOLD (1896 - 1968)	300-5000	F,S,I
BLANEY, DWIGHT (1865 - 1944)	100-2000	L,M
BLANKENSHIP, ROY (1943 -)	*300-1200	L
BLASHFIELD, EDWIN HOWLAND (1848 - 1936)	500-40000	G,F
BLASS, CHARLOTTE L.(1908 -)	100-400	F,L
BLATAS, ARBIT (20TH C)	500-6000	A
BLAUVELT, CHARLES F. (1824 - 1900)	800-6500	G,F
BLECKNER, ROSS (20TH C)	500-3500	A
BLEIMAN, MAX (19TH - 20TH C)	200-1000	L
BLENNER, CARLE JOHN (1864 - 1952)	200-10000	F,S,G,L
BLISS, ROBERT R. (1925-)	100-1200	F,L,M
BLOCH, ALBERT (1882 - 1961)	700-6000	A
BLOCH, JULIUS T. (1888-1966)	200-4800	X(F)
BLOMFIELD, C. (19TH C)	250-1000	L
BLOODGOOD, MORRIS S. (1845 - 1920)	250-2500	L
BLOOM, HYMAN (1913 -)	1000-10000	A
BLOOMER, HIRAM REYNOLDS (1845 - 1911)	200-4800	L
BLOSSOM, EARL (1891 - 1970)	*100-600	I
BLUEMNER, OSCAR F.	*350-20000	
BLUEMNER, OSCAR F. (1867 - 1938)	4000-150000+	A,L
BLUHM, NORMAN	*200-1200	
BLUHM, NORMAN (1920 -)	1200-18000	A
BLUM, JEROME (1884 - 1956)	250-1500	A,L
BLUM, ROBERT FREDERICK	*1000-50000+	
BLUM, ROBERT FREDERICK (1857 - 1903)	2500-220000+	L,F,I
BLUMBERG, YULI (1894-1964)	100-850	L

 * Denotes watercolors, pastels, drawings, and/or mixed media

BLUME, PETER	*500-5000	
BLUME, PETER (1906 -)	1000-30000	A
BLUMENSCHEIN, ERNEST L.	*1500-8000	
BLUMENSCHEIN, ERNEST L. (1874 - 1960)	1500-80000	A,F,I,L
BLUMENSCHEIN, HELEN GREENE (1909 -)	600-3000	X (L)
BLUMENSCHEIN, MARY SHEPHARD (1869-)	1000-12000	F,G
BLUNT, JOHN S. (1798 - 1835)	1500-17000	P (M)
BLYTHE, DAVID GILMOUR (1815 - 1865)	3000-60000	G,F
BOARDMAN, WILLIAM G. (1815 - 1865)	350-5000	L
BOCHERO, PETER (1895 - 1962)	700-6000	P
BODWELL, A.V. (early 20TH C)	100-500	X (L)
BOEHM, HENRY (- 1914)	300-1500	L
BOESE, HENRY (active 1845-65)	400-3000	L
BOGDANOVE, ABRAHAM JACOBI (1887-1941)	300-3500	X(L)
BOGERT, GEORGE HENRY (1864 - 1944)	200-4500	L,F
BOGGS, FRANK MEYERS	*500-4500	
BOGGS, FRANK MEYERS (1855 - 1926)	1500-28000	L,M
BOHAN, RUTH HARRIS (1891 - 1981)	250-1000	X
BOHLER, HANS (20TH C)	100-450	L
BOHM, C. CURRY (20TH C)	200-1200	L
BOHM, MAX (1868 - 1923)	500-5000	G,F
BOHROD, AARON	*200-2800	
BOHROD, AARON (1907 -)	600-10000	G,L,S
BOICE, BRUCE (1941 -)	500-5000	A
BOILEAU, PHILIP	*300-2500	
BOILEAU, PHILIP (1864 - 1917)	400-4500	F,I
BOIS, GUY PENE DU (1884-1958)	3000-75000	G,F
BOIS, YVONNE PENE DU (20TH C)	100-900	X(L)
BOISSEAU, ALFRED (1823 - 1903)	350-3500	X (G,F)
BOIT, EDWARD DARLEY (1840 - 1916)	*350-8500	L
BOIZARD, C.U. (19TH-20TH C)	300-3200	G,F
BOLANDER, KARL S. (1893-)	150-1800	X(L)
BOLEGARD, JOSEPH (20TH C)	*500-3500	I
BOLLENDONK, WALTER (19TH C)	100-900	M
BOLLES, REGINALD FAIRFAX (20TH C)	150-1200	I

* Denotes watercolors, pastels, drawings, and/or mixed media

BOLMER, M. DEFOREST (1854 - 1910)	200-1200	L
BOLOTOWSKY, ILYA (1907 - 1981)	1500-30000	A
BOLSTER, JANETTE WHEELER (1821 - 1883)	200-900	X (L)
BOMBERGER, BRUCE (1918 - 1980)	*100-700	I
BONAR, LESTER M. (20TH C)	100-500	X(L)
BONFIELD, GEORGE R. (1802 - 1898)	500-6000	L,M
BONFIELD, WILLIAM VAN DE VELDE (19TH C)	400-4800	L,M
BONGART, SERGEI R. (20TH C)	300-2500	L
BONHAM, HORACE (1835 - 1892)	600-5000	G
BONIN, R. (20TH C)	600-3000	X
BONNET, LEON (19TH-20TH C)	400-2000	L
BONTECOU, LEE (1931 -)	*500-5000	A
BOOG, CARLE MICHEL (1877 -)	500-9000	X (G)
BOOTH, FRANKLIN (1874 - 1943)	*250-3500	I
BORBINO, J. (1905 - 1964)	800-4800	L,M
BOREIN, EDWARD (1872 - 1945)	*250-30000	G,L
BOREN, JAMES	*2500-25000	
BOREN, JAMES (1921 -)	5000-40000	G,L
BORG, CARL OSCAR (1879 - 1947)	700-14000	L,I
BORGLUM, J. GUTZON (1867 - 1941)	400-2000	X (L)
BORGO, LOUIS (1867 -)	*100-500	I
BORGORD, MARTIN (1869 - 1935)	600-3000	F,G
BORIE, ADOLPHE (1877-1934)	500-15000	F,G
BORNEGAR, PHILIP (19TH-20TH C)	100-600	X(L,F)
BORONDA, LESTER D.(1886 - 1951)	250-2000	L,G
BORRIS, ALBERT (LATE 19TH C)	100-1500	L
BOSA, LOUIS (1905 -)	200-3000	L,G
BOSKERCK, ROBERT WARD VAN (1855 - 1932)	300-7500	L
BOSLEY, FREDERICK A.(1881 - 1942)	2500-38000	F
BOSS, HOMER (1882 - 1956)	250-1500	L
BOSTELLE, THOMAS (1921 -)	*100-500	L
BOSTON, F.D. (20TH C)	200-900	L
BOSTON, FREDERICK JAMES (1855 - 1932)	350-4500	F,L,S
BOSTON, JOSEPH H.(1901 - 1954)	300-2500	L,F
BOTKE, CORNELIUS (1887 - 1954)	300-2000	L,S

* Denotes watercolors, pastels, drawings, and/or mixed media

BOTKE, JESSIE ARMS (1883 - 1971)	500-16000	W,I
BOTT, E.F.E.V. (19TH C)	400-1500	L,G
BOUCHE, LOUIS (1896 - 1969)	600-18000	L,G,I
BOUGHTON, GEORGE HENRY (1833 - 1905)	500-20000	L,G,F
BOUGUEREAU, ELIZABETH G.(1837 - 1922)	1200-25000+	F
BOUNDEY, BURTON SHEPARD (1879 - 1962)	300-2500	L
BOURGEOIS, LOUISE (1911 -)	400-5000	X (F)
BOURNE, GERTRUDE (20TH C)	*150-600	X(L)
BOUTELLE, DEWITT CLINTON (1820 - 1884)	800-30000	L,G,F
BOUVE, ROSAMOND SMITH (20TH C)	500-15000	F
BOVEE, I.A. (19TH - 20TH C)	100-400	L
BOWDOIN, HARRIETTE (19TH - 20TH C)	200-1200	G,I
BOWEN, BENJAMIN JAMES (1859 -)	200-2500	M
BOWER, ALEXANDER	*100-1000	
BOWER, ALEXANDER (1875 - 1952)	300-3200	M,L
BOWER, MAURICE (1889 - 1980)	*300-3200	I
BOWIE, FRANK LOUVILLE (1857 - 1936)	400-3500	L
BOWMAN, ADRIANUS M.(19TH C)	200-900	S
BOWYER, ALAN (19TH - 20TH C)	100-600	X (G)
BOXER, STANLEY ROBERT (1926 -)	2000-10000	A
BOYDEN, DWIGHT F. (1860-1933)	150-900	L
BOYENHART, C. (19TH C)	100-400	X (F)
BOYER, RALPH LUDWIG (1879 - 1952)	200-1000	F,I
BOYES, G.E. (19TH C)	500-5000	F
BOYLE, CHARLES WELLINGTON (1864 - 1925)	600-3000	L
BOYLE, FERDINAND THOMAS LEE (1820 - 1906)	400-3500	F
BOYLE, JOHN J. (1852 - 1917)	600-4500	S,F
BOYLE, W.W. (19TH C)	250-2500	X (L)
BRAAM, G. (19TH C)	*100-500	P
BRACE, REEVES (19TH - 20TH C)	500-2000	L
BRACH, PAUL (1924 -)	800-5000	A
BRACKER, M. LEONE (1885 - 1937)	*100-1000	I
BRACKETT, A. LORING (19TH - 20TH C)	500-3000	X (W)
BRACKETT, SIDNEY LAWRENCE (19TH-20TH C)	300-2500	G,W,L
BRACKETT, WALTER M. (1823 - 1919)	500-8000	W,S

* Denotes watercolors, pastels, drawings, and/or mixed media

BRACKMAN, ROBERT	*200-3000	
BRACKMAN, ROBERT (1898 - 1980)	300-20000	F,S
BRADER, F.A. (19TH C)	*1500-6500	P
BRADFORD, WILLIAM	*400-6000	
BRADFORD, WILLIAM (1823 - 1892)	1200-80000	M,L
BRADISH, ALVA (1806 - 1901)	500-3000	P
BRADLEY, ANNE CARY (1884 -)	300-2500	X(L)
BRADLEY, JOHN (- 1874)	18000-50000	P
BRADLEY, PETER (1940 -)	500-1500	A
BRADSTREET, JULIA E. (19TH C)	200-1500	S,L
BRADY, MATTHEW (1823 - 1892)	*500-2500	F
BRAGG, CHARLES (20TH C)	500-2000	X (G)
BRAINARD, ANN ELIZABETH (19TH C)	100-800	L
BRALEY, CLARENCE (20TH C)	*100-500	M,L
BRALEY, CLARENCE E. (19TH C)	*100-700	M,L
BRANCHARD, EMILE PIERRE (1881 - 1938)	200-3000	L
BRANDIEN, CARL W. (20TH C)	100-700	X
BRANDRETT, ANTHONY (20TH C)	400-2500	M
BRANDRIFF, GEORGE KENNEDY (1890 - 1936)	200-11000	L
BRANDT, CARL LUDWIG (1831 - 1905)	700-8000	L,F
BRANDT, HENRY (1862-)	300-1800	L
BRANNAN, WILLIAM PENN (- 1866)	300-3500	X (F)
BRANSOM, PAUL (1885 - 1979)	*100-750	I
BRANSOM, PAUL (1885 - 1981)	300-4000	I
BRAUN, MAURICE (1877 -1941)	600-8500	L
BRAY, ARNOLD (20TH C)	100-500	X(M)
BRAZINGTON, WILLIAM CAREY (1865 - 1914)	*400-1200	F
BRECHER, SAMUEL (1897 -)	500-7500	X (M)
BRECK, J.H. (20TH C)	150-1200	X(M,L)
BRECKENRIDGE, HUGH HENRY (1870 - 1937)	800-7500	S,L,F
BREDIN, RAY SLOAN (1881 - 1933)	1000-18000+	L,F
BREEM, PAUL (19TH)	300-3500	M
BREENE, ALEXANDER (20TH C)	100-350	M
BREHM, GEORGE (1878 - 1966)	*200-1000	I
BREMER, ANNE (1872-1923)	150-3200	L,F

 * Denotes watercolors, pastels, drawings, and/or mixed media

BRENEISER, STANLEY (1890-)	*150-800	L
BRENNER, CARL CHRISTIAN (1838 - 1888)	800-6000	L
BRENNER, F.H. (19TH C)	200-1000	L
BRENNERMAN, GEORGE W. (1856 - 1906)	500-5000	L,W,I
BRETT, DOROTHY (1882 - 1977)	700-8000	A
BRETT, HAROLD MATHEWS (1880 - 1955)	350-5000	I,G,F
BREUER, HENRY JOSEPH (1860 - 1932)	400-3500	L
BREUER, N.R. (20TH C)	100-1500	F
BREUER, THEODORE A. (19TH - 20TH C)	500-12000	F
BREUL, HUGO (1854 - 1910)	350-3500	F,G
BREVITT, GEORGE (1854 -)	700-5500	L
BREVOORT, JAMES RENWICK (1832 - 1918)	500-4500	L
BREWER, ADRIAN L. (1891 - 1956)	100-1500	X (L)
BREWER, NICHOLAS RICHARD (1857 - 1932)	600-5000	F,L
BREWERTON, GEORGE DOUGLAS	*300-2000	
BREWERTON, GEORGE DOUGLAS (1820 - 1901)	600-5000	L,M
BREWSTER, ANNA RICHARDS (1870 - 1952)	300-4500	L,I
BREWSTER JR., JOHN (1766 - 1854)	5000-160000+	P
BRICE, WILLIAM (1921 -)	5000-20000	A
BRICHER, ALFRED THOMPSON	*500-25000+	
BRICHER, ALFRED THOMPSON (1837 - 1908)	1200-110000	M,L,G,F
BRIDGE, WILLIAM B. (20TH C)	100-900	F
BRIDGEMAN, R. (19TH C)	100-500	P
BRIDGES, CHARLES (active 1730-45)	2500-8000	P
BRIDGES, FEDILIA	*200-3500	
BRIDGES, FIDELIA (1835 - 1923)	1000-6500+	L,W,M
BRIDGMAN, FREDERICK ARTHUR (1847 - 1928)	800-40000	F,L,G
BRIDPORT, HUGH (1794-1868)	500-6500	L,F
BRIGANTI, NICHOLAS P. (1895 -)	350-15000	L,F
BRIGGS, LUCIUS A. (1852 - 1931)	*250-1000	M
BRIGGS, WARREN C. (1867 - 1903)	250-1800	L
BRIGHAM, R. JORDAN (19TH C)	200-3500	F
BRIGHAM, WILLIAM COLE (1870 -)	500-2500	L
BRIGHTWELL, WALTER (1914 -)	200-2000	I
BRILL, GEORGE REITER (1867 - 1918)	100-400	F

BRINDLE, E. MELBOURNE (1904 -)	*600-5000	I
BRINKLEY, HILL (- 1944)	*100-1200	I
BRINLEY, DANIEL PUTNAM (1879 - 1963)	400-5000	L,F
BRISCOE, DANIEL (1826 - 1883)	250-800	X (M)
BRISCOE, FRANKLIN D.(1844 - 1903)	400-7000	M,L,G
BRISTOL, JOHN BUNYON (1826 - 1909)	500-15000	L
BROAD, A.H. (20TH C)	100-300	L
BROCKMAN, ANN (1899 -)	250-3000	X (F)
BRODERSON, MORRIS GAYLORD (1928 -)	500-5000	A
BRODIE, GANDY (1924 - 1975)	200-3500	X (A)
BROMLEY, FRANK C.(19TH C)	200-4200	L
BROMLEY, J.W. (19TH C)	400-1500	F
BROOK, ALEXANDER	*150-850	
BROOK, ALEXANDER (1898 -)	500-6000	F,L
BROOKE, RICHARD NORRIS (1847 - 1920)	250-4500	L,G
BROOKES, SAMUEL MARSDEN (1816 - 1892)	3500-50000	S
BROOKS, ALDEN FINNEY (1840 - 1931)	1000-4800	S,F,G
BROOKS, AMY (19TH - 20TH C)	*100-600	X (G)
BROOKS, CORA SMALLEY (- 1930)	100-500	L
BROOKS, HENRY HOWARD (1898 -)	200-1200	X(L,S)
BROOKS, JAMES (1906 -)	2500-30000	A
BROOKS, NICHOLAS ALDEN (active 1885-1905)	1000-12000+	S
BROUGIER, ADOLF (1870 - 1926)	300-1500	X (L)
BROWERE, ALBERTIS DEL ORIENT (1814 - 1887)	700-18000	G,L,S
BROWN, ANNA M. (19TH - 20TH C)	300-1500	X
BROWN, ANNA WOOD (20TH C)	400-5000	F
BROWN, ARTHUR W. (1881 - 1966)	*100-2000	I
BROWN, BENJAMIN CHAMBERS (1865 - 1942)	350-4800	L
BROWN, BOLTON (1865 - 1936)	400-2000	X (L)
BROWN, BRADFORD (20TH C)	*150-600	X
BROWN, CHARLES V. (1848 -)	500-3000	X (F)
BROWN, DOUGLAS EDWIN (1904 -)	*150-500	X
BROWN, ETHELBERT (1870 -)	100-400	X (G)
BROWN, F. GRISWOLD (20TH C)	100-400	L
BROWN, FLORINNE (19TH C)	200-1800	X (S)

* Denotes watercolors, pastels, drawings, and/or mixed media

BROWN, FRANCIS F.(1891 -)	400-1200	L
BROWN, FRANK A.(1876 -)	150-3500	F,G
BROWN, GEORGE ELMER (1871 - 1946)	250-6000	L
BROWN, GEORGE LORING (1814 - 1889)	500-12000	L,M
BROWN, GRAFTON TYLER (1841 - 1918)	250-1500	L
BROWN, HARLEY (20TH C)	*500-8000	X (F)
BROWN, HARRISON BIRD (1831 - 1915)	300-8500+	L,M
BROWN, J. (active 1800-35)	5000-35000	P
BROWN, J. HENRY (1818 - 1891)	450-2000	F,L
BROWN, J. RANDOLPH (1861 -)	350-2000	X (M)
BROWN, JAMES (mid 19TH C)	700-9000	X (G)
BROWN, JAMES FRANCIS (1862-1935)	200-2500	F
BROWN, JOAN (1938 -)	3000-18000	A
BROWN, JOHN APPLETON (1844 - 1902)	450-15000+	L,M
BROWN, JOHN BUNYAN (1826 - 1909)	400-3500	L
BROWN, JOHN GEORGE (1831 - 1913)	4000-115000+	G
BROWN, MANNEVILLE E.D. (1810 - 1896)	800-9000	L,F
BROWN, MATHER (1761 - 1831)	400-7500	F
BROWN, MAURICE (1877 - 1941)	150-900	X (L)
BROWN, MCALPIN (20TH C)	100-500	F,L
BROWN, P. (19TH - 20TH C)	100-400	X (M)
BROWN, PAUL F. (1871 - 1944)	*200-1800	X
BROWN, ROGER (1941 -)	5000-25000	A
BROWN, ROY (1879 - 1956)	350-3000	L
BROWN, SAMUEL JOSEPH (1907 -)	400-3000	A,F
BROWN, W. WARREN (19TH C ?)	250-1500	M
BROWN, W.H. (active 1875-1890)	200-750	X (L)
BROWN, WALTER FRANCIS (1853 - 1929)	400-4000	L,I
BROWN, WILLIAM ALDEN (1877 -)	100-900	L
BROWN, WILLIAM MARSHALL (1863 - 1929)	750-3000	G
BROWN, WILLIAM MASON (1828 - 1898)	800-25000+	S,L
BROWN, WILLIAM THEO (1919 -)	300-4000	X (F,G)
BROWNE, BYRON (1907 - 1961)	450-15000	A
BROWNE, CHARLES FRANCIS (1859 - 1920)	300-6500	L
BROWNE, GEORGE ELMER (1871 - 1946)	200-7000	M,L,G

BROWNE, HAROLD PUTNAM (1894 - 1931)	*150-400	X (L)
BROWNE, MARGARET FITZHUGH (1884 - 1972)	350-3500	F,L
BROWNE, MATILDA (1896 -)	350-1800	S,L
BROWNELL, CHARLES DE WOLF (1822 - 1909)	650-18000	L,S
BROWNELL, MATILDA AUCHINLOSS (1869-)	300-6000	L
BROWNING, COLLEEN (1927 -)	300-1800	X
BROWNSCOMBE, JENNIE	*300-2500	
BROWNSCOMBE, JENNIE (1850 - 1936)	800-32000	F
BROWNSON, WALTER C. (19TH-20TH C)	100-850	L
BROWNSWORTH, D. (19TH C)	100-750	X(F)
BRUCE, EDWARD (1879 - 1943)	400-10500	L
BRUCE, GRANVILLE (20TH C)	*200-800	X
BRUCE, JAMES CHRISTIE (19TH - 20TH C)	150-600	M
BRUCE, JOSEPHINE (19TH C)	100-300	X (S)
BRUCE, WILLIAM BLAIR (19TH C)	350-11000	L,G
BRUCKMAN, LODEWYK (1903 -)	500-3000	X (S)
BRUESTLE, BERTRAM G. (1902 -)	200-1200	L
BRUESTLE, GEORGE M.(1872 - 1939)	400-6500	L
BRUMBACH, LOUISE UPTON (1929 -)	100-750	L
BRUMIDI, CONSTANTINO (1805 - 1880)	2000-35000	G,F
BRUNDAGE, WILLIAM TYSON (1849 - 1923)	200-2500	M
BRUNET, ADELE LAURE (1879 -)	100-250	F
BRUNNER, FREDERICK SANDS (1886 -)	350-3000	I
BRUNTON, RICHARD (- 1832)	800-4800	P
BRUSH, GEORGE DE FOREST (1855 - 1941)	500-70000	F
BRUTON, MARGARET (1894- 1983)	200-1800	X(L)
BRUZZI, ? (19TH C)	100-500	X (W)
BRYANT, EVERETT LLYOD (1864 - 1945)	300-12000	F,S,L
BRYANT, HAROLD E.(1894 - 1950)	800-4500	X (F)
BRYANT, HENRY C.(1812 - 1881)	1000-7000	L,F
BRYANT, WALLACE (19TH - 20TH C)	150-600	M,F,L
BRYERS, DUANE (20TH C)	*100-500	I
BRYUM, RUTHVEN H. (20TH C)	100-500	L
BUCHTERKIRCH, ARMIN (1859 -)	100-900	F,L,M
BUCK, CLAUDE (1890 -)	200-2000	X (S)

 * Denotes watercolors, pastels, drawings, and/or mixed media

BUCK, CLAUDE (1890 -)	500-3500	X (F)
BUCK, WILLIAM H. (1840 - 1888)	2000-30000	L,G
BUCKLER, CHARLES E. (1869 -)	100-1000	L
BUCKLEY, JOHN MICHAEL (1891-1958)	100-2000	L,M
BUCKLIN, WILLIAM SAVERY (1851-1928)	300-2500	L
BUDGEON, T. (19TH C)	500-3000	L
BUDNER, T. (20TH C)	100-400	X (G)
BUDSEY, ALFRED (20TH C)	*100-500	X (F,L)
BUEHR, G.F. (early 20TH C)	100-400	X (L)
BUEHR, KARL ALBERT (1866-)	300-4500+	L
BUELL, AL (20TH C)	150-900	I
BUFANO, BENIAMINO (1888-1970)	*200-1000	A
BUFF, CONRAD (1886 - 1975)	300-6500	L
BULL, CHARLES LIVINGSTON (1874 - 1932)	*200-2500	I,W,M
BULLARD, OTIS A. (1816 - 1853)	800-4500	F,G,L
BUMANN, SYDNEY W. (19TH C)	150-850	X(F)
BUNCE, WILLIAM GEDNEY (1840 - 1916)	200-1500	L,M
BUNDY, GILBERT (1911 - 1955)	*100-500	I
BUNDY, HORACE (1814 - 1883)	300-5000	P
BUNDY, JOHN ELWOOD (1853 - 1933)	300-3000	L
BUNKER, DENNIS MILLER (1861 - 1890)	1200-45000	F,L,M
BUNNER, ANDREW FISHER (1841 - 1897)	800-7500	L,M
BURBANK, ELBRIDGE AYER (1858 - 1949)	400-10000	F,S
BURCHFIELD, CHARLES E.(1893 - 1967)	*400-150000	L,A
BURDICK, HORACE ROBBINS (1844 - 1942)	100-1000	L,F,S
BUREN, RAEBURN L. VAN (1891 -)	*100-750	I
BURGDORFF, FERDINAND	*100-1200	L
BURGDORFF, FERDINAND (1883 -1975)	200-2500	L
BURGESS, GEORGE H. (1831 -)	400-8000	L
BURGESS, RUTH PAYNE (19TH C)	350-3500	F,S
BURHENNE, MINNIE (19TH-20TH C)	200-3200	X(M)
BURKHARDT, HANS GUSTAV (1904 -)	*200-3000	A
BURLEIGH, SIDNEY RICHMOND	*200-7500	
BURLEIGH, SIDNEY RICHMOND (1853 - 1931)	500-8500	L,F
BURLIN, PAUL (1886 - 1969)	250-5000	A

* Denotes watercolors, pastels, drawings, and/or mixed media

BURLIUK, DAVID	*150-800	
BURLIUK, DAVID (1882 - 1966)	250-20000	G,S,L,F
BURNHAM, THOMAS MICKELL (1818-1866)	1500-30000	G,L,F
BURNS, CHARLES H. (1932 -)	200-1000	X
BURNS, MILTON J.	*100-800	
BURNS, MILTON J. (1853 - 1933)	600-5000	G,M,L
BURNS, PAUL (20TH C)	*100-600	L
BURNSIDE, CAMERON (1887 -)	*250-700	X (L)
BURPEE, WILLIAM PARTRIDGE	*250-1000	
BURPEE, WILLIAM PARTRIDGE (1846 -)	800-8500	M,L
BURR, GEORGE BRAINARD (1876 - 1939)	700-5000	L
BURR, GEORGE ELBERT	*200-750	
BURR, GEORGE ELBERT (1859 - 1939)	600-3000	L,S
BURR, KAROLD SAXTON (1889-1973)	200-1800	L
BURRIDGE, WALTER WILCOX (1857 -)	*200-750	L
BURRILL JR., EDWARD (late 19TH C)	100-2000	G,M
BURROUGHS, BRYSON (1868 - 1934)	500-12000	F
BURT, JAMES (19TH C)	400-4000	L,M
BURWASH, NAT (20TH C)	*100-600	F
BUSBY, C.A. (active 1810-30)	*1000-4000	P ?
BUSCH, CLARENCE FRANCIS (1887 -)	500-2000	X (F)
BUSH, HARRY (1883-)	100-1200	L
BUSH, JACK (1909 - 1977)	5000-65000	A
BUSH, NORTON (1834 - 1894)	400-20000	L,M
BUSSMANN, FRED J. (19TH C)	150-1200	X(S,L)
BUTEAU, W.A. (19TH C)	100-600	L
BUTLER, B.L. (19TH - 20TH C)	100-400	X
BUTLER, CHARLES E. (19TH C)	800-3500	G
BUTLER, EDITH EMERSON (late 19TH C)	*100-400	L
BUTLER, GEORGE BERNARD (1838 - 1907)	700-5000	F,S
BUTLER, H.D. (early 20TH C)	250-800	L
BUTLER, HOWARD RUSSELL (1856 - 1934)	300-4500	L,M,F
BUTLER, MANLEY (20TH C)	100-1000	X(L)
BUTLER, MARY (1865-1946)	100-1000	L,M
BUTLER, PHILLIP A. (19TH C)	200-1500	L

 * Denotes watercolors, pastels, drawings, and/or mixed media

BUTLER, THEODORE EARL (1876 - 1937)	900-62000	L,M,F,S
BUTMAN, FREDERICK (active 1855-70)	350-5500	L
BUTTERFIELD, A. (19TH C)	100-750	X(S)
BUTTERSWORTH, JAMES E.(1817 - 1894)	7500-165000	M
BUTTON, ALBERT PRENTICE (1872-)	300-2300	L
BUTTON, JOHN (1929 -)	400-10000	A
BUXTON, HANNAH P. (19TH C ?)	600-3000	X (F)

C

ARTIST	PRICE	SUBJECT
CABOT, AMY (- 1934)	200-1500	X
CABOT, EDWARD CLARKE (1818 - 1901)	*150-1500	L
CADENASSO, GIUSEPPE (1854 - 1918)	200-2500	L
CADMUS, PAUL	*500-6000	
CADMUS, PAUL (1904 -)	3000-50000+	G,F
CADY, EMMA JANE (19TH C)	*1500-6500	X (S)
CADY, HARRISON (1877 - 1970)	350-3000+	I
CADY, HENRY N.	*150-650	
CADY, HENRY N. (1849 -)	200-3800	M,L
CAFFERTY, JAMES H. (1819 - 1869)	400-6500	G,F,S
CAHILL, WILLIAM VINCENT (- 1924)	750-5000	L
CAHOON, CHARLES (1861 - 1951)	400-14000	L
CAHOON, MARTHA (20TH C)	300-2500	L,S
CAHOON, RALPH (- 1982)	750-20000+	P
CALCAGNO, LAWRENCE (1916 -)	200-1500	A
CALDER, ALEXANDER (1898 - 1976)	1500-75000	A
CALDER, ALEXANDER (1898 - 1976)	*450-25000	
CALDER, ALEXANDER STERLING (1870 - 1945)	*1000-8800	A
CALIFANO, JOHN (1864 -1924)	400-15000+	G
CALIGA, ISAAC HENRY (1857 -)	500-5500	F
CALLAHAN, CAROLINE R. (1871-)	150-1000	X(S)
CALLAHAN, JAMES (20TH C)	*100-400	L

* Denotes watercolors, pastels, drawings, and/or mixed media

CALLE, PAUL	*5000-18000	
CALLE, PAUL (1928 -)	10000-90000	L,I
CALLOWHILL, JAMES (19TH - 20TH C)	150-800	L
CALYO, NICCOLINO VICOMTE (1799 - 1884)	800-6500	L,M
CAMERON, EDGAR SPIER (1862 - 1944)	300-800	L
CAMERON, JOHN (1828 -)	2500-15000	L,M
CAMERON, R.A. (20TH C)	*100-1000	X
CAMERON, WILLIAM ROSS (1893 - 1930)	250-1800	L
CAMP, JOSEPH RODEFER DE (1858 - 1923)	2500-65000	L
CAMPBELL, BLENDON REED (1872 -)	300-1200	I
CAMPBELL, C.M. (active c.1900)	*600-1800	G
CAMPBELL, COLIN (20TH C)	100-300	L
CAMPBELL, GEORGE F. (20TH C ?)	400-1500	X (M)
CAMPBELL, HARRY (20TH C)	100-250	X
CAMPBELL, J.F. (20TH C)	100-700	L
CANFIELD, ABIJAH (1769-1830)	*2000-15000	P
CANIFF, MILTON (1907 -)	*250-850	X (F)
CANTEY, MAURINE (1901 -)	200-1000	X
CANTRALL, HARRIET M. (20TH C)	100-600	M
CAPLES, ROBERT (20TH C)	*200-1000	L
CAPP, AL (20TH C)	2500-18000	A
CARBEE, J.C. (19TH - 20TH C)	400-1200	X (F)
CARBEE, SCOTT CLIFTON (1860 - 1946)	400-3000+	F
CARBONE, CARMINE (20TH C)	100-700	F
CARDELL, MRS. FRANK HALE (1905 -)	200-900	X (S)
CARDENASSO, GIUSEPPE (1858 - 1918)	200-900	L
CARISS, HENRY T. (1840 - 1903)	400-3500+	G,L,M
CARL, KATHERINE AUGUSTA (- 1938)	200-650	F
CARLES, ARTHUR B. (1882 - 1952)	400-80000	A,S,F
CARLETON, ANNE (1878 - 1968)	250-2000	L,F
CARLETON, CLIFFORD (1867 - 1946)	*100-500	I
CARLEY, S.G. (late 19TH C)	100-350	X (S)
CARLIN , ANDREW B. (19TH C)	800-10000	F
CARLIN, JOHN (1813 - 1891)	500-6000	G,L,F
CARLISLE, MARY HELEN (- 1925)	100-900	X(L)

 * Denotes watercolors, pastels, drawings, and/or mixed media

CARLO, GIRARDO DE (20TH C)	100-300	L
CARLSEN, DINES (1901 - 1966)	500-9500	S,L
CARLSEN, SOREN EMIL (1853 - 1932)	650-85000	S,L
CARLSON, JOHN FABIAN (1875 - 1945)	350-16000+	L
CARLTON, ANNE (19TH - 20TH C)	250-2500	L,G
CARLTON, FREDERICK (19TH C)	100-500	L,W
CARLTON, WILLIAM TOLMAN (1816 - 1888)	750-3500	G
CARMER, H. NIMMO (20TH C)	200-3000	L,W
CARMIENCKE, JOHANN HERMANN (1810 - 1867)	300-9000	L
CARPENTER, DUDLEY (1870 -)	100-400	X
CARPENTER, ELLEN MARIA (1836 - 1909)	300-1500	L,F,S
CARPENTER, FRANCIS BICKNELL (1830-1900)	300-3500	X(F)
CARPENTER, FRED GREEN (1882 - 1965)	200-6500	L,F
CARR, JOHN (- 1837)	800-4800	X (S,L)
CARR, LYELL (1857 - 1912)	650-8500	G,F
CARR, SAMUEL S. (1837 - 1908)	800-60000	G,L,W
CARROL, ROBERT (20TH C)	350-2500	X
CARROLL, JOHN WESLEY	*100-850	
CARROLL, JOHN WESLEY (1892 - 1959)	250-2500	F,S
CARSMAN, JON (20TH C)	400-7500	G,L
CARSON, FRANK (1881-)	150-1500	M,L
CARSON, W.A. (early 20TH C)	100-350	L
CARSTAIRS, JAMES STEWART (19TH - 20TH C)	200-900	X (L)
CARTER, CLARENCE HOLBROOK (1904 -)	500-5500	F
CARTER, DENNIS MALONE (1827 - 1881)	250-6000	G,F
CARTER, ESTHER H. (20TH C)	100-600	X (F)
CARTER, GARY (1939 -)	1000-12000	X
CARTER, HENRY (1821 - 1880)	*100-700	X (G)
CARTER, JAMES (1817 - 1873)	350-800	F
CARTER, PRUETT A. (1891 - 1955)	200-4200	I,F
CARY, WM.DE LA MONTAGNE (1840 - 1922)	700-65000	G,S,I
CASE, EDMUND E. (1840 - 1919)	350-2500	L
CASENELLI, VICTOR (1867-1961)	*400-4500	F,G
CASER, ETTORE (1880 - 1944)	400-6500	L,F,S
CASH, HERBERT (19TH - 20TH C)	250-3000	S

* Denotes watercolors, pastels, drawings, and/or mixed media

CASHELL, V. (19TH - 20TH C)	*400-1000	L
CASILEAR, JOHN WILLIAM (1811 - 1893)	1200-20000	L
CASS, GEORGE NELSON (1831 - 1882)	300-3500	W,L,S
CASS, KAE DORN (1901 - 1971)	*100-450	L
CASSATT, MARY	*1500-475000+	
CASSATT, MARY (1844 - 1926)	5000-1250000	F
CASSELLE, JEANNE (20TH C)	100-700	M
CASSIDY, IRA D. GERALD (1879 - 1934)	1000-25000	F,L,I
CASSIN, F.B. (20TH C)	300-1000	X
CASTAIGNE, J. ANDRE (1860 -)	100-1000	I
CASTANO, JOHN (20TH C)	500-2000	X (G)
CASTELLON, FEDERICO (1914 - 1971)	1000-6000	A
CASTLE-KEITH, WILLIAM (19TH - 20TH C)	200-1800	L
CATHCART, JOHN (19TH C)	100-500	X (F)
CATLIN, GEORGE	*2500-35000	
CATLIN, GEORGE (1796 - 1872)	2000-325000	F,L,M
CAULDWELL, LESLIE GRIFFEN (1861 - 1941)	500-4500	F
CAVALLON, GIORGIO	*500-6000	
CAVALLON, GIORGIO (1904 -)	4000-45000	A
CEDERQUIST, ARTHUR E. (1884 - 1955)	250-800	L
CHACE, HELEN B. (20TH C ?)	100-350	X (M)
CHADEAYNE, ROBERT O. (1897-)	300-3500	F,L
CHADWICK, ELLEN N. (?)	100-600	X (L)
CHADWICK, WILLIAM (1879 - 1962)	1000-25000	F,L
CHAESE, EMILIE (18TH C)	800-8000	X (G)
CHAESE, NORA (19TH C)	250-1200	G,F
CHAFFEE, OLIVER (1881 - 1944)	350-3000	X (S)
CHAFFEE, SAMUEL R. (19TH - 20TH C)	*100-900	L
CHALFANT, JEFFERSON DAVID (1846 - 1931)	6500-65000	G,F
CHALIAPIN, BORIS (20TH C)	100-700	X (F)
CHALLEE, S.R. (late 19TH C)	*100-400	X (L)
CHALONER, WALTER L. (20TH C)	600-3000	X (L,M)
CHAMBERLAIN, NORMAN STILES (1887 - 1961)	800-4500	X (L)
CHAMBERLAIN, WYNN (1929 -)	500-8500	F,S
CHAMBERLIN, FRANK TOLLES (1873 - 1961)	*250-800	X

 * Denotes watercolors, pastels, drawings, and/or mixed media

CHAMBERLIN, PRICE A. (19TH C)	*100-400	L
CHAMBERS, C. BOSSERON (1882 -)	250-2500	F,I
CHAMBERS, CHARLES EDWARD (1892 - 1942)	300-2500	I
CHAMBERS, JOSEPH K. (-1916)	200-1800	L
CHAMBERS, THOMAS (1805 - 1866)	1500-35000+	P
CHAMPNEY, BENJAMIN (1817 - 1909)	450-6500	L,G,S
CHAMPNEY, E.G. (19TH C)	200-1200	L
CHAMPNEY, JAMES WELLS	*400-6000	
CHAMPNEY, JAMES WELLS (1843 - 1903)	500-45000	G,F,L
CHAN, GEORGE (20TH C)	200-900	L
CHANDLER, (? late 19TH - 20TH C)	100-350	L,M
CHANDLER, HENRY DALAND (19TH C)	*250-2500	I
CHANDLER, JOSEPH GOODHUE (1813 - 1880)	5000-35000	F
CHANDLER, MRS. JOSEPH G.(1820-1868)	100-1000	X (F,S)
CHANDLER, WINTHROP (1747 - 1790)	10000-75000	P
CHANEY, LESTER JOSEPH (1907 -)	200-650	M
CHANLER, ROBERT WINTHROP (1872 - 1930)	*600-1800	X (W)
CHAPEL, GUY MARTIN (1871 -)	200-850	L
CHAPIN, ALPHEUS (1787 - 1870)	400-1200	F
CHAPIN, BRYANT (1859 - 1927)	150-3500	S,L
CHAPIN, C.H. (active 1850-85)	500-3000	L
CHAPIN, FRANCIS (1899 - 1965)	*100-1500	G,F
CHAPIN, JAMES ORMSBEE (1887 -1975)	300-7000	X (G)
CHAPIN, JOHN R. (1823-)	*150-1000	F,L
CHAPIN, LUCY GROSVENOR (- 1939)	400-4500	F
CHAPLIN, SARAH (19TH C)	*250-650	X (S)
CHAPMAN, CARLTON THEODORE (1860 - 1926)	300-8000	M,L
CHAPMAN, CHARLES SHEPARD (1879 - 1962)	300-4000	F,L,I
CHAPMAN, CONRAD WISE (1842 - 1910)	700-30000	G,L,M
CHAPMAN, CYRUS DURAND (1856 - 1918)	500-30000	X (S)
CHAPMAN, JOHN GADSBY (1808 - 1889)	600-18000	G,L,I,M
CHAPMAN, JOHN LINTON (1839 - 1905)	1000-18000	G,L,M
CHAPMAN, MINERVA JOSEPHINE (1858 -)	300-1200	G,S,L
CHAPPEL, ALONZO	*200-3000	
CHAPPEL, ALONZO (1828 - 1887)	350-1800	F,M

* Denotes watercolors, pastels, drawings, and/or mixed media

CHARTRAND, ESTEBAN (19TH C)	300-3000	L
CHASE, ADELAIDE COLE (1868 - 1944)	100-650	F,S
CHASE, C.H. (19TH C)	400-3000	M
CHASE, FRANK SWIFT (1886 - 1958)	400-4500	L,M
CHASE, HENRY (HARRY) (1853 - 1889)	200-6000	M
CHASE, LILA ELIZABETH (19TH - 20TH C)	350-1500	X (F)
CHASE, WILLIAM MERRITT	*1200-300000+	
CHASE, WILLIAM MERRITT (1849 - 1916)	5000-800000	L,F,S
CHATTERTON, CLARENCE K. (1880 - 1973)	750-18000	L,F
CHATTIN, LOU-ELLEN (1891-1937)	200-1000	X(L,F)
CHECK, R.S. (19TH C)	200-600	F
CHEN, CHI (1912 -)	*350-3200	L
CHEN, GEORGE (20TH C)	100-700	X(F)
CHEN, HILO (20TH C)	1000-6500	X (F)
CHENEY, RUSSELL (1881 - 1945)	100-3500	L,S
CHERNEY, MARVIN (1925 - 1967)	200-1200	A
CHERNOW, ANN (20TH C)	*300-1500	A
CHESTER, C. (19TH C)	150-500	P
CHICHESTER, ARCHIBALD (19TH C)	*100-600	L
CHICHESTER, CECIL (1891 -)	250-3200	L,I
CHICKERING, CHARLES R. (1934 -)	250-650	X (G)
CHILD, EDWIN BURRAGE (1868 - 1937)	250-3000	F,L,I
CHIRIACKA, ERNEST (1920 -)	1000-8500+	L,F
CHITTENDEN, ALICE BROWN (1859 - 1944)	300-5000+	L,F,S
CHRISTENSEN, DAN (1942 -)	1500-20000	A
CHRISTOPHER, WILLIAM (1924 - 1973)	*300-1200	X
CHRISTY, F. EARL (1882 - 1961)	*300-1200	F,I
CHRISTY, HOWARD CHANDLER	*250-5000	
CHRISTY, HOWARD CHANDLER (1873 - 1952)	500-30000+	I,F
CHUEY, ROBERT (20TH C)	500-2500	X(A)
CHUMLEY, JOHN WESLEY (1928 -)	*400-5500	X (L,G)
CHURCH, FREDERIC EDWIN (1826 - 1900)	2500-350000+	L,M
CHURCH, FREDERICK STUART (1842 - 1923)	250-6000	L,I
CHURCHILL, Wm WORCESTER (1858 - 1926)	600-6500	F
CICERI, ERNEST (1817 - 1866)	*150-500	X (M)

* Denotes watercolors, pastels, drawings, and/or mixed media

CIKOVSKY, NICOLAI (1894 - 1934)	100-2500	F,L,S,M
CIMIOTTI, GUSTAVE (1875 -)	250-2000	L
CIPRICO, MARGUERITE (20TH C)	100-850	L
CIRINO, ANTONIO (1889 -)	300-5500	I,M,L
CLAGHORN, JOSEPH C.	*150-1200	
CLAGHORN, JOSEPH C. (1869 -)	900-8000	L
CLAGUE, RICHARD (1816 - 1878)	400-2800	L
CLAIR, R.A. (19TH C)	450-2500	L
CLAITON, J.(19TH - 20TH C)	150-650	X (M)
CLAPP, WILLIAM HENRY (1879 - 1954)	750-6500	L,F
CLARK, ALSON SKINNER (1876 - 1949)	300-20000	F,L,I
CLARK, BENTON (1895 - 1964)	300-3500	I
CLARK, C. MYRON (1876 - 1925)	100-1600	L,M
CLARK, ELIOT CANDEE (1883 - 1980)	300-5200	L
CLARK, EMERSON (19TH C)	200-850	X (G)
CLARK, FRANCIS HERBERT (1876-)	150-2000	X(L)
CLARK, FREEMAN (19TH C)	200-750	L
CLARK, GEORGE MERRITT (- 1904)	350-1500	G
CLARK, MATT (1903 - 1972)	200-1200	I
CLARK, RENE (1886 - 1969)	*200-900	I
CLARK, ROY C. (1889 -)	100-850	L
CLARK, VIRGINIA KEEP (1878 -)	100-400	F
CLARK, WALTER A. (1848 - 1917)	200-2800	L
CLARK, WALTER APPLETON (1876 - 1906)	200-3500+	L,W
CLARK, WALTER LEIGHTON (1859 - 1935)	150-2000	X
CLARKE, BRANDUS J. (20TH C)	100-600	L
CLARKE, J.V. (late 19TH C)	100-600	X (L)
CLARKE, JOHN CLEM (1937 -)	500-18000	A
CLARKE, ROBERT A. (early 19TH C)	3500-25000	G
CLARKSON, EDWARD (active 1845-60)	750-3000	X (G)
CLAUS, WILLIAM A.J. (1862-)	150-1200	F,M
CLAVE, ANTON (20TH C)	*5000-60000 A	
CLAY, MARY F.R. (- 1939)	250-1000	F,L
CLEAVES, W.R. (late 19TH C)	200-800	L
CLIME, WINFIELD SCOTT (1881 - 1958)	450-6000	L

* Denotes watercolors, pastels, drawings, and/or mixed media

CLINEDINST, BENJAMIN WEST	*100-850	
CLINEDINST, BENJAMIN WEST (1859 - 1931)	350-4800	I,G,F
CLINTON, C.F. (19TH C)	500-2000	X (F)
CLONESSY, W. (19TH C)	100-600	X (G)
CLONNEY, JAMES GOODWYN (1812 - 1867)	25000-275000	G,F
CLOSE, E. (19TH C)	100-600	L,W
CLOSSON, WILLIAM BAXTER P.(1848-1926)	250-4000	X (F,G)
CLOUGH, STANLEY THOMAS (1905 -)	100-900	L
CLOUGH,GEORGE L. (1824 - 1901)	400-6500	L,M,F
CLOVER, LEWIS P. (1819 - 1896)	250-1500	F,G
CLURE, W.M. (19TH - 20TH C)	300-1500	L
CLUSMANN, WILLIAM (1859 - 1927)	800-15000	L,F
CLYMER, EDWIN S, (20TH C)	*100-600	X(L)
CLYMER, JOHN FORD (1907 -)	1000-140000	I,G
CLYNE, A.J. (20TH C)	100-500	L
COALE, GRIFFITH BAILAY (1890 - 1950)	300-3500+	I,F
COAST, OSCAR REGAN (1851 - 1931)	200-850	L
COATES, EDMOND C. (1816 - 1871)	500-5000+	L,G,M
COATES, JOHN (19TH C)	400-1500	L,G
COATS, RANDOLPH (1891 -)	150-750	L
COATS, RANDOLPH (1891 -)	300-2800	X
COB, LYMUSES E. (19TH C)	650-2000	X (F)
COBB, CYRUS (1834 - 1903)	150-650	L,F,M
COBB, DARIUS (1834 - 1919)	200-1800	L,S,F,M
COBURN, FREDERICK SIMPSON	*200-2000	
COBURN, FREDERICK SIMPSON (1871 - 1960)	350-30000	L,F
COCHRAN, ALLEN DEAN (1888 - 1935)	150-900	X (F)
COCHRANE, CONSTANCE (20TH C)	150-650	L,M
CODMAN, CHARLES (1800 - 1842)	1000-12000	L,M
CODMAN, EDWIN E. (19TH C)	100-600	M
CODMAN, JOHN AMORY (1824 - 1886)	600-4000	L,M,F
COFFEE, WILL J. (20TH C)	100-350	L,F
COFFIN, ELIZABETH REBECCA (1851 - 1930)	800-4800	F
COFFIN, GEORGE ALBERT (1856 - 1922)	100-850	M
COFFIN, WILLIAM ANDERSON (1855 - 1925)	200-15000	L,M,F

 * Denotes watercolors, pastels, drawings, and/or mixed media

COFFIN, WILLIAM HASKELL	*200-850	
COFFIN, WILLIAM HASKELL (1878- 1941)	250-5000	M,L,F
COGGELSHALL, JOHN I. (1856 - 1927)	250-1500	X (G)
COGGESHALL, K.M. (20TH C)	100-350	L
COGSWELL, WILLIAM (1819 - 1903)	250-2800	F
COHEN, FREDERICK (19TH C)	200-3200	L
COHEN, GEORGE (1919 -)	350-1500	X (G)
COHEN, LEWIS (1857 - 1915)	350-3200	L,F
COIT, CAROLINE (- 1934)	*150-500	M,L
COLBURN, ELANOR (1866-1939)	300-3500	F,G
COLBURN, SAMUEL BOLTON (1909 -)	*100-650	L
COLBY, GEORGE E. (1859 -)	350-1800	L
COLCHIDAS, GUS (20TH C)	300-4000	X(F)
COLE, ALPHAESUS PHILEMON (1876 - 1900)	300-6000	F,L
COLE, CASILEAR (1888-)	800-7500	X(F)
COLE, CHARLES OCTAVIUS (1814-)	600-15000	L,F
COLE, JOSEPH FOXCROFT (1837 - 1892)	200-3500	L,F
COLE, JOSEPH GREENLEAF (1803 - 1858)	350-1500	F
COLE, THOMAS (1801 - 1848)	3500-900000	L
COLE, THOMAS CASILEAR (1888 - 1976)	200-85000	X(F)
COLEGROVE, M.B. (19TH C)	100-650	L
COLEMAN, BLANCHE E. (19TH C)	100-800	X(F)
COLEMAN, CHARLES CARYL (1840 - 1928)	700-100000+	L,G,F
COLEMAN, GLENN O. (1887 - 1932)	3500-25000	L
COLEMAN, HARRY B. (1884 - 1959)	100-1000	L
COLEMAN, LORING W. (20TH C)	150-900	L
COLEMAN, MARION (20TH C)	150-650	X (F)
COLEMAN, MARY DARTER (1894-)	150-1200	L
COLEMAN, R. CLARKSON (1884 -)	200-3000	M
COLEMAN, RALPH PALLEN (1892 -)	100-1200	I,F
COLEMAN, SAMUEL (1832 - 1920)	1500-35000	L,M
COLL, JOSEPH C. (1881 - 1921)	*100-750	I
COLLIER, B.L. (19TH - 20TH C)	100-400	L
COLLIER, WILLIAM R. (19TH C)	*300-1500	X (L)
COLLINS, EARL (1925 -)	400-1800	X (L)

* Denotes watercolors, pastels, drawings, and/or mixed media

COLLINS, EMELIA (20TH C)	*100-800	X
COLLINS, FRANK H. (- 1935)	100-750	X (F)
COLLVER, ETHEL BLANCHARD (1875 - 1955)	750-4500	F
COLMAN, ROY CLARKSON (1884 -)	200-750	L
COLMAN, SAMUEL	*400-3500	
COLMAN, SAMUEL (1832 - 1920)	1500-35000	L,M
COLT, MORGAN (1876 - 1926)	450-4800	L
COLTMAN, ORA	*100-400	
COLTMAN, ORA (1860-)	100-1000	L
COLVON, S.M. (19TH C)	100-700	X(S)
COLYAR, P.M. (19TH-20TH C)	*100-600	M,L
COLYER, VINCENT (1825-1888)	*150-1500	L
COMAN, CHARLOTTE BUELL (1833 - 1924)	350-3500	L
COMEGYS, GEORGE H. (early 19TH C)	350-3500	G
COMINS, ALICE R. (- 1934)	300-650	L
COMINS, EBEN F. (1875-1949)	100-1000	X(F)
COMPERA, ALEXIS (1856 - 1906)	400-1200	L
COMSTOCK, ENOS BENJAMIN (1879 - 1945)	600-3000	X (I)
CONANT, ALBAN JASPER (1821 - 1915)	650-3000	F,M
CONANT, LUCY SCARSBOROUGH (1867 - 1921)	*200-900	L
CONARROE, GEORGE W. (1803 - 1882)	600-2500	F
CONE, MARVIN D. (1891-1964)	700-10000	X(L,F)
CONELY, WILLIAM B. (1830 - 1911)	300-2800	G,S,F
CONGDON, ADAIRENE VOSE (19TH C)	600-1800	X (G)
CONGDON, THOMAS RAPHAEL	*200-750	
CONGDON, THOMAS RAPHAEL (1862 - 1917)	400-4000	X (G)
CONGER, WILLIAM (early 20TH C)	*200-600	X (G)
CONKLIN, S. (19TH - 20TH C)	350-1200	X (M)
CONNAWAY, JAY HALL (1893 - 1970)	250-5500	M,L
CONNELL, EDWIN D. (1859 -)	800-3000	F,W
CONNER, ALBERT CLINTON (1848 - 1929)	150-850	L
CONNER, JOHN ANTHONY (20TH C)	150-600	L,M
CONNORS, BRUCE G. (1909 -)	*250-800	X (L)
CONREY, LEE F. (1883 -)	*100-650	I
CONSTANT, GEORGE (1892 - 1978)	*150-500	I

 * Denotes watercolors, pastels, drawings, and/or mixed media

CONTENT, DANIEL (1902-)	300-4500	I
CONTI, GINO EMILIO (1900 -)	100-350	G
CONWAY, FREDERICK E. (1900 - 1982)	*150-850	L,M
COOK, C.M. (19TH C)	150-1200	M
COOK, CAPTAIN (19TH - 20TH C)	1000-6000	P
COOK, CHARLES BAILEY (early 20TH C)	200-900	X (L)
COOK, DELIA E. (20TH C)	100-400	F,L
COOK, JOHN A. (1870-1936)	*200-850	M
COOK, MARION (19TH C ?)	300-1200	X (L)
COOK, NELSON (1817 - 1892)	300-5000	F
COOK, W.B. (19TH-20TH C)	100-500	L
COOKE, GEORGE (1793 - 1849)	700-4500	L,M
COOKMAN, CHARLES EDWIN (1856 -1913)	250-2000	F
COOLEY, B. (19TH C)	400-3500	X(L)
COOLIDGE, CASSIUS M. (1844-1934)	1000-15000	W
COOLIDGE, JOHN (1882-)	100-900	X(L)
COOLIDGE, JOHN (1918-1984)	150-1500	X(M)
COOMANS, DIANA (19TH-20TH C)	500-6000	F
COOMBS, DELBERT DANA (1850 - 1938)	150-3200	L,M
COOPER, A.L. (19TH C)	100-1000	X(M)
COOPER, ASTLEY D. M.(1856 - 1924)	300-15000	S,L,G,F
COOPER, COLIN CAMPBELL (1856 - 1937)	450-25000+	L,F,G
COOPER, EMMA LAMPERT (- 1920)	*400-1000	F,G
COOPER, GEORGE VICTOR (1810 - 1878)	150-650	L
COOPER, J. (18TH - 19TH C)	200-850	F
COOPER, LILLIAN (19TH-20TH C)	350-4000	G,F
COPE, GEORGE (1855 - 1929)	500-35000	S,L
COPE, GORDON (20TH C)	150-800	L
COPELAND, ALFRED BRYANT (1840 - 1909)	350-8500	G,L,S
COPELAND, CHARLES (1858 - 1945)	*100-900	L,I,M
COPELAND, ELEANOR R. (1875-)	*100-400	X(M)
COPELAND, JOSEPH FRANK (1872 -)	*100-850	L
COPLEY, JOHN SINGLETON (1737 - 1815)	2500-650000	F,M
COPLEY, WILLIAM (BILL) NELSON (1919-)	700-18000	A
COPPEDGE, FERN ISABELL (1888 -)	150-1500	L

* Denotes watercolors, pastels, drawings, and/or mixed media

CORBINO, JON (1905 - 1964)	400-5000	F,G,L
CORCOS, LUCILLE (1908 -)	*500-6000	X(L)
CORDREY, EARL SOMERS (1902 -)	*150-500	X (I)
COREY, BERNARD (20TH C)	250-800	L
CORNE, MICHEL FELICE (1752 - 1845)	*2000-25000	F,M
CORNELL, JOSEPH (1903 - 1972)	1000-20000	A
CORNOYER, PAUL (1864 - 1923)	500-30000	L
CORNWELL, DEAN (1892 - 1960)	400-45000	I
CORSON, ALICE VINCENT (- 1915)	750-3000	X (F)
CORSON, CHARLES SCHELL (- 1921)	400-6000	L
CORWIN, CHARLES ABEL (1857 - 1938)	*500-5500	G,L
COSTELLO, A. (20TH C)	100-500	X(M)
COSTELLO, DAVID (20TH C)	300-800	X
COSTIGAN, JOHN EDWARD (1888 - 1972)	450-15000	L,F
COSTSANEN, J. (1888 -)	1200-6000	G
COTE, ALAN (1937 -)	500-5000	A
COTTINGHAM, ROBERT	*1000-6000	
COTTINGHAM, ROBERT (1935 -)	5000-45000	A
COTTON, WILLIAM H.	*200-1800	
COTTON, WILLIAM H. (1880 - 1958)	350-7500	F,I
COUGHLIN, A.T. (late 19TH C)	400-2000	L
COUGHLIN, H. (20TH C)	*100-800	I
COULON, EMMA (19TH - 20TH C)	800-3500	L,G
COULON, GEORGE DAVID (1823 - 1904)	850-4500	L,F
COULON, PAULINE (19TH C)	*400-1200	X (W)
COULTER, MARY J. (20TH C)	100-700	L
COULTER, WILLIAM ALEXANDER (1849 - 1936)	900-18000	M
COUSE, EANGER IRVING	*500-25000	
COUSE, EANGER IRVING (1866 - 1936)	1000-80000	F,G
COUTER, FRANKLYN C. (19TH C)	700-2000	X (F)
COUTTS, ALICE (1880 - 1973)	400-4000	L,G
COUTTS, GORDON (1880 - 1937)	450-6000+	F,L
COVEY, ARTHUR SINCLAIR (1877-1960)	*100-1000	X(M)
COWAN, SARAH EAKIN (19TH-20TH C)	*150-900	F
COWELL, JOSEPH GROSS (19TH-20TH C)	100-700	X(L,F)

 * Denotes watercolors, pastels, drawings, and/or mixed media

COWLES, FLEUR (20TH C)	250-900	X
COX, ALBERT SCOTT (1863 - 1920)	500-3200	G,L,F,I
COX, ALLYN (1896 - 1982)	100-1500	L,F,S
COX, ARTHUR (late 19TH C)	*150-650	X (L)
COX, CHARLES BRINTON (1864 - 1905)	400-4000	X (G)
COX, KENYON (1856 - 1919)	500-5500	F,I
COX, L. CARR (19TH C)	100-600	X(S)
COX, L.M. (19TH - 20TH C)	100-400	X (L)
COX, WALTER (1866-1930)	100-3000	X(L)
COZZENS, FREDERICK SCHILLER (1846 - 1928)	*300-8500	M,I
CRAFFT, R.B. (active 1835-65)	600-2000	F
CRAIG, CHARLES (1846 - 1931)	850-8500	L,G,F
CRAIG, ISAAC EUGENE (1830 -)	500-2000	F,L
CRAIG, J.W. (20TH C ?)	*100-400	L
CRAIG, ROBERT (19TH C)	200-1000	L
CRAIG, THOMAS BIGELOW (1849 - 1924)	350-4500	L
CRAIG, WILLIAM (1829 - 1875)	*150-650	L
CRAM, ALLEN G. (1886-1947)	500-5000	M,F
CRAMER, FLORENCE BALLIN (1934-)	100-800	X(S)
CRAMER, KONRAD (1888-1963)	1000-12000	A
CRANCH, CHRISTOPHER PEARSE (1813 - 1892)	400-6500	L,F,S
CRANDELL, BRADSHAW (1896 - 1966)	*400-4000	I
CRANE, (ROBERT) BRUCE	*400-6000	
CRANE, (ROBERT) BRUCE (1857 - 1937)	800-30000	L
CRANE, ANN (20TH C)	250-850	L
CRANE, JAMES (20TH C)	800-4500	P
CRANE, STANLEY WILLIAM (1905 -)	450-1800	L,S
CRAVEN, STANLEY W. (1905-)	100-1000	X(S)
CRAWFORD, ALICE BERLE (20TH C)	*100-400	X (L)
CRAWFORD, EARL STETSON (1877 -)	600-3500	F
CRAWFORD, JAMES W. (1832 -)	*150-2500	S,G
CRAWFORD, RALSTON (1906 - 1978)	10000-185000	A
CRAWFORD, W. (1869 - 1944)	*100-900	I
CREE, JAMES (1867-1951)	*150-1400	X(L)
CRIEFELDS, RICHARD (1853 - 1939)	400-2000	S,F

* Denotes watercolors, pastels, drawings, and/or mixed media

CRIPS, G.A. (19TH-20TH C)	150-1200	L
CRISP, ARTHUR WATKINS (1881 -)	600-3000	G,I
CRISS, FRANCIS H.(1901 - 1973)	1000-18000	A,F,L
CRITCHER, CATHERINE CARTER (1868 -)	5000-32000	F
CROCKER, JOHN DENISON (1823 - 1879)	650-6000	L,F
CROCKWELL, DOUGLAS S. (1904 -1968)	600-7500	I
CROCKWELL, SPENCER DOUGLAS (1904 - 1968)	600-6000	I
CROMPTON, EDNA L. (20TH C)	100-500	X
CROMWELL, CHARLES (1838 -)	700-3000	F
CROOKS, R. (20TH C)	400-1500	X (G)
CROPSEY, JASPER FRANCIS (1823 - 1900)	3000-300000+	L,M
CROSBY, GEORGE L. (1833 -)	300-2500	G,M
CROSBY, RAYMOND MOREAU (1875 -)	*150-500	F
CROSKEY, W.H. (19TH C)	500-1500	X (G)
CROSS, HENRY H. (1837 - 1918)	500-22000	L,G,F
CROSSMAN, WILLIAM HENRY (1896 -)	350-1200	L,G
CROW, LOUISE (20TH C)	100-400	X (S)
CROWLEY, DAVID B. (20TH C)	100-650	X(L)
CROWLEY, J.M. (active c.1830-40)	*1200-4000	P
CROWNINGSHIELD, FREDERIC (1845 - 1918)	400-4500	L
CRUSET, SEBASTIEN (20TH C)	700-2000	X (L)
CRUTCHFIELD, WILLIAM (1932 -)	*500-1800	X
CUCARO, PASCAL (1915 -)	100-500	X
CUCCHI, ANTHONY (20TH C)	200-750	X
CUCUEL, EDWARD (1875 - 1951)	1000-38000	F,L
CULLEN, MAURICE GALBRAITH (19TH-20TH C)	350-4000	X(M)
CULLINGANE, A.C. (19TH C)	100-300	P
CULMER, HENRY L.A. (1854 - 1914)	800-3500	X
CULVER, CHARLES (1908 - 1967)	*100-750	L,W,F
CULVERHOUSE, JOHANN MONGELS (19TH C)	3000-23000	G,L
CUMMING, ARTHUR (19TH C)	150-500	X (S)
CUMMING, CHARLES ATHERTON (1858 - 1932)	400-4000	G,L
CUMMINGS, THOMAS SEIR (1804-1894)	700-5000	F
CUNEO, CYRUS C. (1878 - 1916)	150-2800	X (L,G)
CUNEO, RINALDO (RICHARD) (1877 - 1939)	250-3000	L

 * Denotes watercolors, pastels, drawings, and/or mixed media

CUNNINGHAM, EARL (1893 - 1978)	300-3000	P
CUNNINGHAM, FERN FRANCES (1889 -)	100-650	X (L,S)
CUNNINGHAM, PATRICIA S. (1919 -)	200-1500	X (M,L)
CUNNINGHAM (SR), CHARLES C. (1841-1918)	800-3500	M
CUPREIN, FRANK W. (1871 - 1948)	250-3000	L,M
CURRAN, CHARLES COURTNEY (1861 - 1942)	500-70000+	F,L,S
CURRAN, J. (19TH -20TH C)	500-4000	F,L
CURRIER, EDWARD WILSON (1857-1918)	100-950	L
CURRIER, JOSEPH FRANK (1843 - 1909)	600-2500	G,L
CURRIER, WALTER BARRON (1879 - 1934)	250-1600	L
CURRY, JOHN STEUART	*500-6500	
CURRY, JOHN STEUART (1897 - 1946)	700-35000	G,L
CURRY, ROBERT F. (1872 - 1945)	500-2500	L
CURTIN, THOMAS R. (19TH-20TH C)	150-900	L
CURTIS, ALICE MARION (1847-1911)	200-2300	L,S
CURTIS, ASA (- 1858)	100-450	M
CURTIS, C. (19TH C)	100-700	F
CURTIS, CALVIN (1822 - 1893)	250-1200	L
CURTIS, ELIZABETH (1873 -)	100-3000	L,M
CURTIS, EMILE (20TH C)	150-600	X (F)
CURTIS, GEORGE (1826 - 1881)	300-2500	M
CURTIS, LELAND (1897 -)	200-1200	L,M
CURTIS, MARIAN (1912 -)	*100-400	L
CURTIS, RALPH WORMELEY (late 19TH C)	600-40000	F,L
CUSHING, HOWARD GARDINER (1869 - 1916)	600-20000	L,F
CUSHING, J.C. (19TH C)	200-1000	X (S)
CUSHING, LILY (20TH C)	200-1200	X(S)
CUSHING, MARY A. (19TH C)	*200-600	F
CUSHING, OTTO (1871 - 1942)	*100-800	I
CUSHMAN, ALICE (1854-)	*100-650	X(L,M)
CUSTER, E.A. (19TH-20TH C)	100-850	L
CUSTER, EDWARD L. (1837 - 1880)	250-4500	P,W,L
CUSTIS, ELEANOR PARKE (1897 - 1983)	*500-5000	L,G,F
CUTHBERT, VIRGINIA (1908 -)	300-3500	G
CUTTING, FRANCIS HARVEY (1872-1964)	100-800	L,M

* Denotes watercolors, pastels, drawings, and/or mixed media

D

ARTIST	PRICE	SUBJECT
D'ARCANGELO, ALLAN (1930 -)	3000-20000	A
DABB, RAYMOND (19TH C)	650-2000	M
DABO, LEON (1868 - 1960)	250-20000	M,L,F,S
DABO, THEODORE SCOTT (1877 -)	150-900	M,L
DAGGY, RICHARD S. (1892 -)	*200-750	L
DAHLAGER, JULES (20TH C)	700-2500	X
DAHLGREEN, CHARLES W. (1864 - 1955)	400-2000	L
DAHLGREN, CARL CHRISTIAN (1841 - 1920)	300-5000	L
DAHLGREN, MARIUS (1844 - 1920)	400-3500	L
DAINGERFIELD, ELLIOTT (1859 - 1932)	500-6000	L,F,I
DAKEN, SIDNEY TILDEN (1876 - 1935)	100-2000	L
DALBIAC, F. (20TH C)	200-750	F
DALE, GEORGE EDWARD (1840 - 1873)	300-1500	X (G)
DALE, WILLIAM (19TH - 20TH C)	500-2500	L
DALEE, JUSTUS (active 1826-1847)	*300-2000	P
DALLAS, WILLIAM WILKINS (19TH C)	100-600	L
DALLIN, CYRUS EDWIN (1861 - 1944)	200-2000	L
DAMROW, CHARLES (1916 -)	350-4500	G,L
DANA, WILLIAM P.W. (1833-1927)	600-2000	L,G,M
DANIEL, WILLIAM SWIFT (1865 -)	150-900	L
DANIELS, ELMER HARLAND (1905 -)	100-300	L,F
DANLON, F. (JR.) (19TH - 20TH C)	600-5000	X (I,S)
DANNAT, WILLIAM TURNER (1853 - 1929)	500-3500	F,G
DANNER, SARA KOLB (1894 - 1969)	150-1500	L
DAPHNIS, NASSOS (1914 -)	100-1200	A
DARBY, ELIZABETH CLORINDA (- 1906)	500-2500	X (S)
DARBY, MARY (20TH C)	*100-500	X(L)
DARGE, FRED (1900 -)	100-400	G,L
DARLEY, FELIX OCTAVIUS CARR (1822 - 1888)	*100-6500	I,G
DARLING, DAVID T. (20TH C)	100-700	X(L)
DARLING, ROBERT (19TH C)	2500-10000	F
DARLING, WILDER M. (1856 - 1933)	*100-500	L

* Denotes watercolors, pastels, drawings, and/or mixed media

DARRAH, ANN SOPHIA TOWNE (1819 - 1881)	250-3000+	S,L,M
DARRO, TOM (20TH C)	300-2000	F
DART, RICHARD POUSETTE (20TH C)	1500-7000	X (F)
DASBURG, ANDREW	*500-12000	
DASBURG, ANDREW (1887 - 1979)	1200-85000+	A,L
DASH, ROBERT (1932 -)	350-1800	L
DATZ, ABRAHAM MARK (1891 - 1969)	100-450	L
DAUGHERTY, JAMES HENRY	*350-1500	
DAUGHERTY, JAMES HENRY (1889 - 1974)	600-28000	A,I
DAUGHERTY PAUL (1877 - 1947)	700-2800	L
DAVENPORT, HENRY (1882 -)	200-1800	G,L
DAVENPORT, W.S. (19TH - 20TH C)	150-900	X
DAVEY, RANDALL	*1000-28000	
DAVEY, RANDALL (1887 - 1964)	1500-55000	W,F
DAVID, S.S. (DE SCOTT EVANS)(1847 - 1898)	500-30000	S,G,F
DAVIDSON, ALLAN D. (19TH - 20TH C)	100-400	X (G)
DAVIDSON, CHARLES GRANT (1866-1945)	*200-1000	L
DAVIDSON, GEORGE (1889 - 1965)	250-750	L,G
DAVIDSON, GRACE (20TH C)	100-850	L
DAVIDSON, JO (1883 - 1952)	*100-900	F
DAVIDSON, MORRIS (1898 -)	*100-450	A
DAVIES, ALBERT WEBSTER (1889 - 1967)	400-3500	P
DAVIES, ARTHUR BOWEN	*400-6500	
DAVIES, ARTHUR BOWEN (1862 - 1928)	800-40000	A,F,L,
DAVIES, HAROLD CHRISTOPHER (?)	500-3000	X (L)
DAVIES, KEN (1925 -)	800-4500	S
DAVIS, A.C. (19TH - 20TH C)	100-500	X (S)
DAVIS, A.F. (20TH C ?)	150-750	L
DAVIS, ALEXANDER JACKSON (1803 - 1892)	*5000-20000	L
DAVIS, ALICE (1905-)	200-1500	X(L,M)
DAVIS, CHARLES HAROLD (1856 - 1933)	600-15000	L,G
DAVIS, EMMA EARLENBAUGH (1891-)	250-1000	X(S)
DAVIS, F. WATSON (19TH-20TH C)	*100-1500	F,G
DAVIS, FLOYD MACMILLAN (1896 - 1966)	*250-3000	I
DAVIS, GENE (1920 -)	1500-20000	A

* Denotes watercolors, pastels, drawings, and/or mixed media

DAVIS, GLADYS ROCKMORE (1901 - 1967)	500-5000	F
DAVIS, H.A. (19TH C)	500-1800	L
DAVIS, HARRY JR. (20TH C)	350-1500	X (G)
DAVIS, J. A. (active 1830-55)	*1000-9500	P
DAVIS, JAMES EDWARD (1901 -)	900-5000	X (G)
DAVIS, JERROLD (1926-)	100-900	X
DAVIS, JOHN STEEPLE (1844-1917)	300-2500	X (G)
DAVIS, JOSEPH H. (active 1832-37)	*1500-30000	P
DAVIS, LEE E. (1910-)	100-600	X
DAVIS, LEONARD MOORE (1864 - 1938)	300-3500	L
DAVIS, MARY DEFOREST (19TH C)	300-2800	L
DAVIS, RONALD (RON) WENDELL (1937 -)	2500-30000	A
DAVIS, STUART	*1000-100000	
DAVIS, STUART (1894 - 1964)	12000-225000	A
DAVIS, VESTIE E. (1904 - 1978)	400-8500	P
DAVIS, WARREN B.	*100-1200	
DAVIS, WARREN B. (1865 - 1928)	400-6500	F
DAVIS, WILLIAM MOORE (1829 - 1920)	1500-65000	L,G,S
DAVISSON, H.G. (1866-)	*100-500	L,W
DAWES, EDWIN M. (1872 -)	350-1500	L
DAWSON, GEORGE WALTER (1870 -)	300-1200	L,G,S
DAWSON, MARK (19TH C)	100-600	X (L)
DAWSON-WATSON, DAWSON (1864 - 1939)	450-15000	L
DAY, FRANCIS (1863 - 1942)	500-8000	L,G,F
DAY, NELLIE M. (19TH C)	150-850	L,G
DAY, W. PERCY (20TH C)	500-2500	F
DAYNE, EDGAR ALWIN (1882-1947)	400-4500	L
DE CAMP, JOSEPH RODEFER (1858 - 1923)	650-65000	L,F
DE DIEGO, JULIO (1900 - 1979)	*100-750	X
DE HAVEN, FRANKLIN (1856 - 1934)	350-7500	L
DE LEIRIS, JEANNE W. (20TH C)	*150-900	X(S)
DE NERO, ROBERT (1922-)	400-2000	A
DE RIBCOWSKY, DEY (1880 - 1935)	200-1500	M,L
DE THULSTRUP, THURE	*250-2000	
DE THULSTRUP, THURE (1849 - 1930)	700-6500	F,M,I

 * Denotes watercolors, pastels, drawings, and/or mixed media

DEAKIN, EDWIN (1838 - 1923)	350-25000	S,L
DEAN, EDWARD CLARENCE (1879 -)	*250-850	X (L)
DEAN, SOPHIA (19TH C)	800-2500	P
DEAN, WALTER LOFTHOUSE (1854 - 1912)	300-1500	M,G,L
DEARBORN, SAMUEL H. (actice 1800-25)	*200-500	F
DEARTH, HENRY GOLDEN (1864 - 1918)	900-9500	L,F
DEAS, CHARLES	*600-12000	
DEAS, CHARLES (1818 - 1867)	1000-65000	G,F
DEBLOIS, F.B. (19TH C)	400-6500	S
DECAMP, RALPH EARL (1858 - 1936)	400-3000	L
DECHAR, PETER (1942 -)	800-4500	A
DECKER, JOSEPH (1853 - 1924)	3500-165000+	S,L
DECKER, ROBERT M. (1847 -)	300-2500	L
DEFREES, T. (late 19TH C)	200-850	L
DEGREGORIO, L. (19TH-20TH C)	100-700	L
DEHAAS, M.F.H. (1832 - 1895)	500-12000+	M
DEHAVEN, FRANKLIN (1856-1934)	350-5000	L
DEHN, ADOLPH ARTHUR (1895 - 1968)	500-7500	
DEHN,ADOLPH ARTHUR	*350-4500	G,L
DEKLYN, CHARLES F. (20TH C ?)	150-600	L
DELAND, CLYDE OSMER (1872(19TH-20TH C)	250-1200	X(I)
DELANEY, BEAUFORD (1902 - 1979)	250-850	X (M)
DELANEY, JOSEPH (1904 -)	300-1500	X (G)
DELANO, GERARD CURTIS (1890 - 1972)	3500-30000	L,G
DELANOY, ABRAHAM (1740 - 1786)	*750-1500	P,F
DELBOS, JULIUS	*100-850	
DELBOS, JULIUS (1879 -)	250-3000	M,L
DELEROISE, C. (19TH C)	100-650	X (L)
DELLENBAUGH, FREDERICK S. (1853 - 1935)	800-25000	G,L
DELUCE, PERCIVAL (1847-1914)	200-1800	F
DEMEAUX, M. (20TH C)	100-300	F,L
DEMETROPOULOS, CHARLES (1912-1976)	*500-3000	X(L)
DEMING, EDWIN WILLARD	*450-4000	
DEMING, EDWIN WILLARD (1860 - 1942)	500-12000+	F,G,I,W
DEMUTH, CHARLES (1883 - 1935)	*1000-125000	A,F,S,L

* Denotes watercolors, pastels, drawings, and/or mixed media

DENNIS, L. (19TH-20TH C)	100-500	L
DENNIS, ROGERS WILSON (1902-)	200-3000	L
DENNY, GIDEON JACQUES (1830 - 1886)	500-6000	L,G,M,W
DENNY, J.C. (-1900)	250-2000	M
DENSLOW, WILLIAM WALLACE (1856 -)	*100-350	L
DERBY, HORACE B. (19TH C)	*150-850	M
DERIJCKE, J.L. (20TH C)	100-600	X (G)
DERRICK, WILLIAM ROWELL (- 1941)	350-1200	X (L)
DES PORT, A. (19TH C)	750-4500	X (G)
DESATNICK, MIKE (1943 -)	5000-18000	X
DESSAR, LOUIS PAUL (1867 - 1952)	300-4500+	G,L,W
DESVARREUX-LARPENTEUR, J.(1847 -)	400-2000	L,W
DETHLOFF, PETER HANS (1869-)	*100-650	L
DETREVILLE, RICHARD (1864 - 1929)	450-3000	L
DETWILLER, FREDERICK K. (1882 - 1953)	200-1800	I
DEVLAN, F.D. (1835 - 1870)	400-2000	L
DEVOLL, F. USHER (1873 - 1941)	250-3200	L
DEWEY, CHARLES MELVILLE (1849 - 1937)	400-7500	L
DEWEY, EDWARD H. (1850 - 1939)	500-3000	L,W
DEWEY, JAMES (19TH - 20TH C)	100-1000	X(G)
DEWING, MARIA OAKEY (1857 -)	850-18000	G
DEWING, THOMAS WILMER	*650-46000	
DEWING, THOMAS WILMER (1851 - 1938)	3000-20000	F
DEWOLFE, SARAH BINDER (- 1905)	100-750	X (S)
DIAO, DAVID (1943 -)	350-2500	A
DICK, CECIL (1915-)	*200-1200	X(F)
DICK, H.R. (19TH-20TH C)	300-3500	X(F)
DICK, M.G. (19TH - 20TH C)	200-750	X (S)
DICKERMAN, ALBERT (19TH - 20TH C)	250-3000	L
DICKINSON, ANSON (1780 - 1852)	*300-800	F
DICKINSON, DAROL (1942 -)	1500-4500	X (G)
DICKINSON, EDWIN W. (1891 - 1978)	3000-25000	A,L,F
DICKINSON, HOWARD CLINTON (20TH C)	100-700	L,M
DICKINSON, J.S. (19TH C)	150-600	X (G)
DICKINSON, PRESTON	*850-10000	

 * Denotes watercolors, pastels, drawings, and/or mixed media

DICKINSON, PRESTON (1891 - 1930)	1000-75000+	A
DICKINSON, ROSS (1903-)	100-1000	X(L)
DICKINSON, SIDNEY EDWARD (1890-)	450-6500	F
DICKMAN, CHARLES JOHN (1863-1943)	200-1800	L
DIEBENKORN, RICHARD	*7000-115000	
DIEBENKORN, RICHARD (1922 -)	150000-500000	A
DIEGO, JULIO DE (1900-1979)	*100-850	X
DIEHL, ARTHUR VIDAL (1870-1929)	200-3500	M,L
DIELMAN, FREDERICK (1847 - 1935)	*300-5000	I,F
DIETRICH, ADELHEID (1827 -)	5000-80000	S
DIKE , PHILIP LATIMER (1906 -)	100-850	L
DILLAWAY, THEODORE M. (1874 -)	100-850	L
DILLER, BURGOYNE (1906 - 1964)	5000-45000	A
DILLON, JULIA MCENTEE (1834 - 1919)	500-9500	S,L
DILLWORTH, C. (19TH C)	100-750	L
DINE, JIM	*2000-65000	
DINE, JIM (1935 -)	10000-138000	A
DINKEL, GEORGE W. (early 20TH C)	100-650	L
DINNERSTEIN, HARVEY (1928 -)	*200-900	I
DIRK, NATHANIEL (1895-1961)	*100-400	X(M)
DITEMAN, HALL (20TH C)	400-1800	X (L)
DITTMANN, JOHAN (- 1847)	100-850	F
DIX, CHARLES TEMPLE (1838 - 1872)	100-850	L,M,A
DIXON, FRANCIS STILLWELL (1879 - 1967)	200-1800	L
DIXON, L. MAYNARD	*200-10000	
DIXON, L. MAYNARD (1875 - 1946)	750-50000	L,F,I
DOBKIN, ALEXANDER (1908 - 1975)	100-850	X
DODD, LAMAR (1909 -)	400-3200	X (F)
DODDS, PEGGY (1900 -)	*100-400	X (G)
DODGE, CHESTER L. (1880 -)	150-750	L
DODGE, WILLIAM DE LEFTWICH (1867 - 1935)	600-7500	L,S
DODSON, RICHARD WHATCOAT (1812 - 1867)	*350-750	F
DODSON, SARAH BALL (1847 - 1906)	600-3200	L,G,F
DOFFLEMEYER, ? (19TH - 20TH C)	300-900	X (L)
DOHANOS, STEVAN	*400-2800	

* Denotes watercolors, pastels, drawings, and/or mixed media

DOHANOS, STEVAN (1907 -)	800-15000	I
DOLE, WILLIAM (1917 -)	*1000-6000	A
DOLICE, LEON (20TH C)	*100-500	L,M
DOLINSKY, NATHAN (1890 -)	100-750	L,F
DOLPH, JOHN HENRY (1835 - 1903)	750-8500+	W,G,F
DONAGHY, JOHN (1838 - 1931)	500-4800	S,L
DONAHUE, WILLIAM HOWARD (1881-)	300-1800	L
DONATI, ENRICO (1909 -)	800-15000	A
DONLY, EVA BROOK (1867 -)	100-850	L,M
DONNELL, JOHN (early 20TH C)	150-650	F
DONNELLY, THOMAS J. (1893 -)	100-1500	X
DONOHO, GAINES RUGER (1857 - 1916)	500-12000	L
DORAZIO, PIERO (20TH C)	2000-25000	A
DORIAN, C.S. (19TH - 20TH C)	300-1200	X (G,M)
DORIANI, WILLIAM (1891 - 1966)	200-800	G
DORINZ, D. (19TH -20TH C)	*400-1000	X (I)
DORNE, ALBERT (1904 - 1965)	*250-1200	I
DOUGHERTY, PARKE CUSTIS (1867 -)	400-7500	L
DOUGHERTY, PAUL (1877 - 1947)	300-18000	M,L
DOUGHTY , THOMAS (1793 - 1856)	2000-135000	L,M
DOUGLAS, CHESTER (1902 -)	300-1500	X
DOUGLAS, LUTHER (20TH C)	100-400	X
DOUGLAS, WALTER (1864 -)	350-2000	W,L
DOVE, ARTHUR GARFIELD	*2500-150000	
DOVE, ARTHUR GARFIELD (1880 - 1946)	15000-200000+	A,M,I
DOW, ARTHUR WESLEY (1857 - 1922)	400-16000	L
DOW, NELL PIERCE (20TH C)	200-750	L
DOW, OLIN (19TH C ?)	*350-900	L
DOWNAN, E. NEWMAN (19TH C)	100-700	X(F,L)
DOWNES, P.S. (late 19TH C)	*600-4500	P(M)
DOWNING, THOMAS (1928 -)	250-3000	A
DOYLE, WILLIAM M.S. (1769-1828)	400-6500	F
DRAGO, GABRIELLE (20TH C)	100-600	X (M)
DRAKE, CHARLES E. (1865 - 1918)	200-3000	F,L
DRAKE, WILLIAM HENRY (1856 - 1926)	200-900	W,I

* Denotes watercolors, pastels, drawings, and/or mixed media

DRAPER, EDITH (early 20TH C)	100-400	X (F)
DRAPER, WILLIAM FRANKLIN (1912 -)	350-1200	X (L)
DRAVER, ORRIN (20TH C)	100-650	L
DRAYTON, JOHN (1766 - 1822)	*250-800	X (I)
DREIER, KATHERINE S. (1877 - 1952)	*200-750	A
DREW, CLEMENT (1806 - 1889)	500-7500	M
DREW, GEORGE W. (1875 -)	200-3500	L
DREW BEAR, JESSIE (20TH C)	100-650	G,M,S
DREWES, WERNER (1899 - 1965)	700-28000	A
DREXEL, FRANCES MARTIN (1792 - 1863)	500-3500	X (L)
DRIGGS, ELSIE	*300-3500	
DRIGGS, ELSIE (1898 -)	1500-18000	A
DROWN, WILLIAM STAPLES (-1915)	350-3200	L
DRYDEN, HELEN (1887 -)	*200-1200	I
DRYSDALE, ALEXANDER JOHN (1870 - 1934)	400-6500	L
DUBE, MATHIE (1861 -)	350-1500	G,F
DUBOIS, CHARLES E. (1847 - 1885)	200-1000	L
DUBOIS, GUY PENE (1884 - 1958)	3000-72000	G,F
DUBREUIL, VICTOR (19TH - 20TH C)	1200-18000	S
DUCKETT, V.F. (20TH C)	*100-500	L
DUDLEY, FRANK VIRGIL (1868 -)	250-1500	L
DUESBURY, HORACE (1851 - 1940)	200-1200	L
DUESSEL, HENRY A. (19TH-20TH C)	200-2000	L,M
DUFNER, EDWARD	*500-12000	
DUFNER, EDWARD (1872 - 1957)	750-22000	L,F
DUGMORE, A. RADCLYFFE (20TH C)	100-400	X (W)
DUGMORE, EDWARD (1915 -)	700-3000	A
DULL, JOHN J. (1862 -)	*100-500	L
DUMLER, MARTIN GEORGE (1868 - 1934)	150-650	F,S
DUMMER, H. BOYLSTON (1878 -)	100-600	I
DUMMER, JOSEPH OWEN (?)	250-900	L
DUMOND, FRANK VINCENT (1865 - 1951)	400-5500	I,L
DUMONT, JO (19TH - 20TH C)	400-1000	G,F
DUMONT, PAUL (20TH C)	150-700	X (M)
DUNBAR, CARL (20TH C)	100-600	X(L)

* Denotes watercolors, pastels, drawings, and/or mixed media

DUNBAR, HAROLD (1882 -)	150-2000	L,F,I,S
DUNBAR, LILI (20TH C)	450-1200	X (G)
DUNBAR, PATRICK (20TH C)	450-1500	M
DUNBIER, AUGUSTUS WILLIAM (1888 - 1977)	600-1800	L
DUNCANSON, ROBERT SCOTT (1821 - 1872)	400-25000	L
DUNINGTON, A. (19TH C)	200-1400	X(M)
DUNLAP, EUGENE (20TH C)	100-650	L
DUNLAP, MARY STEWART (20TH C)	100-450	L
DUNLAP, WILLIAM (1766 - 1839)	500-3000	F
DUNLOP, DAN (20TH C)	100-400	X (G)
DUNN, HARVEY T. (1884 - 1952)	2000-65000	I
DUNN, JULIA E. (1850 -)	*200-700	F
DUNNING, ROBERT SPEAR (1829 - 1905)	3000-65000+	S
DUNSMORE, JOHN WARD (1856 - 1945)	700-3500	G,F
DUNTON, WILLIAM HERBERT	*100-7000	
DUNTON, WILLIAM HERBERT (1878 - 1936)	2500-60000	I,F,L
DUPONT, ANNE (19TH-20TH C)	*100-700	F
DURAN, BOB (ROBERT)(1938 -)	500-3000	A
DURAND, ASHER BROWN (1796 - 1886)	3000-100000	L
DURAND, ELIAS (19TH C)	100-750	X(L)
DURAND, J.C. (19TH C)	150-900	L
DURAND, JOHN (18TH C)	500-3500	P
DUREAU, GEORGE (1930 -)	500-5500	F
DUREN, KARL (19TH - 20TH C)	500-3000	L
DUREN, TERENCE ROMAINE (1907 -)	300-6500	G
DURRIE, GEORGE HENRY (1820 - 1863)	5000-125000	L,F
DUTANT, CHARLES (1908 -)	150-900	L
DUTHEIL, E. (19TH-20TH C)	150-850	G,M
DUVENECK, FRANK (1848 - 1919)	3000-85000	F,L
DUYCKINCK, GERARDUS (1695 - 1742)	8000-35000	P
DWIGHT, JULIA S. (1870 -)	800-5500	F,L
DWYER, A. (19TH C)	*150-750	I,G
DYE, CHARLIE (1906 - 1973)	10000-85000	L
DYE, CLARKSON (1869 - 1945)	250-3000	L
DYER, C.L. (19TH C)	150-800	X (L)

 * Denotes watercolors, pastels, drawings, and/or mixed media

DYER, CHARLES GIFFORD (1846 - 1912)	*300-1200	L
DYER, ELIZABETH GRIFFIN (19TH C)	100-600	L
DYER, HEZEKIAH ANTHONY	*200-1500	
DYER, HEZEKIAH ANTHONY (1872-1943)	200-1500	L,M
DYER, NANCY A. (1903 -)	*100-850	X (I)
DYER, URIAH N. (19TH C)	350-1200	X (S)
DYKE, SAMUEL P. (active 1855-70)	200-3500	L,G
DYNINGER, F. (20TH C)	100-400	L
DZIGURSKI, ALEXANDER (1910 -)	350-2500	M,L
DZUBAS, FRIEDEL (1915 -)	1500-25000	A

E

ARTIST	PRICE	SUBJECT
EAKINS, SUSAN MACDOWELL (1851 - 1938)	450-6500	F,G
EAKINS, THOMAS	*3500-575000	
EAKINS, THOMAS (1844 - 1916)	8000-2450000	G,F,M
EARHART, JOHN FRANKLIN (1853 - 1938)	300-1500	L
EARL, JAMES (1761 - 1796)	2000-8000	F
EARL, RALPH (1751 - 1801)	800-30000	P
EARL, RALPH E.W. (1786-1838)	5000-35000	P
EARLE, EYVIND (1916 -)	500-3500	L
EARLE, LAWRENCE CARMICHAEL	*250-3000	
EARLE, LAWRENCE CARMICHAEL (1845 - 1921)	400-4500	F,S
EARLY, MILES T. (1886 -)	200-750	X (G)
EASTMAN, EMILY (early 19TH C)	*1000-6000	F
EASTMAN, WILLIAM JOSEPH (1888 - 1950)	100-850	L,S
EATON, CHARLES HARRY (1850 - 1901)	400-4500	L
EATON, CHARLES WARREN	*200-2500	
EATON, CHARLES WARREN (1857 - 1937)	500-14000	L
EATON, JOSEPH ORIEL (1829 - 1875)	350-4500	G,F
EATON, VALOY (1938 -)	800-8000	X(L)
EATON, WYATT (1849 - 1896)	500-6500	F

* Denotes watercolors, pastels, drawings, and/or mixed media

EBERT, CHARLES H. (1873 - 1959)	500-7500	L,M
EBERT, MARY ROBERTS (1873 -)	*200-1200	L,M
EBY, KERR (1889 - 1946)	*200-1200	I
EDDY, DON (1904-)	4000-35000	A
EDDY, HENRY STEPHENS (1878 - 1944)	300-3500	L,M
EDDY, OLIVER TARBELL (1799 - 1868)	400-1500	X (F)
EDE, FREDERIC (1865 -)	400-2800	G,L
EDGERLY, BEATRICE (20TH C)	100-300	X (F)
EDLICH, STEPHEN (1944 -)	*500-10000	A
EDMONDS, FRANCIS WILLIAM (1806 - 1863)	1500-75000	G,L
EDMONDSON, WILLIAM JOHN (1868 -)	150-2500	F,L
EDSTROM, PETER DAVID (1873-1938)	100-2000	L
EDWARD, CHARLES (1797 - 1868)	200-1200	L
EDWARDS, ALICE (19TH C)	200-800	X (L)
EDWARDS, GEORGE WHARTON (1869 - 1950)	300-4500+	G,F,L
EDWARDS, HARRY C. (1868-1922)	200-1500	F,I
EDWARDS, JEANETTE SLOCOMB (20TH C)	100-600	L
EDWARDS, LIONEL (20TH C)	100-600	L
EDWARDS, T.F. (20TH C ?)	200-800	X (G)
EDWARDS, THOMAS (active 1820-55)	500-2500	F,L
EFFIE, WILLIAM (active 1835-50)	700-2000	F
EGAN, ELOISE (20TH C)	300-1000	X (G)
EGGENHOFER, NICK	*450-20000	
EGGENHOFER, NICK (1897 -)	6000-50000	G,F,I
EGGINTON, FRANK (20TH C)	*100-500	L
EGGLESTON, ANNA C. (20TH C)	200-2000	X(F)
EGGLESTON, BENJAMIN OSRO (1867 - 1937)	300-7500	G,F,L,M
EGGMEYER, MAVIC KAUFMANN (20TH C)	100-800	L
EGLAU (EGLAN), MAX (1825 -)	750-5000	L,S
EHNINGER, JOHN WHETTON (1827 - 1889)	1500-30000	G
EICHELBERGER, ROBERT A. (19TH C)	500-3200	G
EICHHOLTZ, JACOB (1776 - 1842)	700-25000	F
EILERS, EMMA (20TH C)	400-3500	X
EILSHEMIUS, LOUIS MICHEL (1864 - 1941)	200-5500	A,F,L
EISELE, CHRISTIAN (19TH - 20TH C)	250-1200	L,F

 * Denotes watercolors, pastels, drawings, and/or mixed media

EISENLOHR, EDWARD G. (1872 - 1961)	200-900	L
EISENMAN, MICHAEL (20TH C)	100-900	F,G,L
ELDER, JOHN ADAMS (1833 - 1895)	500-5000	G,F
ELDRED, LEMUEL D. (1848 - 1921)	500-6000+	M
ELK, ALBERT LOOKING (20TH C)	400-3500	L
ELKINS, HENRY ARTHUR (1847 - 1884)	300-3000	L
ELLINGER, DAVID (20TH C)	*300-3000	P
ELLIOT, LIDIE (19TH C)	100-450	X (F)
ELLIOTT, CHARLES LORING (1812 - 1868)	350-5000	F
ELLIS, A. (active 1830-35)	1000-4500	P
ELLIS, CLYDE GARFIELD (1879 -)	100-300	X (L)
ELLIS, FREMONT F. (1897 -)	800-15000	L
ELLSWORTH, CLARENCE ARTHUR	*350-1800	
ELLSWORTH, CLARENCE ARTHUR (1885 - 1961)	700-10000	F,G
ELLSWORTH, JAMES SANFORD (1802 - 1874)	*500-3000	P(F)
ELTING, N.D. (19TH C)	350-1500	X (S)
ELWELL, D. JEROME (1857 - 1912)	750-3000	X (L)
ELWELL, ROBERT FARRINGTON (1874 - 1962)	300-4000	G,F
ELWELL, W.H. (?)	100-500	M
EMBRY, NORRIS (1921 - 1981)	*500-2500	A
EMBURY, J.H. (19TH C)	200-1500	L
EMERSON, ARTHUR WEBSTER (1885-)	100-1000	X(M,L)
EMERSON, CHARLES CHASE (1874 - 1922)	350-5000	I
EMERSON, William C. (20TH C)	200-1500	F,L
EMERY, JAMES (active 1865-75)	750-4000	M
EMMET, LYDIA FIELD (1866 - 1952)	800-18000+	F,I
EMMONS, ALEXANDER HAMILTON (1816 - 1879)	300-1500	F
EMMONS, CHANSONETTA S.(1858 - 1937)	350-2500	L,F,G,S
EMMONS, DOROTHY STANLEY (1891 -)	350-2800	L
EMPEL, JAN VAN (20TH C)	700-2000	X
ENDERS, FRANK (20TH C)	500-2500	X (F)
ENDERS, OSCAR (19TH C ?)	100-500	L
ENGEL, NISSAN (20TH C)	500-2000	G
ENGELHARDT, WALTER (20TH C)	100-500	L
ENGLE, HARRY L. (1870 -)	200-2500	L

ENGLEHARDT, JOSEPH J. (1859-)	100-1500	L
ENGLEHEART, JOHN C.D. (1783-1862)	100-650	F
ENGLISH, FRANK F.	*150-2200	
ENGLISH, FRANK F. (1854 - 1922)	300-5000	L,G
ENNEKING, JOHN JOSEPH (1841 - 1916)	800-48000+	L
ENNIS, GEORGE PEARCE	*100-800	
ENNIS, GEORGE PEARCE (1884 - 1936)	300-5500	M
ENSER, JOHN F. (1898 -)	150-1000	X (L)
EPPENS, WILLIAM H. (1885-)	100-500	X(L)
ERDELEY, FRANCIS DE (1904 - 1959)	200-2500	G,F
ERICSON, DAVID (1873 - 1946)	250-1800	M,L
ERNESTI, ETHEL H. (19TH-20TH C)	200-1800	F
ERNST, JIMMY	*500-4000	
ERNST, JIMMY (1920 - 1984)	800-25000	A
ERTZ, EDWARD F.	*100-750	
ERTZ, EDWARD F. (1862 -)	300-6200	L,F,I
ESLEY, DONALD W. (20TH C)	*100-700	F
ESNAULT, MAURICE (20TH C)	100-400	L
ESPOY, ANGEL DE SERVICE (1869 - 1962)	150-3500	M,L
ESSIG, GEORGE EMERICK	*150-850	
ESSIG, GEORGE EMERICK (1883 - 1919)	450-4000	M,I
ESTES, RICHARD (1936 -)	3000-150000+	A
ETHERIDGE, C.B. (19TH C)	800-3000	X (S)
ETNIER, STEPHEN MORGAN (1903 -)	200-2500	M
ETTING, EMLEN (1905 -)	200-3000	X
EUBANK, TONY (1939 -)	1000-12000	X
EUGREN, GIL (20TH C)	200-4000	I
EURIGHT, M. W. (1881 - 1966)	*200-2000	I
EVANS, BRUCE (20TH C)	800-3500	A
EVANS, DE SCOTT (S.S.DAVID)(1847 - 1898)	500-30000	S,G,F
EVANS, J. (active 1831-1835)	*1500-5500	P
EVANS, JAMES GUY	*750-7500	
EVANS, JAMES GUY (mid 19TH C)	5000-50000	P(M)
EVANS, JESSIE BENTON (1866 - 1954)	250-1000	L,F
EVANS, RUDULPH (1878 - 1960)	200-850	F

 * Denotes watercolors, pastels, drawings, and/or mixed media

EVERETT, E. DEARBURN (19TH C)	*100-400	L
EVERGOOD, PHILIP	*250-8000	
EVERGOOD, PHILIP (1901-1973)	1800-25000+	A
EVERINGHAM, MILLARD (1912 -)	100-500	X
EVERLY, C. (20TH C)	100-600	X(S)
EVERS, JOHN (1797 - 1884)	400-3500	L,G
EVETT, KENNETH WARNOCK (1913 -)	100-300	X (F)
EYDEN, WILLIAM ARNOLD JR (1893 -)	*200-1200	L
EYLES, D.C. (- 1975)	200-2000	X(F)
EYTINGE, SOLOMON (JR) (1833 - 1905)	700-5000	X (G,I)

F

ARTIST	PRICE	SUBJECT
FABER, JOHN (- 1906)	100-400	L
FABER, LUDWIG E.	*100-600	
FABER, LUDWIG E. (1855 - 1913)	200-1800	L,M
FAGAN, JAMES (1864 -)	100-850	F
FAHNESTOCK, HENRY REIGERT (1830 - 1909)	600-3800	L
FAHNESTOCK, WALLACE WEIR (1877 -)	250-4000	L
FAIRFIELD, HANNAH T. (1808 - 1894)	15000-41000	P
FAIRMAN, JAMES (1826 -1904)	800-15000	L
FALCONER, JOHN M. (1820 - 1903)	1000-6500	L
FALES, P. (late 19TH C)	100-750	X (G)
FALKNER, HENRY (20TH C)	100-700	X
FALTER, JOHN PHILIP (1910 - 1982)	300-20000	I
FANGOR, WOJCIECH (1922 -)	900-3500	A
FARETO, P. (19TH C)	150-1500	X(S)
FARIS, J.A. (late 19TH C)	*350-1200	F
FARLEY, RICHARD BLOSSOM (1875 -)	500-3500	L
FARLOW, HARRY (1882-)	300-3500	X(F)
FARNDON, WALTER (1876 - 1964)	300-4000	M,L
FARNES, W.M. (19TH C)	100-750	X (M)

FARNSWORTH, ALFRED VILLIERS (1858 - 1908)	*200-850	X (G)
FARNSWORTH, JERRY (1895 - 1983)	300-2500	I,F
FARNUM, HERBERT CYRUS (1886 -)	150-1200	M
FARNY, HENRY F.	*1500-230000	
FARNY, HENRY F. (1847 - 1916)	2000-525000	I,G,L
FARRE, HENRI (1871 - 1934)	250-5000	L
FARRER, HENRY (1843 - 1903)	*300-6800	L
FARRINGTON, MRS ARCH (19TH - 20TH C)	500-3000	G
FASONE, PHILIP A. (20TH C)	100-500	L
FASSETT, TRUMAN E. (1885 -)	200-1200	L
FATTON, GEORGE (19TH C)	150-650	X (F)
FAULKNER, HERBERT W. (1860 - 1940)	200-1800	L,G,I
FAURE, MARIE (19TH C)	250-850	W,S
FAUSETT, WILLIAM DEAN (1913 -)	100-800	L
FAWCETT, ROBERT (1903 - 1967)	*250-4500	I
FAY, WILLIAM E. (1882 - 1967)	*200-900	X (G)
FECHIN, NICOLAI I. (1881 - 1955)	4500-65000+	F,G
FEELEY, PAUL (1913 - 1966)	1500-9000	A
FEININGER, LYONEL	*600-35000	
FEININGER, LYONEL (1871 - 1956)	20000-300000	A,I
FEINSTEIN, SAMUEL (20TH C)	*100-300	X (G)
FEKE, ROBERT (1724 - 1769)	800-5000	F
FELINGER, JEAN PAUL (late 19TH C)	200-900	X (F)
FELL, J.R. (20TH C)	100-400	L
FELLOWS, BYRON W. (19TH-20TH C)	100-900	X(M)
FELLOWS, FRANK WAYLAND (1833 - 1900)	200-1000	X (L)
FELLOWS, FRED (1934 -)	2000-18000	X (L)
FENIMORE, T.J. (19TH C)	300-1200	X (L)
FENN, HARRY (1845 - 1911)	*250-2500	I
FENSON, R. (19TH - 20TH C)	200-950	L
FENTON, CHARLES L. (1808 - 1877)	600-2000	X (F)
FENTON, HALLIE CHAMPLIN (1880 - 1935)	100-900	L
FENTON, JOHN WILLIAM (1875-)	150-900	X(S)
FEO, CHARLES DE (1892 - 1978)	*100-500	X (F)
FERBER, HERBERT	*6000-18000	

 * Denotes watercolors, pastels, drawings, and/or mixed media

FERBER, HERBERT (1906 -)	15000-50000	A
FERGUSON, ELEANOR M. (1876 -)	100-900	X (S)
FERGUSON, HENRY A. (1845 - 1911)	400-6500	L
FERREN, JOHN	*300-3500	
FERREN, JOHN (1905 - 1970)	600-12000	A
FERRIS, JEAN LEON JEROME (1863 - 1930)	1000-7500	G
FERY, JOHN (1865 - 1934)	400-6000+	L,W
FEUDEL, ARTHUR (1857 -)	*150-900	L
FEVRET DE ST MEMIN, CHARLES (1770 - 1852)	2500-8000	F
FIEDLER, LEOPOLD (19TH C)	*100-700	X(L)
FIELD, EDWARD LOYAL (1856 - 1914)	250-2000	L
FIELD, ERATUS SALISBURY (1805 - 1900)	1500-35000+	P
FIELD, ROBERT (1769-1819)	700-6000	F
FIELDING, G. (19TH C)	100-1000	X (L,M)
FIENE, ERNEST (1894 - 1965)	200-6500	L,S,F
FILCER, LUIS (20TH C)	100-700	A
FILLEAU, EMERY A. (active 1890-1910)	500-4500	G,L,F
FILMUS, TULLY (1908 -)	*100-700	X (G,F)
FINCH, E.E. (active 1832-1850)	800-20000	P
FINCH, KEITH (1920 -)	150-800	A
FINCH, RUBY DEVOL (19TH C)	1000-4800	F
FINCK, HAZEL (1894 - 1977)	200-850	L
FINCKEN, JAMES H. (1860 - 1943)	150-650	L
FINK, DON (1923-)	100-1000	A
FINK, FREDERICK (1817 - 1849)	500-2500	G,F
FINKELGREEN, DAVID (1888 - 1931)	650-3000	G,F
FINSTER, REVEREND HOWARD (1916 -)	200-2000	P
FIRENZE, PAUL (20TH C)	*1500-3500	X
FISCHER, ANTON OTTO (1882 - 1962)	500-8500	M,G,I
FISH, CARRIE NOELLA (19TH-20TH C)	*100-450	L
FISH, GEORGE G. (1849 -)	*100-850	X (I,M)
FISH, JANET (1938 -)	4000-45000	A
FISHER, ALVAN (1792 - 1863)	1500-18000	L,G,F,M
FISHER, ANNE S. (- 1942)	*100-750	M,L
FISHER, D.A. (19TH C)	100-500	L,M

* Denotes watercolors, pastels, drawings, and/or mixed media

FISHER, GEORGE H. (19TH C ?)	*400-1500	L
FISHER, HARRISON (1875 - 1934)	*400-22000	I
FISHER, HUGO ANTOINE (1854 - 1916)	*250-2500	L,W
FISHER, HUGO MELVILLE (1876 - 1946)	100-1200	L,M
FISHER, MAC S. (20TH C)	*100-600	L
FISHER, MARK (WILLIAM MARK)(1841 - 1923)	500-9500	L,F
FISK, HARRY T. (20TH C)	500-1200	X
FISKE, GERTRUDE (1879 - 1961)	500-9500	F,L
FITLER WILLIAM CROTHERS (1857 - 1915)	250-3000	L
FITZ, ALLEE C. (19TH - 20TH C)	300-1500	X (S)
FITZ, BENJAMIN RUTHERFORD (1855 - 1891)	400-2500	X (G)
FITZGERALD, HARRINGTON (1847 - 1930)	150-1500	M,L
FITZGERALD, JAMES (1899-)	*100-650	L
FLAGG, H. PEABODY (1859 -)	*100-750	L,M,G
FLAGG, JAMES MONTGOMERY	*150-2500	
FLAGG, JAMES MONTGOMERY (1877 - 1960)	800-10000	I
FLAGG, MONTAGUE (1842 - 1915)	400-1200	X (S)
FLAHERTY, THORPE (19TH - 20TH C)	300-750	L
FLANNAGAN, JOHN B. (1898 - 1942)	*450-3500	X (F)
FLANNERY, VAUGHN (20TH C)	250-1000	X (G)
FLAVELLE, GEOFF H. (19TH - 20TH C)	*150-650	L,M
FLAVIN, DAN (1933 -)	*750-7500	A
FLECK, JOSEPH A. (1892 - 1977)	1000-9000	L,F
FLEISCHBEIN, FRANCOIS (1804 - 1862)	350-8000	F
FLEMING, CAPEN A. (20TH C)	100-500	L
FLENEAR, J.W. (19TH C)	100-800	X(L)
FLETCHER, AARON DEAN (1817-1902)	300-3200	X(F)
FLETCHER, CALVIN (1882 -)	200-850	L,M
FLOCH, JOSEPH (JOSEF) (1894 - 1977)	200-750	F
FLOETER, KENT (1937 -)	*300-700	A
FLORIAN, WALTER (1878 - 1909)	600-1500	L,F
FLORIMONT, AUSTIN (active 1775-95)	*800-1800	F
FLORSHEIM, RICHARD ABERLE (1916 - 1979)	150-650	X
FOERSTER, EMIL (1822-1906)	500-12000	F
FOGARTY, THOMAS (1873 - 1938)	*150-3500	I

 * Denotes watercolors, pastels, drawings, and/or mixed media

FOLAWN, THOMAS JEFFERSON (1876 - 1934)	*100-900	X (F)
FOLINSBEE, JOHN FULTON (1892 - 1972)	500-5000	L
FOLLETT, FOSTER O. (1872 -)	500-1800	S
FONDA, HARRY STUART (1864-1942)	100-800	L
FOOTE, JACK (20TH C)	250-900	X
FOOTE, WILL HOWE (1874 - 1965)	300-7000	L,F
FORBES, CHARLES S. (1860 -)	150-2500	L,F,I
FORBES, EDWIN (1839 - 1895)	750-4500	L,W,M
FORD, ELISA (20TH C)	100-600	X(S)
FORD, HENRY CHAPMAN (1828 - 1894)	200-900	L
FORD, LOREN (1891 -)	350-1200	X (G)
FORD, NEILSON (- 1931)	200-800	X (F)
FORDNEY, B.F. (1873-)	400-4500	F,G
FOREST, LOCKWOOD DE (1850 - 1932)	150-1000	L,M
FOREST, ROY DE (20TH C)	500-7500	A
FOREST, WESNER LA (20TH C)	700-4800	F
FORESTER, ? (19TH C)	100-400	X (S)
FORESTORR, ? (20TH C)	*100-600	X (G)
FORKER, EDWIN (20TH C)	100-600	L
FORKUM, ROY (20TH C)	100-1500	A
FORRESTAL, F.J. (20TH C)	250-1200	L
FORRESTER, L. (19TH-20TH C)	100-650	L
FORSTER, GEORGE (19TH C)	1000-15000	S,G
FORSYTHE, VICTOR CLYDE (1885 - 1962)	400-6000	L,G
FORTUNE, E. CHARLTON (1885 - 1969)	500-15000	L,F
FOSBURGH, JAMES WHITNEY (1910 -)	100-2400	X
FOSS, HARRIEET CAMPBELL (1860 - 1938)	150-1200	X(F)
FOSS, OLIVIER (1920 -)	200-900	L
FOSS, PETER OLIVER (1865 - 1932)	450-3000	P
FOSTER, ALAN (1892 - 1934)	700-4500	I
FOSTER, ARTHUR TURNER (1877-)	100-750	X(L,S)
FOSTER, BEN	*200-1200	
FOSTER, BEN (1852 - 1926)	200-6000 +	L,S
FOSTER, CHARLES (1850 - 1931)	300-1800	L
FOSTER, G.S. (20TH C)	200-750	L

* Denotes watercolors, pastels, drawings, and/or mixed media

FOSTER, H.K. (19TH C)	400-1800	L
FOSTER, JOHN (1648 - 1681)	*500-950	F,I,L
FOSTER, WILL (1882 -)	150-1200	F,S
FOUJIOKA, NOBOM (20TH C)	100-600	L
FOULKE, CAPTAIN B.F. (19TH - 20TH C)	100-400	X (M)
FOULKES, LLYN (1934 -)	1000-5000	A
FOUNTAIN, GRACE R. (1857-1942)	100-900	L
FOURNIER, ALEXIS JEAN (1865 - 1948)	500-5000	L
FOWLER, FRANK (1852 - 1910)	200-2500	F
FOWLER, O.R. (early 19TH C)	900-5000	P
FOWLER, TREVER THOMAS (1830 - 1871)	400-2000	G,F
FOX, ROBERT ATKINSON (1860 - 1927)	350-2000	L,G,I
FRANCA, MANUEL JOACHIM DE (1808 - 1865)	450-7500	F,G
FRANCE, EURILDA LOOMIS (1865 - 1931)	200-5500	L,I
FRANCE, JESSE LEACH (1862 -)	100-950	L,M
FRANCIS, JOHN F. (1808 - 1886)	1500-75000	S,F
FRANCIS, JOHN JESSE (1889-)	*100-500	L
FRANCIS, MRS. JYRA (19TH C)	200-700	X (M)
FRANCIS, SAM	*2000-130000	
FRANCIS, SAM (1923 -)	15000-825000	A
FRANCISCO, J. BOND (1863 - 1931)	400-4500	L
FRANK, CHARLES L. (19TH - 20TH C)	100-600	L
FRANK, E.C. (19TH-20TH C)	100-1000	F
FRANK, GERALD A. (1888 -)	100-900	X (G)
FRANK, MARY (1933 -)	*200-1500	A
FRANKENBERG, H. (19TH C)	150-1400	G
FRANKENSTEIN, GODFREY N.(1820 - 1873)	500-5000+	L
FRANKENTHALER, HELEN (1928 -)	2500-100000	A
FRANSIOLI, THOMAS ADRIAN (1906 -)	600-5500	A
FRANZEN, AUGUST	*300-1800	
FRANZEN, AUGUST (1863 - 1938)	3500-9000	G,F
FRASCONI, ANTONIO M. (1919 -)	*100-850	I
FRASER, CHARLES A. (1782 - 1860)	600-4500	L,F
FRASER, THOMAS DOUGLAS (1885-1955)	300-2800	L
FRAZER, WILLIAM (18TH - 19TH C)	400-1500	M

 * Denotes watercolors, pastels, drawings, and/or mixed media

FRAZIER, KENNETH (1867 - 1949)	300-4000	L,F
FREDERICK, FRANK FOREST (1866 -)	250-1000	L
FREDERICKS, ALFRED (19TH C)	150-800	I
FREDERICKS, ERNEST (1877 -)	100-900	L
FREEDLANDER, ARTHUR R. (1875 - 1940)	100-450	L,F
FREEDLEY, DURR (1888 -1938)	500-5000	X (F)
FREEDMAN, MAURICE (1904 -)	300-1000	X (S)
FREELAND, ANNA C. (1837 - 1911)	100-500	F,G,S
FREEMAN, CHARLES H. (1859-1918)	400-3500	X
FREEMAN, DON (1908 -)	500-8500	G
FREEMAN, GEORGE (1787-1868)	400-2800	F
FREEMAN, JAMES EDWARD (1808 - 1884)	500-2000	F,G
FREEMAN, STEWART (20TH C)	100-400	X
FREEMAN, WILLIAM (1925 -)	500-2000	X (W)
FREER, FREDERICK WARREN	*250-1500	
FREER, FREDERICK WARREN (1849-1908)	350-3000	L
FREEZOR, W.H.M. (20TH C)	100-600	X (F)
FREILICHER, JANE (1924 -)	200-1000	L
FREITAG, CONRAD (active 1875-95)	300-1200	M
FRELINGHUYSEN, SUZY (1912 -)	2500-18000	A
FRENCH, FRANK (1850 - 1933)	300-1200	A (G)
FRENCH, JARED (1905 -)	1500-65000	G,I
FRENZENY, PAUL (19TH C)	*200-1200	F
FRERICHS, WILLIAM C. A. (1829 - 1905)	600-12000+	L,M,S
FRESQUIS, PEDRO ANTONIO (active 1810-40)	100-850	X (G)
FREY, JOSEPH (1892 - 1977)	200-1500	L
FRIEDENTHAL, DAVID (20TH C)	*200-850	X (L)
FRIEDMAN, ARNOLD (1879 - 1946)	850-12000	L,F,S
FRIEDMAN, MARTIN (1896 -)	100-300	M
FRIEND, WASHINGTON F. (1820 - 1881)	*150-1000	L
FRIES, CHARLES ARTHUR (1854 - 1940)	150-2500	L,I
FRIESEKE, FREDERICK CARL (1874 - 1939)	4000-450000+	F,L
FRITZ, HENRY EUGENE (1875-)	300-2500	G
FROHER, ROWLAND (20TH C)	*100-600	X (G)
FROMKES, MAURICE (1872 - 1931)	100-1500	F,S

FROMUTH, CHARLES HENRY (1861 - 1937)	*350-1800	X
FROST, ARTHUR BURDETT	*300-18000	
FROST, ARTHUR BURDETT (1851 - 1928)	2000-18000	I
FROST, FRANCIS S. (late 19TH C)	300-2500	L
FROST, GEORGE ALBERT (1843 -)	400-2800	L,G
FROST, JOHN (1890 - 1937)	600-18000	F,L
FROST, JOHN ORNE (1852 - 1928)	500-18000	P,M
FROTHINGHAM, JAMES (1786 - 1864)	700-4800	F
FRY, JOHN HEMMING (1860 - 1946)	400-1800	L
FRYMIRE, JACOB (1770 - 1822)	5000-15000	P
FUCHS, ERNEST (20TH C)	100-600	X (F)
FUECHSEL, HERMANN (1833 - 1915)	600-15000	L,M
FUERTES, LOUIS AGASSIZ (1874 - 1927)	*500-10000+	W
FUGLISTER, FRITZ (20TH C)	350-1500	X (F)
FUHR, ERNEST (1874 - 1933)	*200-850	I
FULDE, EDWARD (19TH - 20TH C)	600-2800	X (G)
FULLER, A. (19TH C)	800-8000	L
FULLER, ARTHUR D. (1889 - 1966)	*200-1000	I
FULLER, CHARLES O. (19TH C)	200-1000	X(M)
FULLER, G.F. (19TH C)	150-700	X (L)
FULLER, GEORGE (1822 - 1884)	500-2500	L,F
FULLER, LEONARD (1822 - 1871)	300-1500	X
FULLER, S.W. (19TH C)	100-750	L
FULLICK, E. (early 20TH C)	100-600	L,F
FULOP, KAROLY (1898 -)	*250-1200	X (G)
FULTON, FITCH (20TH C)	100-700	L
FULTON, H.D. (20TH C)	100-600	L
FURLMAN, FREDERICK (1874 -)	100-850	L
FURLONG, CHARLES WELLINGTON (1874-)	500-7500	I
FURSMAN, FREDERICK F. (1874-1943)	400-4500	F
FUSSELL, CHARLES LEWIS (1840 - 1905)	*800-15000	G,F,M

 * Denotes watercolors, pastels, drawings, and/or mixed media

G

ARTIST	PRICE	SUBJECT
GAENNSLEN, OTTO ROBERT (1876 -)	150-1000	X
GAERTNER, CARL F. (1898 - 1952)	100-1200	L,F,I
GAG, WANDA HAZEL (1893 - 1946)	*200-1200	L,G,I
GAGE, GEORGE WILLIAM (1887 - 1957)	200-2500	I
GAGE, HARRY LAWRENCE (1887 -)	100-1200	M
GALLAGHER, SEARS	*100-1800	
GALLAGHER, SEARS (1869 - 1955)	400-3500	L,M,F
GALLATIN, ALBERT EUGENE (1882 - 1952)	*1000-18000	A
GALLI, STANLEY (1912-)	100-750	X (L)
GALLISON, HENRY HAMMOND (1850 - 1910)	300-4500	L
GALLO, FRANK (1933 -)	*100-850	F
GAMBIER, M. (19TH C)	100-750	L
GAMBLE, EDNA (19TH - 20TH C)	*100-450	X (S)
GAMBLE, JOHN MARSHALL (1863 - 1957)	500-18000	L
GAMBLE, ROY C. (1887 - 1972)	150-1500	G,F,L
GAMMELL, ROBERT HALE IVES (1893 -)	350-4500	F,G,L
GANNAM, JOHN (1897 - 1965)	*300-1500	I
GANSO, EMIL	*150-2500	
GANSO, EMIL (1895 - 1941)	400-12000	F,L,M
GARBER, DANIEL (1880 - 1958)	3500-85000	L
GARDENER, ROBERT (early 19TH C)	*1000-3000	X (L)
GARDINER, DONALD (20TH C)	150-750	X (G)
GARDNER, ARCHIBALD S. (1904 -)	200-800	M
GARDNER, SHEILA (20TH C)	*500-2000	L
GARMAN, ED (20TH C)	1000-15000	A
GARRATT, J.H.(19TH - 20TH C)	*100-500	X (L)
GARRETSON, DELLA (1860 -)	*100-600	X(L)
GARRETT, EDMUND HENRY	*150-1500	
GARRETT, EDMUND HENRY (1853 - 1929)	200-2500	I,L
GARSON, ETTA CORBETT (1898 - 1968)	200-900	L
GASKE, F.J. (19TH - 20TH C)	*200-850	X (L)
GASKINS, LEE	*100-800	

* Denotes watercolors, pastels, drawings, and/or mixed media

GASKINS, LEE (1882-1935)	300-3500	X(M,W)
GASPARD, LEON S.(1882 - 1964)	2000-60000	L,F
GASSER, HENRY MARTIN	*150-1200	
GASSER, HENRY MARTIN (1909 - 1981)	400-5500	L,M
GASSETTE, GRACE (19TH - 20TH C)	100-700	X (M)
GASSIM, MARY W. (19TH C)	150-750	L
GATCH, LEE	*300-3500	
GATCH, LEE (1902 - 1968)	700-15000	A
GATTER, OTTO (1892 - 1926)	400-2500	X (I,L)
GAUEN, M. (early 20TH C)	100-600	F
GAUGENGIGL, IGNAZ MARCEL (1855 - 1932)	1000-25000+	F
GAUL, (WILLIAM)GILBERT (1855-1919)	600-32000	G,F,L
GAUL, ARRAH LEE (1888-1980)	200-2000	X (M,L)
GAULEY, ROBERT DAVID (1875 - 1943)	350-4000	F
GAULT, MARY D. (early 19TH C)	500-4750	X (L)
GAVENCKY, FRANK J. (1888 -)	250-1000	X (L)
GAW, WILLIAM A. (1891 - 1973)	100-1500	X (S,F)
GAY, AUGUST (20TH C)	100-500	X (W)
GAY, EDWARD (1837 - 1928)	500-10000+	L
GAY, GEORGE HOWELL	*100-3200	
GAY, GEORGE HOWELL (1858 - 1931)	200-2000	M,L
GAY, PATRICIA (1876 - 1965)	400-5000	L
GAY, WALTER (1856 - 1937)	500-25000+	G,L,S
GAY, WINCKWORTH ALLAN (1821 - 1910)	350-3500	L,M
GAYER, A. (19TH C)	200-1000	L
GAYLOR, SAMUEL WOOD (1883 -)	*200-5500	I
GAZE, HAROLD (20TH C)	*450-1500	I
GECHTOFF, LEONID (20TH C)	100-400	X (L)
GEDEOHN, PAUL (20TH C)	250-1500	X (G)
GEHRY, P. (19TH C)	100-700	X (S)
GELLENBECK, ANN P. (19TH - 20TH C)	250-1500	X(L,W)
GELWICKS, D.W. (20TH C)	100-650	L,F
GENTH, LILLIAN MATILDE (1876 - 1953)	400-6500+	F,L
GEOFFROI, HARRY (19TH - 20TH C)	250-1200	X
GEORGE, A. (late 19TH C)	100-500	L

* Denotes watercolors, pastels, drawings, and/or mixed media

GEORGE, VESPER (1865-1934)	*200-1000	X(L)
GEORGES, PAUL (1923 -)	5000-35000	A
GEORGHI, EDWIN A. (1896 - 1964)	100-1000	I
GEORGI, EDWIN A. (1896 - 1964) 150-1200	F,I	
GERBI, CLAUDIO (20TH C)	100-600	X (S)
GERBINO, ROSARIO U. (19TH - 20TH C)	200-900	L
GERLASH, ANTHONY (19TH C)	200-3000	L
GERRY, SAMUEL LANCASTER (1813 - 1891)	500-7000+	L
GETMAN, WILLIAM (1917 - 1972)	*100-400	X (S)
GEYER, HERMAN (19TH C)	150-2000	L
GIACOMO, ELSIO SAN (20TH C)	100-750	M
GIBBS, E.T. (19TH C)	*100-400	L
GIBBS, GEORGE	*100-850	
GIBBS, GEORGE (1870 - 1942)	200-1200	I
GIBBS, H. (20TH C)	100-500	A
GIBBS, MARY ANN (19TH C)	*400-1800	F
GIBSON, CHARLES DANA	*300-5500	
GIBSON, CHARLES DANA (1867 - 1944)	500-5000	I,F
GIBSON, WILLIAM ALFRED (1866-1931)	200-1000	L
GIBSON, WILLIAM HAMILTON (1850 - 1896)	*100-850	L,I
GIDDINGS, FRANK A. (1882 -)	*100-500	X
GIES, JOSEPH W. (1860 - 1935)	100-5000	F,L
GIFFORD, CHARLES HENRY	*200-3500	
GIFFORD, CHARLES HENRY (1839 - 1904)	500-8500	M,L
GIFFORD, EDWARD C. (20TH C)	100-400	L
GIFFORD, PAULINE (19TH - 20TH C)	200-900	X (S)
GIFFORD, ROBERT GREGORY (1895 -)	*100-500	I
GIFFORD, ROBERT SWAIN (1840 - 1905)	450-8500	L
GIFFORD, SANFORD ROBINSON (1823 - 1880)	1800-275000	L
GIGNOUX, REGIS FRANCOIS (1816 - 1882)	1500-30000	L
GIHON, ALBERT DAKIN (1866 -)	200-900	L
GIHON, CLARENCE MONTFORT (1871 - 1929)	500-8000	L
GIKOW, RUTH (1913 - 1983)	200-1200	A
GILBERT, A. (19TH C)	100-500	L
GILBERT, ARTHUR HILL (1894 -)	300-2500	L,G

* Denotes watercolors, pastels, drawings, and/or mixed media

GILBERT, C. IVAR (20TH C)	*100-450	X
GILBERT, CHARLES ALLAN (1873-1929)	*100-800	F
GILCHRIST, WILLIAM WALLACE (1879 - 1926)	700-15000+	F,L
GILDER, ROBERT F. (1856 - 1946)	200-1500	L
GILE, SELDON CONNOR (1877 - 1947)	1000-7500	L
GILES, HORACE P.	*100-800	
GILES, HORACE P.(19TH C)	250-3200	L
GILL, ANN (early 19TH C)	*100-800	X
GILL, DELANCEY W. (1859 - 1940)	200-4500	L
GILL, JAMES (1934 -)	500-2500	A,F
GILL, MARIQUITA (20TH C)	500-3000	X (L)
GILL, TOM (1899 -)	*200-900	L
GILLETTE, WILLIAM B. (1864-1957)	*100-650	M
GILLIAM, SAM JR. (1933 -)	1500-15000	A
GILSON, ROGER E. (20TH C)	100-500	X (L)
GIOBBI, EDWARD (1926 -)	*200-1800	X
GIOVANNI, N. (20TH C)	100-600	L
GIRADET, KARL (1813 - 1871)	1000-65000	G,F,L
GIRARDIN, FRANK J. (1856 -)	250-1400	L
GISEVIUS, GERHARD (20TH C)	100-600	L
GISIKE, IDA (20TH C)	150-650	X (L)
GISSON, ANDRE (1928 -)	400-4500	F,L,S
GIURGOLA, ROMALDO (19TH - 20TH C)	*200-800	I
GLACKENS, LOUIS M (1866 - 1933)	*200-1800	I
GLACKENS, WILLIAM JAMES	*150-25000	
GLACKENS, WILLIAM JAMES (1870 - 1938)	2500-425000+	F,L,I
GLARNER, FRITZ (1899 - 1972)	2500-85000+	A
GLASER, ELIZABETH (active 1830-40)	*500-7500	P
GLASGOW, BERNO (19TH-20TH C)	200-1200	X
GLASS, F.R. (20TH C)	*100-500	X
GLASS, JAMES WILLIAM (1825 - 1857)	450-2500	G,F
GLAVE, C.L. (20TH C)	100-700	M
GLEASON, JOE DUNCAN (1881 - 1959)	200-1800	I
GLEW, EDWARD LEES (1817 - 1870)	1000-10000	L,F
GLINTENCAMP, HENRY	*100-600	

 * Denotes watercolors, pastels, drawings, and/or mixed media

GLINTENCAMP, HENRY (1887 - 1946)	150-2500	I,L
GLUCKMANN, GRIGORY (1898-)	400-4500	F
GODARD, GABRIEL (1933 -)	100-850	X
GODDARD, MARGARET E. (1882 -)	200-1200	X (S)
GODFREY, E. (19TH C)	100-500	L
GODFREY, FRANK T. (1873 -)	100-600	I
GODWIN, FRANK (1889 - 1959)	*150-1200	
GOEBEL, ROD (20TH C)	500-2800	L
GOETSCH, GUSTAV F. (1877 - 1969)	100-850	F,L
GOETZ, EDITH (19TH-20TH C)	*100-400	X
GOETZ, HENRI (1909 -)	*100-650	A
GOETZ, RICHARD V. (20TH C)	100-1200	X(S)
GOINGS, F. (19TH C)	100-600	L
GOINGS, RALPH (1928 -)	2000-25000	A
GOLD, ALBERT (1916 - 1972)	100-900	I
GOLDBERG, MICHAEL (1924 -)	750-12000	A
GOLDBERG, RUBE (1883 - 1970)	*250-2000	I
GOLDEN, ROLLAND (1931 -)	*200-850	X (L)
GOLDING, CECIL (20TH C)	100-900	X
GOLDING, WILLIAM O. (1874 - 1943)	*600-2500	P
GOLDINGHAM, J.B. (19TH C)	100-400	L
GOLDSTEIN, HYMAN (20TH C)	*100-500	L
GOLDTHWAITE, ANNE (1875 - 1944)	*100-700	L,F
GOLLINGS, WILLIAM ELLING	*400-7000	
GOLLINGS, WILLIAM ELLING (1878 - 1932)	700-35000	G,F
GOLUB, LEON ALBERT (1922 -)	1500-12000	A
GONSKE, WALT (20TH C)	200-1200	X(L)
GONZALES, XAVIER (1899-)	100-900	A
GOODALL, W. (early 19TH C)	*100-1000	W
GOODE, JOE	*500-2500	
GOODE, JOE (1937 -)	600-6500	A
GOODELL, IRA CHAFFEE (1800 - 1875)	3000-25000	P (F)
GOODES, EDWARD A. (active 1855-85)	500-3000	X (M)
GOODMAN, H.K. (active 1845-50)	2500-32000	P
GOODMAN, SYDNEY (1936 -)	500-5500	X (G)

GOODNOUGH, ROBERT (1917 -)	500-8000	A
GOODWIN, (RICHARD) LABARRE (1840 - 1910)	600-15000+	S,W,L
GOODWIN, ARTHUR C.	*400-7000	
GOODWIN, ARTHUR C. (1864 - 1929)	500-35000	L,M
GOODWIN, BELLE (19TH C)	800-3500	X (S)
GOODWIN, EDWIN WEYBURN (1800 - 1845)	400-35000	X (F)
GOODWIN, PHILIP RUSSELL (1882 - 1935)	500-15000	G,L,I
GOODYEAR, C. (19TH C)	*100-500	X (S)
GORBINO, ROSARIO (20TH C)	100-800	X
GORCHOV, RON (1930 -)	800-6000	A
GORDER, LUTHER EMERSON VAN (1861 - 1931)	150-750	G,L
GORKY, ARSHILE	*3000-375000+	
GORKY, ARSHILE (1904 - 1948)	5000-575000	A
GORLICH, SOPHIE (1855 - 1893)	1000-9000	G
GORMAN, R.C. (1933 -)	*400-1800	X (F)
GORSON, AARON HENRY (1872 - 1933)	700-14000	L
GOTLIEB, JULES (1897 -)	200-3500	I
GOTTLIEB, ADOLPH	*1500-40000	
GOTTLIEB, ADOLPH (1903 - 1974)	8000-325000+	A
GOTTLIEB, HARRY (1895-)	300-1800	X(L)
GOTTLIEB, LEOPOLD (?)	*350-1200	X
GOTTWALD, FREDERICK C. (1860 - 1941)	500-4500	G,L
GOULD, JOHN F. (1906 -)	*100-700	I
GOULD, WALTER (1829 -)	4000-110000	G,F
GOULD, WILLIAM FRANK (20TH C)	*100-400	X (L)
GOURNSEY, C. (19TH C)	*250-1200	X (L)
GRABACH, JOHN R. (1880 - 1981)	700-30000	F,G,L
GRACE, F. (19TH C)	100-900	L
GRACE, GERALD (1918 -)	100-900	X (G)
GRAHAM, GEORGE (19TH - 20TH C)	*100-400	X (G)
GRAHAM, JOHN D. (1881 - 1961)	3000-150000+	A
GRAHAM, RALPH W. (1901 -)	*100-800	G
GRAHAM, ROBERT ALEXANDER (1873 - 1946)	500-9000	F,L
GRAHAM, WILLIAM (1841 - 1910)	400-2000	L
GRAILLY, VICTOR DE (1804 - 1889)	400-10000	L,F

 * Denotes watercolors, pastels, drawings, and/or mixed media

GRAMATKY, HARDIE (1907 -)	*250-1200	I
GRAND, HENRY LE (19TH C)	600-4500	L
GRANDEE, JOE RUIZ (1929 -)	400-2800	F
GRANER Y ARUFFI, LUIS (1867 - 1929)	300-4800	F,G,L
GRANT, CHARLES HENRY (1866 - 1938)	250-2500	M
GRANT, CLEMENT ROLLINS (1849 - 1893)	300-8500	L,F
GRANT, DWINELL (20TH C)	500-3800	X (A?)
GRANT, FREDERIC M. (1886 -)	800-8500+	I,L
GRANT, GORDAN HOPE	*300-1800	
GRANT, GORDON HOPE (1875 - 1962)	500-15000	M,I
GRANT, J. JEFFREY (1883 - 1960)	300-2600	L,M
GRANT, JAMES (1924 -)	*300-1000	A
GRANT, WILLIAM (mid 19TH C)	*1000-3000	P
GRANVILLE-SMITH, WALTER	*150-3500	
GRANVILLE-SMITH, WALTER (1870 - 1938)	350-35000	L,F,I
GRAUER, WILLIAM C. (1896-)	300-4000	L,M
GRAVES, ABBOTT FULLER (1859 - 1936)	1000-40000	F,S,G,L
GRAVES, MORRIS COLE	*600-13000	
GRAVES, MORRIS COLE (1910 -)	1000-30000	A
GRAVES, NANCY	*2000-30000	
GRAVES, NANCY (1940 -)	8000-50000	A
GRAVES, O.E.L. (1912 -)	150-2500	F,W
GRAY, (HENRY) PERCY	*450-12500	
GRAY, (HENRY) PERCY (1869 - 1952)	400-7500	L,M
GRAY, BESSIE (19TH C)	*100-750	X(L)
GRAY, CHARLES A. (1857 -)	200-1000	F
GRAY, CLEVE (1918 -)	500-6500	A
GRAY, FREDERICK G. (19TH-20TH C)	100-750	X (F,G)
GRAY, HENRY PETERS (1819 - 1877)	300-2500	F
GRAY, JACK L. (20TH C)	1500-20000	X
GRAY, M. MAY (20TH C)	100-350	X (F)
GRAY, MARY (20TH C)	100-500	L
GRAY, MARY M. (20TH C)	100-500	L
GRAY, RALPH W. (1880-1944)	*150-800	X(F,L)
GRAY, U.L. (20TH C)	200-1200	X(L,S)

* Denotes watercolors, pastels, drawings, and/or mixed media

GRAY, URBAN (20TH C ?)	150-650	X (L)
GRAY, WILLIAM F. (1866 -)	150-750	X (M)
GRAZIA, TED DE	*250-800	
GRAZIA, TED DE (1909 -)	300-2500	W
GRAZIANI, SANTE (1920 -)	800-3000	A
GREACEN, EDMUND WILLIAM (1877 - 1949)	1000-35000+	F,S,L
GREACEN, NAN (20TH C)	100-700	X (S)
GREASON, DONALD CARLISLE (20TH C)	100-1500	L
GREASON, WILLIAM (1884 -)	200-800	L
GREATOREX, KATHLEEN HONORA (1851-)	600-2200	S,I
GREAVES, HARRY E.(1854-1919)	100-1000	L
GREEN, CHARLES EDWIN LEWIS (1844 -)	500-4500	L,M
GREEN, EDITH JACKSON (1876 - 1934)	100-850	X (L)
GREEN, FRANK RUSSELL (1856 - 1940)	350-8600	S,L
GREEN, ROLAND (20TH C)	*200-1000	W,L
GREEN, ROSE (19TH C)	100-500	S
GREEN, WILLIAM BRADFORD (1871 - 1945)	100-900	L
GREENBAUM, JOSEPH DAVID (1864-1940)	200-1000	L,F
GREENE, BALCOMB (1904 -)	500-4000	A
GREENE, STEPHEN (1918 -)	800-3500	A
GREENE, WALTER L. (19TH-20TH C)	*100-850	L,M,I
GREENFIELD, EVAN JOHN FORREST(1866-)	100-1500	X
GREENLEAF, JACOB I. (1887 - 1968)	100-1500	L,M
GREENWOOD, ETHAN ALLEN (1779 - 1856)	750-8500	F
GREENWOOD, JOHN (1727 - 1792)	400-2000	P
GREENWOOD, JOSEPH H. (1857 - 1927)	250-3000	L
GREENWOOD, MARION (1909 - 1970)	500-3000	G
GREER, A.D. (19TH-20TH C)	100-800	X(S)
GREER, JAMES EMERY (19TH C)	100-900	L
GREGOR, HAROLD (1929 -)	900-15000	A,L
GREGORY, ELIOT (1854 - 1915)	100-850	F
GREIG, DONALD (20TH C)	100-1000	X(F)
GRELL, LOUIS FREDERICK (1887 -)	*100-850	X
GREMKE, DICK (19TH - 20TH C)	200-1000	L
GREMKE, HENRY DIEDRICH (1860-1933)	300-3800	L

 * Denotes watercolors, pastels, drawings, and/or mixed media

GREMKE, M.D. (20TH C)	400-1500	L
GRIFFIN, THOMAS BAILEY (19TH C)	300-2500	L
GRIFFIN, WALTER (1861 - 1935)	500-8500	L
GRIFFIN, WILLIAM (1861 -)	600-5000	L
GRIFFIN, WORTH DICKMAN (1892 -)	100-850	X (M)
GRIFFITH, BILL (20TH C)	*100-600	X
GRIFFITH, JULIE SULZER (- 1945)	100-400	M
GRIFFITH, LOUIS K. (20TH C)	*100-600	X (G)
GRIFFITH, LOUIS OSCAR (1875 -)	100-850	L,F
GRIFFITH, WILLIAM A. (1866 - 1940)	400-3000	L,F
GRIGGS, SAMUEL W. (1827 - 1898)	200-2800	L,S
GRILLEY, ROBERT (1920 -)	200-850	X
GRILLO, JOHN (1917 -)	600-1200	A
GRIMM, PAUL (1892-1974)	300-3500	L
GRINNELL, GEORGE VICTOR (- 1934)	100-1000	L
GRIOMARE, EDWARD T. (20TH C)	300-1200	X
GRISWALD, CASIMIR C. (1834 - 1918)	250-2500	L
GROESBECK, DANIEL SAYRE (20TH C)	*100-1200	F
GROLL, ALBERT LOREY (1866 - 1952)	250-6500	L
GROOMS, FRANK R. (19TH C)	100-1500	X(G)
GROOMS, MIMI (20TH C)	*100-500	X
GROOMS, RED (1937 -)	*1000-20000+	A
GROPPER, WILLIAM	*250-5000	
GROPPER, WILLIAM (1897 - 1977)	600-15000	G,F,I
GROS, D. (early 19TH C)	300-1200	L
GROSE, DANIEL C. (active 1865-90)	200-4500	L
GROSE, HARRIET ESTELLE (- 1914)	400-2000	X (S)
GROSS, CHAIM (1904 -)	*100-1000	A,M,L
GROSS, G. (20TH C)	200-1200	G,F
GROSS, JULIET WHITE (1882 - 1934)	400-1800	X
GROSS, OSKAR (1871 - 1963)	500-1800	X (A?)
GROSS, PETER ALFRED (1849 - 1914)	150-1500	L,G
GROSSENHEIDER, RICHARD PHILIP (1911-1975)	*800-4500	X
GROSSETE, L. (19TH C)	100-700	L
GROSSMAN, EDWIN BOOTH (1887 - 1957)	100-900	L,M

GROSSMAN, JOSEPH (1899-)	200-2500	L
GROSZ, GEORGE (1893 - 1959)	*500-45000	A
GROTH, JOHN (1908 -)	*200-1200	I
GROVER, OLIVER DENNET (1861 - 1927)	250-3000	L,G
GRUELLE, RICHARD BUCKNER (1851 - 1915)	200-1200	L,S
GRUGER, FREDERIC RODRIGO (1871 - 1953)	*200-1200	I
GRUNER, CARL (active 1850-65)	700-2000	F
GRUPPE, CHARLES PAUL (1860 - 1940)	300-12000	L,M
GRUPPE, EMILE ALBERT (1896 - 1978)	350-8500	L,M
GUE, DAVID JOHN (1836 - 1917)	300-4000	L,M,F
GUELLOW, W. (19TH C)	200-3500	X
GUERELSON, A.M. (20TH C ?)	700-4000	X
GUERIN, JOSEPH (1889 -)	300-1800	L,M
GUERIN, JULES (1866 - 1946)	*400-4500	F,I
GUERRERO, JULES (1914 -)	800-6500	X (A?)
GUGLIELMI, LOUIS O. (1906 - 1956)	3000-25000	A
GUIFON, LEON (19TH C)	400-2000	X (L)
GUILFORD, MARGARET (19TH C)	100-600	A
GUILLAUME, L. (19TH C)	*150-750	L,F
GUION, MOLLY (1910 -)	200-1800	G,S
GUISE, M.H. (19TH C)	100-800	L
GUISTO, REGINA (20TH C)	100-700	A
GULAGER, CHARLES (active 1860-80)	250-1200	X (M)
GULLAGER, CHRISTIAN (1762 - 1826)	400-7000	F
GUMPEL, HUGH (20TH C)	*100-400	L
GUNN, EDWIN H. (1876-1940)	*200-1500	X(M)
GURGIN, W. (19TH C)	350-1200	X (W)
GUSSOW, BERNARD (1881 - 1957)	300-5000	L,F
GUSTAVSON, HENRY (1864 - 1912)	250-900	L
GUSTEMER, G. (19TH C)	4000-25000	F
GUSTON, PHILIP (1912 - 1980)	4500-250000	A
GUTHERSON, F. JEROME (20TH C)	*100-600	X (L)
GUY, FRANCIS (1760 - 1820)	4000-60000	L
GUY, SEYMOUR JOSEPH (1824 - 1910)	3000-125000	G,F
GWATHMEY, ROBERT	*600-3000	

 * Denotes watercolors, pastels, drawings, and/or mixed media

GWATHMEY, ROBERT (1903 -)	1000-8500+	A,G,F
GYBERSON, INDIANA (19TH - 20TH C)	500-1800	F

H

ARTIST	PRICE	SUBJECT
HAAPPANEN, JOHN NICHOLS (1891 -)	300-2500	L,M
HABERLE, JOHN	*800-8500	
HABERLE, JOHN (1856 - 1933)	7500-300000+	S,F
HADDOCK, ARTHUR (20TH C)	700-2000	L
HAELEN, JOHN A. (19TH - 20TH C)	100-500	F
HAERST, G. (19TH C) - 1887)	100-850	L
HAES JANVIER, FRANCES DE (1775 - 1824)	450-2000	F
HAESELER, ALICE P. SMITH (19TH - 20TH C)	*200-700	M,L
HAGAMAN, JAMES (20TH C)	150-900	G,L
HAGBERG, C.J. (19TH C)	100-400	M
HAGEFUL, H. (19TH-20TH C)	200-1000	X(M)
HAGERBRUNNER, DAVID (20TH C)	*400-2800	X (W)
HAGERUP, NELS (1864 - 1922)	300-3800	M
HAGNY, J. (19TH C)	100-400	P
HAHN, KARL WILHELM (1829 - 1887)	4000-60000	G
HAHN, WILLIAM (1840-1890)	1500-40000	G
HAINES, RICHARD (1906 -)	100-800	X (L)
HALBERG, CHARLES EDWARD (1855 -)	100-800	M
HALE, ELLEN DAY (1855 - 1940)	1000-28000	F,L
HALE, GERARD VAN BARKALOO (1886-1958)	100-750	X(F)
HALE, LILIAN WESTCOTT (1881 - 1953)	800-7500	F
HALE, MARY POWELL HELME (1862 - 1934)	100-900	X (L)
HALE, PHILIP LESLIE (1865 - 1931)	700-45000+	F
HALE, ROBERT BEVERLY (1901-)	*100-850	X
HALL, ANNE (1792 - 1863)	700-4500	F
HALL, E. W. (19TH C)	300-1200	L
HALL, FREDERICK GARRISON (1879 - 1946)	150-1000	X (G,F)

HALL, GEORGE HENRY (1825 - 1913)	600-22000+	G,S,F
HALL, HENRY BRYAN (1808 - 1884)	500-3500	F,S
HALL, HOWARD HILL (1887 - 1933)	500-10000	X (G)
HALL, PETER (1828 - 1895)	*100-900	F
HALL, THOMAS VICTOR (20TH C)	*100-600	X (G)
HALL, WILLIAM SMITH (19TH C)	800-4500	F
HALLETT, HENDRICKS A.	*100-1000	
HALLETT, HENDRICKS A. (1847 - 1921)	350-4500+	M,L
HALLOWAY, GEORGE (20TH C)	100-600	X (L)
HALLOWELL, ANNA D. (19TH C)	*200-2000	X(M)
HALLOWELL, GEORGE HAWLEY (1871 - 1926)	500-6500	L
HALLOWELL, ROBERT (1886 - 1939)	*100-2200	X (M,S)
HALLWIG, OSCAR (1858 - 1880)	300-1500	X (F)
HALOW, E.J. (19TH-20TH C)	150-1000	L
HALOWAY, EDWARD STRATTON (- 1939)	100-800	X (M)
HALPERT, SAMUEL T.	*200-1800	
HALPERT, SAMUEL T. (1884 - 1930)	350-8000	L,F,S
HALSALL, WILLIAM FORMBY (1841 - 1919)	400-5200	M,L
HALTON, MINNIE HOLLIS (20TH C)	100-750	X (G)
HAMBIDGE, JAY (1867 - 1924)	*200-1500	I
HAMBLEN, STURTEVANT J. (active 1835-55)	3000-45000	P
HAMBLETT, THEORA (1895 -)	250-1200	P
HAMBRIDGE, JAY (1867 - 1924)	350-2500	F,I,S
HAMILTON, EDGAR SCUDDER (1869 - 1903)	400-2000	X (G)
HAMILTON, EDWARD WILBUR DEAN (1862-)	500-4800	L,F
HAMILTON, HAMILTON (1847 - 1928)	500-14000+	L,F
HAMILTON, HELEN (19TH - 20TH C)	300-1500	L
HAMILTON, HILDEGARD (1906 -)	100-600	L
HAMILTON, JAMES (1819 - 1878)	500-12000+	M,L,I
HAMILTON, JOHN MCLURE (1853 - 1936)	200-1800	I,F,S
HAMILTON, ROBERT (1877 - 1954)	250-1500	G,L,F
HAMILTON, WILLIAM R.(1810 - 1865)	700-6500+	F
HAMMER, JOHN J. (1842 - 1906)	350-1800	G,L
HAMMERSTAD, JOHN H. (19TH C)	100-700	X (M,L)
HAMMOND, ARTHUR J. (1875 - 1947)	300-4200	M,L,S

* Denotes watercolors, pastels, drawings, and/or mixed media

HAMPTON, JOHN W. (1918 - 1976)	*300-6000	
HAMPTON, JOHN W. (1918 - 1976)	400-11000	X (I,L,W)
HANARTY, ALICE E. (late 19TH C)	100-500	X (L)
HANAU, JEAN (1899 - 1966)	*300-1000	X (I)
HANDWRIGHT, GEORGE (1873 - 1951)	*200-1000	X
HANE, ROGER (1938 - 1974)	200-1500	I
HANKS, JERVIS F. (1799 -)	500-2000	P
HANKS, LON (19TH - 20TH C)	200-850	X (M)
HANLEY, J.B. (active 1870-85)	500-4000	G
HANLEY, SARAH E. (-1958)	100-2000	L,F
HANNA JR, THOMAS KING (1872 - 1951)	*200-1200	I
HANSEN, ARMIN CARL (1886 - 1957)	900-30000	L,F
HANSEN, EJNAR (1884 - 1965)	500-15000	F
HANSEN, HANS PETER (1881 - 1967)	100-1500	G,F
HANSEN, HAROLD (20TH C)	*100-400	L
HANSEN, HERMAN WENDELBORG	*2500-50000	
HANSEN, HERMAN WENDELBORG (1854 - 1924)	5000-55000	G,F
HANSON, D. (19TH C)	100-600	M
HANSON, R. (19TH C)	100-600	X (S)
HARBESON, GEORGIANA BROWN (1894-)	*350-1500	G,F,I
HARDENGERGH, GERARD R.(1856 - 1915)	*100-850	L
HARDING, CHESTER (1792 - 1866)	500-9000	F
HARDING, GEORGE MATTHEWS	*250-1500	
HARDING, GEORGE MATTHEWS (1882 - 1959)	450-4000	I
HARDING, H.H. (late 19TH C)	200-1200	M
HARDING, JOHN L. (1835 - 1882)	500-3500	F
HARDWICK, MELBOURNE H.	*300-750	
HARDWICK, MELBOURNE H. (1857 - 1916)	400-4500	M,L,G
HARDY, ANNA ELIZABETH (1839 - 1934)	200-2800	S,L
HARDY, JEREMIAH P.(1800 - 1888)	350-1500	F
HARDY, WALTER MANLEY (1877 -)	*150-900	L,I
HARDY, WILLIAM F. (19TH - 20TH C)	150-900	L
HARE, JOHN KNOWLES	*100-800	
HARE, JOHN KNOWLES (1882 - 1947)	200-1800	I,M,L

* Denotes watercolors, pastels, drawings, and/or mixed media

HARE, WILLIAM (active 1820-50)	3000-15000	M,F
HARGENS, CHARLES (1893 -)	100-800	G
HARIS, T. (20TH C)	100-750	L
HARLOW, LOUIS KENNEY (1850 - 1913)	*100-500	L,M
HARMAN, FRED (1902 -)	*200-4500	I
HARMER, ALEXANDER F. (1857 - 1925)	400-9500	G,F
HARMON, CHARLES H. (- 1936)	100-1200	L,F
HARMON, W.S. (19TH C)	400-1500	L
HARNDEN, WILLIAM (1920-1983)	200-1800	X(L)
HARNETT, WILLIAM MICHAEL (1848 - 1892)	1000-300000	S
HARNEY, PAUL E. (1850 - 1915)	350-2000	W,L,F
HARPER, WILLIAM ST. JOHN	*1000-53000	
HARPER, WILLIAM ST. JOHN (1851 - 1910)	400-7500	I,F,G
HARRA, M.A. (19TH C)	300-1500	X (S)
HARRINGTON, E. (20TH C)	100-900	L,F
HARRINGTON, GEORGE (1832-1911)	300-2500	L
HARRINGTON, OLIVER W. (1913 -)	100-500	X (L)
HARRINGTON, RUFUS (20TH C)	100-600	X (M)
HARRIS, C. GOODWIN (1893-1981)	*100-1000	X(M)
HARRIS, CHARLES GORDON (1891-)	300-2000	X(L)
HARRIS, CHARLES X. (1856 -)	700-8500	F,G
HARRIS, LAWREN STUART (1885 - 1970)	800-28000	L,I
HARRIS, MARIAN D. (1904 -)	*100-850	L,F
HARRIS, ROBERT GEORGE (1911 -)	400-3500	I,F
HARRIS, SAM HYDE (1889-1977)	200-2500	L
HARRIS, W. (19TH C)	100-500	L
HARRISON, (THOMAS)ALEXANDER (1853-1930)	450-6000	M,L
HARRISON, BIRGE (1854 - 1929)	500-30000	L
HARRISON, CHARLES (19TH-20TH C)	100-500	X(L)
HARRISON, MARK ROBERT (1819 - 1894)	500-5000	L,G
HARRISON, THOMAS ALEXANDER (1853 - 1930)	300-5560	M,L,G,F
HART, GEORGE O. ("POP" HART)(1868 - 1933)	*250-3500	L,G
HART, J. (19TH-20TH C)	300-1500	X(L)
HART, JAMES MCDOUGAL (1828 - 1901)	500-25000	L,G
HART, LETITIA BONNET (1867-)	400-3500	F,L

 * Denotes watercolors, pastels, drawings, and/or mixed media

HART, MARY THERESA (1872-1921)	300-3500	X(S)
HART, SALOMON ALEXANDER (1806 - 1881)	600-15000	G
HART, T.H. (19TH C ?)	100-850	L
HART, WILLIAM HOWARD (1863 - 1934)	400-4500	L
HART, WILLIAM M. (1823 - 1894)	800-28000+	L,W
HARTIGAN, GRACE (1922 -)	1500-12000	A
HARTLEY, ELAINE (20TH C)	100-500	X
HARTLEY, MARSDEN	*500-30000	
HARTLEY, MARSDEN (1878 - 1943)	1500-100000	A,S
HARTLEY, RACHEL (1884 -)	100-650	G,I
HARTMAN, BERTRAM	*200-1500	
HARTMAN, BERTRAM (1882 - 1960)	400-3500	L,S
HARTMAN, GEORGE (- 1934)	100-900	X (F)
HARTMAN, SYDNEY K. (1863 -)	*100-450	I,L
HARTRATH, LUCIE	*100-800	
HARTRATH, LUCIE (19TH - 20TH C)	100-1500	L
HARTSHORNE, HOWARD MORTON (20TH C)	200-1200	X
HARTSLY, A. (19TH C)	100-700	L
HARTSON, WALTER C. (1866 -)	*100-700	L
HARTWICH, HERMAN (1853 - 1926)	250-3500	L,W,F
HARTWICK, GEORGE GUNTHER (active 1845-60)	600-7500	L
HARTWIG, HEINE (1937-)	250-3000	L
HARVEY, A.T. (19TH C)	100-1500	(X)F,G
HARVEY, ELI (1860 - 1957)	450-1800	L,F
HARVEY, GEORGE	*200-5000	
HARVEY, GEORGE (1800 - 1878)	1000-50000+	L,F
HARVEY, GEORGE W.	*100-1500	
HARVEY, GEORGE W. (1835 - 1920)	300-12000	L,F
HARVEY, GERALD (1933 -)	8000-100000	L,G
HARVEY, HENRY T. (19TH C)	250-1500	L,F
HASBROUCK, DU BOIS FENELON	*100-600	
HASBROUCK, DU BOIS FENELON (1860 - 1934)	500-2500	L
HASELTINE, CHARLES FIELD (1840 -)	100-1500	L
HASELTINE, WILLIAM STANLEY (1835 - 1900)	350-18000	L
HASENFUS, RICHARD C. (20TH C)	500-4000	X (M)

* Denotes watercolors, pastels, drawings, and/or mixed media

HASKELL, ERNEST (1876 - 1925)	*250-900	L
HASKELL, IDA C. (1861 - 1932)	500-3500	G
HASKELL, JOSEPH ALLEN (1808 - 1894)	200-2500	P
HASKELL, T.R. (late 19TH C)	100-500	L
HASKINS, GAYLE PORTER (1887 - 1962)	500-3000	X (G)
HASLER, WILLIAM N. (1865 -)	200-1500	L
HASSAM, FREDERICK CHILDE	*2500-125000	
HASSAM, FREDERICK CHILDE (1859 - 1935)	4500-330000+	L,F
HASSAN, E. (19TH C)	100-600	X(W,L)
HASSELBUSH, LOUIS (1863 -)	600-1500	X (F)
HASTINGS, HOWARD L. (20TH C)	100-700	L
HASTINGS, MATTHEW (1834 - 1919)	250-1500	F,G
HATFIELD, JOSEPH HENRY (1863 - 1928)	300-2000	F,L
HATFIELD, PAULINE (early 20TH C)	100-500	X (S)
HATHAWAY, GEORGE M.	*100-650	
HATHAWAY, GEORGE M. (1852 - 1903)	300-2800	M
HATHAWAY, RUFUS (1770 - 1822)	5000-90000	P
HATHERELL, WILLIAM (20TH C)	*100-1000	I
HAUGH, N. (19TH C)	*100-800	X (S)
HAUPT, ERIK GUIDE (1891 -)	800-6500	L,F
HAUPT, THEODORE G. (1902-)	*200-1000	A
HAUSER, JOHN	*600-18000	
HAUSER, JOHN (1858 - 1913)	1000-20000	L,F
HAUSHALTER, GEORGE M. (1862 -)	100-750	G
HAUSMAN, CHAUNCEY (19TH C)	100-700	F
HAVARD, JAMES PICKNEY (1937 -)	1000-40000	A
HAVELL, ROBERT JR (1793 - 1878)	1500-38000	L
HAVEN, FRANKLIN DE (1856 - 1934)	450-4000+	L
HAWES, CHARLES (20TH C)	*100-500	X(M,L)
HAWKINS, JOHN (20TH C)	200-700	X (M)
HAWLEY, HUGHSON (1850 - 1936)	*300-2800	X (L,I)
HAWSKWORTH, E.J. (19TH C)	100-700	X(S)
HAWTHORNE, CHARLES WEBSTER (1872 - 1930)	1000-95000+	F,G
HAWTHORNE, E.D. (19TH C)	600-7500	G
HAYDEN, CHARLES HENRY (1856 - 1901)	300-3500	L

 * Denotes watercolors, pastels, drawings, and/or mixed media

HAYDEN, EDWARD PARKER (- 1922)	300-1500	L
HAYDEN, ELLA FRANCES (1860 -)	*100-750	L
HAYNIE, WILBUR (1929 -)	100-400	A
HAYS, BARTON STONE (1826-1914)	350-3500	S,L,W,F
HAYS, GEORGE A. (1854 -)	250-2500	L,W
HAYS, WILLIAM JACOB JR (1872 - 1954)	700-4500	L,G
HAYS, WILLIAM JACOB SR (1830 - 1875)	800-10000+	W,S
HAYTER, CHARLES (1761 - 1835)	*700-2000	F
HAYWARD, FRANK (1867 -)	250-1200	L
HAYWARD, PETER (1905-)	150-1000	X(M)
HAYWARD, ROGER (1899 - 1979)	*150-650	A
HAZARD, ARTHUR MERTON (1872 - 1930)	300-4000	L,F,I
HAZELL, S.N. (19TH C)	400-1500	G
HAZELTON, MARY BREWSTER (early 20TH C)	400-1200	F
HAZLITT, JOHN (1767-1837)	200-1000	F
HEAD, J. (19TH C)	100-600	L
HEADE, MARTIN JOHNSON (1819 - 1904)	7500-450000+	L,S,F
HEALY, ARTHUR K.D. (1902-)	*100-800	F,L
HEALY, GEORGE PETER A. (1813 - 1894)	300-12000+	F
HEASLIP, WILLIAM JOHN (1898-1965)	200-1200	L
HEATH, FRANK L. (1857-1921)	500-4500	L,M
HEATH, W.A. (late 19TH C)	150-750	X (L)
HEATON,AUGUSTUS GEORGE G.1844-1931)	500-5000	F,G
HEATON OF ALBANY, JOHN (18TH C)	1000-6500	P
HEBERER, C. (early 20TH C)	150-700	L
HECHT, ZOLTAN (1890-1968)	100-900	L
HECKSHER, E. (19TH-20TH C)	100-500	X(S)
HEDGES, ROBERT D. (1878 -)	100-850	M
HEDINGER, ELISE (1854 -)	800-4800	X (S)
HEFFRON, M. (19TH C)	400-1800	X
HEICHER, FORD (late 19TH C)	100-900	G
HEIL, CHARLES EMILE	*150-650	
HEIL, CHARLES EMILE (1870 -)	200-2800	L,I
HEITH, V. (20TH C ?)	100-750	L
HEITZEL, GEORGE (1826 - 1906)	*100-400	L

* Denotes watercolors, pastels, drawings, and/or mixed media

HEIZER, MICHAEL (20TH C)	2000-14000	A
HEKKING, JOSEPH ANTONIO (active 1860-80)	800-20000	L
HELCK, PETER CLARENCE (1897 -)	*400-4800	I
HELD, AL (1928 -)	4000-100000	A
HELD, JOHN (JR) (1889 - 1958)	*300-3500	I
HELDNER, KNUTE (1884 - 1952)	400-3800	X (L,G)
HELIKER, JOHN EDWARD (1909 -)	400-3500	A,I,L
HELLER, E. (20TH C)	200-1000	L
HELLER, JOHN M. (20TH C)	350-2500	X (I)
HELLER, S. (20TH C)	100-600	X
HELMICK, HOWARD (1845 - 1907)	400-4500	I
HENDERSON, WILLIAM P. (1877-1943)	*400-2500	F,G
HENDRICKS, DAVID (20TH C)	*100-400	X(L)
HENNESSY, TIMOTHY (1925 -)	200-750	A
HENNESSY, WILLIAM JOHN (1839 - 1917)	500-30000	G,L,I
HENNINGS, ERNEST MARTIN (1886 - 1956)	1000-80000	G,F,L
HENRI, ROBERT	*350-15000	
HENRI, ROBERT (1865 - 1929)	1000-75000+	F,G
HENRICI, JOHN H. (19TH -20TH C)	250-4000	G,F
HENRY, EDWARD LAMSOM	*400-12000	
HENRY, EDWARD LAMSON (1841 - 1919)	700-175000+	G,L,F
HENSHAW, GLENN COOPER (1881 - 1946)	200-700	L,M
HERBST, FRANK C. (20TH C)	200-1500	I
HERGENRODER, EMILE (19TH - 20TH C)	100-700	X (F)
HERGESHEIMER, ELLA S. (1873 - 1943)	250-1200	F,S
HERGET, H. (19TH - 20TH C)	200-1500	X (G)
HERING, HARRY (1887 -)	100-800	G,F
HERKOMER, HERMAN G. (1863 -)	500-3000	G,F
HERRERA, VELINO SHIJE (1902 - 1973)	*250-1200	X (L)
HERRICK, HENRY W. (1824 - 1906)	*250-1200	L,F
HERRICK, MARGARET COX	*100-1000	
HERRICK, MARGARET COX (1865 - 1950)	200-1800	L,M,F,S
HERRING, LEE (20TH C)	100-1000	X(L,F)
HERRMANN, FRANK S. (1866 - 1942)	*350-2000	L
HERRMANN, NORBERT (1891 - 1966)	100-850	L

* Denotes watercolors, pastels, drawings, and/or mixed media

HERSCH, LEE F. (20TH C)	500-5000	L,F
HERTER, ADELE (1869 - 1946)	400-7500	F,S
HERTER, ALBERT	*900-6500	
HERTER, ALBERT (1871 - 1950)	2000-90000	F,G,L
HERZEL, PAUL (1876 -)	100-750	I
HERZOG, HERMANN (1832 - 1932)	1500-70000	L,M
HERZOG, LOUIS (1868 -)	150-850	L
HERZOG, MAX (19TH - 20TH C)	200-1000	X (S)
HESS, J.N. (late 19TH C)	400-2000	X (G)
HESS, SARA M. (1880 -)	500-3500	L
HESSE, EVA (1936 - 1970)	*2500-30000	A
HESSELIUS, JOHN (1728 - 1778)	2500-45000	F
HESTHAL, WILLIAM J. (1908 -)	150-1500	I
HETHERINGTON, CHARLES (20TH C)	100-700	M
HETZEL, GEORGE (1826 - 1906)	450-15000	S,L,F
HEUEL, BOB (20TH C)	100-500	X (F)
HEUSTIS, LOUISE LYONS (19TH C)	350-1500	F
HEWETT, EDWARD (1874 -)	150-650	X (A)
HEWINS, AMASA (1785 - 1855)	1000-6500	G,F,L
HIBBARD, ALDRO THOMPSON (1886 - 1972)	750-15000	L
HIBBARD, MARY (19TH - 20TH C)	100-600	F,G
HIBEL, EDNA (1917 -)	400-6000	F
HICKOK, CONDE WILSON (19TH -20TH C)	400-2200	L
HICKS, EDWARD (1770 - 1849)	25000-350000	P
HICKS, GEORGE (20TH C)	200-1000	X (L)
HICKS, SIDNEY S. (19TH C)	*150-750	X (M)
HICKS, THOMAS (1823 - 1890)	500-6500	F,L,G
HIDLEY, JOSEPH H. (1830 - 1872)	5000-80000	P
HIGGINS, CARLETON (1848 - 1932)	350-1800	L,G
HIGGINS, EUGENE	*100-1500	
HIGGINS, EUGENE (1874 - 1958)	300-4500	G,F,L
HIGGINS, GEORGE FRANK (active 1855-85)	350-2500	L
HIGGINS, WILLIAM VICTOR	*500-12000	
HIGGINS, WILLIAM VICTOR (1884 - 1949)	800-40000	L,F
HIGHWOOD, CHARLES (19TH - 20TH C)	500-2000	L

HIKKIMG, J.A. (19TH C)	700-4000	X (L)
HILDA, E. BAILY (19TH - 20TH C)	400-1800	X
HILDEBRANDT, HOWARD LOGAN (1872 - 1958)	400-6000	F,G,S
HILDEBRANT, CORNELIA E. (20TH C)	100-600	F
HILER, HILAIRE (1898 -)	100-650	L,G
HILL, ANDREW P. (19TH C)	350-1800	L,G
HILL, ANNA GILMAN (20TH C)	350-1500	L
HILL, ARTHUR TRUMBULL (1868 -)	500-2500	L,F
HILL, BESSIE M. (19TH C?)	400-3500	X (S)
HILL, EDWARD (1843 - 1923)	250-2500	L
HILL, EDWARD RUFUS (1852 - 1908)	300-5000	L,G
HILL, HOMER (-1968)	100-850	L,G
HILL, HOWARD (19TH C)	600-7500	W
HILL, JOHN HENRY (1839 - 1922)	*200-9000	L
HILL, JOHN WILLIAM	*800-8500+	
HILL, JOHN WILLIAM (1812 - 1879)	1000-30000	L,G,S
HILL, POLLY KNIPP (1900-)	*100-900	X(I)
HILL, THOMAS (1829 - 1908)	500-80000	L,F,S
HILL, W.R. (19TH C)	100-500	L
HILLERN, BERTHA VON (19TH C)	150-900	X (L)
HILLIARD, F. JOHN (1886 -)	400-2000	F
HILLIARD, WILLIAM HENRY (1836 - 1905)	300-3500	L,M,F
HILLINGS, JOHN (- 1894)	5000-35000	P
HILLS, ANNA ALTHEA (1882 - 1930)	400-1200	L,F
HILLS, LAURA COOMBS (1859 - 1952)	*1000-11000	S
HILLSMITH, FANNIE (1911-)	150-1500	L
HILLYER, WILLIAM (JR.) (early 19TH C)	500-2000	F
HILTON, JOHN WILLIAM (1904 -)	400-1500	L
HILTON, ROY (19TH - 20TH C)	500-4000	X
HINCKLEY, THOMAS HEWES (1813 - 1896)	350-7500+	W,L,S
HIND, WILLIAM GEORGE R.(1833-1888)	*100-750	L
HINES, BOB (20TH C)	*100-600	X(W,L)
HINES, PAUL (19TH - 20TH C)	300-1500	L,F
HINKLE, CLARENCE KEISER (1880 - 1960)	500-15000	L,S
HINMAN, CHARLES (1932 -)	1000-18000	A

 * Denotes watercolors, pastels, drawings, and/or mixed media

HINTERMEISTER, HENRY (1897 -)	400-6000	I
HINTON, W.H. (20TH C)	200-900	I
HIRSCH, JOSEPH (1910 - 1981)	500-25000	A,G,F,I
HIRSCH, STEFAN (1899 -)	800-6500	A
HIRSCHBERG, CARL (1854 - 1923)	1000-15000	L,F,M,S
HIRSCHFELD, ALBERT (1903 -)	*300-2000	I
HIRSH, ALICE (1888 - 1935)	200-1500	L
HIRSHFIELD, MORRIS (1872 - 1946)	5000-45000	P
HIRST, CLAUDE RAGUET	*400-15000	
HIRST, CLAUDE RAGUET (1855 - 1942)	1000-25000	G,S,M
HISLOP, ANDREW (20TH C)	100-600	X(F,G)
HITCHCOCK, DAVID HOWARD (1861 - 1943)	350-1800	L,I
HITCHCOCK, GEORGE	*250-4500	
HITCHCOCK, GEORGE (1850 - 1913)	700-35000+	F,L,M
HITCHCOCK, LUCIUS WOLCOTT (1868 - 1942)	350-4500	L,F,I
HITCHINGS, HENRY (-1903)	*100-2800	L
HITCHINS, JOSEPH (19TH C)	400-2000	X (L)
HOBART, CLARK	*100-900	
HOBART, CLARK (1880 - 1948)	200-3500+	L
HOBBS, GEORGE THOMPSON (1846 -)	300-1500	L
HOBBS, MORRIS HENRY (1892 -)	*200-900	X
HOCKNEY, DAVID (1937 -)	7500-450000	A
HODGDON, L. W. (20TH C)	100-700	M
HODGDON, SYLVESTER PHELPS (1830 - 1906)	300-3500	L,F
HODGKIN, HOWARD (1932 -)	7000-225000	A
HODGKINS, A.W. (19TH - 20TH C)	*100-600	L
HODGKINS, S. (19TH - 20TH C)	100-600	L
HODRIDGE, R.D. (19TH-20TH C)	200-1200	L
HOEBER, ARTHUR (1854 - 1915)	300-7500	L,F
HOEGGER, AUGUSTUS (1848 - 1908)	100-850	X (S)
HOEN, L. (20TH C)	*100-500	L
HOERMAN, CARL (1885 -)	100-850	L
HOFF, MARGO (1912 -)	*200-1200	X
HOFFBAUER, CHARLES C. J.	*200-3500+	
HOFFBAUER, CHARLES C. J. (1875 - 1957)	400-10000	M,F,G

* Denotes watercolors, pastels, drawings, and/or mixed media

HOFFMAN, ARNOLD (1886 -)	250-2000	L
HOFFMAN, CHARLES (1820 - 1882)	15000-80000+	P(L)
HOFFMAN, FRANK B. (1888 - 1958)	600-3500	I
HOFMANN, HANS	*500-25000	
HOFMANN, HANS (1880 - 1966)	6500-450000+	A
HOFSTETTER, WILLIAM A. (1884 -)	*100-500	L
HOGAN, JEAN (20TH C)	100-600	X
HOGG, A.W. (early 20TH C)	100-700	L
HOGNER, NILS (1893 -)	300-1500	G
HOIT, ALBERT GALLATIN (1809 - 1856)	500-9000	F,L
HOKINSON, HELEN E. (1893-1949)	*150-700	I
HOLBERG, RICHARD A.	*100-600	
HOLBERG, RICHARD A. (1889-1942)	150-1800	F,M
HOLBERG, RUTH LANGLAND (1891 -)	250-2000	L
HOLBERTON, WAKEMAN (1839 - 1898)	200-1200	L
HOLBROOK, L.T. (19TH C)	200-900	L
HOLCOMB, ALICE WHITE (19TH C)	300-2000	X(F)
HOLDEN, JAMES ALBERT (19TH - 20TH C)	*200-1200	L
HOLDEN, JAMES ALBERT (19TH-20TH C)	100-500	X(F,L)
HOLDING, JOHN (late 19TH C)	*100-400	X (I?)
HOLDREDGE, RANSOME G. (1836 - 1899)	350-8500	L,F
HOLL, H.H. (19TH C)	100-1000	L
HOLLAND, A. (20TH C)	100-600	X (F)
HOLLOWAY, EDWARD STRATTON (- 1939)	250-1800	L,I
HOLMER, CHARLES J. (20TH C)	100-600	X (M)
HOLMES, JOHN F. (20TH C)	200-1500	X
HOLMES, RALPH (1876 - 1963)	250-3200	L,I
HOLMES, ROSINDA SELLERS (20TH C)	100-600	X(F)
HOLMES, WILLIAM HENRY (1846 - 1933)	*200-1800	M,L,F
HOLSLAG, EDWARD J. (1870 - 1925)	100-750	X
HOLT, NELL (20TH C)	*200-800	G
HOLTY, CARL ROBERT	*350-3000	
HOLTY, CARL ROBERT (1900 - 1973)	800-8000	A
HOMER, WINSLOW	*3500-770000	
HOMER, WINSLOW (1836 - 1910)	10000-2000000	M,G,F,L,I

 * Denotes watercolors, pastels, drawings, and/or mixed media

HONDIUS, GERRIT (1891 - 1970)	200-1500	F,L
HONDO, K. (20TH C)	*100-400	F
HOPE, JAMES (1818 - 1892)	900-15000	L,G,F
HOPE, THOMAS H. (- 1926)	750-5500	S,L
HOPKIN, ROBERT (1832 - 1909)	300-4500	M,L
HOPKINS, A. (19TH C)	*100-500	X(G,I)
HOPKINS, BUDD (1931 -)	400-3500	A
HOPKINS, C.E. (1886 -)	*100-600	L
HOPKINS, GEORGE E. (1855 -)	*200-1800	X (L)
HOPKINS, PETER (1911-)	500-5000	G,F
HOPKINS, W. (19TH C)	2000-7500	P
HOPKINSON, CHARLES SYDNEY	*200-2500	
HOPKINSON, CHARLES SYDNEY (1869 - 1962)	600-18000	F,L
HOPPENRATH, C. (20TH C)	100-500	L
HOPPER, EDWARD	*1000-110000	
HOPPER, EDWARD (1882 - 1967)	4500-1350000+	G,L
HOPPIN, THOMAS FREDERICK (1816 - 1872)	400-3000	G,I
HORD, DONALD (1902-)	100-850	X(L)
HOROWITZ, LOUISE MCMAHON (20TH C)	100-500	G,M
HORSFALL, ROBERT BRUCE (1869-)	*100-600	X(W)
HORSFORD, A.J. (-1877)	100-1600	X(L,F)
HORSTMEIER, ALBERT (20TH C)	400-6500	L,F
HORTER, EARL	*100-1200	
HORTER, EARL (1881 - 1940)	400-7500+	S,L
HORTON, ELIZABETH S. (1902 -)	200-1000	G,L
HORTON, WILLIAM SAMUEL	*300-4500	
HORTON, WILLIAM SAMUEL (1865 - 1936)	600-40000	G,L,F,S
HOSKINS, GAYLE PORTER (1887 - 1962)	100-3500	I
HOUSTON, FRANCES C.	*200-2000	
HOUSTON, FRANCES C. (1867 - 1906)	400-4500	F
HOVENDEN, THOMAS (1840 - 1895)	1000-35000	G,F
HOW, KENNETH G. (1883 -)	150-1500	L,G
HOWARD, B.K. (1872-)	150-1800	L
HOWARD, CHARLES (1899 -)	400-3500	A
HOWARD, HENRY MOWBRAY (1873 -)	200-18000	M,L

* Denotes watercolors, pastels, drawings, and/or mixed media

HOWARD, MARION (1883 -)	300-3500	L
HOWE, E.R. (19TH C)	100-800	L
HOWE, H.H. (20TH C)	100-600	M,L
HOWE, R.O. (19TH C)	100-800	L
HOWE, WILLIAM HENRY (1846 - 1929)	250-3000	L,G
HOWELL, FELICIE WALDO (1897 -)	500-8000	L,F
HOWELL, WILLIAM H. (1860 - 1925)	400-3000	L
HOWITT, JOHN NEWTON (1885 - 1958)	100-1800	I,L
HOWLAND, ALFRED CORNELIUS (1838 - 1909)	400-5000	G,L
HOWLAND, GEORGE	*100-800	
HOWLAND, GEORGE (1865 - 1928)	400-3500	F,L
HOWLAND, ISABELLA (1895 -)	*100-400	X
HOWLAND, JOHN DARE (19TH - 20TH C)	500-4500	W,L
HOYLE, RAPHAEL (1804 - 1838)	600-5000	L
HUBACEK, WILLIAM (1866-1958)	200-2000	L,S
HUBARD, WILLIAM JAMES (1807 - 1862)	3500-18000	F
HUBBARD, CHARLES (1801 - 1865)	400-4500	M,L
HUBBARD, F.M.B. (1869 - 1930)	200-1000	X (S)
HUBBARD, RICHARD WILLIAM (1816 - 1888)	400-5000	L,M,F
HUBBELL, CHARLES H. (20TH C)	100-750	X
HUBBELL, HENRY SALEM (1870 - 1949)	700-38000	F
HUDDLE, REBA E. (20TH C)	100-600	G,F,L
HUDSON, CHARLES BRADFORD (1865 -)	200-2500	X (L)
HUDSON, CHARLES WILLIAM (1871 - 1943)	*150-750	L,F
HUDSON, ERIC ELMER FOREST (1862 -)	*100-850	X (G)
HUDSON, GRACE CARPENTER (1865 - 1937)	1000-56000	F,L
HUDSON, JOHN BRADLEY JR (1832 - 1903)	400-4500	L,G
HUFFINGTON, JOHN C. (1864 - 1929)	*200-1200	M,L
HUGE, JURGAN FREDERICK (1809 - 1878)	*10000-35000	P
HUGENTOBLEN, E. J. (20TH C)	250-1800	L
HUGGINS, M.W. (20TH C)	100-500	L,S
HUGHES, DAISY MARGUERITTE (1883 - 1968)	100-900	L
HUGHES, GEORGE (1907 -)	100-3500	I
HULBERT, CHARLES ALLEN	*100-600	
HULBERT, CHARLES ALLEN (19TH-20TH C)	100-1000	L

 * Denotes watercolors, pastels, drawings, and/or mixed media

HULBERT, KATHERINE ALLMOND (- 1961)	200-1000	X
HULDAH, (20TH C)	350-2000	F
HULISTON, J.D. (early 20TH C)	100-500	L
HULLENKREMER, ODON (20TH C)	350-1200	X
HULTBERG, JOHN (1922 -)	*100-1500	A
HUMMELL, ANTHONY (20TH C)	*150-1000	X
HUMPHREY, RALPH (1932 -)	1000-9000	A
HUMPHREY, WALTER BEACH (1892 -)	150-3500	I
HUMPHREYS, CHRALES S. (19TH C)	400-7000	X
HUNLEY, KATHERINE JONES (1883-1964)	200-1500	L,I
HUNT, CHARLES D. (1840 - 1914)	250-1800	L
HUNT, HENRY P. (19TH C)	500-3500	L,G
HUNT, LYNN BOGUE	*300-5000	
HUNT, LYNN BOGUE (1878 - 1960)	500-4500	W,G,I
HUNT, SAMUEL VALENTINE (1803 - 1893)	500-3500	L,S
HUNT, THOMAS L. (1882 - 1938)	400-1800	L
HUNT, WILLIAM MORRIS	*500-8500	
HUNT, WILLIAM MORRIS (1824 - 1879)	800-65000	F,L
HUNTER, CLEMENTINE (1880 -)	250-1200	P
HUNTER, FRANCIS T. (1896 - 1957)	*150-1200	I
HUNTER, FRED LEO (19TH - 20TH C)	100-1200	M,L
HUNTER, ISABEL (1878-1941)	400-4000	L
HUNTER, JOHN YOUNG (1874 - 1955)	500-12000	X (G)
HUNTER, LIZBETH C. (1868-)	*100-750	X(S)
HUNTER, MAX (19TH - 20HT C)	100-400	L
HUNTINGTON, C. LYMAN (19TH C)	200-850	X (F)
HUNTINGTON, D.W. (19TH - 20TH C)	*100-700	W,G
HUNTINGTON, DANIEL	*300-2400	F,G
HUNTINGTON, DANIEL (1816 - 1906)	900-8500	F,G
HUNTINGTON, ELIZABETH H. T.(1878-1963)	150-750	L,M
HUNTINGTON, JIM (1941 -)	600-4500	A
HURD, PETER	*400-18000	
HURD, PETER (1904 - 1984)	1000-20000	L,I,G
HURDLE, GEORGE LINTON (1868 - 1922)	*100-850	L
HURLEY, WILSON (1924 -)	500-25000	L

* Denotes watercolors, pastels, drawings, and/or mixed media

HURTING, J.D. (19TH - 20TH C)	*100-400	L
HURTT, ARTHUR R. (1861 -)	250-1500	L,I
HUSTON, WILLIAM (late 19TH C)	500-3000	L
HUTCHENS, FRANK TOWNSEND (1869 - 1937)	350-7000+	F,L
HUTCHINS, A. (20TH C)	100-850	G,I,M
HUTCHINSON, D.C. (20TH C)	100-850	I
HUTCHISON, ELLEN WALES (1867 - 1937)	150-1500	L
HUTCHISON, FREDERICK W.(1871 - 1953)	200-3000	L
HUTT, HENRY (1875 - 1950)	*150-1200	I
HUTTY, ALFRED HEBER (1877 - 1954)	*300-4000	G,L
HUWITSIT, JESSE (20TH C)	100-800	L
HYDE, H. H. (20TH C)	100-1000	X (S)
HYDE, WILLIAM HENRY (1858 - 1943)	200-1800	F,L
HYND, FREDERICK S.	*100-600	
HYND, FREDERICK S. (1905-)	200-1200	M
HYNEMAN, HERMAN N. (1859 - 1907)	600-4500	F,S
HYNEMAN, JULIA (19TH - 20TH C)	250-1000	L

I

ARTIST	PRICE	SUBJECT
IDELL, MARGARET C. (20TH C)	*100-400	L,M
ILIGAN, RALPH W. (20TH C)	300-2000	X(L)
ILLAWAY, H. (19TH C)	100-700	L
ILSLEY, FREDERICK JULIAN (1855 - 1933)	200-900	L,M
ILYIN, CALEB (20TH C)	100-700	X
ILYIN, PETER (1887 - 1950)	200-900	L,M
IMHOF, JOSEPH A. (1871 - 1955)	*250-6500	F,G
INDIANA, ROBERT (1928 -)	4500-35000	A
INGALLS, WALTER J. (1805 - 1874)	250-1500	F,S,G
INGEMANN, KEITH (20TH C)	300-2500	X
INGEN, HENRY A. VAN (1833 - 1898)	500-4800	L,W
INGERLE, RUDOLPH F. (1879 - 1950)	350-1200	L,G

 * Denotes watercolors, pastels, drawings, and/or mixed media

INGHAM, CHARLES CROMWELL (1796 - 1863)	600-2000	F
INGHAM, WILLIAM (active 1855-1860)	700-4800	F,S
INMAN, HENRY (1801 - 1846)	350-15000	F,L,G
INMAN, JOHN O'BRIEN (1828 - 1896)	400-11000	G,F,S
INNESS, GEORGE (1825 - 1894)	800-225000	L
INNESS (JR), GEORGE (1853-1926)	300-12000	L
INSLEY, ALBERT B. (1842 - 1937)	350-5000	L
INUKAI, KYOHEI (1934 -)	400-3500	A
IPCAR, DAHLOV (1917 -)	*100-1200	X
IPSEN, ERNEST LUDWIG (1869 - 1951)	200-800	F
IRELAND, LEROY (1889 -)	400-3000	G,S,F
IRVINE, WILSON HENRY	*200-3500	
IRVINE, WILSON HENRY (1869 - 1936)	600-18000	L,M,F
IRVING, JOHN BEAUFAIN (1825 - 1877)	600-3500	F,G
IRWIN, BENONI (1840-1896)	250-2000	X(F)
IRWIN, ROBERT (1928 -)	5000-55000	A
ISHAM, SAMUEL (1855 - 1914)	200-3000	F
ITLEY, PAUL (20TH C)	100-500	L,M
ITTNER, RICHARD R. (20TH C)	*100-600	X(W)
IVES, FREDERICK EUGENE (1856 - 1937)	250-1000	F
IVES, PERCY (1864 -)	250-4500	G,F

J

ARTIST	PRICE	SUBJECT
JACKSON, CHARLES AKERMAN (1857 -)	100-850	L
JACKSON, ELBERT McGRAN (1896 -)	300-3200	I
JACKSON, ELIZABETH LESLEY (1867 - 1934)	*100-600	M,L
JACKSON, HERBERT W. (late 19TH C)	200-900	F
JACKSON, JOHN EDWIN (1876-)	*100-800	X(M)
JACKSON, LEE (1909 -)	400-3800	G,L
JACKSON, LUCY ATKINS (19TH - 20TH C)	300-1500	X (G)
JACKSON, MARIAN W. (20TH C)	*100-500	L

* Denotes watercolors, pastels, drawings, and/or mixed media

JACKSON, ROBERT (1891-)	150-1400	X(F)
JACKSON, ROBERT L. (20TH C)	100-450	X
JACKSON, WILLIAM FRANKLIN (1850 - 1936)	300-2000	L
JACKSON, WILLIAM H. (1832 -)	*250-2500	L
JACOB, MICHEL (1877 -)	700-3500	F,S
JACOB, NED	*900-4500	
JACOB, NED (1938 -)	5000-30000	G,F
JACOBS, MILNE (early 20TH C)	100-1800	L
JACOBS, TED SETH (1927-)	200-6000	F
JACOBSEN, ANTONIO	*800-6000	
JACOBSEN, ANTONIO (1850 - 1921)	1200-45000+	M
JACOBSON, OSCAR BROUSSE (1882 - 1934)	150-1500	M,L,G
JAHAM, M.DE (20TH C)	100-600	G
JAHNKE, WILLIAM (1937 -)	100-400	X (L)
JAKOBSEN, KATHY (1952 -)	6000-17000	P
JAMBOR, LOUIS (1884 - 1954)	150-900	G,F
JAMES, ALICE A. S. (1870 -)	100-600	X (L)
JAMES, FREDERICK (1845 - 1907)	500-6000	X(F)
JAMES, H. (19TH C)	*300-1500	X
JAMES, WILLIAM (19TH-20TH C)	200-1200	X(F)
JAMESON, JOHN (1842 - 1864)	500-5500	L
JAMISON, PHILIP (1925 -)	*200-4000	L,S
JANSEN, LEO (20TH C)	100-400	X (F)
JANSSON, ALFRED (1863 - 1931)	300-3000	L
JARVIS, JOHN WESLEY (1780 - 1840)	1500-35000+	F
JECT-KEY, D. WU (20TH C)	100-500	X (L)
JEFFERSON, JOSEPH IV (1829 - 1905)	250-2000	L
JEN, PANG (20TH C)	100-400	F
JENKINS, CHARLES WALDO (1820 -)	600-1500	F
JENKINS, GEORGE WASHINGTON (1816 - 1907)	250-3000	G,F,L,S
JENKINS, J. LeBRUN (1876 - 1951)	150-850	L,G
JENKINS, JOHN ELLIOT (1868 -)	100-600	L
JENKINS, PAUL	*300-6000	
JENKINS, PAUL (1923 -)	1000-65000	A
JENNIN, JONATHAN (active 1830-40)	*1500-5500	P

* Denotes watercolors, pastels, drawings, and/or mixed media

JENNINGS, RICHARD (19TH C)	800-3500	F
JENNYS, WILLIAM (active 1795-1805)	1500-20000	P
JENSEN, ALFRED J.(1903 - 1981)	2500-50000+	A
JENSEN, GEORGE (1878 -)	200-2000	L
JENSEN, THOMAS M. (1831 - 1916)	300-1800	X (F,M)
JEWETT, WILLIAM SMITH (1812-1873)	2000-45000	L
JEX, GARNET W. (1895 - 1979)	150-900	L,G
JICHA, JOE (20TH C ?)	100-500	L
JOHANSEN, JEAN MACLANE (1878-1964)	1000-10000+	F
JOHANSEN, JOHN CHRISTIEN (1876 - 1966)	250-3500	L,G
JOHNS, CLARENCE M. (1843-1925)	400-4500	L
JOHNS, JASPER (1930 -)	*10000-350000+	A
JOHNS, JOSEPH W.	*5000-75000	
JOHNS, JOSEPH W. (1833 - 1877)	2500-12000	L,G
JOHNSON, ARTHUR (1874 - 1954)	700-6000	F,L
JOHNSON, AVERY F. (1906 -)	*200-1500	I
JOHNSON, BEN (1902 -)	900-3000	A
JOHNSON, CAROLINE R. (19TH-20TH C)	150-1000	F
JOHNSON, CHARLES H. (20TH C)	*150-1500	I
JOHNSON, CONTENT (- 1949)	200-1500	L,G
JOHNSON, DAVID (1827 - 1908)	750-45000+	L
JOHNSON, EASTMAN	*2500-110000	
JOHNSON, EASTMAN (1824 - 1906)	750-375000	G,F
JOHNSON, FRANCIS NORTON (1878 - 1931)	200-1000	X
JOHNSON, FRANK TENNEY (1874 - 1939)	1000-140000	F,G,I
JOHNSON, GUY (1927 -)	500-3000	A
JOHNSON, HARVEY (1920 -)	3000-28000	G
JOHNSON, HORACE (1820 - 1890)	100-950	F,G
JOHNSON, J. (19TH C)	500-2500	M
JOHNSON, J.W.A. (19TH-20TH C)	250-2000	X(W)
JOHNSON, JOSHUA (active 1800-1824)	5000-150000+	P(F)
JOHNSON, LESTER	*500-5000	
JOHNSON, LESTER (1919 -)	1000-20000	A
JOHNSON, LUCAS (1940 -)	300-1200	A
JOHNSON, MARSHALL (1850 - 1921)	400-5000	M

* Denotes watercolors, pastels, drawings, and/or mixed media

JOHNSON, PAUL (20TH C)	*100-600	X
JOHNSON, RAY (1927 -)	*500-5000	A
JOHNSON, SAMUEL FROST (1835-)	400-5000	X(S)
JOHNSON, WILLIAM H. (1901-)	100-900	X
JOHNSTON, DAVID C. (1797 - 1867)	400-5000	X (I)
JOHNSTON, EASTMAN (19TH C)	400-5000	F,L
JOHNSTON, FRANK HANS (1888-1949)	200-1500	L
JOHNSTON, JOHN (1753 - 1818)	650-3000	F
JOHNSTON, JOHN HUMPHREYS (1857 -)	400-3500	L
JOHNSTON, JOHN R. (active 1850-75)	500-3500	F,L
JOHNSTON, REUBEN LE GRANDE (1850 - 1914)	250-1000	L,W
JOHNSTON, RICHARD T. (20TH C)	100-650	L
JOHNSTON, ROBERT E. (1885 - 1933)	300-2500	I
JOINER, HARVEY (1852 - 1932)	400-2500	L
JOLLEY, GWILT (1859 -)	100-900	X (F)
JOLLY, WADE L. (1909-)	100-500	L
JONES, F. EASTMAN (19TH C)	350-1500	L,W
JONES, FRANCIS COATES (1857 - 1932)	750-20000	F
JONES, HUGH BOLTON (1848 - 1907)	350-25000	L
JONES, J. WATKINS (19TH C)	100-500	X(F)
JONES, JOE (or JOSEPH JOHN) (1909 - 1963)	400-4500	G,F
JONES, LEON FOSTER (1871 - 1940)	300-3500	L
JONES, MARY E.H. (mid 19TH C)	*300-1200	P
JONES, NORA (20TH C)	*100-600	X(F)
JONES, PAUL (1860 -)	450-1500	W,F
JONES, ROBERT EDMOND (1887 -)	*400-4500	I
JONES, SETH C. (1853 - 1930)	*100-1000	I
JONES, SUSAN (1897 -)	250-1200	X (I,S)
JONES, WELL CHOATE (1879-)	100-1200	L,F,S
JONES, WILLIAM F. (19TH C)	1200-8000	W,G
JONNEVOLD, CARL HENRIK (1856 - 1930)	250-1800	L
JONNIAUX, ALFRED (1882-)	150-2500	F
JONSON, RAYMOND (1891 -)	600-8500	X
JONTINEL, J.H.R. (19TH C)	500-3000	X (L)
JORDAN, GUS (19TH - 20TH C)	350-1800	X (M)

 * Denotes watercolors, pastels, drawings, and/or mixed media

JORDAN, MARGUERITE (20TH C)	*100-900	X (F)
JORGENSEN, CHRISTIAN	*200-2500	
JORGENSEN, CHRISTIAN (1860 - 1935)	400-4500	L
JORGENSON, WILLIAM (20TH C)	400-1800	X (G)
JOSEPH, RICHARD (2OTH C)	800-4500	A
JOSEPHI, ISAAC (19TH - 20TH C)	450-1800	L,F
JOUETT, F.S. (19TH C)	350-2500	X (M)
JOUETT, MATTHEW HARRIS (1787 - 1827)	400-4000	F
JOULLIN, AMEDEE (1862 - 1917)	350-5500	F,G
JOULLIN, LUCILLE (1876-1924)	100-800	L
JOYLES, C.S. (19TH C)	300-1200	X (M)
JUDD, DONALD (1928 -)	*600-5000	A
JUDSON, ALICE (-1948)	300-3500	L,M
JUDSON, C. CHAPEL (1864 -)	100-800	L,M
JUDSON, MINNIE LEE (1865 - 1939)	100-650	L
JUDSON, WILLIAM LEES	*200-1200	
JUDSON, WILLIAM LEES (1842 - 1928)	400-3500	L,G,F
JUERGENS, ALFRED (1866 - 1934)	200-7000	F,M,L

K

ARTIST	PRICE	SUBJECT
KACERE, JOHN C. (1920 -)	5000-20000	A
KACZUROWSKI, MICHAEL (20TH C)	*100-500	L
KAELIN, CHARLES SALIS	*300-5000	
KAELIN, CHARLES SALIS (1858 - 1929)	400-7500	M,L
KAHILL, JOSEPH B. (1882 - 1957)	300-1500	F
KAHN, WOLF (1927 -)	1000-18000	A
KALBFUS, GEORGE (19TH C)	1000-6500	G,F
KALI, MRS. HENRYK WEYNEROWSKI (20TH C)	200-1200	X (F)
KALIN, VICTOR (1919 -)	250-1500	I
KALISKI, HENRY (19TH C)	300-4500	L
KALISKI, HENRY (19TH C)	400-4500	L

* Denotes watercolors, pastels, drawings, and/or mixed media

KALLEM, HENRY (1912 -)	100-600	X
KALMENOFF, MATTHEW (1905 -)	250-1200	L
KAMP, ANTON (20TH C)	100-400	X (L,S)
KANE, JOHN (1860 - 1934)	1500-28000	G,F,L
KANE, THEODORA (1906-)	*100-500	L
KANTOR, MORRIS	*150-600	
KANTOR, MORRIS (1896 - 1974)	200-1800	A
KAPPES, ALFRED (1850 - 1894)	500-10000	X (G)
KAPPES, KARL A. (1861-1943)	100-1000	L
KARFIOL, BERNARD (1886 - 1952)	250-4500	L,F
KAROLY-SZANTO, ? (20TH C)	*100-600	X
KARRAS, SPIRO JOHN (1897 -)	200-1600	L
KATZ, ALEX	*800-7000	
KATZ, ALEX (1927 -)	1000-50000	A
KAUFFMANN, GEORGE F. (19TH C)	*100-400	X (F)
KAUFFMANN, ROBERT (1893 -)	200-1500	I
KAUFMANN, THEODORE (1814 - 1887/90)	5000-45000	G
KAULA, LEE LUFKIN (19TH - 20TH C)	500-32000	F,L
KAULA, WILLIAM JURIAN (1871 - 1953)	500-18000	L
KAUMEYER, G.F. (20TH C)	100-700	L
KAUTZKY, TED (20TH C)	*200-1000	L
KAY, GERTRUDE (20TH C)	*150-600	X(L)
KAYE, OTIS (1885-1974)	2000-25000	S
KAYN, HILDE BAND (1906 - 1950)	200-1200	X (G)
KAZ, NATHANIEL (1917-)	*100-500	X
KEARL, STANLEY (20TH C)	100-450	X (F)
KEAST, SUSETTE SCHULTZ (1892-1932)	250-3000	L
KEEP, A.L. (20TH C)	100-400	X (L)
KEFFER, FRANCES (1881 - 1954)	200-1000	W,L
KEIFFER, EDWIN L. (1921 -)	300-1500	X (L)
KEINHOLZ, EDWARD (1927-)	*100-800	A
KEITH, CASTLE (19TH - 20TH C)	300-1800	L
KEITH, ELIZABETH (1887 -)	500-4800	X (S)
KEITH, WILLIAM (1839 - 1911)	350-32000	L,F
KELLER, ARTHUR IGNATIUS (1866 - 1924)	*200-3500	I

* Denotes watercolors, pastels, drawings, and/or mixed media

KELLER, CHARLES FREDERICK (19TH - 20TH C)	200-1000	L
KELLER, CLYDE LEON (1872 - 1941)	200-1800	L
KELLER, HENRY GEORGE	*100-1200	
KELLER, HENRY GEORGE (1870 - 1949)	300-3000	L,G,S
KELLEY, RAMON (1939 -)	*400-15000	X
KELLOGG, HARRY J. (19TH C)	300-2500	X(S)
KELLOGG, MARY KILBORNE (1814 - 1889)	150-650	X (L)
KELLOGG, NOAH J. (19TH C)	100-600	L
KELLY, CLAY (19TH - 20TH C)	100-400	X (F)
KELLY, ELLSWORTH	*4000-20000	
KELLY, ELLSWORTH (1923 -)	10000-175000+	A,F,S
KELLY, FRANCIS ROBERT (1927 -)	200-1500	X
KELLY, GRACE VERONICA (1884-)	*100-750	X(F)
KELLY, J. REDDING (1868 - 1939)	150-900	F,L
KELPE, PAUL (1902 - 1985)	4000-20000+	A
KEMBLE, EDWARD W. (1861 - 1933)	*100-1800	I
KEMP, OLIVER (1887 - 1934)	400-12000	I
KEMPER, HENRY W. (19TH C)	600-4500	L,F
KEMPTON, ELMIRA (20TH C)	100-900	X
KENDALL, KATE (-1915)	*100-900	X(M)
KENDALL, WILLIAM SERGEANT (1869 - 1938)	800-8000+	F
KENDRICK, DANIEL (20TH C)	100-500	X
KENNEDY, DAVID (active 1840-55)	*5000-15000	P(L)
KENNEDY, EDWARD L. (20TH C)	100-900	X (M)
KENNEDY, WILLIAM W. (1817 - 1870)	1500-12000+	P(F)
KENNON, C.H. (19TH C)	100-600	L
KENSETT, JOHN FREDERICK (1818 - 1872)	1500-150000+	M,L
KENSIL, WILLIAM H. (19TH C)	400-1500	X (S)
KENT, H.H. (19TH C)	200-2400	L
KENT, ROCKWELL	*350-6500	
KENT, ROCKWELL (1882 - 1971)	900-65000	L,F,I
KEPES, GYORGY (1906-)	400-3000	A
KEPLINGER, LONA MILLER (1876-1956)	*150-700	X(M)
KEPPLER, JOSEPH (1838 - 1894)	*100-850	I
KERKAM, EARL (1890 - 1965)	150-2000	A,F

KERN, HERMAN (19TH C)	400-7500	G,F
KERNAN, JOSEPH F. (1878 - 1958)	400-2800	I
KERR, H.M. (19TH C)	200-750	X(S)
KESTER, LENARD (1917 -)	100-850	X (L)
KETT, EMILE (1828 - 1880)	400-3500	L,S
KEY, JOHN ROSS (1837 - 1920)	500-20000+	L
KIENBUSCH, WILLIAM (1914 -)	300-1000	X
KIENHOLZ, EDWARD	*200-1200	
KIENHOLZ, EDWARD (1927 -)	1500-7000	A
KIESALAK, J. (19TH C)	300-1000	X (L)
KIHN, WILFRED LANGDON (1898 - 1957)	1500-12000	L,F
KILEY, GLENN (19TH C)	100-400	X (L)
KILLGORE, CHARLES P. (20TH C)	200-1000	X (L)
KILM, WILFRED LANGDON (1898-)	200-3500	F,L
KILPATRICK, AARON EDWARD (1872-1953)	250-1500	L
KILVERT, B. CORY (1881 - 1946)	*100-1500	I,M
KIMBALL, CHARLES FREDERICK	*100-600	
KIMBALL, CHARLES FREDERICK (1835 - 1907)	250-2500	L,M
KIMBEL, RICHARD M. (1865-1942)	350-3000	L,M
KING, ALBERT F. (1854 - 1934)	300-20000	S,L
KING, CHARLES BIRD	*300-5500	
KING, CHARLES BIRD (1785 - 1862)	500-30000+	F,G,S
KING, EMMA B. (20TH C)	300-1500	X (G)
KING, GEORGE W. (1836-1922)	400-5000	L
KING, HAMILTON (1871 - 1952)	*100-800	I
KING, JOE (20TH C)	400-1800	F
KING, PAUL (1867 - 1947)	400-10000	L,M
KINGMAN, CHARLES R. (1895-)	*100-500	X(L)
KINGMAN, DONG M. (1911 -)	*400-12000	A,I,L
KINGSBURY, EDWARD R. (- 1940)	200-1800	L,M
KINGSTEIN, JONAH (1923 -)	100-400	X
KINGWOOD, CHARLES (20TH C)	*100-500	X (L)
KINNARD, H. (19TH - 20TH C)	100-500	X (M)
KINSELLA, JAMES (1857 - 1923)	100-850	L
KINSEY, ALBERTA (1875 - 1955)	100-1500	F

 * Denotes watercolors, pastels, drawings, and/or mixed media

KINSTLER, EVERITT RAYMOND (1926 -)	*400-7500	I
KIPNESS, ROBERT (20TH C ?)	100-600	X (A?)
KIRK, ELIZABETH (1866 -)	100-750	L
KIRK, RICHARD (20TH C)	100-400	X
KIRKPATRICK, FRANK LE BRUN (1853 - 1917)	500-4500	F,G,I
KIRKPATRICK, WILLIAM A. (1880-)	250-3500	F,I
KIRMSE, MARGUERITE (1885 - 1954)	*200-700	I
KIRTLEY, F.W. (19TH C)	100-700	L
KISSACK, R.A. (1878 -)	*100-500	F
KISSEL, ELEANORA (1891 - 1966)	250-4000	L,S
KITAJ, RONALD B. (1932 -)	5000-275000+	A
KITCHELL, HUDSON M. (1862 - 1944)	100-1800	L,M
KITCHELL, JOSEPH GRAY (1862 -)	150-1200	L
KITELL, ROBERT (20TH C)	100-400	X (I)
KITTELL, NICHOLAS BIDDLE (1822 - 1894)	200-1200	L,F
KIVETT, B. CORY (20TH C)	200-900	X
KLACKNER, C. (19TH C)	400-2500	X (G)
KLAGSTAD, ARNOLD (1898 -)	100-500	X (L)
KLEEMAN (KLEMANN?), RON (1937 -)	1000-12000	A
KLEIN, KATHY M. (20TH C)	*100-500	L
KLEIN, M.J. (20TH C)	100-300	X (L)
KLEINHOLTZ, FRANK (20TH C)	100-700	X(L)
KLEMPNER, ERNEST S. (1867 - 1962)	500-3500	F,I
KLINE, FRANZ	*600-48000	
KLINE, FRANZ (1910 - 1962)	4500-900000	A
KLIREN, H.C. (20TH C)	100-400	L
KLITGAARD, GEORGINA (1893 -)	*150-800	S,L
KLOSS, F. (20TH C)	*200-1000	X(L)
KLOTZ, EDWARD (20TH C)	100-400	L
KLUMKE, ANNA ELIZABETH (1856-1942)	*500-6000	F
KLUMPP, GUSTAV (1902 -1980)	1000-7500	P
KNAP, JOSEPH DAY (1875-)	*200-1500	W,I
KNAPER, G.H. (20TH C ?)	100-500	X (L)
KNAPP, CHARLES W. (1823 - 1900)	450-9000	L
KNATHS, KARL	*150-1800	

* Denotes watercolors, pastels, drawings, and/or mixed media

KNATHS, KARL (1891 - 1971)	450-12000	A
KNEEDLER, J. (20TH C)	100-500	X
KNIGHT, CHARLES ROBERT (1874 - 1953)	*200-5000	W,L
KNIGHT, CLAYTON (1891 - 1969)	*100-700	I
KNIGHT, DANIEL RIDGWAY	*600-3500	
KNIGHT, DANIEL RIDGWAY (1839 - 1924)	2500-75000	F,G
KNIGHT, JOHN A. (1825 -)	100-750	M,L
KNIGHT, LOUIS ASTON (1873 -1948)	400-12000+	L
KNOBLAUCH, L.V. (20TH C)	100-500	X(S)
KNOPF, NELLIE AUGUSTA (1875 - 1962)	100-850	M,L
KNOWLES, FARQUHAR M. (1860 - 1932)	350-5000	M,L,I
KNOWLES, JOE (20TH C)	*100-500	X (G)
KNOWLTON, HELEN M. (1832-1913)	150-1000	L
KNOX, FRANK (20TH C)	*100-600	X(L)
KNOX, JAMES (1866-)	100-1800	X
KNOX, SUSAN RICKER (1874 - 1960)	150-2000	F
KOCH, GERD (1929 -)	100-600	X (L)
KOCH, JOHN (1909 - 1978)	1200-55000	F,S,G
KOCH, PYKE (20TH C)	2500-20000	X
KOCH, SAMUEL (1887 -)	100-900	X (S)
KOCHER, MARY (20TH C)	100-500	X (L)
KOEHLER, PAUL R. (1866 - 1909)	200-1000	L
KOEHLER, ROBERT (1850 - 1917)	500-15000	F
KOENIGER, WALTER (1881 -)	400-7000	L
KOERNER, HENRY (1915 -)	600-4800	A
KOERNER, P.K. (19TH C)	100-500	X (L)
KOERNER, WILLIAM HENRY D. (1878-1938)	1000-45000	I
KOHLER, WILLIAM EIFFE V.R. (19TH C)	300-1500	X (L)
KOLLNER, AUGUSTUS (1813 - 1870)	*300-2000	M,L
KOLLOCK, MARY (1840 - 1911)	500-3500	L,F,S
KOONING, ELAINE DE (1920 -)	600-5000	A
KOONING, WILLEM DE	*3000-250000+	
KOONING, WILLEM DE (1904 -)	7500-3000000+	A
KOOPMAN, AUGUSTUS (1869 - 1914)	300-1500	X (L)
KOOPMAN, JOHN R. (1881 - 1949)	*100-600	X (L,M)

* Denotes watercolors, pastels, drawings, and/or mixed media

KOPF, MAXIM (20TH C)	100-500	X
KOPMAN, BENJAMIN D. (1887 - 1965)	200-1200	F,G
KOPPLEMAN, DOROTHY (1920-)	100-500	X
KORAB, KARL (1937 -)	2500-20000	A
KORSAKOFF, S. DE (20TH C)	100-400	X (M)
KOSA (JR), EMIL JEAN (1903 - 1968)	300-3000	F,G
KOSKI, ? (20TH C)	*100-400	X (F)
KOST, FREDERICK WILLIAM (1861 - 1923)	200-1200	L,G
KOTIN, ALBERT (1907 -)	200-1000	A
KOTZ, DANIEL (1848-1933)	200-2800	L
KRAFFT, CARL RUDOLPH (1884 - 1938)	200-6000	L,G,S
KRASNER, LEE	*600-8000	
KRASNER, LEE (1911 -)	4500-165000	A
KRASNOW, PETER (1890 - 1979)	500-3500	X
KREHBIEL, ALBERT H. (1875 - 1945)	150-2400	G,L
KREPP, FRIEDRICH (19TH C)	200-700	X (F)
KRESS, FREDERICK B. (1888-1970)	400-4500	L
KRETZINGER, CLARA JOSEPHINE (1883 -)	200-3000	X (G)
KREUTER, WERNER (20TH C)	*100-400	X (F)
KRIEGHOFF, CORNELIUS (1812-1872)	600-40000	G,F
KRIMMEL, JOHN LEWIS (1787 - 1821)	10000-150000+	G,F
KROGH, PER LASSON (1889 -)	200-2000	F
KROLL, ABRAHAM (1919 -)	400-3200	F,G
KROLL, LEON	*250-5000	
KROLL, LEON (1884 - 1974)	700-30000+	F,L
KRONBERG, LOUIS	*300-4000	
KRONBERG, LOUIS (1872 - 1964)	400-8000+	F,G
KROTTER, R. (20TH C)	100-400	L
KRUEGER, E. (19TH - 20TH C)	150-750	X (G)
KRUGER, RICHARD (20TH C)	150-600	L
KRUIF, HENRI GILBERT DE (1882 - 1944)	200-1000	X
KRUPPENDORF, FRANZ (20TH C)	100-500	L
KRUSHENICK, NICHOLAS (1929 -)	400-4500	A
KUBIK, KAMIE (20TH C)	*200-1200	X (L)
KUEHNE, MAX (1880 - 1968)	700-25000	L,M,S

KUENSTLER, G. (20TH C)	100-400	X (L)
KUHLMANN, G. EDWARD (1882 - 1934)	100-900	L,F
KUHN, WALT	*600-12000	
KUHN, WALT (1877 - 1949)	900-65000+	A,S,F,L
KULICKE, ROBERT (1924 -)	200-1000	X
KULLOCK, M. (19TH C)	100-500	X (L)
KUNDERT, B. (19TH - 20TH C)	300-1200	L
KUNIYOSHI, YASUO	*200-5000	
KUNIYOSHI, YASUO (1893 - 1953)	5000-250000+	A,F,L
KUNSTLER, MORT (1931 -)	300-8500	I,F
KUNTZ, KARL (18TH - 19TH C)	350-1500	X (G)
KURLANDER, H.W. (20TH C)	150-650	X (F)
KWAL, PAUL (20TH C)	100-600	L
KYLE, JOSEPH (1815 - 1863)	300-1200	F,G,S

L

ARTIST	PRICE	SUBJECT
L'ENGLE, WILLIAM (1884-1957)	100-1200	X(G)
LA CHAISE, EUGENE A. (1857-1925)	600-18000	F
LA CHANCE, GEORGE (1888 -)	200-1500	L,F
LA FARGE, JOHN	*750-50000	
LA FARGE, JOHN (1835 - 1910)	3000-80000	S,F
LA FARGE, JULES (19TH C)	150-850	L
LA GATTA, JOHN (1894 - 1977)	300-5000	I
LABRIE, ROSE (1916 -)	1000-5000	P
LACHAISE, GASTON (1882-1934)	*500-4500	F
LACHMAN, HARRY B. (1886 - 1974)	250-3000	L
LACROIX, PAUL (active 1855-70)	1000-15000	S
LADD, C. (19TH-20TH C)	150-1200	L
LAER, ALEXANDER T. VAN	*150-1000	
LAER, ALEXANDER T. VAN (1857 - 1920)	300-1500	L,M
LAGERBERG, DON (1938 -)	400-1500	A

 * Denotes watercolors, pastels, drawings, and/or mixed media

LAHEY, RICHARD FRANCIS (1893 - 1979)	*200-800	G,F
LAING, GERALD (20TH C)	500-4500	A
LAMASURE, EDWIN (1886- 1916)	*100-750	L
LAMB, ADRIAN (1901-)	200-1200	X(F)
LAMB, F. MORTIMER (1861 - 1936)	400-3500	L,F,W
LAMB, KATE B. (20TH C)	100-500	X (L)
LAMB, RUBEN G. (19TH C)	500-2500	X(S)
LAMBDIN, GEORGE COCHRAN (1830 - 1896)	1200-48000	S,F,G
LAMBDIN, JAMES REID (1807 - 1889)	700-15000	F
LAMBERT, TED R. (1905 - 1960)	3000-18000	X (L)
LANCASTER, MARK (1938 -)	400-3000	A
LANCKEN, FRANK VON DER (1872 - 1950)	350-3000	F,G
LAND, ERNEST ALBERT (20TH C)	150-850	X
LANDERYOU, R. (late 19TH C)	100-750	L
LANE, EMMA (late 19TH C)	100-400	X (S)
LANE, ERNEST (19TH C)	100-700	X (L)
LANE, FITZ HUGH (1804 - 1865)	20000-375000	L,M
LANE, MARTELLA CONE (1875-1962)	100-1000	L
LANG, LOUIS (1814 - 1893)	750-60000	F,G,L
LANGE, ERNA (1896-)	200-1800	X(L)
LANGERFELDT, THEODORE O. (1841-)	*100-600	L
LANGLEY, EDWARD	*100-750	
LANGLEY, EDWARD (20TH C)	300-3500	L
LANGWORTHY, WILLIAM H. (late 19TH C)	300-1200	G,L
LANMAN, CHARLES (1819 - 1895)	350-4500	L
LANSIL, WALTER FRANKLIN (1846 - 1925)	300-4500	M,L
LANSIL, WILBUR H. (19TH-20TH C)	250-3500	L
LARENCE, R.J. (19TH - 20TH C)	*100-500	L
LARIMER, BARBARA (20TH C)	100-800	L
LARSEN, L. (19TH-20TH C)	100-800	L
LARSEN, MIKE (20TH C)	*100-700	X (F)
LARSEN, MORTEN (20TH C)	100-750	L
LARSON, EDWARD (1931 -)	1000-8500	P
LARSSON, KARL (20TH C)	*100-400	X
LARSSON, MARCUS (1825 - 1864)	400-2000	X (L)

* Denotes watercolors, pastels, drawings, and/or mixed media

LASCARI, SALVATORE (1884 -)	100-800	X (F)
LASSNER, N.T. (19TH C)	150-850	X(F)
LASSONDE, OMER (1903 - 1980)	100-900	X (A,S)
LATHROP, IDA PULIS (1859-1937)	200-1500	L,M,F
LATHROP, WILLIAM LANGSON (1859 - 1938)	500-10000	L
LATIMER, F.R. (19TH-20TH C)	*100-500	X(F)
LATIMER, LORENZO PALMER	*150-1000	
LATIMER, LORENZO PALMER (1857 - 1941)	300-2500	L
LATOIX, GASPARD	*1000-6000	
LATOIX, GASPARD (19TH - 20TH C)	1000-12000	F
LAUDIN, MARGARET E. (19TH-20TH C)	150-1200	X(S)
LAUFMAN, SYDNEY (1891-)	100-950	X (F,L)
LAUGHLIN, EDWARD (20TH C)	100-650	X
LAUGHNER, L.M. (20TH C)	100-500	X
LAURENCE, SYDNEY M. (1865 - 1940)	700-40000	L,F
LAURENT, JOHN (20TH C)	250-1000	F
LAURENT, ROBERT (1890 - 1970)	*100-750	X (W)
LAURITZ, JACK (20TH C)	100-600	L
LAURITZ, PAUL (1889 - 1975)	400-3500	L
LAUSSUCQ, HENRI (20TH C)	*100-400	X
LAUTERER, ARCH (20TH C)	*200-600	I
LAUX, AUGUST (1847 -1921)	400-6000	S,W
LAVALLE, JOHN	*100-750	
LAVALLE, JOHN (1896 -)	500-8500	G,F
LAVALLEY, JONAS JOSEPH (1858 - 1930)	500-3500	S
LAVIGNE, AUDREY RAE (19TH C)	*100-400	X
LAW, HARRY V. (20TH C)	100-700	L
LAWLESS, CARL (1896 - 1934)	300-5000	L
LAWLOR, GEORGE WARREN (1848 -)	200-6000	F,G
LAWMAN, JASPER HOLMAN (1825 - 1906)	700-6500	L,F
LAWRENCE, EDNA W. (1898-)	*150-900	X(M,L)
LAWRENCE, JACOB (1917 -)	*1000-32000	A
LAWRENCE, VAIL EUGENE (1856 - 1934)	2000	
LAWRIE, ALEXANDER (1828 - 1917)	600-3500	F,L
LAWSON, ERNEST (1873 - 1939)	1000-220000	L

 * Denotes watercolors, pastels, drawings, and/or mixed media

LAWSON, MARK (20TH C)	650-2500	I
LAZARUS, JACOB HART (1822 - 1891)	200-1000	F
LAZZARIO, PIETRO (1898 -)	*200-1000	A
LAZZELL, BLANCHE (- 1956)	600-9000	A,L,M
LEA, TOM (1907 -)	800-4800	I
LEACH, FREDERICK (20TH C)	*100-500	X(F)
LEAKE, GERALD (1885 -)	400-1800	X (F)
LEAR, LAVIN (20TH C)	*100-400	X (F)
LEAVITT, EDWARD CHALMERS (1842 - 1904)	400-12000	S,L
LEAVITT, J.A. (20TH C)	*100-800	X (M)
LEAVITT, JOHN FAUNCE (1905 - 1974)	*250-2000	M
LEAVITT, R.C. (20TH C ?)	200-900	X (M)
LEAVITT, SHELDON (JR) (19TH C ?)	500-3500	X
LEBDUSKA, LAWRENCE H. (1894 - 1966)	300-5000	P
LEBRUN, RICO	*200-4800	
LEBRUN, RICO (1900 - 1964)	300-2500	A
LECHAY, MYRON (1898 -)	150-950	L,F
LECLEAR, THOMAS (1818 - 1882)	300-5000	G,F,M
LECOQUE, ALOIS (1891-1981)	200-4500	X
LEE, BERTHA STRINGER (1873 - 1937)	100-1800	L,M
LEE, CHEE CHIN S. CHEUNG (20TH C)	100-800	X
LEE, DORIS EMRICK (1905 - 1983)	500-6000+	L,G
LEE, LAURA (1867 -)	300-2400	L
LEE, MANNING DE VILENEUE (20TH C)	200-1600	X
LEE, MATTIE (19TH C)	100-600	L
LEE, SAMUEL M. (- 1841)	300-1500	L,F
LEEDY, LAURA A. (1881 -)	150-850	X (L)
LEETEC, EDGAR (20TH C)	400-3200	F
LEFEVRE, LAURA (19TH C)	300-3800	L
LEGANGER, NICOLAY TYSLAND (1832 - 1894)	250-3000	L,M
LEGRAND, HENRY (active 1855-85)	400-5000	L,F
LEHR, ADAM (1853 - 1924)	150-1200	S
LEIGH, WILLIAM ROBINSON (1866 - 1955)	2000-160000	I,F
LEIGHTON, KATHRYN W.(1876 - 1952)	800-15000	F
LEIGHTON, SCOTT (1849 - 1898)	300-30000	W,F,L

* Denotes watercolors, pastels, drawings, and/or mixed media

LEIKER, W. (19TH C)	150-600	X (L)
LEISSER, MARTIN B. (1845 -)	500-3000	L
LEITCH, RICHARD P. (19TH C)	*100-600	L
LEITH-ROSS, HARRY	*200-2000	
LEITH-ROSS, HARRY (1886 - 1973)	400-10000	L,S
LEITNER, LEANDER (1873 -)	100-1200	X (L)
LELAND, HENRY (1850 - 1877)	600-5000	G,F
LEMAIRE, CHARLES (20TH C)	*200-1000	X (I)
LEMMENMEYER, M. (20TH C)	100-400	X
LENHART, A. (20TH C)	100-600	L
LESLIE, ALFRED (1927 -)	2500-50000	A
LESLIE, FRANK (see HENRY CARTER)		
LESLIE, G. (late 19TH C)	300-1200	L
LEU, AUGUST WILHELM (1819 - 1887)	1000-7500	L
LEUTZE, EMANUEL GOTTLIEB (1816 - 1868)	600-30000	F,G,M
LEVER, RICHARD HAYLEY	*100-4800	
LEVER, RICHARD HAYLEY (1876 - 1958)	300-40000	M,L
LEVI, JULIAN (1874 -)	250-3000	F,M,G
LEVIER, CHARLES (1920 -)	250-1800	L,M,S
LEVINE, DAVID (1926 -)	*150-5500	I,L,F
LEVINE, JACK	*250-6500	
LEVINE, JACK (1915 -)	1000-45000	A,G,F
LEVY, ALEXANDER OSCAR (1881 - 1947)	500-8500	L,F,I
LEVY, NAT (20TH C)	*100-700	X (L,M)
LEVY, WILLIAM AUERBACH (1889 - 1964)	200-1500	X (F,L)
LEWANDOWSKI, EDMUND D. (1914 -)	800-4500	X
LEWIN, JAMES MORGAN (1836-1877)	500-3000	X(S)
LEWIS, C.H.	*100-650	
LEWIS, C.H. (19TH C)	400-2500	F,M
LEWIS, EDMUND DARCH	*150-4500	
LEWIS, EDMUND DARCH (1835 - 1910)	400-20000	M,L
LEWIS, EMERSON (20TH C)	*100-900	I
LEWIS, GEORGE JEFFREY (20TH C)	150-700	X (L,F)
LEWIS, H. EMERSON (1892-)	100-950	L
LEWIS, MARTIN (1883 - 1962)	*500-9500	G,L

 * Denotes watercolors, pastels, drawings, and/or mixed media

LEWIS, V. (20TH C)	100-900	X(L)
LEWITT, SOL (1928 -)	*500-5000	A
LEYENDECKER, FRANCIS X. (1877 - 1924)	500-7500	I
LEYENDECKER, JOSEPH C. (1874 - 1951)	700-40000	I
LIBBY, FRANCIS ORVILLE (1884 -)	100-1000	X (L)
LIBERMAN, ALEXANDER (1912 -)	800-7000	A
LIBERTE, JEAN (20TH C)	100-400	X (L,F)
LICHTENAUER, JOSEPH M. (1876-)	200-1200	X(F)
LICHTENBERG, MANES (20TH C)	300-2200	L
LICHTENSTEIN, ROY	*3000-575000	
LICHTENSTEIN, ROY (1923 -)	7000-600000+	A
LIE, JONAS (1880 - 1940)	650-40000	M,L
LILJESTROM, GUSTAVE (1882-)	200-2000	X(W,L)
LIMARZI, JOSEPH (1907-)	100-1500	X(F)
LINCOLN, EPHRAIM F. -)	800-4500	M
LINDE, OSSIP L. (19TH-20TH C)	300-2500	X(L)
LINDENMUTH, TOD (1885 -)	300-1000	L,G,M
LINDER, HENRY (1854 - 1910)	100-900	L
LINDGREN, MARJORIE REED (20TH C)	300-1500	X
LINDHOLM, W. (19TH C)	300-1000	X (M)
LINDIN, CARL OLAF ERIC (1869 - 1942)	100-750	X (M)
LINDNER, E. (20TH C)	*100-500	X (L)
LINDNER, RICHARD	*800-35000	
LINDNER, RICHARD (1901 - 1978)	1500-350000	A (F)
LINDNEUX, ROBERT OTTOKAR (1871 - 1970)	100-1800	F,L
LINDSAY, THOMAS CORWIN (1845 - 1907)	300-3000	L,F
LINFORD, CHARLES (1846 - 1897)	400-2500	L
LINGLE, BENJAMIN (20TH C)	*100-600	L
LINSON, CORWIN KNAPP (1864 - 1934)	600-7500	L,I
LINTON, FRANK BENTON ASHLEY (1871 - 1944)	300-900	X (F)
LINTOTT, EDWARD BERNARD (1875 - 1951)	300-5000	F,L,S
LINTOTT, EDWARD BERNARD)	*150-850	
LIPPINCOTT, WILLIAM HENRY (1849 - 1920)	400-18000	F,L,I
LIPSKY, PAT (1941 -)	500-2500	X
LITTLE, A.P. (19TH C)	100-1000	X (S)

* Denotes watercolors, pastels, drawings, and/or mixed media

LITTLE, ARTHUR (20TH C)	500-4500	X
LITTLE, JOHN WESLEY (1867 - 1923)	*100-850	L,M
LITTLE, NATHANIEL STANTON (1893 -)	500-4800	L,M
LITTLE, PHILIP	*100-850	
LITTLE, PHILIP (1857 - 1942)	500-9000+	M,L
LITTLEFIELD, WILLIAM HORACE (1902 - 1969)	100-650	A
LITTLEWOOD, JOHN (19TH C)	100-600	X (G)
LITZINGER, DOROTHEA M. (1889-1925)	500-7500	L,S
LLOYD, SARA (20TH C)	450-3500	L,F
LOCHRIE, ELIZABETH DAVEY (1890 - 1976)	350-1500	X (F,G)
LOCK, F.W. (mid 19TH C)	*400-2500	L,F
LOCKE, W.R. (20TH C)	100-800	L
LOCKWOOD, JOHN WARD (1894 - 1963)	*100-1200	L
LOCKWOOD, WILTON (ROBERT) (1862 - 1914)	300-3000	F,S
LOEB, LOUIS (1866 - 1909)	150-5000	F,G,I
LOEBERS, ADRIAN (20TH C)	100-850	X (L)
LOEMANS, ALEXANDER FRANCOIS (19TH C)	400-3500	L
LOFTEN, RICHARD (20TH C)	100-600	X
LOGAN, FRANCES (20TH C)	200-1000	X(S)
LOGAN, MAURICE	*300-1200	
LOGAN, MAURICE (1886 - 1977)	300-2500	F,M,L
LOGAN, ROBERT FULTON (1889 - 1959)	500-4500	G,L
LOGAN, ROBERT HENRY (1874 - 1942)	500-5500	F
LOHREDL, G.S. (20TH C)	150-700	X
LONE WOLF,	*600-12000	
LONE WOLF, (1882 - 1970)	1000-18000	X (F)
LONG, STANLEY M. (1892 - 1972)	*100-1000	F,G
LONGFELLOW, ERNEST W. (1845 - 1921)	300-2000	L
LONGFELLOW, MARY KING (1852 - 1945)	*200-1500	L,M
LONGO, ROBERT (1923 -)	*800-2500	A
LONGPRE, PAUL DE	*600-3200	
LONGPRE, PAUL DE (1855 - 1911)	600-15000	S
LOOMIS, (WILLIAM)ANDREW (1892-1959)	250-2500	I
LOOMIS, CHARLES RUSSELL (1857 - 1936)	*200-1800	M,L,F
LOOMIS, CHESTER R. (1852 - 1924)	400-3500	L,F

 * Denotes watercolors, pastels, drawings, and/or mixed media

LOOMIS, JESSIE PARROTT (?)	*100-700	X (L?)
LOOMIS, P.L. (early 20TH C)	100-300	X (S)
LOOMIS, W.H. (early 20TH C)	*300-1200	X (F)
LOOP, HENRY AUGUSTUS (1831 - 1895)	100-800	F,L
LOOP, JEANETTE SHEPPERD H. (1840-1909)	100-1000	F
LOOP, JENNIE (19TH C)	400-1200	X (F)
LOPEZ, CARLOS (20TH C)	150-1200	X (F)
LOPEZ-LOZA, LUIS (1939 -)	700-2800	A
LORENZ, RICHARD (1858 - 1915)	500-32000	G,F,L
LORING, FRANCIS WILLIAM (1838 - 1905)	300-1500	G,F,L
LORING, WILLIAM CUSHING (1879-)	250-3000	F
LORSKI, BORIS LOVET- (1894-1973)	*400-1200	X(F)
LOTHROP, GEORGE EDWIN (20TH C)	600-3000	X (A?)
LOTICHIUS, ERNEST (late 19TH C)	400-2500	G,L,W
LOTT, E. (19TH C)	100-400	X (L)
LOTZ, MATILDA (1858-1923)	300-3500	X(W,M)
LOUDERBACK, WALT (1887 - 1941)	100-3000	I
LOUGHEED, ROBERT ELMER (1910 - 1982)	800-35000	L,G,W,I
LOUIS, MORRIS (1912 - 1962)	7500-450000	A
LOVE, GEORGE PATTERSON (1887 -)	*100-600	X (F)
LOVEJOY, RUPERT (20TH C)	350-4000	L,M
LOVELL, KATHERINE ADAMS (19TH - 20TH C)	250-1200	L,F,S
LOVELL, TOM (1909 -)	1500-125000	I,F,G
LOVEN, FRANK W. (1869 - 1941)	250-4000	L,I
LOVERIDGE, CHARLES (19TH C)	300-1800	L
LOVERIDGE, CLINTON (1824 - 1902)	1000-10000+	L
LOVEWELL, ROMINER (1853-1932)	*300-1200	M,L,F
LOW, LAWRENCE GORDON (1912 -)	150-3500	F,S,I
LOW, MARY L.F. MACMONIES (1858-1946)	500-7500+	F
LOW, WILL HICOCK (1853 - 1932)	400-18000	I
LOW, WILLIAM GILMAN (19TH - 20TH C)	500-3000	X (L,W)
LOWE, R. (19TH - 20TH C)	100-400	X
LOWELL, MILTON H. (1848 - 1927)	200-1200	L
LOWELL, ORSON BYRON	*300-2000	
LOWELL, ORSON BYRON (1871 - 1956)	500-5000	I

LOWES, H.C. (19TH C)	200-800	X (W)
LOWING, M. (19TH C)	100-1000	L
LOWNES, ANNA (19TH C)	400-2500	X (S)
LOWRY, WILLIAM J. (19TH C)	100-700	L
LOZIER, AIMEE A. (20TH C)	100-600	F
LOZOWICK, LOUIS (1892 - 1973)	1000-45000+	A
LUCAS, ALBERT PIKE (1862 - 1945)	350-10000	L
LUCE, MOLLY (1896 -)	500-11000	G,F,L
LUCE, PERCIVAL DE (1847 - 1914)	250-1000	X (L)
LUCIONI, LUIGI (1900 -)	500-7800	S,L
LUKS, GEORGE BENJAMIN	*200-8000	
LUKS, GEORGE BENJAMIN (1867 - 1933)	1500-27550000	G,F,L
LUM, BERTHA BOYNTON (1879-1954)	350-3500	F
LUMIS, HARRIET RANDALL (1870 - 1953)	500-250000	L,M
LUMLEY, ARTHUR (1837 - 1912)	300-2000	F,I
LUND, HAROLD (1904-)	100-850	X(M)
LUNDBERG, AUGUST FREDERICK (1878-1928))	500-40000	G,M
LUNDBORG, A.F. (20TH C)	100-900	X(L)
LUNDBORG, FLORENCE (1871 - 1949)	*150-850	X (I)
LUNDEAN, J. LOUIS (20TH C)	300-2000	X (W)
LUNDEBERG, HELEN (1908 -)	200-3500	M,G,F
LUNGREN, FERNAND HARVEY (1857 - 1932)	*500-4500	L,I
LURIE, NAN (20TH C)	100-700	X
LUTKINS, MARGARET (20TH C)	100-500	L
LUTZ, DAN (1906 - 1978)	100-1500	A
LUX, THEODORE F. (1910 -)	300-2000	X (M)
LUYTIES, JAN VAN (19TH C)	100-800	L
LYFORD, PHILIP (1887 - 1950)	200-2000	F,L,I
LYMAN, JOSEPH (JR) (1843 - 1913)	500-3500	L
LYNN, DAVID (20TH C)	100-700	L
LYONNEL, A. (19TH - 20TH C)	100-700	L

* Denotes watercolors, pastels, drawings, and/or mixed media

M

ARTIST	PRICE	SUBJECT
MAAR, DORA (20TH C)	250-1200	X (L)
MACALLISTER, CARRIE R. (19TH - 20TH C)	400-4000	L
MACAULIFFE, JAMES J. (1848 - 1921)	500-9500	G,M,L
MACCAMERON, ROBERT LEE (1866-1912)	500-15000	F,G
MACCARTHY, FRANK (1924 -)	*100-900	G,F,L
MACCAY, WILBUR (20TH C)	100-700	X (L)
MACCORD, CHARLES WILLIAM (1852 - 1923)	300-1200	L
MACCORD, ELIZABETH (19TH - 20TH C)	100-600	X
MACCORD, MARY NICHOLENA (20TH C)	500-6500	X (L)
MACDONALD, HAROLD L. (1861 -)	100-1500	G,F
MACDONALD, JAMES EDWARD H.(1873-1932)	2000-65000	L
MACDONALD, L.W. (19TH - 20TH C)	150-900	X(F)
MACDONALD-WRIGHT, STANTON	*500-8500	
MACDONALD-WRIGHT, STANTON (1890 - 1973)	600-30000	A,F,S
MACDOUGALL, JOHN ALLAN (1843 -)	100-900	F
MACEWEN (MCEWEN), WALTER	*200-7500	
MACEWEN (MCEWEN), WALTER (1860 - 1943)	450-10000	G,F,L
MACGILVARY, NORWOOD HODGE (1874 - 1950)	300-7500	L,F
MACGINNIS, HENRY R. (1875 - 1962)	700-4500	F
MACHEFERT, ADRIAN C. (1881 -)	*100-500	L,F
MACHEN, WILLIAM HENRY (1832 - 1911)	350-2500	W,S
MACHESNEY, CLARA TAGGART (1860 -)	150-850	X (L)
MACINNIS, CHARLES (19TH C)	300-1200	G,F
MACIVER, LOREN (1909 -)	1000-18000	A
MACKENDRICK, LILIAN (1906 -)	300-2500	X (F)
MACKENZIE, RODERICK D. (1865-1941)	600-13000	F,L
MACKNIGHT, DODGE (1860 - 1934)	*200-5000	L
MACKUBIN, FLORENCE (1866 - 1918)	*100-900	F,W
MACKY,CONSTANCE L.J. (1883-1961)	*100-800	L
MACLAUGHLIN, CHARLES J. (20TH C)	150-900	X (L)
MACLAUGHLIN, GERALD (20TH C)	200-1000	X
MACLEOD, WILLIAM (active 1840-65)	800-6500	L

MACMONNIES, FREDERICK WILLIAM (1863 - 1936)	1000-40000	G,F
MACMONNIES, MARY FAIRCHILD (19TH C)	1000-18000	F
MACNEAL, FREDERICK A. (early 20TH C)	*100-500	L
MACOMBER, MARY LIZZIE (1861 - 1916)	400-10000	F
MACRAE, ELMER LIVINGSTON	*200-3500	
MACRAE, ELMER LIVINGSTON (1875 - 1952)	500-30000	M,L,G,F
MACRAE, EMMA FORDYCE (1887-1974)	400-4500	X(F,S)
MACRUM, GEORGE H. (20TH C)	500-6800	L,F
MACSOUD, NICHOLAS S. (1884 -)	100-850	L,F
MACY, WENDELL FERDINAND -)	350-3000	L
MACY, WILLIAM STARBUCK (1853 - 1916)	400-5500	L,G
MADER, LOUIS (1842 - 1892)	2500-25000	P
MAENTEL, JACOB (1763 - 1863)	*2000-35000+	P
MAGEE, JAMES C.	*100-350	
MAGEE, JAMES C. (1846 - 1924)	250-5000	L
MAHAFFEY, NOEL (1944 -)	1500-18000	X (G)
MAHER, KATE HEATH (1860-1946)	300-3200	L
MAHOLY-NAGY, LAZLO	*600-25000	
MAILLOT, VICTORIA (early 20TH C)	300-1500	X (S)
MAJOR, B. (19TH - 20TH C)	100-800	L
MAJOR, ERNEST LEE (1864 - 1950)	400-3500	F,L,S
MAKO, B. (1890 -)	100-1200	X
MALBONE, EDWARD GREENE (1777-1807)	1500-10000	F
MALCOLM, LLYOD R. (19TH C)	*150-900	X (M,L)
MALCOM, ELIZABETH (20TH C)	*100-500	X (F)
MALHERBE, WILLIAM (1884 - 1951)	300-6000	L,F,S
MAN-RAY,	*300-75000	
MAN-RAY, (Emmanuel Radinski) (1890 - 1976)	1500-325000+	A
MANGOLD, ROBERT	*400-15000	
MANGOLD, ROBERT (1937 -)	3500-90000	A
MANGRAVITE, PEPPINO (1896 -)	*400-3000	A,F
MANIGAULT, EDWARD M.(1887 - 1922)	500-18000	X
MANLEY, THOMAS R. (1853 -)	100-650	L
MANN, PARKER (1852 - 1918)	100-1800	L

 * Denotes watercolors, pastels, drawings, and/or mixed media

MANNHEIM, JEAN (1863 -1945)	300-5500	L,F
MANNING, RUSSEL G. (- 1982)	*100-600	X (G)
MANOIR, IRVING K. (1891-)	150-750	L
MAPES, JAMES J. (1806 - 1866)	200-1500	X (F)
MARATTA, HARDESTY GILLMORE (1864 -)	*200-1000	X (L,W)
MARBLE, JOHN NELSON (1855 - 1918)	100-650	L,F
MARBOEUF, V. (20TH C)	100-900	X(M)
MARCA-RELLI, CONRAD (1913 -)	*600-10000	A
MARCHAND, JOHN NORVAL (1875 - 1921)	*300-4500	I
MARCHANT, EDWARD DALTON (1806 - 1887)	700-10000	F
MARCIUS-SIMONS, PINCKNEY (1867 - 1909)	500-7500	G,F
MARCY, WILLIAM (20TH C)	*100-300	X
MARDEN, BRICE (1938 -)	*1000-65000	A
MARGESON, GILBERT TUCKER (1852-)	100-1200	M
MARGO, BORIS (1902 -)	300-3000	A
MARGULIES, JOSEPH	*100-900	
MARGULIES, JOSEPH (1896 -)	400-3000	G,F,L,M
MARIA, WALTER DE (1935 -)	*1000-10000	A
MARIN, JOHN	*500-50000	
MARIN, JOHN (1870 - 1953)	6000-40000	A,M,L
MARINKO, GEORGE (1908 -)	100-1000	X (F)
MARIS, WALTER DE (1877 -)	300-2000	X
MARK, GEORGE WASHINGTON (1795 - 1879)	800-10000	P
MARK, LOUIS (1867 - 1942)	100-1500	F
MARKHAM, CHARLES C. (1837 - 1907)	1000-10000	G,S
MARKHAM, KYRA (1891 -)	300-2500	X (F)
MARKOS, LAJOS (1917 -)	500-10000	F,G
MARLATT, H. IRVING (- 1929)	250-1200	M,L
MARPLE, WILLIAM (1827-1910)	200-2000	L
MARPLE, WILLIAM L. (1827 - 1910)	500-4000	L
MARR, CARL RITTER VON (1858-1936)	200-6000	F
MARSDEN, THEODORE (20TH C)	500-12000	W
MARSH, FELICIA MEYER (20TH C)	100-500	F,L
MARSH, FREDERICK DANA (1872 - 1961)	200-1500	F,G
MARSH, REGINALD	*300-45000	

* Denotes watercolors, pastels, drawings, and/or mixed media

MARSH, REGINALD (1898 - 1954)	600-60000+	G,F,I
MARSHALL, CLARK S. (19TH - 20TH C)	100-450	L
MARSHALL, FRANK HOWARD (1866 -)	100-850	M,L
MARSHALL, THOMAS W. (1850 - 1874)	500-4800	G,L
MARSHALL, WILLIAM EDGAR (1837 - 1906)	500-7500	F
MARTENET, MARJORIE D. (19TH - 20TH C)	100-600	X
MARTENS, G. (early 19TH C)	100-850	X(F)
MARTIN, A. (19TH C)	100-400	L
MARTIN, AGNES (1912 -)	*1000-150000	A
MARTIN, EMMA (19TH C)	*600-3800	X(F)
MARTIN, FLETCHER	*200-4000	
MARTIN, FLETCHER (1904 - 1979)	600-5000	G,F
MARTIN, GILL (20TH C)	100-900	L
MARTIN, HELEN DOAK (19TH - 20TH C)	100-600	L
MARTIN, HOMER DODGE (1836 - 1897)	700-25000+	L
MARTIN, J.H. (19TH C)	150-950	X (L)
MARTIN, KEITH (20TH C)	*100-650	X(G,F)
MARTIN, KNOX (1923 -)	400-5000	A
MARTIN, L.B. (19TH C)	400-2500	X (M)
MARTINEZ, XAVIER	*200-1200	
MARTINEZ, XAVIER (1874 - 1943)	800-8500	X (L,F)
MARTINI, JOSEPH DE (1896 -)	*100-400	G,L
MARTINO, ANTONIO PIETRO (1902 -)	200-3500	L
MASON, ALICE TRUMBULL (1904 - 1971)	800-18000+	A
MASON, FRANK H. (1921 -)	200-2000	L,G
MASON, GEORGE CHAMPLIN (1820 - 1894)	400-6500	L
MASON, L.D. (19TH C)	100-900	X(L,W)
MASON, MAUD MARY (1867 - 1956)	100-750	X (L,S)
MASON, ROY MARTELL (1886 -)	*100-500	X (G)
MASON, SANFORD (1798 - 1862)	500-3200	F
MASON, WILLIAM SANFORD (1824 - 1864)	800-6500	G,F
MASSEY, RAYMOND (20TH C)	300-2400	M
MASTERS, FRANK B. (1873-)	*250-3000	I
MASTERS, WALTER (20TH C)	100-1000	F
MATHEUS, A. (19TH - 20TH C)	100-700	L

 * Denotes watercolors, pastels, drawings, and/or mixed media

MATHEWS, ARTHUR FRANK	*500-4500	
MATHEWS, ARTHUR FRANK (1860 - 1945)	850-30000	F,G,L
MATHEWS, J. (early 19TH C)	2500-12000	P
MATHEWS, JOSEPH (1863 - 1893)	350-2800	X (F)
MATHEWSON, FRANK CONVERS (1862 - 1941)	200-2200	F,L,S
MATSON, VICTOR (20TH C)	100-800	L
MATTESON, TOMPKINS HARRISON (1813 - 1884)	600-9000	G,F
MATTHEWS, W.T. (19TH - 20TH C)	100-500	X (F,S)
MATTSON, HENRY ELLIS (1887 - 1971)	100-900	X (F,L)
MATULKA, JAN	*400-6500	
MATULKA, JAN (1890 - 1972)	800-10000	A
MATZAL, LEOPOLD C. (1890 -)	150-850	F
MAURER, ALFRED HENRY	*600-7500	
MAURER, ALFRED HENRY (1868 - 1932)	700-190000	A,F,L
MAURER, LOUIS (1832 - 1932)	2500-65000	G,F,W
MAXFIELD, CLARA (1879-1959)	100-1000	S
MAXFIELD, JAMES E. (1848 -)	300-7500	L
MAXWELL, EDDA (19TH - 20TH C)	400-4500	F
MAXWELL, PAUL (20TH C)	*100-500	X
MAY, J. (19TH-20TH C)	200-1000	L
MAYER, CONSTANT (1829 - 1911)	500-24000	G,F
MAYER, FRANK BLACKWELL (1827 - 1899)	400-30000	G,F
MAYER, PETER BELA (1888 -)	500-20000	L,M
MAYFIELD, ROBERT B. (1869 - 1935)	100-600	X
MAYNARD, GEORGE W.(1843 - 1923)	*300-3500	X (M,F)
MAYNARD, RICHARD FIELD (1875 -)	500-3500	X (F)
MAYS, PAUL KIRTLAND (1887 - 1961)	200-1200	L
MAZZONOVICH, LAWRENCE (1872 - 1946)	500-12000	L
MCAULIFFE, JAMES J. (1848 - 1921)	300-18000+	G,M,L
MCBEY, JAMES (1883 - 1959)	*200-2000	L
MCCALL, CHARLES (20TH C)	200-1200	X (F)
MCCARTER, HENRY (1865 - 1943)	*100-2500	I,L
MCCARTHY, FRANK (1924 -)	450-55000	I
MCCARTHY, HELEN K. (1884 -)	100-300	X (M)
MCCHESNEY, CLARA T. (early 20TH C)	*100-500	F,L

MCCHESNEY, ROBERT (1913-)	100-900	A
MCCLELLAND, BARCLAY (1891 - 1943)	*100-500	X
MCCLOSKEY, J. BURNS (20TH C)	200-1500	X (G)
MCCLOSKEY, WILLIAM J. (1859 - 1941)	6000-165000+	S
MCCOLLUM, ALLAN (20TH C)	400-1200	A
MCCOMAS, FRANCIS JOHN	*600-7500	
MCCOMAS, FRANCIS JOHN (1874 - 1938)	750-22000	L,M
MCCOMAS, GENE FRANCES (20TH C)	*100-500	F
MCCONNELL, GEORGE (1852 - 1929)	100-1200	M,L
MCCORD, CHARLES W. (1852-1923)	100-1500	L
MCCORD, GEORGE HERBERT	*250-1500	
MCCORD, GEORGE HERBERT (1848 - 1909)	400-6000	L,M
MCCOY, LAWRENCE R. (1888 -)	150-850	X (F)
MCCRACKEN, JOHN HARVEY (1934 -)	400-4500	A
MCCREA, SAMUEL HARKNESS (1867 -)	500-3500	L
MCCULLEN, A. (19TH C)	*350-2500	X (L)
MCCUTCHEON, JOHN T. (1870 -)	*100-500	I
MCDERMOTT, A. (20TH C)	100-800	X(L)
MCDERMOTT, J.R. (1919 - 1977)	100-1000	I
MCDONALD, MASON (1880-1961)	400-2500	X(M)
MCDONNOUGH, JAMES (19TH C)	100-800	X(F,G)
MCDORMAN, DONALD (20TH C)	400-8000	G
MCDOUGALL, J.A. JR (1843 -)	500-2500	X (G)
MCDOUGALL, JOHN ALEXANDER (1810-1894)	400-3500	F
MCENTEE, JERVIS (1828 - 1891)	700-60000	L
MCENTEE, WILLIAM H. (1857-1919)	400-3500	F
MCEVOY, EUGENIE (20TH C)	100-600	X (L)
MCEWAN, WILLIAM (19TH C)	400-3500	X (L)
MCFARLAND, R. (early 19TH C)	700-6500	G,L
MCFARLANE, DUNCAN (19TH C)	7000-25000	M
MCFEE, HENRY LEE	*200-3000	
MCFEE, HENRY LEE (1886 - 1953)	500-7000	F,L,S
MCGARREL, JAMES (1930 -)	800-10000	A
MCGRATH, CLARENCE (1938 -)	3000-12000	X
MCGRATH, JOHN (1880 - 1940)	100-900	X

 * Denotes watercolors, pastels, drawings, and/or mixed media

MCGREW, RALPH BROWNELL	*900-10000	
MCGREW, RALPH BROWNELL (1916 -)	7000-55000	X (F)
MCGUINNESS, C.W. (early 19TH C)	*1000-5000	P
MCILHENNEY, CHARLES MORGAN (1858 - 1904)	300-7500	L,M
MCILWORTH, THOMAS (actice 1755-65)	400-1500	F
MCINTOSH, PLEASANT RAY (1897 -)	350-3200	L
MCINTOSH, ROBERT J. (20TH C)	100-800	X (F)
MCKAIN, BRUCE (1900-)	350-2500	M,L
MCKAY, M.R. (19TH C)	150-1000	L
MCKENNEY, HENRIETTA F.(1825 - 1877)	400-2500	L
MCKEY, EDWARD MICHAEL (1877 - 1918)	100-850	X
MCKILLOP, WILLIAM (20TH C)	400-2500	X(S)
MCKINLEY, HAZEL (20TH C)	*100-600	X
MCKNIGHT, THOMAS (20TH C)	300-6500	A
MCLAUGHLIN, JOHN (1898 - 1976)	5000-20000	A
MCLEAN, HOWARD (19TH - 20TH C)	1200-18000	G,F
MCLEAN, RICHARD (1934 -)	5000-40000	A
MCLOUGHLIN, GREGORY (20TH C)	100-900	X (S)
MCMANUS, GEORGE (1884 -)	*200-1000	I
MCMANUS, JAMES GOODWIN (1882 -)	*100-800	F
MCMEE, J.W. (19TH C)	2000-15000	G,F
MCMEIN, NEYSA (1890 - 1949)	*200-2000	I
MCNAIR, WILLIAM HUGH (1867 -)	100-650	L
MCNALTY, WILLIAM CHARLES (1889-)	200-1200	X(L)
MCNEIL, WILLIAM (19TH C)	100-1000	F
MCNETT, W. BROWN (19TH - 20TH C)	100-700	L
MEAD, T. (19TH C)	100-700	X(F)
MEADE, WILLIAM (20TH C)	200-1000	X
MEAKIN, LEWIS HENRY (1853 - 1917)	500-11000	L
MECHAU, FRANK (1904 - 1946)	500-3500	G,W,L
MEEKER, JOSEPH RUSLING (1827 - 1887)	800-16000	L
MEEKS, EUGENE (1843 -)	350-4500	G
MEESER, LILLIAN BURK (1864 - 1942)	100-1500	L,S
MEGARGEE, LON (1883 - 1960)	350-1500	F,L
MEIRHANS, JOSEPH (1890-1981)	800-4500	A

* Denotes watercolors, pastels, drawings, and/or mixed media

MELBY, G. (19TH C)	300-1200	X (M)
MELCHER, GEORGE HENRY (19TH - 20TH C)	100-500	L
MELCHERS, JULIUS GARI (1860 - 1932)	1000-80000	F,L
MELEGA, FRANK (1906 -)	100-500	X
MELLEN, MARY (19TH C)	500-7500	L,M
MELLON, ELEANOR (1894 -)	200-1500	F,L
MELROSE, ANDREW W. (1836 - 1901)	800-30000+	L,M
MELTSNER, PAUL R. (1905 -)	200-2000	F,L
MELTZER, ANNA ELKAN (1896 -)	300-2500	X(F)
MELTZER, ARTHUR (1893 -)	400-12000	L,F
MENDENHALL, EMMA (20TH C)	*100-600	F,L
MENDENHALL, JACK (1937 -)	3000-18000	A
MENKES, SIGMUND (1896 -)	300-5500	F,S
MENTE, CHARLES (19TH - 20TH C)	200-2000	X (I)
MENZLER-PEYTON, BERTHA S. (1874 -)	400-6000	L,F
MERKIN, RICHARD (1938 -)	*200-1500	A
MERRILD, KNUD (1894 - 1954)	150-800	X (A)
MERRILL, FRANK THAYER (1848 -)	200-1500	I
MERRILL, ROBERT S. (1842 - 1924)	150-900	M
MERRITT, ANNA LEA (1844 - 1930)	500-3000	F
MERSFELDER, JULES (1865-1937)	100-2200	L,G
MESCHES, ARNOLD (20TH C)	100-700	X(F)
MESSER, EDMUND CLARENCE (1842 -)	300-1500	L,F
MESTROVIC, IVAN (1883 - 1962)	*100-850	F
METCALF, ARTHUR W. (1874 -)	*100-700	M
METCALF, ELIAB (1785 - 1834)	800-3500	F
METCALF, WILLARD LEROY	*400-6000	
METCALF, WILLARD LEROY (1858 - 1925)	600-160000	L
METEYARD, THOMAS BUFORD (1865 - 1928)	300-3500	L,I
METHVEN, H. WALLACE (1875 -)	400-2800	X (L)
METZ, GERRY (1943-)	300-5000	G
MEUCCI, ANTHONY (early 19TH C)	400-1800	F
MEURER, CHARLES ALFRED (1865 - 1955)	250-5000	F,S,L
MEUTTMAN, WILLIAM (19TH - 20TH C)	*500-3500	X (L)
MEYER, CHRISTIAN (1838 - 1907)	500-4000	L,F

* Denotes watercolors, pastels, drawings, and/or mixed media

MEYER, ERNEST (1863 - 1961)	300-2000	L
MEYER, GWEN (20TH C)	100-700	X(S)
MEYER, HERBERT (1882 - 1960)	500-4800	G,L,S
MEYER, RICHARD MAX (late 19TH C)	400-3200	G,L
MEYER-KASSEL, HANS (20TH C)	*100-500	F
MEYEROWITZ, WILLIAM (1898 - 1981)	200-4500	L,M,S,F
MEYERS, HARRY MORSE (1886 - 1961)	400-2000	I
MEYERS, RALPH (1885 - 1948)	500-3500	L,F
MEYERS, ROBERT WILLIAM (1919-1970)	500-11000	L
MEZA, ENRIQUE (20TH C)	100-600	X (L)
MICEU, VIRGINIA (19TH C)	400-2000	L
MICHAELIS, H. VON (20TH C)	300-1000	X
MIDDLETON, STANLEY GRANT (1852 -)	400-9000	F,L
MIELATZ, CHARLES F. W. (1864 - 1919)	200-1200	M
MIELZINER, JO (1901 - 1976)	*100-1500	I
MIERUM, GEORGE H. (20TH C)	800-4500	X (L)
MIFFLIN, JOHN HOUSTON (1807 - 1888)	400-3500	F
MIFFLIN, LLYOD (1846 - 1921)	400-3500	L
MIGNOT, LOUIS REMY (1831 - 1870)	600-35000+	L,F
MIKUS, ELEANORE (1927 -)	100-800	A
MILARSKY, A. (20TH C)	150-900	L
MILBURN, JOHN (19TH C)	500-4500	P
MILBURN, OLIVER (1883 - 1934)	400-2000	X
MILDER, JAY (1934 -)	200-2500	A
MILDWOFF, BEN (20TH C)	*100-500	X (L)
MILES, JOHN C. (19TH C)	100-850	F,G
MILES, S.S. (19TH C)	300-1500	L
MILLAR, ADDISON THOMAS (1860 - 1913)	300-7500	F,G,L,S
MILLAR, JAMES (18TH C)	500-25000	F
MILLER, A.R. (20TH C)	100-500	A
MILLER, ALFRED JACOB	*3000-125000	
MILLER, ALFRED JACOB (1810 - 1874)	15000-200000	L,F
MILLER, BARSE (1904 -)	*100-800	L
MILLER, CHARLES HENRY (1842 - 1922)	200-4500	M,L
MILLER, EVYLENA NUNN (1888-1966)	100-1500	X(L)

MILLER, FRANCIS H. (1855 - 1930)	400-9500	F,L,S
MILLER, HENRY (1897-)	*300-2000	X (L)
MILLER, J.C. (20TH C)	100-600	L
MILLER, KENNETH HAYES (1876 - 1952)	300-12000	F,G,S,L
MILLER, LAURA (20TH C)	100-600	X(F)
MILLER, MARGUERITE C. (20TH C)	100-600	X(F)
MILLER, MELVIN (1937 -)	250-1500	L,G
MILLER, MILFRED BUNTING (1892 - 1964)	1000-15000	F
MILLER, PHIL (20TH C)	*100-600	X(M)
MILLER, RALPH DAVISON (1858 - 1945)	200-3500	L
MILLER, RICHARD EMIL (1875 - 1943)	500-275000	F,S,L
MILLER, THOMAS OXLEY (1854-1909)	200-1500	L
MILLER, WILLIAM RICKARBY	*600-4500	
MILLER, WILLIAM RICKARBY (1818 - 1893)	1000-40000	L,F,M,S
MILLER-URY, ADOLPH (1882-)	200-1000	X(S)
MILLESON, ROYAL HILL (1849 -)	100-2000	L
MILLET, CLARENCE (1897 - 1959)	600-7000	L
MILLET, FRANCIS DAVID	*500-6500	
MILLET, FRANCIS DAVID (1846 - 1912)	1000-65000	F,I
MILLET, GERALDINE REED (19TH-20TH C)	250-1800	F
MILLETT, G. VAN (1864-)	100-2500	F,G,L
MILONE, G. (19TH C)	300-2500	L,F
MINAMOTO, KANAME (20TH C)	100-800	F
MINNEGERODE, MARIETTA (19TH C)	*100-800	X (F)
MINNELLI, VINCENTE (1910 -)	*300-1500	I
MINOR, ANNE ROGERS (1864 -)	150-1200	L
MINOR, ROBERT CRANNELL (1839 - 1904)	300-4000	L
MIRA, ALFRED S. (20TH C)	300-1800	X (L)
MITCHELL, ALFRED R. (1886 - 1972)	350-2000	X
MITCHELL, ARTHUR (1864 -)	150-1200	L
MITCHELL, ARTHUR R. (1889-1977)	700-8500	L,F
MITCHELL, BRUCE (1908-1963)	*100-850	L
MITCHELL, C.T. (19TH - 20TH C)	100-400	L
MITCHELL, CHARLES DAVID (1887-1940)	100-900	X(M)
MITCHELL, E.T. (19TH C)	200-1200	L

 * Denotes watercolors, pastels, drawings, and/or mixed media

MITCHELL, GEORGE BERTRAND (1872 - 1966)	300-5500	L,F
MITCHELL, GLEN (1894-1972)	*300-3500	X(L)
MITCHELL, JAMES III (20TH C)	100-1200	M
MITCHELL, JOAN (1926 -)	2500-100000	A
MITCHELL, JOHN CAMPBELL (1862 - 1922)	250-1500	L
MITCHELL, THOMAS JOHN (1875 -)	200-1500	X (L)
MIZEN, FREDERICK KIMBALL (1888 - 1964)	400-1800	I,F
MOCHARANAK, MARY (20TH C)	100-500	X (F,L)
MODRA, THEODORE B. (1873 - 1930)	*100-700	X (W)
MOELLER, LOUIS CHARLES (1855 - 1930)	1800-40000	G,F
MOFFETT, ROSS E. (1888-1971)	100-2000	X(L,I)
MOHLERS, R.H. (19TH C)	100-900	X(L,F)
MOHOLY-NAGY, LAZLO (1895 - 1946)	10000-95000	A
MOHRMANN, JOHN HENRY (1857 - 1916)	1000-4500	M
MOLARSKY, A. (1883 - 1951)	100-500	X (L)
MOLARSKY, MAURICE (1885 - 1950)	400-6500	F,S
MOLINA, VALENTIN (1880 -)	400-1500	X
MOLINARY, ANDREAS (1847 - 1915)	700-5000	X (L)
MONEGAR, CLARENCE BOYCE (20TH C)	*100-500	L,G
MONKS, JOHN AUSTIN SANDS	*100-600	
MONKS, JOHN AUSTIN SANDS (1850 - 1917)	250-1500	W,L
MONSEN, G. (19TH C)	100-600	X (M)
MONTAGUE, FARLEIGH L. (19TH C)	100-800	L
MONTALANT, JULIUS O. (active 1850-60)	300-2000	L
MONTGOMERY, ALFRED (1857 - 1922)	400-3000	G,S,L
MONTGOMERY, T. (19TH-20TH C)	*100-600	X(M)
MONTRICHARD, RAYMOND D. (20TH C)	100-1000	X(S)
MOON, CARL (1878 - 1948)	400-5500	X (F)
MOOR, C.H. (20TH C)	*100-400	L
MOORE, ABEL BUEL (19TH C)	400-1500	F
MOORE, BENSON BOND (1882 - 1974)	200-3500	L
MOORE, EDWIN AUGUSTUS (1858 - 1925)	1000-6500	X (S)
MOORE, FRANK MONTAGUE (1877 - 1967)	300-2500	L,M
MOORE, GUERNSEY (1874 - 1925)	*500-3500	X (F)
MOORE, H.W. (19TH C)	150-1200	X (L)

MOORE, HARRY HUMPHREY	*150-1800	
MOORE, HARRY HUMPHREY (1844 - 1926)	1500-15000+	F,M
MOORE, HERBERT (20TH C)	300-2400	X(F)
MOORE, JACOB BAILY (1815 - 1893)	*500-2500	F
MOORE, JAMES HENRY (1854 - 1913)	*100-600	X (L)
MOORE, NELSON AUGUSTUS (1824 - 1902)	250-4500	L,F
MOORE, R. H. (20TH C)	100-500	L
MOORE, W.J. (19TH C)	250-1000	X (M)
MORA, FRANCIS LUIS	*200-2500	
MORA, FRANCIS LUIS (1874 - 1940)	500-30000	F,L,I
MORALES, ARMANDO	*1500-6000	
MORALES, ARMANDO (1927 -)	600-18000	A
MORAN, ANNETTE (19TH C)	500-4000	X(G)
MORAN, EDWARD (1829 - 1901)	800-30000+	M,G,F
MORAN, EDWARD PERCY (1862 - 1935)	250-15000	F,G,L
MORAN, H. (19TH C)	400-1800	L
MORAN, LEON (JOHN LEON)	*200-2000	
MORAN, LEON (JOHN LEON) (1864 - 1941)	450-9000	F,G,L
MORAN, PAUL NIMMO (1864 - 1907)	500-6000	F,G
MORAN, PETER (1841 - 1914)	700-35000	W,L
MORAN, THOMAS	*1000-190000	
MORAN, THOMAS (1837 - 1926)	1500-700000	L,M
MORAN, VICTOR (19TH C)	150-1000	X(G)
MORATZ, FRANK (20TH C)	100-500	X (F)
MORGAN, ANNIE LAURIE (19TH C?)	400-2000	X (S)
MORGAN, JANE (1832 - 1898)	300-2000	G
MORGAN, MARY DENEALE (1868-1948)	350-4000	L,M
MORGAN, PATRICK (1904 -)	100-800	X (S)
MORGAN, RANDALL (1920 -)	300-1000	L,F
MORGAN, SISTER GERTRUDE (1900 - 1980)	200-3500	P
MORGAN, T. (19TH-20TH C)	*100-600	X(L)
MORGAN, THEODORE J. (1872 -)	300-1500	L,S
MORGAN, WALLACE (1873 - 1948)	*100-900	I
MORGAN, WILLIAM (1826 - 1900)	400-7500	F,G
MORLEY, MALCOLM	*1500-25000	

 * Denotes watercolors, pastels, drawings, and/or mixed media

MORLEY, MALCOLM (1931 -)	2500-10000+	A
MORO, PAUL (20TH C)	300-1800	L,S
MORONI, F. (early 20TH C)	100-750	F
MORRELL, EDITH WHITCOMB (19TH C)	100-750	X(M)
MORRELL, WAYNE BEAM (1923 -)	200-2000	L,M
MORRIS, A. (19TH - 20TH C)	200-900	L
MORRIS, ANDREW (active 1845-55)	400-1500	F
MORRIS, C.D. (19TH - 20TH C)	350-2000	L
MORRIS, CARL (20TH C)	200-1200	A
MORRIS, GEORGE (20TH C)	100-600	L
MORRIS, GEORGE FORD (20TH C)	600-3000	X (F)
MORRIS, GEORGE L.K. (1905 - 1975)	1500-20000	A
MORRIS, KYLE (1918 - 1979)	1000-7000	A
MORRIS, NATHALIE (19TH - 20TH C)	300-900	X (F)
MORRIS, ROBERT (1931 -)	*500-15000	A
MORRISON, DAVID (1885 - 1934)	*100-850	X (M,S)
MORRO, SYDNE (20TH C)	*100-500	L
MORSE, EDWARD LIND (1857 - 1923)	400-1500	X (L,G)
MORSE, GEORGE FREDERICK (1834 -)	200-2000	L,M
MORSE, GEORGE R. (19TH C)	100-600	L
MORSE, HENRY DUTTON (1826 - 1888)	400-6500	W
MORSE, I.B. (20TH C)	200-800	L
MORSE, J.B. (active 1875 - 1890)	100-1500	L
MORSE, SAMUEL F.B. (1791 - 1872)	800-35000	F,M
MORSE, VERNON JAY (1898 - 1965)	250-1400	L
MORSE, W. (19TH C)	100-1000	X(L)
MORTON, CHRISTINA (20TH C)	100-700	X(F)
MORTON, WILLIAM E. (1843 - 1916)	500-5000	L
MORVILLER, JOSEPH (active 1855-70)	450-10000	L
MOSER, FRANK H. (1886-1964)	*100-2400	X(L)
MOSER, JAMES HENRY (1854 - 1913)	400-4800	F,L
MOSERT, ZOE (20TH C)	*400-1500	X (F)
MOSES, ("GRANDMA") (1860 - 1961)	1500-125000	P
MOSES, ED (1926 -)	*700-21000	A
MOSES, FORREST K. (1893 - 1974)	300-3500	G,L

* Denotes watercolors, pastels, drawings, and/or mixed media

MOSES, THOMAS G. (1856 - 1934)	100-750	L
MOSES, THOMAS PALMER (19TH C)	*100-700	X (L)
MOSES, WALTER FARRINGTON (1874 -)	100-1000	L
MOSLER, GUSTAVE H. (1875 - 1906)	100-1000	G,L
MOSLER, HENRY (1841 - 1920)	300-12000	F,G
MOSLER, JOHN HENRY (19TH C)	*100-800	X (L)
MOSS, R.F. (1898 - 1954)	300-1500	L
MOSTEL, ZERO (20TH C)	100-1200	X (F)
MOTE, MARCUS (1817 - 1890)	2000-20000	F,L
MOTHERWELL, ROBERT	*600-50000	
MOTHERWELL, ROBERT (1915 -)	3000-275000	A
MOTTET, JEANIE GALLUP (1884 - 1934)	400-4000	F
MOULTON, FRANK B. (1847-)	150-1200	L,S
MOUNT, EVILINA (19TH C)	500-2500	L
MOUNT, NINA (1837-1920)	300-4500	X(L)
MOUNT, SHEPARD ALONZO (1804 - 1868)	750-18000	F,L,W
MOUNT, WILLIAM SIDNEY (1807 - 1868)	4000-900000	G,F,L,S
MOUNTFORT, ARNOLD (1873 - 1942)	300-12000	F
MOWBRAY, HENRY SIDDONS (1858 - 1928)	1000-48000	F
MOYERS, WILLIAM (1916 -)	400-5200	X
MOYLAN, LLOYD (1893 -)	500-3500	F,L
MUE, MAURICE AUGUSTE DEL (1875-1955)	100-1200	L
MUELLER, ALEXANDER (1872 - 1935)	300-8500	F,L
MUHLENFELD, S.L.R.(active 1895-1905)	500-8500	M
MULERTT, CAREL EUGENE	*250-1500	
MULERTT, CAREL EUGENE (1869 - 1915)	600-3500	F,L
MULHAUPT, FREDERICK JOHN (1871 - 1938)	750-25000	M,L,F,S
MULLER, DANIEL (1888 - 1977)	300-1800	X (I,L)
MULLER, HEINRICH (1823 - 1853)	700-6500+	L
MULLER, JAN (1922 - 1958)	400-3000	X (F,L)
MULLER, KARL (19TH C)	*100-400	X
MULLER-URY, ADOLF FELIX (1862 -)	100-1800	F,L,S
MULLICAN, LEE (1919 -)	100-800	A
MULLIGAN, C.L.(20TH C)	100-600	X(F)
MUMFORD, R.T. (19TH - 20TH C)	100-400	L

 * Denotes watercolors, pastels, drawings, and/or mixed media

MUNGER, GILBERT DAVIS (1837 - 1903)	600-8500	L,F
MUNN, P.S. (19TH-20TH C)	*300-2500	G,L
MUNROE, ALBERT F. (19TH - 20TH C)	300-1500	X (S)
MUNSON, H. (19TH C)	100-800	L
MUNSON, KNUTE (20TH C)	*150-750	F,L
MURA, FRANK (1861 -)	300-3000	X (L)
MURCH, WALTER TANDY (1907 - 1967)	2000-45000	A,S
MURPHY, ADAH CLIFFORD (early 20TH C)	200-1000	X (F,I)
MURPHY, C.A. (early 20TH C)	100-300	L
MURPHY, CHRISTOPHER JR (1902 - 1973)	200-3000	L,F,G
MURPHY, CHRISTOPHER P.H. (1869-1939)	200-2500	F,L
MURPHY, HERMAN DUDLEY (1867 - 1945)	400-8000	S,L
MURPHY, JOHN FRANCIS	*300-7000	
MURPHY, JOHN FRANCIS (1853 - 1921)	600-15000+	L
MURRAY, ELIZABETH (1940 -)	500-2500	A
MURRAY, GEORGE (1822 -)	200-1000	L
MURRY, J.E. (19TH C)	200-1500	X (S)
MUSGRAVE, ARTHUR (1880-)	150-900	L
MUSGRAVE, HELEN G. (1890 -)	100-500	X
MUSGRAVE, INNOCK (19TH C)	100-600	X(F)
MUSGRAVE, SYLVESTER (19TH C)	400-5000	F
MUSS-ARNOLT, GUSTAV (1858 - 1927)	500-6500	W
MYERS, FRANK H. (1899-1956)	400-4000	L,M,S
MYERS, IRWIN O. (1888-)	*100-500	X(L)
MYERS, JEROME	*400-7500	
MYERS, JEROME (1867 - 1940)	600-35000	G,F
MYGATT, ROBERTSON K. (-1919)	100-1000	L

N

ARTIST	PRICES	SUBJECT
NADELMAN, ELIE (1882 - 1946)	*500-5000	A,F
NADHERNY, E.V. (20TH C)	100-1200	I
NAGEL, HERMAN F. (1876 -)	350-1500	X (W)
NAGLER, EDITH KROGER VAN (1895 - 1978)	100-2500	F,I
NAGLER, FRED A. (1891 - 1934)	*100-500	X (F)
NAHL, CHARLES CHRISTIAN (1818 - 1878)	1500-100000	G,F,L,W
NAHL, H.W. ARTHUR (1833-1889)	500-3500	X(S)
NAHL, VIRGIL THEODORE (1876 - 1930)	400-4500	I,L,F
NAILOR, GEROLD (1917 - 1952)	*100-800	X (F)
NAKAGAWA, HIROMI (20TH C)	100-800	X(L)
NAKIAN, REUBEN (1897 -)	*500-3000	A
NANGERONI, CARLO (1922 -)	250-1000	A
NANKIVELL, FRANK A. (1869-1959)	300-8500	L
NARJOT, ERNEST (1827 - 1898)	600-22000	L,F
NASH, WILLARD AYER (1898 - 1943)	*100-1500	F,L,S
NASON, GERTRUDE (1890 - 1968)	250-1000	X (S)
NAST, THOMAS	*200-4500	
NAST, THOMAS (1840 - 1902)	1800-60000	I
NATKIN, ROBERT	*900-6000	
NATKIN, ROBERT (1930 -)	500-25000	A
NAUMAN, BRUCE (1941 -)	*1000-45000	A
NEAGLE, JOHN (1796 - 1866)	500-7500	F
NEAL, DAVID DALHOFF (1838 - 1915)	1000-4500	F
NEALE, A. (19TH - 20TH C)	100-500	X (M)
NEAVES, DOROTHY P. (20TH C)	*150-650	X(S)
NEEDHAN, D. (19TH-20TH C)	100-2000	L
NEEL, ALICE (1901 -)	500-12000	A,S,F
NEHLIG, VICTOR (1830 - 1910)	700-6500	F,G,L
NEILL, FRANCIS ISABEL (1871 -)	100-1000	L
NEILSON, RAYMOND PERRY R.(1881-1964)	600-22000	G,F
NEIMAN, LEROY	*350-12000	
NEIMAN, LEROY (1926 -)	750-40000	A

* Denotes watercolors, pastels, drawings, and/or mixed media

NELAN, CHARLES (1859 - 1904)	*100-750	X (I)
NELKE, ALEXANDER (19TH-20TH C)	100-500	L
NELL, MISS TONY (20TH C)	*100-850	X (I)
NELLE, ANTHONY (19TH - 20TH C)	*1200-3500	I
NELSON, A. PATRICK (20TH C)	*100-600	I
NELSON, EDWARD D. (- 1871)	1200-6500	L
NELSON, ERNEST BRUCE (1888 - 1952)	800-18000	L,M
NELSON, GEORGE LAURENCE (1887 - 1978)	250-8000	F,L
NELSON, J. (late 19TH C)	300-1200	X (G)
NELSON, JOHN G.(19TH C)	100-700	L
NELSON, RALPH LEWIS (1885 -)	100-500	X (L)
NELSON, WILLIAM (1861 - 1920)	*100-4800	F,G,L
NEMETHY, ALBERT (19TH-20TH C)	300-4500	G,L,M
NEMETHY, GEORGE (20TH C)	450-3500	M
NEMETHY, H. (20TH C)	*150-400	L
NESBITT, LOWELL (1933 -)	500-25000	A
NESBITT, ROBERT H. (20TH C)	200-1500	X
NESBITT, VICTOR (20TH C)	200-1500	I
NESEMANN, ENNO (1861-)	100-1500	L
NETTLETON, WALTER (1861 - 1936)	300-2400	L
NEUFELD, WOLDEMAR (1909-)	300-2500	L,I
NEUHAUS, EUGEN (1879 - 1963)	*100-800	L
NEUMAN, ROBERT S. (1926 -)	150-850	X (L)
NEUVILLE, BARONESS HYDE DE (1779-1849)	*500-5000	F,G
NEVELSON, LOUISE (1900 -)	*600-6500	A,F
NEWBERRY, JOHN STRONG (1822 - 1892)	*100-900	I,F
NEWELL, GEORGE GLENN (1870 - 1947)	300-3500	W,L
NEWELL, HUGH (1830 - 1915)	700-4500+	G,F,L
NEWELL, IDA H. (20TH C)	100-500	X (F)
NEWELL, PETER SHEAF (1862 - 1924)	*100-1000	I
NEWHALL, HARRIOT B. (1874 -)	*300-1500	G
NEWHAM, JOHN DEEING (19TH - 20TH C)	300-1200	X (L)
NEWMAN, BARNETT	*10000-60000	
NEWMAN, BARNETT (1905 - 1970)	20000-275000+	A
NEWMAN, CARL (1858 - 1932)	300-2000	F,L

* Denotes watercolors, pastels, drawings, and/or mixed media

NEWMAN, GEORGE A. (20TH C)	100-1500	X (L)
NEWMAN, HENRY RODERICK (1833-1918)	*100-850	X
NEWMAN, ROBERT LOFTIN (1827 - 1912)	500-7500	F
NEWMAN, S. (19TH C)	*700-7000	X
NEWMAN, WILLIE BETTY (1864 -)	100-900	F,L
NEWTON, A.PARKER (20TH C)	200-1200	X(M,L)
NEWTON, GILBERT STUART (1794 - 1835)	300-6000	G,F
NEY, LLOYD (1893-)	*150-700	X (A)
NIBLETT, GARY (1943 -)	5000-35000	L,F
NICHOLAS, GRACE (19TH C)	100-600	P
NICHOLAS, P. (19TH C)	100-500	L,F
NICHOLAS, THOMAS (20TH C)	*300-1500	X (W)
NICHOLLS, RHODA HOLMES (1854 - 1930)	200-1500	X (G)
NICHOLLS, RHODA HOLMES (19TH C)	*500-4800	F
NICHOLS, BURR H. (1848 - 1915)	250-2000	G,F,L
NICHOLS, CELESTE BRUFF (active 1885-1910)	200-1000	X (S)
NICHOLS, DALE WILLIAM	*500-3800	
NICHOLS, DALE WILLIAM (1904 -)	400-12000	G,F,L
NICHOLS, H.D. (19TH C)	*100-750	L
NICHOLS, HENRY HOBART (1869 - 1962)	300-12000	L
NICHOLS, HUBLEY (19TH C)	350-2500	X (M)
NICHOLS, SPENCER BAIRD (1875 - 1950)	400-5000	F,L
NICHOLSON, CHARLES W. (20TH C)	100-1000	X (S)
NICHOLSON, EDWARD HORACE (1901 - 1966)	250-1500	M,F,L
NICHOLSON, GEORGE W.(1832 - 1912)	400-12000	L,F
NICKOLSON, LILLIE MAY (1884-1964)	250-3500	M,L
NICOLL, JAMES CRAIG (1846 - 1918)	300-10000	M
NICOLL, NICOL (1923 -)	*200-1200	X (G)
NICOLS, AUDLEY DEAN (20TH C)	400-2000	L
NIEMEYER, JOHN HENRY (1839 - 1932)	400-4500+	F
NILES, GEORGE E. (1837 - 1898)	200-1000	X (G)
NIRO, ROBERT DE (1922 -)	400-1800	X (S)
NISBET, ROBERT H.	*100-800	
NISBET, ROBERT H. (1879 - 1961)	300-3500	L,F
NOBLE, JOHN (1874 - 1935)	750-4800	M,F

 * Denotes watercolors, pastels, drawings, and/or mixed media

NOBLE, THOMAS SATTERWHITE (1835 - 1907)	400-9500	F
NOGUCHI, ISAMU	*500-4500	
NOGUCHI, ISAMU (1904 -)	1000-85000	F
NOHEIMER, MATHIAS (20TH C)	400-3500	A
NOLAN, E.B. (19TH - 20TH C)	*100-500	X (L)
NOLAND, KENNETH (1924 -)	5000-350000	A,L
NOLF, JOHN (1871 -)	100-1200	I
NOLF, THEODORE E. (20TH C)	100-600	X(L)
NOLL, CHARLES (20TH C)	*100-500	M
NOONAN, JAMES (20TH C)	*100-400	L
NORBERG, C. ALBERT (1895-)	250-1500	L,F
NORDELL, CARL J. (1885 -)	500-7500+	F,L,S
NORDELL, EMMA PARKER (20TH C)	150-1200	X(F)
NORDELL, POLLY (19TH - 20TH C)	*100-600	F
NORDFELDT, BROR JULIUS O.	*450-2500	
NORDFELDT, BROR JULIUS O.(1878-1955)	500-30000	L,G,F,S
NORDHAUSEN, AUGUST HENRY (1901 -)	150-1600	F
NORDSTROM, CARL HAROLD (1876 - 1934)	200-2500	M,L
NORFOLK, WALTER (19TH - 20TH C)	100-500	X
NORMAN, MABEL (20TH C)	100-400	X (G)
NORRIS, S. WALTER (1868-)	*100-400	X(L)
NORSE, STANSBURY (19TH C)	150-800	L
NORTH, NOAH (1809 - 1880)	2000-15000+	P
NORTHCOTE, JAMES (1822 - 1904)	250-6500	F,L,M
NORTON, L.D. (19TH - 20TH C)	100-900	X (L,M)
NORTON, WILLIAM EDWARD	*200-2500	
NORTON, WILLIAM EDWARD (1843 - 1916)	450-14000	M,L
NORTWICK, EVAN (20TH C)	100-400	X (F,G)
NOTT, RAYMOND (20TH C)	*100-1000	L
NOURSE, ELIZABETH	*500-45000	
NOURSE, ELIZABETH (1859 - 1938)	1500-60000	F
NOVAK, LOUIS (1903-)	*100-750	L,M
NOVROS, DAVID (1941-)	400-25000	A
NOWAK, FRANZ (19TH C)	*500-3500	S
NOYES, BERTHA (1876-1966)	150-850	X (F)

* Denotes watercolors, pastels, drawings, and/or mixed media

NOYES, GEORGE LOFTUS (1864 - 1951)	350-28000	L
NUDERSCHER, FRANK B. (1880 - 1959)	400-4000	L,I
NUHLER, AUGUSTUS W. (- 1920)	*100-600	X (M)
NUNAMAKER, KENNETH (1890 - 1957)	900-18000	L
NURSTRUM, C. (20TH C)	*100-600	X (M)
NUYTTENS, JOSEF PIERRE (1880 -)	*100-700	X (F)
NYE, EDGAR H.(1879 - 1943)	200-1200	L
NYE, MOSES (19TH C)	200-1200	X(M)

O

ARTIST	PRICE	SUBJECT
O'DONOVAN, WILLIAM RUDOLPH (1844 - 1920)	*150-600	L
O'GRADY, DONN (20TH C)	300-1200	X
O'HAGEN, JOHN L. (20TH C)	100-500	X
O'HARA, ELIOT (1890 - 1969)	*200-1000	L
O'HIGGINS, PABLO	*600-1500	
O'HIGGINS, PABLO (1904 -)	500-4500	X (F)
O'KEEFFE, GEORGIA	*1500-250000	
O'KEEFFE, GEORGIA (1887 -)	8000-775000+	A
O'KELLEY, MATTIE LOU (1907 -)	3500-15000	P
O'KELLY, ALOYSIUS (1853 -)	350-3500	F,L
O'LEARY, ANGELA (1879 - 1921)	*200-1500	L
O'LEARY, GALBRAITH (20TH C)	400-2000	L
O'NEAL, J. (20TH C)	150-850	X(L)
O'NEIL, ROSE CECIL (1875 - 1944)	*400-1800	I
O'SHEA, JOHN (active 1925-40)	100-800	L
O'SHEA, KAREN (20TH C)	100-600	X (S)
O'SULLIVAN, PAUL F. (20TH C)	*300-900	X (M)
OAKES, WILBUR (1876 -)	150-1000	X (M)
OAKLEY, THORNTON	*250-3000	
OAKLEY, THORNTON (1881 - 1953)	400-6000	I
OAKLEY, VIOLET (1874 - 1961)	*100-1200	F,S,I

 * Denotes watercolors, pastels, drawings, and/or mixed media

OATES, MERRITT L.C. (19TH - 20TH C)	100-300	X (F)
OBATA, CHUIRA (20TH C)	*100-500	X (L)
OBERTEUFFER, GEORGE (1878 - 1940)	800-20000	L,M
OCHTMAN, LEONARD (1854 - 1934)	700-12000+	L
OCHTMAN, MINA FUNDA (1862 - 1924)	200-1800	X (L)
ODDIE, WALTER M. (1808 - 1865)	500-6000	L
OELSHIG, AUGUSTA (20TH C)	300-1000	A
OERTEL, JOHANNES A. S. (1823 - 1909)	1000-21000	G,F
OF, GEORGE F. (1876 -)	500-6500	L,S
OGDEN, FREDERICK D. (19TH C)	400-1500	L,I
OGDEN, J. WILLIAM (19TH C)	100-700	L
OGLIVIE, JOHN CLINTON (1838 - 1900)	600-18000	L,M
OKADA, KENZO (1902 -)	2000-45000	A
OKAMURA, ARTHUR (1932 -)	350-6500	A
OLDENBURG, CLAES THURE (1929 -)	*1000-45000	A
OLESEN, OLAF (1837 -)	500-4000	L
OLINSKY, IVAN GREGOREVITCH (1878 - 1962)	750-9000+	F
OLINSKY, TOSCA (1909 -)	100-600	X (S)
OLITSKI, JULES (1922 - 1964)	2000-110000	A
OLIVEIRA, NATHAN	*500-4500	
OLIVEIRA, NATHAN (1928 -)	1000-40000	A
OLIVER, DAVID (20TH C)	100-500	X(L,F)
OLIVER, JEAN NUTTING (1883 -)	100-1000	X (F)
OLIVER, THOMAS CLARKSON (1827 - 1893)	400-6500	M
OLSEN, HENRY (1902 - 1983)	200-1000	L,M,S
OLSEN, HERB (1905 - 1973)	*100-650	L
OLSON, J. OLAF	*200-1200	
OLSON, J. OLAF (1894 - 1979)	400-5000	L,F
OLSON, JOSEPH OLAF (1894 - 1979)	300-4000	L,F
ONDERDONK, JULIAN (1882 - 1922)	500-23000	L
ONGLY, W. (19TH C)	150-800	L,F
OPERTI, ALBERT JASPER (1852 - 1922)	*350-2500	M
OPPENHEIM, DENNIS A. (1938 -)	800-3500	A
OPPER, JOHN (1908 -)	*200-2500	A
ORCULL, A.C. (late 19TH C)	100-500	L

* Denotes watercolors, pastels, drawings, and/or mixed media

ORD, JOSEPH BIAYS (1805 - 1865)	2000-18000	F,S
ORGAN, MARJORIE (1886 - 1931)	400-3500	I
ORMSBY, DOROTHY (19TH - 20TH C)	400-1800	L,F
ORR, ALFRED EVERITT (1886 -)	*100-500	L,I
ORR, ELLIOT (1904 -)	100-900	X (F)
OSBURN, SALLY (20TH C)	*100-650	F
OSCAR, CHARLES	*200-1800	
OSCAR, CHARLES (20TH C)	200-900	X (F)
OSHIVER, HARRY JAMES (1888 -)	200-1500	X (S)
OSSORIO, ALFONSO ANGEL (1916 -)	*400-6500	A
OSTHAUS, EDMUND HENRY	*500-12000	
OSTHAUS, EDMUND HENRY (1858 - 1928)	500-16000	W
OSTRANDER,WILLIAM CHESEBOURGH (1858-)	*350-1200	X (L)
OSTROWSKY, SAM (1885 -)	100-1200	F,S
OSVER, ARTHUR (1912-)	100-1000	X
OTIS, BASS (1784 - 1861)	800-6500	F
OTIS, GEORGE DEMONT	*200-1500	
OTIS, GEORGE DEMONT (1877 - 1962)	500-7500	L,M
OTTINGER, GEORGE MORTON (1833 - 1917)	800-18000	G
OUREN, KARL (1882 - 1943)	200-2000	L
OVEREND, WILLIAM HEYSMAN (1851 - 1898)	500-6500	M,I
OWEN, BILL (1942 -)	6500-35000	G,F,L
OWEN, CARLOS J. (19TH C)	*100-500	X (L)
OWEN, FRANK EDWARD (1907 -)	400-2000	A
OWEN, GEORGE (active 1855-75)	400-3500	G,F
OWEN, JOEL (20TH C)	*100-500	L
OWEN, ROBERT EMMETT (1878 - 1959)	300-8000+	L
OWLES, ALFRED (1896-)	*150-800	S

P

 * Denotes watercolors, pastels, drawings, and/or mixed media

ARTIST	PRICE	SUBJECT
PAALEN, ALICE (20TH C)	*150-750	A
PACE, STEPHEN (1918 -)	500-5000	A
PACH, WALTER (1883 - 1958)	400-2500	X (F)
PACKARD, MABEL (19TH - 20TH C)	500-2500	X (L)
PADDOCK, ETHEL LOUISE (1887 -)	*100-900	G,F,M
PAGE, ELIZABETH AMIE (1908 -)	100-850	L
PAGE, JOSEPHINE A. (20TH C)	100-1200	L
PAGE, MARIE DANFORTH (1869 - 1940)	900-18000	F
PAGE, WALTER GILMAN (1862 - 1934)	450-18000	F,L,M,S
PAGE, WILLIAM	*400-5000	
PAGE, WILLIAM (1811 - 1885)	1000-18000+	F,L,G,M
PAGES, JULES EUGENE (1867 - 1946)	700-20000	L,F,G
PAGINTON, (19TH - 20TH C)	200-1800	L
PAIL, EDOUARD (1851 -)	300-2000	L
PAIN, WILLIAM BOWYER (1856-1930)	*100-700	L
PAINE, GEORGE S. (19TH C)	*100-700	L
PAINE, H.H. (19TH C)	1500-6000	P
PAINE, SUSANNAH (1792 - 1862)	1000-7500	F,L
PAIRPOINT, NELLIE M. (19TH - 20TH C)	100-750	L,W
PALFRIES, J. (19TH C)	100-600	X (L)
PALMER, ADELAIDE (19TH - 20TH C)	150-750	X (S)
PALMER, ERATUS DOW (1817 - 1904)	*100-300	F
PALMER, PAULINE (1865 - 1938)	250-4000	L,F
PALMER, SAMUEL (19TH C)	*100-1200	X (W)
PALMER, WALTER LAUNT	*500-7500	
PALMER, WALTER LAUNT (1854 - 1932)	900-20000+	L,F,M
PALMER, WILLIAM C. (1906 -)	*100-1000	X (L,I)
PALMORE, THOMAS DALE (1940-)	150-1500	X(S)
PANCOAST, MORRIS HALL (1877 -)	150-1000	L,I
PANSING, FRED (active 1885-1905)	1000-25000+	M,L
PAPPAS, JOHN L. (1898 -)	100-300	X (L)
PAPPE, CARL (20TH C)	100-500	L
PARADISE, JOHN (1783 - 1833)	200-3000	P
PARADISE, PHILLIP (1905 -)	*250-1800	X (M)

* Denotes watercolors, pastels, drawings, and/or mixed media

PARCELL, MALCOLM S. (1896 -)	500-3500	L,G
PARIS, WALTER (1842-1906)	*300-1800	L
PARISEN, WILLIAM DE (1800 - 1832)	100-850	F
PARISH, JANE (19TH C)	800-3000	S
PARK, DAVID	*800-18000	
PARK, DAVID (1911-1960)	1000-30000	A
PARK, ROSWELL (active 1820's)	*5000-25000	X (L)
PARKS, JAMES DALLAS (1907 -)	500-5000	X (F)
PARKER, CHARLES STEWART (1860 - 1930)	200-2000	L,M,F
PARKER, EDGAR (1840 - 1892)	800-6000	L,F
PARKER, JOHN ADAMS (1829 - 1905)	400-4500	L
PARKER, JOHN F. (1884 -)	100-800	X (S)
PARKER, KAY PETERSON (20TH C)	*100-500	X
PARKER, LAWTON S. (1868 - 1954)	400-28000	L,F
PARKER, RAYMOND (RAY) (1922 -)	500-7500	A
PARKER, S. PERKINS (1862-1942)	200-2000	M,L
PARKHURST, H. (20TH C)	100-400	X (G)
PARKINGTON, J. (19TH C)	100-750	L
PARRISH, CLARA WAEVER (- 1925)	*150-850	L,F
PARRISH, DAVID BUCHANAN (1939 -)	2000-10000	A
PARRISH, MAXFIELD FREDERICK	*200-10000	
PARRISH, MAXFIELD FREDERICK (1870 - 1966)	1500-75000+ I	
PARRISH, STEVEN WINDSOR (1846 - 1938)	250-3500	L
PARROT, A. (19TH C)	100-500	L
PARROTT, WILLIAM SAMUEL (1844 - 1915)	500-6500	L
PARSHALL, DEWITT (1864 - 1956)	200-1800	L,M
PARSHALL, DOUGLAS EWELL (1899 -)	400-2000	L
PARSONS, A. (19TH C)	150-1200	X (L,M)
PARSONS, BETTY B. (20TH C)	*100-650	L
PARSONS, CHARLES (1821 - 1910)	400-3500	M,G
PARSONS, M.A. (19TH C)	*800-2500	L
PARSONS, ORRIN SHELDON (1866 - 1943)	200-4500	L
PARSONS, PHILLIP B. (1896-1977)	100-1500	L
PARSONS, THEOPHILUS (1876 - 1934)	100-900	L,F
PARTEE, MCCULLOUGH (20TH C)	*200-1000	X(F)

 * Denotes watercolors, pastels, drawings, and/or mixed media

PARTINGTON, RICHARD L. (1868 - 1929)	400-2000	L
PARTON, ARTHUR B.(1842 - 1914)	450-18000	L
PARTON, ERNEST (1845 - 1933)	500-7000	L
PARTON, HENRY WOODRIDGE (1858 - 1933)	600-4500	F,L
PARTON, HULDA (19TH-20TH C)	100-500	X(L)
PASCIN, JULES	*700-60000	
PASCIN, JULES (1885 - 1930)	2500-100000+	A,F
PASKELL, WILLIAM	*100-650	
PASKELL, WILLIAM (1866 - 1951)	250-1500+	L,M
PATECKY, ALBERT (20TH C)	100-800	L,F
PATTEN, MARION (1889 - 1941)	100-900	M,L
PATTERSON, AMBROSE M. (1877 - 1930)	400-3500	L
PATTERSON, CHARLES ROBERT (1878 - 1958)	400-8000	M
PATTERSON, HOWARD ASHMAN (1891 -)	100-750	L,F
PATTERSON, MARGARET JORDAN (1867 - 1950)	*200-2500	I,L
PATTERSON, ROBERT (1898 - 1981)	100-800	I
PATTISON, JAMES WILLIAM (1844 1915)	600-4500	L,F
PATTON, KATHERINE (19TH - 20TH C)	300-1500	X (M,L)
PATTY, WILLIAM ARTHUR (1889 - 1961)	100-650	X (M)
PAUL, JEREMIAH (- 1830)	2000-65000	G,F
PAULI, RICHARD (1855 - 1892)	300-1500	L
PAULL, GRACE (20TH C)	*100-500	G,F
PAULSON, O. (19TH C)	400-4500	L
PAULUS, FRANCIS PETRUS (1862 - 1933)	200-4000	G,L,S
PAUS, HERBERT ANDREW (1880 - 1946)	*200-2500	I
PAVIL, ELIE ANATOLE (1873 - 1948)	300-3500	L,F
PAXSON, EDGAR SAMUEL	*500-35000	
PAXSON, EDGAR SAMUEL (1852 - 1919)	5000-70000	F,G,I
PAXSON, ETHEL (1885 -)	150-1500	L,F,I
PAXTON, ELIZABETH V.O. (1877-1971)	500-7000	X(L,F)
PAXTON, JOHN (19TH - 20TH C)	500-6000	F
PAXTON, WILLIAM A. (19TH - 20TH C)	200-1200	L
PAXTON, WILLIAM MCGREGOR	*200-20000	
PAXTON, WILLIAM MCGREGOR (1869 - 1941)	2000-100000+	F,L,S
PAYNE, EDGAR ALWIN (1882 - 1947)	700-18000+	L,M

PAYNE, HILMA M. (20TH C)	250-1000	L
PEABODY, RUTH EATON (1898-1967)	200-2500	X(L)
PEAKE, CHANNING (1910 -)	*100-700	X (F)
PEALE, CHARLES WILLSON (1741 - 1827)	15000-????+	F
PEALE, HARRIET CARY (1800 - 1869)	600-7500	F
PEALE, JAMES (1749 - 1831)	1500-375000	S,F,L,M
PEALE, MARY JANE (1826 - 1902)	700-11000	S,F
PEALE, RAPHAELLE (1774 - 1825)	8000-500000	S,F
PEALE, REMBRANDT (1778 - 1860)	3000-380000+	F
PEALE, RUBENS (1784 - 1865)	700-10000	S,W
PEALE, SARAH MIRIAM	*100-900	
PEALE, SARAH MIRIAM (1800 - 1885)	600-3500	F,S
PEALE, TITIAN RAMSEY	*700-15000	
PEALE, TITIAN RAMSEY (1799 - 1885)	1000-40000	I,W,L
PEARCE, CHARLES SPRAGUE (1851 - 1914)	600-70000+	F
PEARCE, EDGAR LEWIS (1885 -)	200-1200	X (F)
PEARL, MOSES P. (20TH C)	250-1800	L
PEARLSTEIN, PHILIP	*500-15000	
PEARLSTEIN, PHILIP (1924 -)	2500-48000	A,F
PEARSON, CORNELIUS (1805 - 1891)	*200-1500	L
PEARSON, HENRY (1914 -)	200-1000	X (A?)
PEARSON, JAMES (1900 -)	100-500	X
PEARSON, MARGUERITE STUBER (1898 - 1978)	600-28000	F,S
PEARSON, ROBERT (- 1891)	500-3500	X (M)
PEASE, G.M. (19TH C)	200-1500	X (L)
PEBBLES, FRANK MARION (1839 - 1928)	200-2500	F,L,M
PECK, CHARLES E. (1827-1900)	300-1800	L
PECK, HENRY JARVIS (1880 - 1964)	200-1200	I
PECK, SHELDON (1797 - 1868)	5000-100000	P
PECKHAM, (DEACON) ROBERT	*300-1200	
PECKHAM, (DEACON) ROBERT (1785 -)	2000-55000	F
PECKHAM, LEWIS (1788 - 1822)	500-6000	F
PEDERSON, ROBERT HOLM (1906-)	200-1200	X(M)
PEELE, JOHN THOMAS (1822 - 1897)	1000-18000	G,F,W
PEETERS, E. (19TH C)	*100-700	X (L,S)

 * Denotes watercolors, pastels, drawings, and/or mixed media

PEIRCE, H. WINTHROP (1850 - 1935)	300-4500	F,L,I
PEIRCE, WALDO (1884 - 1970)	300-6000	G,S,F
PEIXOTTO, ERNEST CLIFFORD (1869 - 1940)	300-2500	I,L
PEIXOTTO, FLORIAN (19TH C)	300-1500	X (L)
PELL, ELLA FERRIS (1846 -)	400-2000	X (F,I)
PELL, J. (19TH-20TH C)	200-1500	L
PELTON, AGNES (1881 - 1961)	100-5000	X (F)
PENE DU BOIS, GUY (1884 - 1958)	3000-60000	G,F
PENFIELD, EDWARD (1866 - 1925)	*200-2500	I
PENFOLD, FRANK C. (19TH-20TH C)	400-3800	F
PENNELL, HARRY (early 20TH C)	250-3500	L
PENNELL, JOSEPH (1860 - 1926)	*250-2500	I
PENNEY, FREDERICK D. (1900-)	150-900	L
PENNIMANN, JOHN RITTO (1782-1841)	2500-30000	G,F
PENNINGTON, HARPER (1854 - 1920)	500-7500	F
PENNOYER, ALBERT SHELDON (1888 - 1957)	200-2500	L,F
PENT, ROSE MARIE (- 1954)	100-600	L
PEPPER, BEVERLY (1924 -)	*500-3500	A
PEPPER, CHARLES HOVEY (1864 - 1950)	*100-800	L
PERBANDT, CARL VON (1832 - 1911)	300-2500	L
PERBANDT, CARL VON (1832 - 1911)	400-4500	L
PERCIVAL, EDWIN (1793 -)	400-1000	F
PERCONI, D.F. (20TH C)	400-2000	X (G)
PERCY, LORAN (20TH C)	100-500	L
PEREIRA, IRENE RICE	*100-5000	
PEREIRA, IRENE RICE (1901 - 1971)	400-7500	A
PERELLI, ACHILLE (1822 - 1891)	400-3000	S,W
PERILLO, GREGORY (1932-)	400-9000	F,G
PERKINS, D.H. (20TH C)	*100-700	X (L)
PERKINS, GRANVILLE	*200-2800	
PERKINS, GRANVILLE (1830 - 1895)	600-20000	L,M,I
PERKINS, RUTH HUNTER (1911 -)	300-2500	P
PERKINS, SARAH	*500-3000	
PERKINS, SARAH (1771 - 1831)	1000-20000	P(F)
PERLAR, L. (19TH C)	300-1500	X

* Denotes watercolors, pastels, drawings, and/or mixed media

PERLE, F. (early 20TH C)	100-850	X (M)
PERRAULT, JOSEPH (20TH C)	100-300	X (M)
PERREIRA, JOAN (20TH C)	100-700	A
PERRINE, VAN DEARING (1869 - 1955)	900-5000	A
PERRY, CLARA FAIRFIELD (- 1941)	200-1000	L
PERRY, CLARA GREENLEAF (1871 - 1960)	300-1800	L,G
PERRY, ENOCH WOOD	*500-6000	
PERRY, ENOCH WOOD (1831 - 1915)	500-48000	F,G,L
PERRY, F.C. (19TH C)	100-700	L
PERRY, LILLA CABOT (1848 - 1933)	1000-35000	F,L
PERRY, WILLIAM C. (20TH C)	100-600	X
PERSSON, FRITIOF (20TH C)	100-600	L
PERU, ALTO (18TH C)	1500-8000+	F
PESCE, GIRLO (20TH C)	100-800	X (M)
PETERDI, GABOR (1915 -)	*100-700	A
PETERIS, J.H. (20TH C)	100-700	X (M)
PETERS, CARL WILLIAM (1898-1980)	300-4000	L
PETERS, CHARLES ROLLO (1862 - 1928)	500-7000	L,M
PETERSEN, CARL (1885 -)	150-900	L
PETERSEN, L. (19TH C)	1000-4500	M
PETERSEN, THOMAS (20TH C)	300-1200	X (M)
PETERSON, JANE	*500-18000+	
PETERSON, JANE (1876 - 1965)	800-35000	M,F,L,S
PETERSON, ROLAND (1926-)	150-1000	X
PETICOLAS, ARTHUR EDWARD (1793 - 1853)	3000-18000	L
PETO, JOHN FREDERICK (1854 - 1907)	4000-275000+	S
PETROFF, GILMER (1913-)	*200-800	X(F)
PETRUS, P. (19TH - 20TH C)	100-800	X(L)
PETRY, VICTOR (1903-)	400-3000	X(S)
PETRYN, ANDREW (20TH C)	100-1500	X (I)
PETTET, WILLIAM (1942 -)	300-5000	A
PETTIBONE, RICHARD (1938 -)	150-950	X
PETTY, GEORGE (20TH C)	*300-3500	I
PEW, GERTRUDE (20TH C)	*100-1200	X (F)
PEYRAUD, FRANK C. (1858 - 1948)	300-5000	L,F

 * Denotes watercolors, pastels, drawings, and/or mixed media

PEYSTER, EVA DE (early 19TH C)	*400-1000	P
PFEIFFER, FRITZ (1875 - 1960)	500-4500	X
PHARES, FRANK (20TH C)	100-600	I
PHELAN, CHARLES T. (1840 -)	200-1500	W,L
PHELAN, HAROLD LEE (1881 -)	100-800	L
PHELPS, EDITH CATLIN (1875 - 1961)	200-5600	F
PHELPS, WILLIAM PRESTON (1848 - 1923)	300-7000	L,G
PHILBRICK, OTIS (1888-1973)	300-2000	X(S,F)
PHILIP, FREDERICK WILLIAM (1814 - 1841)	400-3500	F,S
PHILIPP, ROBERT (1895 - 1981)	400-21000	F,G,M,S
PHILIPPOTEAUX, PAUL D. (1846 -)	700-5500	G,F,L
PHILIPS, FRANK ALBERT (19TH C)	400-3500	X
PHILLIPS, AARON FRANCIS (1848 - 1899)	300-1500	L,F
PHILLIPS, AMMI (1788 - 1865)	3000-250000+	P
PHILLIPS, BERT GREER (1868 - 1956)	1000-70000	F,L,S,I
PHILLIPS, C. (mid 19TH C)	100-800	X (S)
PHILLIPS, C.E. (19TH C)	100-1000	L
PHILLIPS, COLES	*300-7000	
PHILLIPS, COLES (1880-1927)	800-10000	I
PHILLIPS, GORDON (1927 -)	1000-18000	G,F
PHILLIPS, JOHN CAMPBELL (1873 - 1949)	100-1800	F,L
PHILLIPS, MARORIE (1895-)	200-3000	G,F,S
PHILLIPS, R. (20TH C)	200-1000	X (S)
PHILLIPS, S. GEORGE (- 1965)	100-1200	L,F
PHILLIPS, WALTER JOSEPH (1884 - 1963)	*800-8500	L
PHIPPEN, GEORGE (1916 - 1966)	10000-60000	I,L,F
PIAZZONI, GOTTARDO (1872 - 1945)	300-5000	L
PICKARD, C.G. (20TH C)	100-800	L
PICKETT, JOSEPH (1848 - 1918)	8000-35000	P
PICKNELL, GEORGE W. (1864 - 1943)	200-1500	L
PICKNELL, WILLIAM LAMB (1853 - 1897)	700-15000+	F,L
PIENE, OTTO (1928 -)	300-1200	A
PIENKOWSKI, JONI (20TH C)	300-1200	X
PIERCE, CHARLES FRANKLIN (1844 - 1920)	300-2000	L,W
PIERCE, WALDO	300-3500	

PIERCE, WALDO (1884-1970)	400-5000+	F,S
PIERCEY, A. (20TH C)	100-500	X
PIERSON, ALDEN (1874 - 1921)	600-4500	X (L)
PIG, ROBERT (20TH C)	100-700	X (M)
PIKE, MARION HEWLETT (1914 -)	300-1200	X (S)
PILES, L.M. (late 19TH C)	300-2500	L
PILLSBURY, FRANKLIN C. (20TH C)	100-500	X (F)
PINE, ROBERT EDGE (1720-1788)	1000-6500	F
PINE, THEODORE E. (1828 - 1905)	250-1200	F
PINNEY, EUNICE (1770 - 1849)	*500-12000	P
PIPPIN, HORACE (1888 - 1946)	7500-75000+	P
PITTMAN, HOBSON L. (1900 - 1972)	600-5000	X (I)
PITZ, HENRY CLARENCE (1895 - 1976)	300-2500	I,L
PLATT, CHARLES ADAMS (1861 - 1933)	400-6800	M,G,F
PLEASONTON, RUTH (20TH C)	100-500	X (F)
PLEGER, E. (20TH C)	100-400	X(L,W)
PLEISSNER, OGDEN MINTON	*700-32000	
PLEISSNER, OGDEN MINTON (1905 - 1983)	2500-55000	G,L
PLETCHER, GERRY (20TH C)	*100-600	X
PLETKA, (20TH C)	100-600	F,L
PLIMPTON, W.E. (early 20TH C)	100-400	X (L)
PLUMB, HENRY GRANT (1847 - 1936)	*400-3000	X (F)
PLUMMER, ETHEL (19TH C)	*100-500	L
PLUMMER, WILLIAM H. (19TH - 20TH C)	100-4000	M,L
PODCHERNIKOFF, ALEXIS M. (1912 -)	300-4500	L,F
POEHLMANN, THEO (20TH C)	100-500	X (F)
POGANY, "WILLY" (1882 - 1955)	*150-1200	F,I
POHL, EDWARD H. (19TH - 20TH C)	200-1200	L
POHL, HUGO DAVID (1878 - 1960)	200-2000	I,F
POINCY, PAUL (1833 - 1909)	700-7500	G,F
POINDEXTER, JAMES THOMAS (1832 - 1891)	800-3500	F
POLINSKIE, KENNETH (20TH C)	*100-400	X
POLK, ANITA (19TH C)	400-1000	X (F)
POLK, CHARLES PEALE (1767 - 1822)	2000-110000	F,G
POLLACK, MARK A. (20TH C)	100-600	X (S)

 * Denotes watercolors, pastels, drawings, and/or mixed media

POLLOCK, CHARLES CECIL (1902 -)	700-5000	L
POLLOCK, JACKSON	*4500-575000+	
POLLOCK, JACKSON (1912 - 1956)	7500-325000+	A
POLLOCK, JAMES ARLIN (1898-1949)	100-1500	L
POND, DANA (1880 - 1962)	100-1500	F,L
POND, MABEL E. DICKINSON (early 20TH C)	100-700	X (L)
PONSEN, TUNIS (1891-1968)	250-3500	F,M
POOLE, E. ABRAM (1883 - 1961)	200-1800	L,F
POOLE, EARL LINCOLN (1891 - 1934)	*100-600	W,I
POONS, LARRY (1937 -)	2000-75000	A
POOR, ANN (1887 - 1970)	100-900	X (F)
POOR, HENRY VARNUM	*100-750	
POOR, HENRY VARNUM (1888 - 1970)	300-4800	L,S
POORE, HARRY (19TH C)	200-1200	X
POORE, HENRY RANKIN (1859 - 1940)	300-8500	L,G,W
POPE, ALEXANDER (1849 - 1924)	500-15000+	S,W,F
POPE, ARTHUR (1880 -)	*100-600	X (L)
POPE, JOHN (1820 - 1886)	100-2000	L,G,F
POPE, THOMAS BENJAMIN (- 1891)	300-3000	L,G,S
PORAY, STANISLAUS P. (1888 - 1948)	150-750	X (S)
PORIN, T. (19TH C)	100-600	X (M)
PORTER, DAVID (1780 - 1843)	2000-18000	M
PORTER, E. (19TH-20TH C)	100-400	X(M)
PORTER, FAIRFIELD	*600-30000	
PORTER, FAIRFIELD (1907 - 1975)	6000-165000+	L,M,F
PORTER, MARY KING (1865 - 1930)	*100-600	X (F,L)
PORTER, R.W. (19TH - 20TH C)	*100-600	X (L)
PORTER, RUFUS (1792 - 1884)	4000-60000+	P
PORTER, S.R. (19TH C)	300-1200	L
PORTER, V.F. (20TH C)	200-800	X (M)
PORTINOFF, ALEXANDER (1887 - 1949)	*100-500	X (L)
PORTZLINE, FRANCIS (1800-1847)	*1000-9000	X
POSEN, STEPHEN (1939 -)	8000-25000	A
POSSNER, HUGO A.(20TH C)	100-600	X
POST, CHARLES JOHNSON (1873 -)	300-1500	X (L,I)

* Denotes watercolors, pastels, drawings, and/or mixed media

POST, EDWARD C. (active 1850-60)	600-7000	L
POST, GEORGE BOOTH (1906 -)	*100-1000	L
POST, WILLIAM MERRITT (1856 - 1935)	250-3200	L
POTTER, EDNA (20TH C)	100-750	L
POTTER, HARRY SPAFFORD (1870 -)	100-850	L,I
POTTER, LOUIS MCCLELLAN (1873 - 1912)	600-5000	G,F
POTTER, MARY HELEN (1862 - 1950)	100-800	L,S
POTTER, WILLIAM J. (1883 - 1964)	400-2000	F,L,M
POTTHAST, EDWARD HENRY	*300-30000	
POTTHAST, EDWARD HENRY (1857 - 1927)	2000-200000	G,F,L
POTTS, WILLIAM SHERMAN (1867 - 1927)	100-900	F
POULSON, M.B. (19TH C)	300-3000	X (M)
POUSETTE-DART, NATHANIEL J. (1886 - 1965)	*100-600	X (F)
POUSETTE-DART, RICHARD (1916 -)	7500-60000	A
POWELL, ACE	*200-3500	
POWELL, ACE (1912 - 1978)	700-6500	F
POWELL, ARTHUR JAMES EMERY (1864 - 1956)	250-3000	L
POWELL, LICIEN WHITING	*200-3500	
POWELL, LUCIEN WHITING (1846 - 1930)	200-4500	L
POWELL, M. (- 1711)	700-3500	F
POWER, JAMES P. (19TH C)	100-600	G,L
POWERS, A.G. (active 1845-65)	1500-6500	F
POWERS, AMANDA (active 1835)	3000-66000	P(F)
POWERS, ASAHEL LYNDE (1813 - 1843)	2500-20000	P
POWERS, MARION KIRKPATRICK (20TH C)	250-3500	F
POWIS, PAUL (19TH - 20TH C)	300-2500	X (S,L)
POZZATTI, RUDY (1926-)	100-600	X
PRATHER, WILLIAM E. (19TH - 20TH C)	100-750	X (S)
PRATT, A.M. (19TH C)	300-1500	X (L)
PRATT, CATHERINE (19TH C)	300-1200	X (S)
PRATT, HENRY CHEEVER (1803 - 1880)	1000-5000	F,L,M
PRATT, JOHN F. (20TH C)	100-600	X (F)
PRATT, MATTHEW (1734 - 1805)	5000-25000	F
PRATT, ROBERT M. (1811 - 1888)	700-25000	G,F,S
PRENDERGAST, CHARLES E. (1868 - 1948)	*800-30000	L,F

 * Denotes watercolors, pastels, drawings, and/or mixed media

PRENDERGAST, MAURICE BRAZIL	*3500-450000	
PRENDERGAST, MAURICE BRAZIL (1861 - 1924)	4000-485000	A,L,F
PRENTICE, GILBERT M. (20TH C)	100-400	M
PRENTICE, LEVI WELLS (1851 - 1935)	800-28000+	S,L
PRENTISS, LILLIAN (20TH C)	100-700	X (G)
PRESCOTT, F.R. (early 19TH C)	100-700	X (L)
PRESSER, JOSEF (1907-)	*100-600	X
PRESTON, JESSE GOODWIN (1880-)	100-900	L
PRESTON, MAY WILSON	*250-1500	
PRESTON, MAY WILSON (1873 - 1949) 500-9000	F,I	
PRESTON, WILLIAM (20TH C)	*150-1000	X
PRESTOPINO, GREGORIO (1907 -)	500-14000	F
PREVOST, EUGENE (20TH C)	400-1500	X (S)
PREY, JUAN DE' (20TH C?)	*100-600	X (L)
PRICE, CLAYTON S. (1874 - 1950)	1500-18000	F,G
PRICE, GARRETT (20TH C)	*150-900	F,S
PRICE, L.A. (19TH - 20TH C)	200-800	X (W)
PRICE, M. ELIZABETH (20TH C)	100-900	X (L,M)
PRICE, NORMAN MILLS (1877 - 1951)	*200-2500	I
PRICE, WILLIAM HENRY (1864 - 1940)	100-1200	L,F
PRIEBE, KARL (1914 -)	*100-2000	F,G
PRIESTMAN, BERTRAM WALTER (1868 -)	100-1000	M,L
PRINCE, L.E. (late 19TH C)	100-750	L
PRINCE, WILLIAM MEAD (1893-1951)	200-1000	I
PRINGLE, JAMES FULTON (1788 - 1847)	2500-12000	M
PRIOR, WILLIAM MATTHEW (1806 - 1873)	1000-40000+	P
PRITCHARD, GORDON THOMPSON (1878 - 1962)	300-3000	L,G,F
PRITCHARD, J. AMBROSE (1858 - 1905)	300-2000	L
PRITCHARD, ZARAH H. (20TH C)	*100-500	L
PROBST, JOACHIM (1913 -)	100-900	X
PROBST, THORWALD A. (1886 - 1948)	100-4500	X (I)
PROCTOR, ALEXANDER PHIMISTER (1862-1950)	*200-2500	W,F,L
PROCTOR, BURT (19TH-20TH C)	500-8500	X(F)
PROHASKA, JOSEPH (20TH C)	150-1000	L
PROHASKA, RAYMOND (1901 - 1981)	200-1500	I

* Denotes watercolors, pastels, drawings, and/or mixed media

PROOM, AL (1933 -)	100-800	X (S)
PROPER, IDA SEDGWICK (1876-1957)	1000-32000	F,L
PROUDFOOT, WILLIAM A. (20TH C)	150-900	L
PUDOR, HEINRICH (19TH C)	400-2000	F
PURDY, ALBERT J.(1835-1909)	400-3000	F
PURDY, DONALD ROY (1924 -)	100-750	F,L,S
PURDY, ROBERT (20TH C)	100-600	X(S)
PURWIN, SIGMUND (20TH C)	100-500	X
PUSHMAN, HOVSEP T. (1877 - 1966)	2500-25000	F,S
PUTHUFF, HANSON DUVALL (1875 - 1972)	300-6000	L
PUTMAN, DONALD (1927 -)	500-4500	F
PYLE, HOWARD	*500-10000	
PYLE, HOWARD (1853 - 1911)	2000-20000+	I

Q

ARTIST	PRICE	SUBJECT
QUARTLEY, ARTHUR (1839 - 1886)	450-9800	M
QUIDOR, JOHN (1801 - 1881)	15000-175000	F,L
QUIGLEY, EDWARD B. (1895 -)	500-6000	G,F
QUINCY, EDMUND (1903-)	400-6500	L,M
QUINLAN, WILL J. (1877 -)	250-1200	L
QUINN, EDMOND T. (1868 - 1926)	200-1000	F
QUIRT, WALTER W. (1902 -)	300-1800	A

R

 * Denotes watercolors, pastels, drawings, and/or mixed media

ARTIST	PRICE	SUBJECT
RAAB, GEORGE (1866 - 1943)	*100-300	L
RABES, MAX (1868-1944)	900-6000	F,G
RABORG, BENJAMIN (1871 - 1918)	100-800	L
RACHMIEL, JEAN (1871 -)	150-1000	X
RACKOW, LEO (1901-)	*200-1200	X
RAFFAEL, JOSEPH	*600-9000	
RAFFAEL, JOSEPH (1933 -)	2000-55000	A
RAGAN, LESLIE D. (1897-)	100-500	X
RAIN, CHARLES WHEEDON (1911 -)	200-2500	X (S)
RALEIGH, CHARLES SIDNEY (1830 - 1925)	2500-35000	P(M)
RALEIGH, HENRY PATRICK (1880 - 1945)	*200-1500	I,F,M
RAMAGE, JOHN (1748-1802)	700-6000	F
RAMESCH, E. (19TH C)	100-900	X(F)
RAMME, H. (early 20TH C)	150-850	X (F)
RAMOS, MEL (1935 -)	3000-25000	A
RAMSDELL, FRED WINTHROP (1865 - 1915)	300-2500	L,F
RAMSEY, MILNE (1846 - 1915)	600-35000	S,L
RAND, ELLEN G. EMMET (1876 - 1941)	*100-700	X (F)
RAND, HENRY ASBURY (1886 -)	250-1200	L
RANDELL, ASA GRANT (1869-)	*250-1500	L
RANDOLPH, JOHN (19TH - 20TH C)	200-1200	X (W)
RANDOLPH, LEE FRITZ (1880 - 1956)	300-2000	L,F
RANGER, HENRY WARD	*250-6000	
RANGER, HENRY WARD (1858 - 1916)	600-25000	L
RANN, VOLLIAN BURR (1897 - 1956)	150-1000	X (F)
RANNEY, WILLIAM TYLEE (1813 - 1857)	8000-300000+	G,F
RANSOM, ALEXANDER (19TH C)	300-1500	L,F
RANSOM, CAROLINE L. ORMES (1838 - 1910)	400-3500	L,S,F
RAPHAEL, JOSEPH (1872 - 1950)	700-24000	L,F
RAPP, J. (19TH - 20TH C)	200-1200	X (L)
RAQUERE, THOMAS J. (20TH C)	*100-700	X (L)
RARPHARO, J. (20TH C)	100-600	X(W,L)
RASCHEN, HENRY (1854 - 1937)	3000-60000	G,F,L
RASER, J. HEYL (19TH C)	250-1500	X (L)

* Denotes watercolors, pastels, drawings, and/or mixed media

RASKIN, JOSEPH (1897 -)	100-900	X (L,F)
RASMUSSEN, JOHN (1828 - 1895)	1000-45000	X (L)
RATNER, JOHN RYKOFF (1934 -)	500-6000	X (A)
RATTNER, ABRAHAM (1895 - 1978)	400-18000	A
RATTRAY, ALEXANDER W. (1849 - 1902)	300-1800	L,F
RAUGHT, JOHN WILLARD (20TH C)	300-1000	X (L)
RAULAND, ORLAND (20TH C)	400-4500	X (M)
RAUSCHENBERG, ROBERT	*1500-425000+	
RAUSCHENBERG, ROBERT (1925 -)	18000-175000	A
RAVLIN, GRACE (1885 - 1956)	600-5000	G,F
RAWSON, ALBERT LEIGHTON (1829 - 1902)	400-3000	L
RAWSON, CARL W. (1884 - 1970)	100-900	L,F
RAY, MAN (see MAN RAY)		
RAY, RUTH (20TH C)	100-500	A
RAYMOND, GRACE RUSSELL (1877 -)	100-900	X (M)
REA, LEWIS EDWARD (1868 -)	300-1200	L
READ, JAMES B. (1803 - 1870)	500-2500	F
READ, RALPH (20TH C)	150-700	X(L)
READ, THOMAS BUCHANAN (1822 - 1872)	600-4800	F
REAM, CARDUCIUS PLANTAGENET (1837 - 1917)	800-8000+	S
REAM, MORSTON CONSTANTINE (1840 - 1898)	600-12000	S
REASER, WILBUR AARON (1860 - 1942)	*150-1800	L,F
RECKHARD, GARDNER ARNOLD (1858 - 1908)	300-4000	S,L,F
REDEIN, ALEX (1912 - 1965)	100-400	X (F)
REDELIUS, F.H. (20TH C)	100-900	X (S)
REDFIELD, EDWARD WILLIS (1869 - 1965)	1000-70000+	L,M
REDMAN, B. (19TH - 20TH C)	700-3000	M
REDMOND, CHARLES (19TH C)	100-500	X (G)
REDMOND, GRANVILLE (1871 - 1935)	400-15000+	L,M
REDMOND, JOHN J. (19TH C)	150-1200	F,L
REDMOND, MARGARET (1867 - 1948)	300-4500	F,S
REDWOOD, ALLEN CARTER	*400-2500	
REDWOOD, ALLEN CARTER (1834 - 1922)	800-7500	F,G,I
REED, ALICE (20TH C)	100-300	S
REED, EARL H. (1863 -)	600-3000	L,W

 * Denotes watercolors, pastels, drawings, and/or mixed media

REED, ETHEL (1876 -)	*200-1200	F
REED, MARJORIE (1915 -)	150-850	G,F
REED, PETER FISHE (1817 - 1887)	200-1000	L,F
REEDER, DICKSON (20TH C)	*100-500	X
REEDY, LEONARD HOWARD	*300-2000	I
REEDY, LEONARD HOWARD (1899 - 1956)	500-4500	I
REESE, BERNARD (JR) (19TH - 20TH C)	150-850	X (F)
REGAN, GREGORY T. (20TH C)	100-400	L
REHN, FRANK KNOX MORTON	*150-1500	
REHN, FRANK KNOX MORTON (1848 - 1914)	150-3000+	M,L
REICHARDT, FERDINAND (1819-1895)	1000-7500+	L
REICHARST, T. (19TH C)	500-6000	L
REICHMAN, FRED (1925-)	100-850	X(W)
REID, J.B. (20TH C)	*200-1000	L,F
REID, JAMES (1907-)	100-850	X(M)
REID, JOHN T. (19TH C)	200-2000	X(F)
REID, ROBERT LOUIS	*300-38000	
REID, ROBERT LOUIS (1862 - 1929)	1500-125000	F,L
REID, VICTOR E. (20TH C)	100-700	X (M)
REIFFEL, CHARLES (1862 - 1942)	600-3000	L
REILLY, FRNAK JOSEPH (1906 - 1967)	300-2500	I
REIMERS, JOHANNES (20TH C)	*100-500	L
REINDEL, EDNA (1900 -)	800-4000	X (S)
REINEZ, S.A. (19TH C)	*100-400	G,F
REINHARDT, AD	*1500-25000	
REINHARDT, AD (1913 - 1967)	5000-265000	A
REINHARDT, SIEGFRIED GERHARD (1925-)	600-6000	A
REINHART, BENJAMIN FRANKLIN (1829 - 1885)	1000-20000	G,F,L
REINHART, CHARLES STANLEY (1844 - 1896)	*200-1500	I
REINHART, STEUART 1897-)	150-1200	X(F)
REISS, FRITZ WINOLD (1886 - 1953)	*300-18000	F
REISS, H. (19TH-20TH C)	150-1000	X(G)
REISS, LIONEL S. (1894-)	*100-600	X
REITER, CHRISTIAN (1864 -)	300-1500	F
RELYEA. CHARLES M. (1863 -)	100-900	L,I

* Denotes watercolors, pastels, drawings, and/or mixed media

REMENICK, SEYMOUR (1923 -)	250-2000	A
REMINGTON, FREDERIC S.	1200-150000	
REMINGTON, FREDERIC S. (1861 - 1909)	12000-630000	G,F
REMINGTON, S.J. (19TH C)	400-2500	L
REMISOFF, NICOLAI (1887 -)	*100-900	I
RENOUARD, GEORGE (19TH - 20TH C)	100-650	M,F
RENSHAW, ALICE (19TH C)	*100-500	X (F)
RESNICK, MILTON (1917 -)	800-18000	A
RETTIG, JOHN (1860-1932)	200-1500	F,L
REULANDT, LE GRANDE de (19TH C)	1000-15000+	M
REUSSWIG, WILLIAM	*300-4000	
REUSSWIG, WILLIAM (1902 - 1978)	400-9000	I,G,F
REUTERDAHL, HENRY	*300-3500	
REUTERDAHL, HENRY (1871 - 1925)	400-6000	M,I
REYNARD, GRANT TYSON (1887 - 1968)	*100-1500	I
REYNOLDS, FREDERICK T. (1882 -)	400-5000	G,F,L
REYNOLDS, J.F. (19TH-20TH C)	100-600	X(S,M)
REYNOLDS, JAMES (1926 -)	1500-60000	X (G)
REYNOLDS, W.S. (19TH - 20TH C)	700-10000+	S
REYNOLDS, WELLINGTON JARED (1866 -)	*500-6500	X (F)
RHEAD, LOUIS JOHN (1857 - 1926)	*200-5000	X (I,F)
RHONE, P. (19TH C)	100-500	L
RIBA, PAUL (1912-1977)	200-3500	L,S
RIBAK, LOUIS (1902 - 1979)	1000-7500	G,F
RIBCOWSKY, DEY DE (1880 - 1935)	200-1800	M,L,F
RICCIARDI, CAESARE (1892 -)	100-900	L,S,F
RICE, G.S. (late 19TH C)	500-5000	F
RICE, HENRY W. (1853 - 1934)	*100-500	X (M,G)
RICE, WILLIAM CLARKE (1875 - 1928)	150-950	F,I
RICE, WILLIAM MORTON JACKSON (1854 - 1922)	500-3000	S,F
RICE-PEREIRA, IRENE	*100-5000	
RICE-PEREIRA, IRENE (1901 - 1971)	400-7500	A
RICH, JOHN HUBBARD (1876 - 1954)	900-34000	F,S
RICHARDS, ELLA E. (19TH-20TH C)	150-750	X (G)
RICHARDS, FREDERICK DEBOURG (1822 - 1903)	700-10000	L,M

 * Denotes watercolors, pastels, drawings, and/or mixed media

RICHARDS, JOHN (1935 -)	100-650	X (F)
RICHARDS, THOMAS ADDISON (1820 - 1900)	1000-25000	L,F,S,I
RICHARDS, WILLIAM TROST	*500-40000	
RICHARDS, WILLIAM TROST (1833 - 1905)	1500-145000+	M,L,S,F
RICHARDSON, ALLAN (early 20TH C)	500-3500	X (F)
RICHARDSON, FRANCIS HENRY (1859 - 1934)	250-4000	M,L,F
RICHARDSON, HARRY L. (20TH C)	*100-500	X
RICHARDSON, JOHN (20TH C)	150-900	X (F)
RICHARDSON, L.H. (1853-1923)	200-1500	L,M
RICHARDSON, MARGARET FOSTER (1881-)	700-6500	F
RICHARDSON, MARY CURTIS (1848 - 1931)	300-9500	F
RICHARDSON, MARY NEAL (1877-)	100-1000	X(F)
RICHARDSON, THEODORE J.	*250-1000	
RICHARDSON, THEODORE J. (1855 - 1914)	500-3500	L
RICHARDSON, VOLNEY A. (20TH C)	100-700	X(S)
RICHARDT, FERDINAND J.(1819-1895)	600-7500+	L
RICHENBURG, ROBERT B. (1917 -)	500-6500	A
RICHERT, CHARLES HENRY	*100-400	
RICHERT, CHARLES HENRY (1880 -)	100-1200	L,M
RICHES, WILLIAM J. (late 19TH C)	100-600	X (F)
RICHMOND, AGNES M. (1870 - 1964)	300-15000	F
RICHTER, HANS (20TH C)	*500-1500	A
RICHTER, HENRY L. (1870 -)	100-850	L
RICKARDS, F. (early 19TH C)	600-3000	F
RICKLE, T. (early 19TH C)	400-2000	X (L)
RICKMAN, PHILIP (1891 -)	*400-2000	X (W)
RICKS, DOUGLAS (20TH C)	1000-6500	L,G
RIDDEL, JAMES (- 1928)	*100-700	X
RIDER, ARTHUR G. (1886 -)	400-5800	X (M)
RIDER, HENRY ORNE (1860 -)	100-850	L
RIECKE, GEORGE A.E. (1848 - 1930)	250-3500	L,W
RIECKE, JOHANN GEORGE L.(1817-1898)	300-2500	L,G,W
RIESENBERG, SIDNEY (1885 - 1962)	350-3500	I
RIFKIN, LOUIS (19TH C)	100-500	X(L)
RIGGS, ROBERT (1896 - 1970)	700-8500	G,F,I

* Denotes watercolors, pastels, drawings, and/or mixed media

RILEY, KENNETH (1919 -)	700-60000	I
RILEY, MARY G. (1883 - 1939)	100-600	X (L)
RILEY, NICHOLAS F. (1900 - 1944)	*200-1500	I,F
RIMMER, WILLIAM (1816 - 1879)	2500-60000	G,F,L
RINCK, ADOLPH D. (active 1835-60)	200-800	F
RING, ALICE BLAIR (1869-)	300-7000	F,L
RIPLEY, AIDEN LASSELL	*250-5500	
RIPLEY, AIDEN LASSELL (1896 - 1969)	300-18000	W,L,F
RIPLEY, LUCY PERKINS (19TH - 20TH C)	200-1200	X (F,A)
RISING, C.P. (early 20TH C)	*100-850	L
RITMAN, LOUIS (1889 - 1963)	1000-80000	F
RITSCHEL, WILLIAM P. (1864 - 1949)	600-26000	M,L,S
RITTENBERG, HENRY R. (1879 -)	500-5500	S,F
RITTER, ALONZO W. (1898 -)	100-400	X (F)
RITTER, HENRY (1816 - 1853)	1000-6000	G,F
RITTER, PAUL (1829-1907)	400-7500	L
RIVERS, GEORGIE THURSTON (1878 -)	*100-400	X (F,L)
RIVERS, LARRY	*1000-75000	
RIVERS, LARRY (1923 -)	5000-165000	A
RIX, JULIAN WALGRIDGE (1850 - 1903)	500-14000	L
ROBBINS, ELLEN (1828 - 1905)	*300-3000	S
ROBBINS, H. (20TH C)	100-600	X(S)
ROBBINS, HORACE WOLCOTT (1842 - 1904)	700-18000	L
ROBBINS, RAIS A. (20TH C)	300-2000	X
ROBERTI, ROMOLO (1896-)	*100-400	X(G)
ROBERTS, BLANCHE GILROY (1871 -)	100-900	L
ROBERTS, ELIZABETH W. (1871-1927)	600-16000	X(M)
ROBERTS, MORTON (1927 - 1964)	800-15000	I
ROBERTS, NATHAN B. (19TH C)	600-3500	F
ROBERTS, VIRGINIA (20TH C)	100-600	X(M)
ROBERTSON, ANNA MARY (see "MOSES")		
ROBERTSON, ANNE L. (1844 - 1933)	600-45000	G,F
ROBERTSON, ARCHIBALD (1765 - 1835)	*450-3500	F
ROBERTSON, FREDERICK E. (1878-1953)	100-1000	X(L)
ROBERTSON, ROBERT (20TH C)	150-750	I

 * Denotes watercolors, pastels, drawings, and/or mixed media

ROBINS, LOUISA (1898-)	*100-600	X(F)
ROBINSON, ALEXANDER (1867 - 1940)	*100-3200	M,L
ROBINSON, BOARDMAN (1876 - 1952)	*100-900	I
ROBINSON, CHARLES DORMAN (1847 - 1933)	500-14000	L,M
ROBINSON, FLORENCE VINCENT (1874 - 1937)	*200-2000	L,F
ROBINSON, GLADYS LLOYD (20TH C)	100-500	X (S)
ROBINSON, HAL (1875 - 1933)	200-4000	L
ROBINSON, MRS. A.K. (19TH C)	200-1000	X (W)
ROBINSON, THEODORE (1852 - 1896)	7500-375000+	L,F
ROBINSON, THOMAS (1835 - 1888)	200-1800	L,G,W
ROBINSON, WILLIAM S. (1861 - 1945)	400-13000	F,L,M
ROBINSON, WILLIAM T. (1852 -)	150-2000	L,G,M
ROBUS, HUGO	*500-7500	
ROBUS, HUGO (1885 - 1964)	1000-40000	A
ROCKLINE, VERA (1896 - 1934)	600-3800	F
ROCKMORE, NOEL DAVIS (1928-)	300-1200	X
ROCKWELL, AUGUSTUS (19TH C)	400-3500	L,F
ROCKWELL, CLEVELAND	*300-5000	
ROCKWELL, CLEVELAND (1837 - 1907)	800-35000+	M,L
ROCKWELL, FREDERIC (20TH C)	100-900	F,A
ROCKWELL, NORMAN	*1000-50000	
ROCKWELL, NORMAN (1894 - 1978)	2000-150000+	I
RODNEY, H.C. (19TH C)	500-5000	X(G)
RODRIGUEZ, A.C. (19TH C)	100-1000	L
ROE, CLARENCE (19TH C)	100-600	L
ROE, NICHOLAS (19TH C)	250-3000	L
ROEDING, FRANCES (1910 -)	300-1200	X (F)
ROESEN, SEVERIN (1815 - 1872)	8000-100000+	S
ROGER, CHARLES A. (1866 - 1907)	100-900	L,F
ROGERS, FRANKLIN WHITING (1854 -)	200-1200	W,L
ROGERS, GRETCHEN W. (1881-1967)	400-5000	F
ROGERS, NATHANIEL (1788-1844)	400-2000	F
ROGERS, S.D. (19TH C)	300-3500	L
ROGERS, WILLIAM (19TH-20TH C)	100-700	X(M)
ROGERS, WILLIAM ALLEN (1854 - 1931)	*300-2000	I

ROHDE, H. (20TH C)	100-600	L,W
ROHLAND, PAUL (20TH C)	100-400	X (S)
ROHOWSKY, MEYERS (1900 - 1974)	350-1500	X
ROHRHIRSCH, RICHARD (1833-1892)	400-2800	X(S)
ROLFE, EDMUND (19TH - 20TH C)	350-1800	S
ROLLE, AUGUST H.O. (1875 - 1941)	250-2800	L,M
ROLLINS, WARREN E. (1861 - 1962)	500-6500	F,L
ROLSHOVEN, JULIUS (1858 - 1930)	500-16000	F,L
ROMANO, UMBERTO (1905 -)	200-1200	F
ROMANOVSKY, DIMITRI (20TH C)	100-600	X
ROMANSKI, HARRY (1861 -)	200-1200	X (L)
RONDEL, FREDERICK (1826 - 1892)	600-15000+	G,L
RONEY, HAROLD ARTHUR (1899-)	200-2500	X(L)
ROOS, PETER (1850 -)	200-1500	L
ROOSEVELT, S. MONTGOMERY (1863 - 1929)	*100-600	X (F)
ROPES, JOSEPH (1812 - 1885)	400-2000	L
RORPHURO, J. (20TH C)	100-500	X(F)
ROSAR, M. (19TH C)	100-900	L
ROSAS, CHARLES (20TH C)	200-1500	L
ROSATI, JAMES (1912 -)	*100-900	A
ROSE, ANTHONY LEWIS DE (1803 - 1836)	350-1200	F
ROSE, GUY (1867 - 1925)	1000-30000	L
ROSE, HERMAN (1909 -)	450-5000	L
ROSE, HORACE L. (19TH - 20TH C)	100-600	X(L)
ROSE, IVOR (20TH C)	100-700	X(G,F)
ROSE, W. (- 1938)	300-1800	X
ROSELAND, HARRY (1868 - 1950)	700-35000+	G,F
ROSEN, CHARLES (1878 - 1950)	500-12000	L
ROSEN, ERNEST T. (1877-1926)	150-1000	X(F)
ROSEN, STEPHEN (19TH C)	100-400	F,L
ROSENBAUM, RICHARD (19TH C)	*100-850	X (G,I)
ROSENBERG, HENRY MORTIKAR (1858 - 1947)	150-1000	X (F)
ROSENBERRY, O.W. (20TH C)	*100-600	X
ROSENKRANZ, CLARENCE C. (19TH - 20TH C)	200-1000	L
ROSENQUIST, JAMES	*2000-85000	

 * Denotes watercolors, pastels, drawings, and/or mixed media

ROSENQUIST, JAMES (1933 -)	5000-250000+	A
ROSENTHAL, ALBERT (1863 - 1939)	200-3500	F
ROSENTHAL, DORIS (1895 - 1971)	150-600	G,F,L
ROSENTHAL, MAX (1833 - 1918)	300-1500	F,M
ROSENTHAL, TOBY EDWARD (1848 - 1917)	700-25000	F,G
ROSNER, CHARLES (1894 - 1975)	*150-500	M
ROSS, ALEX (1909 -)	*100-700	I
ROSS, CARRIE (20TH C)	200-1200	X(F,L)
ROSS, CHANDLER R. (20TH C)	400-2500	S
ROSS, DENMAN WALDO (1853 - 1935)	400-1500	L
ROSS, GORDON (20TH C)	*100-600	X(G)
ROSS, HARRY LEITH (1886 -)	1000-6500	L,M
ROSS, LILLI (20TH C)	100-300	X
ROSS, SANFORD (20TH C)	*100-600	X(L)
ROSSEAU, PERCIVAL LEONARD (1859 - 1937)	500-28000	W,L
ROSSITER, THOMAS PRITCHARD (1818 - 1871)	900-9000	G,F,L,M
ROTCH, BENJAMIN SMITH (1817 - 1882)	400-2000	L
ROTENBERG, HAROLD (1905-)	100-1200	X(L)
ROTERS, CARL G.(20TH C)	*100-600	L
ROTH, ERNEST DAVID (1879 - 1964)	250-3500	L
ROTHBORT, SAMUEL (1882 - 1971)	200-2500	L
ROTHERMEL, PETER FREDERICK (1817 - 1895)	300-4000	F
ROTHKO, MARK	*1500-90000	
ROTHKO, MARK (1903 - 1970)	3000-950000+	A
ROTHSTEIN, E. (1907 -)	100-400	X (G)
ROUILLION, M.W. (19TH - 20TH C)	100-900	X (L)
ROULAND, ORLANDO (1871 - 1945)	200-2500	M,L
ROUSSEFF, W. VLADMIR (1890 - 1934)	100-850	X (L)
ROUX, A. (19TH C)	100-900	L
ROUZEE, W. (19TH C)	100-600	L,M
ROWE, J. STAPLES (1856 - 1905)	*100-350	X (F)
ROY, FRANK (20TH C)	100-800	L
ROYCE, WOODFORD (1902-)	150-1800	X(L,S)
RUBEN, RICHARD (1925 -)	150-800	A
RUBINS, HARRY W. (1865 - 1934)	100-900	X

RUCKER, ROBERT (20TH C)	200-1000	X (L)
RUDELL, PETER EDWARD (1854 - 1899)	150-1500	L
RUDOLPH, ERNEST (19TH - 20TH C)	400-2000	X (L)
RUFF, BEATRICE (20TH C)	100-650	X (L)
RUGE, CARL (20TH C)	*250-1000	X
RUGGLES, ELIZA E. (19TH C)	*150-950	X(L)
RUIZ, B.YAMERO -)	200-2500	L,G,F
RUMMELL, RICHARD (1848 - 1924)	*350-3800	M
RUNGIUS, CARL	*500-15000	
RUNGIUS, CARL (1869 - 1959)	1000-80000	W,L
RUSALL, J.L. (19TH C)	100-500	L
RUSCHA, EDWARD	*600-15000	
RUSCHA, EDWARD (1937 -)	2500-150000	A
RUSH, OLIVE (20TH C)	*100-650	X (L)
RUSS, C.B. (active 1880-1920)	350-2500	L
RUSSELL, ALFRED (20TH C)	100-500	L,F
RUSSELL, BENJAMIN (1804 - 1885)	*2500-7500	M
RUSSELL, CHARLES MARION	*1500-175000	
RUSSELL, CHARLES MARION (1865 - 1926)	15000-275000	G,F,I
RUSSELL, EDWARD (1832 - 1906)	*400-2500	M,F
RUSSELL, EDWARD JOHN (1832 - 1906)	*1000-3000	M
RUSSELL, EDWIN (19TH C)	200-900	F
RUSSELL, GEORGE D. (19TH C)	*100-500	L
RUSSELL, GRACE L. (20TH C)	100-500	X (M)
RUSSELL, HILDA (20TH C)	100-800	X
RUSSELL, MORGAN (1886 - 1953)	3500-35000	A
RUSSELL, MOSES B. (1810-1884)	150-1000	L,F
RUSSELL, WALTER (1871 - 1963)	400-10000	F,M,I
RUSSELL, WILLIAM GEORGE (1860 -)	*100-850	X (M)
RUTHERFORD, HARRY (19TH C)	300-2500	F,L
RUTLEDGE, JANE (20TH C)	100-500	X (L)
RUTTAN, C.E. (20TH C)	100-800	X
RYAN, ANNE (1889 - 1954)	*1800-9500	A
RYAN, TOM	*2500-40000	
RYAN, TOM (1922 -)	3500-50000	I

 * Denotes watercolors, pastels, drawings, and/or mixed media

RYDEN, HENNING (1869 - 1939)	250-3000	F,M,L
RYDER, ALBERT PINKHAM (1847 - 1917)	3500-????	F,L,M
RYDER, CHAUNCEY FOSTER (1868 - 1949)	600-18000+	L,F
RYDER, HENRY ORNE (19TH C)	200-1200	L,M
RYDER, PLATT POWELL (1821 - 1896)	600-15000	G,F
RYDER, WORTH (1884 - 1960)	*150-600	L,F
RYLAND, ROBERT KNIGHT (1873 - 1951)	600-8500	F,I
RYMAN, ROBERT (1930 -)	*3000-45000	A
RYNERSON, BEULAH (20TH C)	100-700	X

S

ARTIST	PRICE	SUBJECT
SABELA, H.J. (19TH-20TH C)	200-900	X (S)
SACCO, LUCA (1858 - 1912)	300-3000	G,F,L
SACKS, JOSEPH (1887 -)	300-2500	L
SACKS, WALTER T. (1895 -)	*100-800	L
SADONA, MATTEO (1881 - 1964)	*150-1200	X (L)
SAGE, KAY (1898 - 1963)	1200-25000	A
SAGER, HERMAN (20TH C)	100-600	L
SAINT-PHALLE, NIKI DE (1930 -)	*650-4800	A
SALEMME, ATTILIO (1911 - 1955)	1500-10000	A
SALINAS, PORFIRIO (1910 - 1972)	800-25000	L
SALING, PAUL E. (1876-1936)	100-1800	L
SALLA, SALVATORE (20TH C)	200-1200	X (L)
SALLE, DAVID (20TH C)	2000-40000+	A
SALMON, ROBERT (1775 - 1848)	3500-125000	M,L
SALT, JOHN (1937 -)	4000-25000	A
SALTONSTALL, ELIZABETH (1900 -)	100-500	X
SALTZMAN, LINDA B. (1903 -)	200-800	A
SALVI, EDWARD (20TH C)	200-1200	A
SALZMANN, E. (19TH C)	500-1800	X (L)
SAMARAS, LUCAS (1936 -)	*1000-6000	A

SAMBROOK, RUSSELL (20TH C)	200-1500	X (G)
SAMMONS, CARL (1886-1968)	150-2500	L,M
SAMMONS, FREDERICK H. C.(1853-1917)	400-2000	X (S)
SAMPLE, PAUL STARRETT	*300-2500	
SAMPLE, PAUL STARRETT (1896 - 1974)	450-18000	G,L,M,I
SAMPSON, ALDEN (1853-)	*100-500	L
SAMUELS, IRVING K. (20TH C)	*100-600	X (L)
SANBORN, PERCY (1849 - 1929)	700-8000	M
SAND, PERCY TSISETE (1918 -)	*100-300	X (F)
SANDER, LUDWIG (1906 - 1975)	750-5500	A
SANDERSON, CHARLES WESLEY (1838 - 1905)	*100-450	L
SANDHAM, HENRY (1842-1912)	*100-700	L
SANDZEN, SVEN BIRGER (1871 - 1954)	400-4800	L
SANFORD, GEORGE T. (active 1840-1850)	*800-4500	M
SANGER, JOSEPH (20TH C)	150-600	X (G)
SANGER, WILLIAM (1875 -)	*100-600	X (F)
SANTRY, DANIEL (1858 - 1915)	200-2500	L
SARG, TONY (1882 - 1942)	*100-750	I
SARGENT, HENRY (1770 - 1845)	3000-25000	G,F
SARGENT, JOHN SINGER	*600-135000+	
SARGENT, JOHN SINGER (1856 - 1925)	3000-550000+	F,L
SARGENT, PAUL TURNER (1880 -)	1500-12000	X (L)
SARGENT, WALTER (20TH C)	100-800	L
SARISKY, MICHAEL (1906-)	100-850	F,S
SARKISIAN, SARKIS (1909 - 1977)	200-1500	F,S
SARNOFF, ARTHUR (20TH C)	*100-1500	X
SARRAZIN, LOUISE (20TH C)	*100-600	X
SARTAIN, WILLIAM (1843 - 1924)	200-1800	L
SARTELLE, HERBERT (20TH C)	100-700	L
SASLOW, HERBERT (1920 -)	200-1000	X (S)
SATTERLEE, WALTER	*400-1200	
SATTERLEE, WALTER (1844 - 1908)	400-3500	G,F
SAUER, WILLIAM (20TH C)	200-1000	L,F
SAUERWEIN, FRANK PETER	*650-2500	
SAUERWEIN, FRANK PETER (1871 - 1910)	1000-10000	L,G,F

 * Denotes watercolors, pastels, drawings, and/or mixed media

SAUL, PETER (1934 -)	700-20000	A
SAURA, ANTONIO (20TH C)	3000-30000	A
SAVAGE, EUGENE FRANCIS (1883 -)	200-1800	G,F
SAVAGE, R.A. (19TH C)	200-1500	X (F)
SAVITSKY, JACK (1910 -)	350-1800	P
SAWTELLE, ELIZABETH A. (20TH C)	200-1200	X (S)
SAWTELLE, MARY BERKELEY (1872 -)	500-4500	X
SAWYER, HELEN ALTON (1900 -)	100-850	L,S
SAWYER, W.B. (20TH C)	250-1500	L
SAWYER, WELLS M. (1863 - 1961)	100-800	M,L
SAWYERS, MARTHA (1902 -)	*100-900	
SAYER, RAYMOND (19TH - 20TH C)	100-800	M,L
SAYRE, FRED GRAYSON (1879 - 1938)	400-6500+	L
SAYRES, S.T. (19TH C)	100-700	X(L)
SCALELLA, JULES (1895 -)	100-450	X (L)
SCHABELITZ, RUDOLPH F.(1884- 1959)	100-3000	G,I
SCHAEFFER, MEAD (1898 - 1980)	500-8500	I
SCHAETTE, LOUIS (- 1917)	200-2000	F
SCHAFER, FREDERICK F.(1841 - 1917)	300-8500	L
SCHALDACH, WILLIAM J.	*100-600	
SCHALDACH, WILLIAM J. (19TH - 20TH C)	400-2500	W
SCHAMBERG, MORTON L.(1881-1918)	2500-40000+	A
SCHANKER, LOUIS (1903 - 1981)	700-6500	A
SCHANS, S.V.D. (19TH C)	3000-25000	F
SCHARY, SUSAN (20TH C)	100-600	X (F)
SCHATER, F. (19TH C)	500-4000	X (L,F)
SCHATTENSTEIN, NIKOL (1877 - 1954)	400-4000	F
SCHELL, FRANCIS H. (1834 - 1909)	*100-600	I
SCHELL, FREDERICK H. (1838 - 1905)	*400-5000	M
SCHEUERLE, JOE (1873 - 1948)	*350-2800	F
SCHIAVO, A.J. (20TH C)	*100-500	X(F)
SCHINDLER, A. ZENO (1815 - 1880)	*700-4500	L,F
SCHLAIKJER, JES WILLIAM (1897 -)	400-4500	F,L
SCHLECT, RICHARD (20TH C)	100-600	L
SCHLEETER, HOWARD BEHLING (1903 -)	100-750	X (L)

* Denotes watercolors, pastels, drawings, and/or mixed media

SCHLEGEL, FRIDOLIN (19TH C)	400-1200	F
SCHLEMM, BETTY LOU (1934-)	*100-500	M
SCHLEMMER, FERDINAND L. (1893 - 1947)	100-800	X (L)
SCHLENIER, T.M. (1820 - 1880)	200-1200	L
SCHMEDTGEN, WILLIAM HERMAN (1862 - 1936)	*150-900	I
SCHMID, RICHARD ALLAN (1934 -)	150-1000	L,F
SCHMIDT, CHRISTAIN F.(18TH-19TH C)	400-3500	G,F,L
SCHMIDT, J.W. (20TH C)	450-2500	M
SCHMIDT, JAY (1929-)	200-2000	X(G)
SCHMIDT, KARL (1890 - 1962)	*100-1500	X (M)
SCHMIDT, M.A. (20TH C)	100-1000	X (L)
SCHMITT, ALBERT FELIX (1873 -)	300-1500	X (S)
SCHMITT, CARL (1889 -)	200-3500	S,L
SCHMITT, PAUL A. (1893-)	100-900	L
SCHNAKENBERG, HENRY (1892 - 1970)	400-5500	W,L,S
SCHNEIDAU, CRISTIAN VON (1893 - 1976)	100-900	X (F)
SCHNEIDER, ARTHUR (20TH C)	100-700	L,I
SCHNEIDER, FRANK (1935 -)	100-1200	X (M)
SCHNEIDER, GERARD (1896 -)	2500-32000	A
SCHNEIDER, OTTO H. (20TH C)	100-600	X(L)
SCHNEIDER, SUSAN HAYWARD (1876 -)	100-900	X (L)
SCHNEIDER, THEOPHOLE (1872 -)	100-400	X
SCHNEIDER, WILLIAM G. (1863-1912)	*200-1500	X(F)
SCHOEN, CELESTE (20TH C)	100-500	F
SCHOEN, EUGENE (1880 - 1957)	200-3000	X (F)
SCHOFIELD, WALTER ELMER (1867 - 1944)	1000-55000	L
SCHOLDER, FRITZ (1937 -)	1000-30000	A
SCHONZEIT, BEN (1942 -)	2000-25000	A
SCHOONOVER, FRANK EARLE (1877 - 1972)	600-28000	I
SCHOTT, MAX (19TH - 20TH C)	700-3500	X (F)
SCHOTTLE, MARK (20TH C)	100-850	X
SCHRAG, KARL (1912 -)	*300-3500	A
SCHREIBER, GEORGES	*150-2500	
SCHREIBER, GEORGES (1904 - 1977)	500-6500	G,M,I
SCHREYVOGEL, CHARLES (1861 - 1912)	3000-200000	G,F,L

 *** Denotes watercolors, pastels, drawings, and/or mixed media**

SCHUCKER, JAMES W. (1903-)	100-900	X(F)
SCHUELER, JON R. (1916-)	100-1000	A
SCHUESSLER, MARY (20TH C)	100-700	X (L)
SCHULTE, ANTOINETTE (1897 - 1981)	100-800	X (S)
SCHULTZ, CARL (19TH C)	*400-2500	F
SCHULTZ, GEORGE F. (1869 -)	150-4000	F,L,M
SCHULTZ, ROBERT E. (1928-1978)	400-7500	X
SCHULZ, TONY (19TH C)	100-750	L
SCHUMACHER, CHARLES J. (19TH C)	250-1500	L
SCHUMACHER, WILLIAM E. (1870 - 1931)	200-2000	L
SCHUSSELE, CHRISTIAN	*400-2500	
SCHUSSELE, CHRISTIAN (1824 - 1879)	600-20000	G,F,L
SCHUSTER, DONNA N. (1883 - 1953)	350-5500	F,L
SCHUYLER, REMINGTON (1887 - 1955)	250-3500	F,G
SCHWABE, HENRY AUGUST (1843 - 1916)	200-1500	F
SCHWARTZ, A.W. (20TH C)	300-1200	L,M
SCHWARTZ, ANDREW THOMAS (1867 - 1942)	100-1000	L,M
SCHWARTZ, DANIEL (1929 -)	200-1500	I
SCHWARTZ, DAVIS F. (1879-1969)	150-3500	L
SCHWARTZ, WILLIAM S. (1896 - 1977)	500-6500	G,F
SCHWEIDER, ARTHUR (1884-)	100-600	X (M)
SCHWINN, BARBARA E. (1907 -)	*100-700	I
SCIOCCHETTI, L. (20TH C)	100-600	X (L)
SCIVER, PEARL A. VAN (1896-)	250-1500	L,S
SCOFIELD, K.M. (19TH C)	100-400	X (L)
SCOFIELD, WILLIAM BACON (1864 - 1930)	300-1800	L
SCOTT, CHARLES T. (1876 -)	400-2500	L,F
SCOTT, EDITH A. (1877-1978)	300-4000	F
SCOTT, EDWIN (19TH-20TH C)	500-4500	X(L)
SCOTT, EMILY MARIA SPAFORD (1832 - 1915)	*200-1500	S
SCOTT, FRANK EDWIN (1863 - 1929)	400-4500	G,F
SCOTT, G. (19TH C)	150-1200	L
SCOTT, HOWARD (1902 - 1983)	200-1500	I
SCOTT, JOHN WHITE ALLEN (1815 - 1907)	300-5500	L,M,F
SCOTT, JULIAN (1846 - 1901)	500-8500+	F,L

* Denotes watercolors, pastels, drawings, and/or mixed media

SCOTT, THOMAS J. (19TH C)	200-900	X (W)
SCOTT, WILLIAM EDOUARD (1884 -)	150-2500	X
SCOTT, WILLIAM J. (1879 - 1940)	*400-2500	F
SCREYER, C.H. (19TH-20TH C)	150-950	L
SCUDDER, JAMES LONG (1836-1881)	350-4500	X(L,S)
SEARLE, ALICE T. (1869-)	300-2000	X (S)
SEARLE, HELEN (19TH C)	1000-8500	X (S)
SEARLE, HELEN R. (1830 - 1889)	1000-20000	S
SEARS, CARRIE (19TH C)	100-900	L,M
SEAVEY, E. LEONE (19TH C)	250-1800	X
SEAVEY, GEORGE W. (1841 - 1916)	350-4000	X (S)
SECOR, DAVID PELL (1824 - 1909)	100-450	X (M)
SECUNDA, ARTHUR (20TH C)	300-1500	L,F
SEERY, JOHN (1941 -)	300-7500	A
SEGAL, GEORGE (1924 -)	*500-4500	F
SEGALMAN, RICHARD (20TH C)	*150-600	X (F)
SEIBERT, J.O. (19TH - 20TH C)	100-500	X (F)
SEIDEL, A. (19TH C)	*100-500	X(S)
SEIFERT, PAUL A. (1840 - 1921)	*4000-15000	L
SELDEN, DIXIE (20TH C)	200-1000	L
SELDEN, HENRY BILL (1886 - 1934)	150-2500	L,F
SELF, COLIN (1941 -)	*400-2000	F
SELIGER, CHARLES (1926-)	100-1000	A
SELINGER, JEAN PAUL (1850 - 1909)	400-4500	F,M,S
SELLAER, VINCENT (20TH C)	*400-7500	F
SELLERS, ANNA (1824 - 1905)	700-3500	X (S)
SELTZER, OLAF CARL (1877 - 1957)	*2000-80000	G,F
SELZER, F. (19TH - 20TH C)	200-1200	X (F)
SENAT, PROSPER LOUIS (1852 - 1925)	200-4000	M,L
SENNHAUSER, JOHN (20TH C)	*400-3500	A
SENSEMAN, RAPHAEL (1870 - 1965)	*100-500	X (L)
SEPESHY, ZOLTAN L. (1898 - 1934)	150-3500	F,S,L
SERGER, FREDERICK B. (1889 - 1965)	100-850	X (F)
SERISAWA, SUEO (1910 -)	350-2000	L
SERRA, RICHARD	*1200-18000	

 * Denotes watercolors, pastels, drawings, and/or mixed media

SERRA, RICHARD (1938 -)	4000-25000	A
SERRA-BADUE, DANIEL (1914 -)	400-2000	X
SERRES, J.T. (19TH C)	200-2500	L,M
SESSIONS, JAMES (1882-1962)	*400-2800	L,F,M
SETHER, G. (early 20TH C)	*150-900	L
SEVERN, ARTHUR (?)	*100-350	X (M)
SEWARD, JAMES (20TH C)	100-900	X(F)
SEWELL, AMANDA BREWSTER	400-4500	F
SEWELL, AMOS (1901 - 1983)	250-1500	I
SEWELL, ROBERT VAN VORST (1860 - 1924)	200-5000	F,L
SEXTON, FREDERICK LESTER (1889 -)	100-1500	L,I,F
SEYFFERT, LEOPOLD (1887 - 1956)	300-3200	F,S
SEYMOUR, RUTH (20TH C)	100-600	L,S
SHACKENBERG, HENRY E. (19TH C)	150-900	X (L)
SHACKLETON, CHARLES (- 1920)	250-1000	X (L)
SHADE, WILLIAM AUGUST (1848 - 1890)	800-4500	F,G
SHAFER, S. P. (19TH C?)	200-1500	X (S)
SHAHN, BEN	*600-65000	
SHAHN, BEN (1898 - 1969)	3500-150000	A,I
SHALLENBERGER, MARTIN C. (1912-)	*100-650	M
SHANNON, JAMES JEBUSA (19TH-20TH C)	800-26000	F
SHAPLEIGH, FRANK HENRY (1842 - 1906)	400-18000	L,M
SHARP, JAMES CLEMENT (1818 - 1897)	2000-35000	X (S)
SHARP, JOSEPH HENRY	*3500-20000	
SHARP, JOSEPH HENRY (1859 - 1953)	1500-125000	F,I
SHARP, LOUIS HOVEY (1875 - 1946)	250-2000	L,F
SHARP, W.A. (20TH C)	*100-300	X (L)
SHARP, WILLIAM (active 1840-90)	800-8000	G,I
SHARPLES, FELIX THOMAS (1786 -)	*500-5000	F
SHARPLES, JAMES (1751 - 1811)	*6500-30000	F
SHATTUCK, AARON DRAPER (1832 - 1928)	500-12000	L,F,W
SHAW, CHARLES GREEN (1892 - 1974)	500-8500+	A
SHAW, G. (19TH C)	800-6500	L
SHAW, JOSHUA (1777 - 1860)	3500-75000	L,F,S,W
SHAW, SUSAN M. (19TH C)	600-2500	X (S)

SHAW, SYDNEY DALE (1879 - 1946)	350-4500	X(L)
SHAW,GLEN (1891-)	100-900	X(M)
SHAYLOR, H.W. (19TH C)	*100-400	M
SHEARER, CHRISTOPHER H. (1840 - 1926)	100-4000	L,F,M
SHEARER, VICTOR (1872-1951)	200-1500	L
SHEBLE, H. (20TH C)	*300-2500	F
SHEELER, CHARLES	*600-50000+	
SHEELER, CHARLES (1883 - 1965)	3500-200000+	A,L
SHEETS, MILLARD (1907 -)	*500-22000	A,L
SHEFFER, GLEN C. (1881 - 1948)	250-3200	F,M
SHEFFERS, PETER W. (1894 - 1949)	200-1500	X
SHEFFIELD, ISAAC (1798 - 1845)	6000-45000	P(F)
SHELTON, ALPHONSE J. (1905-1976)	300-3000	M,L
SHEPHARD, CLARENCE E. (1869 -)	100-1500	L,F
SHEPHERD, J. CLINTON (1888 - 1975)	300-2500	F,G
SHEPLEY, ANNIE B. (19TH C)	350-2000	X (F)
SHEPPARD, JOSEPH SHERLY (1930 -)	250-1000	X
SHEPPARD, WARREN (1858 - 1937)	350-6000+	M
SHEPPARD, WILLIAM LUDLOW (1833 - 1912)	*400-2800	F,G,I
SHERMUND, BARBARA (20TH C)	*100-800	X (F)
SHERRY, WILLIAM G.(1914 -)	300-3000	L
SHERWOOD, MARY CLARE (1868 - 1943)	1500-7500	L,F
SHERWOOD, WALTER (19TH-20TH C)	350-2000	L,F
SHERWOOD, WILLIAM ANDERSON (1875-1951)	400-2500	L
SHIELDS, THOMAS W. (1850 - 1920)	600-8000	X
SHIKLER, AARON (1922 -)	500-6000	F
SHILLING, ALEXANDER (1859-)	150-2000	L
SHINN, EVERETT	*400-80000	
SHINN, EVERETT (1876 - 1953)	2500-125000+	G,F,I
SHIRK, JEANETTE C. (19TH-20TH C)	*100-900	X
SHIRLAW, WALTER	*100-1500	
SHIRLAW, WALTER (1838 - 1909)	200-7000+	F,G,I
SHITE, JULIA (20TH C)	*200-1000	X (F)
SHIVELY, DOUGLAS (1896-)	150-1500	L
SHOKLER, HARRY (1896 -)	200-1500	X (L)

 * Denotes watercolors, pastels, drawings, and/or mixed media

SHOOK, NEVIL (20TH C)	100-600	X
SHOOK, WILLIS (20TH C)	100-400	X (L)
SHOPE, SHORTY (1900 -)	500-8500	X (F)
SHOTWELL, HELEN H, (1908-)	200-2000	F
SHOVE, JOHN J. (19TH C)	*700-3500	X
SHRADER, EDWIN ROSCOE (1879 - 1960)	350-1200	X (I)
SHRIVER, CRANE (late 19TH C)	300-1500	X
SHUCKER, JAMES W. (19TH - 20TH C)	100-500	X (F)
SHULL, DELLA (19TH - 20TH C)	300-1800	F
SHULTZ, ADOLPH ROBERT (1869 - 1963)	150-3200	L,S
SHURTLEFF, ROSWELL MORSE (1838 - 1915)	300-2800	L,M,I
SHUSTER, WILLIAM HOWARD (1893 - 1969)	400-3500	L,F
SHUTE, R.W. and S.A.(circa 1803-1836)	*3000-45000	P
SIBBEL, SUSANNA (active 1800-15)	*2000-8500	P
SIEBEL, FRED (20TH C)	*150-750	X (G)
SIEBERT, EDWARD S. (1856 - 1938)	250-2000	L,F
SIEGRIEST, LUNDY (19TH - 20TH C)	*200-1200	X (F)
SIENKIEWICZ, CASIMIRE A. (1890-1974)	100-1500	L,M
SIES, WALTER (19TH C)	400-2500	L,F
SIEVAN, MAURICE (1898 -)	100-900	X (L)
SIGLING, GEORGE ADAM (19TH - 20TH C)	300-1500	F
SILLSBY, CLIFFORD (1896 -)	100-500	X (S)
SILVA, FRANCIS AUGUSTUS	*1500-30000	
SILVA, FRANCIS AUGUSTUS (1835 - 1886)	2500-150000	M,L
SILVA, WILLIAM POSEY (1859 - 1948)	250-6000	L
SIMKHOVITCH, SIMKA (1893 - 1949)	100-2500	F,G,L
SIMMONS, EDWARD EMERSON (1852 - 1931)	750-18000+	G,F,L
SIMON, HOWARD (1902 - 1979)	100-850	I
SIMON, MOLLY (1890-)	100-800	X(G)
SIMPSON, CHARLES (19TH C)	100-600	X (G)
SIMPSON, JAMES ALEXANDER (1775 - 1848)	800-3500	F
SIMROCK, E. (19TH C)	200-3000	G,F
SIMS, F. (19TH C)	300-1800	F,L
SINCLAIR, GERRIT VAN W. (1890 - 1955)	100-1200	L
SINCLAIR, IRVING (20TH C)	100-850	X (M,L)

* Denotes watercolors, pastels, drawings, and/or mixed media

SINDALL, H.S. (19TH C)	400-6000	L
SINGER, CLYDE (1908-)	200-4500	G
SINGER, WILLIAM HENRY (JR) (1868 - 1943)	*500-8500	L
SIPORIN, MITCHELL (1910 -)	*100-900	F,I
SISSON, FREDERICK R. (1893-)	*100-600	L
SISSON, LAWRENCE P. (1928 -)	*250-1800	L,M
SITZMAN, EDWARD R. (1874 -)	100-800	L
SKEELE, HANNAH BROWN (1829 - 1901)	400-1200	F
SKELTON, LESLIE JAMES (1848 - 1929)	300-4500	L
SKIDMORE, THORNTON (1884 -)	600-4500	I,L
SKILLING, WILLIAM (20TH C)	500-3000	X (W)
SKINNER, CHARLES (19TH C)	*200-900	I,F
SKIRVING, JOHN (active 1835-65)	300-1800	M
SKLAR, DOROTHY (20TH C)	*100-800	G,F,L
SKOU, SIGURD	*200-1800	
SKOU, SIGURD (- 1929)	600-4200	A,M,L
SKYNNER, THOMAS (early 19TH C)	2500-60000	P (F)
SLADE, CALEB ARNOLD (1882 - 1961)	250-2500	L,F
SLADE, CONRAD (1871 - 1949)	150-900	X
SLAFTER, THEODORE S. (late 19TH C)	100-700	L
SLAYTON, M.E. (1901-)	300-4000	X(L)
SLOAN, JOHN	*600-7500	
SLOAN, JOHN (1871 - 1951)	700-150000	G,F,I
SLOAN, SAMUEL (1815 - 1884)	*350-3000	F
SLOANE, ERIC (1910 - 1985)	500-15000	L,W,I
SLOANE, MARIAN P. (19TH - 20TH C)	100-2500	L
SLOMAN, JOSEPH (1883 -)	150-750	I
SLOUN, FRANK J. VAN	*100-700	
SLOUN, FRANK J. VAN (1879 - 1938)	500-3500	F,G,L
SLUSSER, JEAN PAUL (1886 -)	500-6500	X (L)
SMALL, ARTHUR (20TH C)	500-4000	M
SMEDLEY, WILL LARYMORE (1871 - 1958)	100-900	X (L,I)
SMEDLEY, WILLIAM THOMAS (1858 - 1920)	350-6500	F,I
SMIBERT, JOHN (1688 - 1751)	2000-35000	F
SMILEY, HOWARD P. (20TH C)	*100-450	L

 * Denotes watercolors, pastels, drawings, and/or mixed media

SMILLIE, GEORGE HENRY	*100-3000	
SMILLIE, GEORGE HENRY (1840 - 1921)	300-15000	L
SMILLIE, HELEN SHELDON J. (1854-1926)	400-2500	X(F,L)
SMILLIE, JAMES (1807 - 1885)	700-3000	F,L
SMILLIE, JAMES DAVID	*250-8500	
SMILLIE, JAMES DAVID (1833 - 1909)	400-8000	L,I
SMITH, ALBERT (1862 - 1940)	100-500	L
SMITH, ALFRED E. (1863 - 1955)	400-16000	L,S,I
SMITH, ANITA MILLER (1893-)	300-2500	L
SMITH, ARCHIBALD CARY (1837 - 1911)	2500-17000	M
SMITH, BISSELL PHELPS (1892 -)	100-800	L
SMITH, CALVIN RAE (1850 - 1918)	600-3500	X (F)
SMITH, CHARLES L.A.	*100-450	
SMITH, CHARLES L.A. (1871 - 1937)	150-1500	L
SMITH, CHARLES WILLIAM (1893 -)	300-1800	I
SMITH, CHARLOTTE H. (20TH C)	100-650	X(L)
SMITH, DAN (1865 - 1934)	*200-1200	I
SMITH, DAVID	*1000-20000	
SMITH, DAVID (1906 - 1965)	10000-750000+	A
SMITH, DE COST (1864-1939)	900-8500+	F,I
SMITH, DUNCAN (1877 - 1934)	100-900	X (F)
SMITH, E. GREGORY (1881 - 1963)	300-3500	L
SMITH, ELLA TANNER (1877-1918)	100-900	L
SMITH, ELMER BOYD (1860 - 1943)	800-21000	F,I
SMITH, ERIK JOHAN (20TH C)	*100-750	L
SMITH, FRANCIS HOPKINSON (1838 - 1915)	*600-20000+	L
SMITH, FRANK HILL (1841 - 1904)	400-2000	F,L
SMITH, FRANK VINING	*400-2000	
SMITH, FRANK VINING (1879 - 1967)	400-6500	M
SMITH, FREDERICK CARL (1868 - 1955)	250-1200	X (F)
SMITH, GEAN (1851 - 1928)	250-3000	W,F,G
SMITH, HARRY KNOX (1879 - 1934)	*100-950	F
SMITH, HASSEL W. (1915 -)	500-5000	A
SMITH, HENRY PEMBER	*200-3500	
SMITH, HENRY PEMBER (1854 - 1907)	400-8500	L,M

SMITH, HENRY S. (early 19TH C)	*400-3000	M
SMITH, HOPE (1879 -)	300-1800	L
SMITH, HOUGHTON C.(19TH - 20TH C)	150-950	L
SMITH, HOWARD EVERETT (1885 - 1970)	350-3500	I,F,L
SMITH, JACK WILKINSON (1873 - 1949)	250-3500+	L,M
SMITH, JEROME HOWARD (1861 - 1941)	100-850	X (L)
SMITH, JESSIE WILCOX (1863 - 1935)	600-20000	I
SMITH, JOHN FRANCIS (1868 - 1941)	250-3000	L,M
SMITH, JOHN RUBENS (1775-1849)	500-6500	L,M,F
SMITH, JOSEPH B. (1798 - 1876)	2500-12000+	M
SMITH, JOSEPH LINDON (1863 - 1950)	150-4500	F,L
SMITH, LANGDON (1870-1959)	*150-850	F,L
SMITH, LEON POLK	*350-3000	
SMITH, LEON POLK (1906 -)	1000-10000	A
SMITH, LETTA CRAPO (1862 - 1921)	400-2500	L,S
SMITH, LILLIAN GERTRUDE (19TH - 20TH C)	*300-1000	L
SMITH, LOWELL ELLSWORTH (1924 -)	*3000-20000	L,F,G
SMITH, MAE (19TH C)	100-800	X(S)
SMITH, MARY (1842 - 1878)	600-12000	W,L,S
SMITH, MORTIMER L. (late 19TH C)	500-15000	L,M
SMITH, OLIVER (1896 -)	*450-2000	X (F)
SMITH, OLIVER PHELPS (1867 - 1953)	*300-2500	L
SMITH, PAUL WILLIAMSON (- 1949)	150-900	L,S
SMITH, ROSAMOND LOMBARD (20TH C)	300-1500	X(F)
SMITH, ROYAL BREWSTER (1801-1855)	4000-20000	P
SMITH, RUFUS WAY (1900 -)	300-1200	L
SMITH, RUSSELL (1812 - 1896)	300-5000	L,M,F
SMITH, THOMAS LOCHLAN (1835 - 1884)	500-4500	G,L
SMITH, WALTER GRANVILLE	*150-3500	
SMITH, WALTER GRANVILLE (1870 - 1938)	350-35000	L,F,I
SMITH, WUANITA (1866 -)	*100-900	I
SMITH, XANTHUS (1839 - 1929)	500-38000	M,L,F
SMITHSON, ROBERT (1938 -1973)	500-2000	A
SMUKLER, BARBARA (20TH C)	*100-650	A
SMUTNY, JOSEPH (1855 - 1903)	300-1200	X (F)

 * Denotes watercolors, pastels, drawings, and/or mixed media

SMYTHE, EUGENE LESLIE (1857 - 1932)	150-2000	L,G
SMYTHE, SAMUEL G. (1891 -)	200-1000	I
SNELGROVE, WALTER (1924 -)	300-2000	A
SNELL, HENRY BAYLEY (1858 - 1943)	400-5000	M,L
SNELL, IDA (19TH C)	400-2500	X (S)
SNIDOW, GORDON	*2500-45000	
SNIDOW, GORDON (1936 -)	10000-55000	G,F
SNOW, EDWARD TAYLOR (1844 - 1913)	800-9500	X (S)
SNOW, P. (19TH C)	100-900	X(S)
SNOWE, FRANK (19TH-20TH C)	100-1000	L
SNYDER, BLADEN TASKER (1864-1923)	150-2500	L
SNYDER, CLARENCE (1873 -)	*100-450	X (L)
SNYDER, JOAN (1940-)	*800-25000	A
SNYDER, WESLEY (20TH C)	*100-500	
SNYDER, WILLIAM HENRY (1829 - 1910)	700-8000	G,L
SOBLE, JOHN JACOB (20TH C)	600-4800	X (L,F)
SODERSTON, LEON (20TH C)	100-850	L
SOELEN, THEODORE VAN (1890 - 1964)	450-6000	L,F
SOGLOW, OTTO (1900 -)	*100-850	X (I)
SOHIER, ALICE RUGGLES (1880 -)	400-7800	F
SOLDIER, ANDREW STANDING (20TH C)	100-600	X (F)
SOLING, PAUL (20TH C)	300-1200	L
SOLMAN, JOSEPH (1909 -)	700-5000	A
SOLOMON, HARRY (1873 -)	350-1200	X (F)
SOLOMON, HYDE (1911 -)	200-2500	A
SOMERBY, LORENZO (early 19TH C)	1200-5000	L
SOMMER, CARL A. (1834 - 1921)	400-3800	L
SOMMER, CHARLES A. (1829 - 1894)	450-3000	L
SOMMER, OTTO (19TH C)	450-3200	W,L
SOMMER, WILLIAM	*150-1500	
SOMMER, WILLIAM (1867 - 1949)	250-6800	L,F
SONN, ALBERT H. (1869 - 1936)	*150-1200	X (F)
SONNTAG, WILLIAM LOUIS (JR.)(1870 -)	*350-4500+	L,F
SONNTAG, WILLIAM LOUIS (SR.)	*500-2800	
SONNTAG, WILLIAM LOUIS (SR.)(1822 - 1900)	1000-25000+	L

* Denotes watercolors, pastels, drawings, and/or mixed media

SOREN, JOHN JOHNSTON (- 1889)	400-4500	M,L
SOULAGES, PIERRE (20TH C)	2500-40000	A
SOULE, CARLETON (1911-)	150-850	M,L
SOULEN, HENRY JAMES (1888 - 1965)	350-3000	I
SOUTER, JOHN B. (19TH - 20TH C)	500-3000	F,L
SOUTHWARD, GEORGE (1803 - 1876)	300-4500	L,S,F
SOYER, ISAAC (20TH C)	300-1800	G,L
SOYER, MOSES	*200-3500	
SOYER, MOSES (1899 - 1974)	500-15000	F
SOYER, RAPHAEL	*500-5000	
SOYER, RAPHAEL (1899 -)	1500-95000+	F
SPACKMAN, CYRIL SAUNDERS (1887 -)	400-3500	X (F)
SPADER, WILLIAM EDGAR (1875 -)	200-1000	F,I
SPAHR, JOHN (20TH C)	150-800	X (L)
SPANG, FREDERICK (1834 - 1891)	100-900	X (F)
SPARHAWK-JONES, ELIZABETH (1885 -)	500-8500	F
SPARKS, ARTHUR WATSON (1870 - 1919)	350-4500	L,F
SPARKS, WILL (1862 - 1937)	350-3500	L,M,F
SPAT, GABRIEL (19TH-20TH C)	700-3500	G,F
SPAULDING, HENRY PLYMPTON (1868-)	*100-750	M,L
SPEAR, ARTHUR PRINCE (1879 - 1959)	400-7500	F,L
SPEAR, THOMAS TRUMAN (1803 - 1882)	300-2000	F
SPEER, WILLIAM W. (1877 -)	100-900	L
SPEICHER, EUGENE EDWARD (1883 - 1962)	600-18000	F,L,S
SPEIGHT, FRANCIS (1896 -)	250-1200	L
SPELMAN, JOHN A. (1880 -)	100-850	L
SPENCER, ASA (1805 -)	100-900	X (L)
SPENCER, FREDERICK R. (1806 - 1875)	300-3200	F,G
SPENCER, HOWARD BONNELL (1888-1967)	400-4000	L,M
SPENCER, JOHN C.(19TH - 20TH C)	500-3500	S,W
SPENCER, LILLY MARTIN (1822 - 1902)	1500-32000+	F,S
SPENCER, MARGARET FULTON (1882 -)	150-900	S
SPENCER, NILES (1893 - 1952)	2000-45000	A
SPENCER, ROBERT S. (1879 - 1931)	600-38000	L,M,G
SPICUZZA, FRANCESCO J.	*100-600	

 * Denotes watercolors, pastels, drawings, and/or mixed media

SPICUZZA, FRANCESCO J. (1883 - 1962)	100-1500	F,M,L,S
SPIEGAL, A. (20TH C)	200-900	X
SPIERS, HARRY	*100-650	
SPIERS, HARRY (1869 - 1934)	250-1500	L,F
SPIRO, EUGENE (1874 - 1972)	200-1500	L
SPRINCHORN, CARL	*150-2500+	
SPRINCHORN, CARL (1887 - 1971)	500-5000	A,L
SPRINGER, CHARLES HENRY (1857 - 1920)	100-800	M
SPRUANCE, BENTON M. (1904 -)	*400-2000	X (L)
SQUINT-EYE, (active 1880-90)	*150-800	X
SQUIRE, E.P. (19TH C)	500-3000	X (L)
SQUIRE, MAUD H. (early 20TH C)	150-800	F,L
SRULL, DONALD (20TH C)	100-500	X
STABLER, ? (1871-1943)	150-650	X (L)
STACEY, ANNA LEE (early 20TH C)	250-2000	L
STACEY, JOHN FRANKLIN (1859-)	100-900	L
STAGER, B. (19TH - 20TH C)	100-600	X (L)
STAHL, BENJAMIN ALBERT (1910 -)	200-7500	I
STAHLEY, JOSEPH (20TH C)	100-600	X (F)
STAHR, PAUL C. (1883 - 1953)	400-6000	I
STAIGER, PAUL (1941 -)	600-5000	A
STAIGG, RICHARD MORRELL (1817 - 1881)	400-3500	G,F,L
STAMOS, THEODOROS	*1000-18000	
STAMOS, THEODOROS (1922 -)	5000-125000	A
STANCLIFF, J.W. (1814 - 1879)	500-5500	M,L
STANCZAK, JULIAN (1928 -)	700-9000	A
STANGE, EMILE (1863-1943)	200-2000	L,F
STANLAWS, PENRHYN (1877 - 1957)	400-8000	I
STANLEY, CHARLES ST.GEORGE (active 1870-80)	*200-800	F
STANLEY, JANE C. (1863-)	*100-700	L
STANLEY, JOHN MIX (1814 - 1872)	2500-40000	F,L
STANLEY, ROBERT (BOB) (1932 -)	400-1000	A
STANTON, GEORGE CURTIN (1885 -)	200-1200	L,F
STANTON, JOHN A. (1857-1929)	150-1200	X(F)
STANWOOD, FRANKLIN (1856 - 1888)	350-3000	L,M,S

* Denotes watercolors, pastels, drawings, and/or mixed media

STAPPEN, BARBARA VAN (20TH C)	100-450	X(L)
STARK, OTTO (1859 - 1926)	500-15000	F,L,I
STARKWEATHER, WILLIAM E. B. (1879 - 1969)	150-900	L,F
STARR, SIDNEY (1857 - 1925)	*250-3000	X (F)
STARRETT, WILLIAM K. (20TH C)	*100-500	I
STAUFFER, E. (20TH C)	100-500	F,L
STEARNS, JUNIUS BRUTUS (1810 - 1885)	1500-30000+	G,F,L
STEBBINS, ROLAND STEWART (1883-1974)	300-2500	X(G)
STEELE, THEODORE CLEMENT (1847 - 1926)	700-18000	L,F
STEELE, THOMAS SEDGWICK (1845-1903)	500-3500	X(S)
STEELE, ZULMA (1881-1979)	200-3000	X(L,M)
STEENE, WILLIAM (1888 - 1965)	200-4000	F
STEENKS, GUY L. (19TH - 20TH C)	200-1800	X (L)
STEFAN, ROSS (20TH C)	600-4500	X (G,F)
STEICHEN, EDWARD J. (1879 - 1973)	1500-35000	L
STEIG, WILLIAM (1907 -)	*100-700	I
STEIN, LEO (19TH - 20TH C)	200-950	L
STEIN, WALTER (1924-)	*100-600	X
STEINBERG, SAUL (1914 -)	*1000-32000+	A
STELLA, FRANK	*2000-475000	
STELLA, FRANK (1936 -)	4800-275000+	A
STELLA, JOSEPH	*600-25000	
STELLA, JOSEPH (1877 - 1946)	2500-50000+	L,S,F
STELLE, MARIAN WILLIAMS (1916-)	250-1500	M
STENGEL, G.L. (1872 - 1937)	200-1200	X (L)
STEPHAN, GARY	*500-4500	
STEPHAN, GARY (1942 -)	1000-18000	A
STEPHENS, ALICE BARBER (1858 - 1932)	*300-4000	I
STEPHENS, ANSON R. (19TH C)	100-600	X
STERN, J. (19TH C)	300-1200	X (G)
STERNE, HEDDA (1916 -)	800-7500	A
STERNE, MAURICE	*300-2500	
STERNE, MAURICE (1878 - 1957)	600-14000	A,L
STERNER, ALBERT EDWARD	*200-5500	
STERNER, ALBERT EDWARD (1863 - 1946)	300-5000	F,S,L,I

* Denotes watercolors, pastels, drawings, and/or mixed media

STERNER, HERALD (20TH C)	300-1500	M
STERRIS, JEROME L. (19TH - 20TH C)	100-700	X (L)
STETSON, CHARLES WALTER (1858 - 1911)	400-6200	F,L,S
STETTHEIMER, FLORINE (1871 - 1944)	*400-1500	X (S)
STEVENS, JOHN CALVIN (1855 -)	250-1200	X (L)
STEVENS, VERA (1867-1950)	150-1200	F
STEVENS, WILLIAM CHARLES (1854 - 1917)	150-1000	L
STEVENS, WILLIAM LESTER	*150-1500	
STEVENS, WILLIAM LESTER (1888 - 1969)	600-7500+	L,M,S
STEVENSON, ALFRED (19TH C)	300-1000	L,F
STEVER, JOSEPHINE (19TH C)	200-1000	X (L)
STEWARD, JOSEPH (1753 - 1822)	5000-40000	P
STEWARD, SETH W. (19TH - 20TH C)	400-4500	L,S
STEWART, JAMES LAWSON	*400-3000	
STEWART, JAMES LAWSON (1855 - 1919)	700-35000	F
STEWART, JEANETTE (1867 -)	250-1200	X (L,F)
STEWART, JULIUS L.	*400-18000	
STEWART, JULIUS L. (1855 - 1919)	1000-38000+	F,G
STEWART, MALCOLM (1829 - 1916)	300-1200	X (F)
STEWART, RON (20TH C)	*200-900	X(L,F)
STICK, FRANK (1884 - 1966)	300-2000	L,G
STICKROTH, HENRY I. (-1922)	100-1000	X(F)
STILL, CLYFFORD (1904 - 1980)	4500-825000	A
STILLMAN, WILLIAM JAMES (1828 - 1901)	150-1200	L
STIMSON, JOHN WARD (1850 - 1930)	200-1200	F,I
STINSON, CHARLES (20TH C)	100-700	X (L)
STITES, JOHN RANDOLPH (1836-)	300-2500	G,L,F
STITT, HERBERT D. (1880 -)	400-3500	X (L)
STIX, MARGUERITE (20TH C)	150-650	X(F)
STOBIE, CHARLES (1854-1926)	400-4500	F,G
STOCK, ERNEST (20TH C)	100-700	X (L)
STOCK, FRANK (20TH C)	300-1000	X
STOCK, JOSEPH WHITING (1815 - 1855)	5000-45000+	P
STODDARD, ALICE KENT (1893 -)	800-10000	F
STODDARD, FREDERICK LINCOLN (1861 - 1940)	350-2500	F,L,I

* Denotes watercolors, pastels, drawings, and/or mixed media

STOKES, FRANK WILBERT (1858 -)	300-2000	X (L)
STOLL, JOHN THEODORE E. (1889 -)	150-1500	F,L,I
STOLTENBERG, HANS J. (1879 -)	100-900	L
STONER, HARRY A. (1880 -)	100-750	I
STOOPS, HERBERT MORTON (1888 - 1948)	500-30000	I
STORER, CHARLES (1817-1907)	300-3000	L,M,S
STORRS, JOHN BRADLEY	*600-4800	
STORRS, JOHN BRADLEY (1887 - 1966)	3500-10000	A
STORY, GEORGE HENRY (1835 - 1923)	1200-18000	F,G
STORY, JULIAN RUSSEL (1857 - 1919)	400-7500	F
STOTT, W.R.S. (20TH C)	400-8000	F,L
STRAIN, DANIEL (active 1865-90)	300-2000	F
STRANG, RAY C. (1893 - 1957)	300-7000	I
STRAUS, F. (19TH C)	300-1500	L
STRAUS, MEYER (1831 - 1905)	500-7500+	L,M
STRAUSS, CARL SUMNER (1873 -)	600-3500	X (L)
STRAYER, PAUL (1885-1981)	300-2500	X(F)
STREATOR, HAROLD A. (1861 - 1926)	400-2000	L
STREET, FRANK (1893 - 1944)	250-2000	I,L,F
STREET, ROBERT (1796 - 1865)	1200-30000	L,F
STRISIK, PAUL (1918 -)	*400-5000	L,M
STROBEL, OSCAR (1891-)	100-900	X (L)
STRONG, ELIZABETH (1855 - 1941)	600-10000	F,L,S
STRONG, JOSEPH D. (1852 - 1900)	400-2500	L,F
STROUD, IDA WEELS (1869-)	*400-2500	M,L
STRUCK, HERMAN (1887 - 1954)	300-1800	X (L,G)
STUART, ALEXANDER CHARLES (1831 - 1898)	400-4500	M
STUART, GILBERT (1755 - 1828)	1500-????+	F
STUART, JAMES EVERETT (1852 - 1941)	300-6500	L
STUART, JANE (1812 - 1888)	1500-4800	F
STUBBS, WILLIAM PIERCE (1842 - 1909)	1000-9500	M,G
STUBER, DEDRICK BRANDES (1878 - 1954)	350-4500	L,M
STUECKMANN, FREDERICK C. (20TH C)	600-2500	X (F)
STUEMPFIG, WALTER (1914 - 1970)	300-10000	L,S,M,F
STULL, HENRY (1851 - 1913)	500-15000+	W

 * Denotes watercolors, pastels, drawings, and/or mixed media

STURGIS, KATHERINE (1904 -)	150-1500	X (F)
STURTEVANT, HELENA (1872 - 1946)	100-1000	L,M
SULLIVAN, DENIS (19TH C)	*100-600	X (G)
SULLIVAN, EDMUND J. (20TH C)	*100-650	I
SULLIVANT, THOMAS STARLING (1854 - 1926)	*100-500	I
SULLY, ALFRED (1820 - 1879)	400-3800	F
SULLY, JANE COOPER (1807 - 1877)	350-1500	X (F)
SULLY, THOMAS	*800-18000	
SULLY, THOMAS (1783 - 1872)	1000-60000	F
SUMMERS, IVAN (-1964)	100-900	L
SUNDBLOM, HADDON HUBBARD (1899 - 1976)	600-14000	I
SUPLIN, ANN (19TH C)	150-850	P
SURBER, PAUL (20TH C)	*200-900	X(L,F)
SURENDORF, CHARLES FREDERICK (1906-)	*100-500	L,F,G
SUTER, E.V. (19TH - 20TH C)	*100-700	X (F)
SUTTER, SAMUEL (1888-)	100-850	L
SUTTERLIN, CHARLES (20TH C)	100-700	L
SUTTON (JR), HARRY (1897-1984)	300-4000	L,F,S
SUTZ, ROBERT	*300-2500	
SUTZ, ROBERT (19TH - 20TH C)	1000-8500	F
SUYDAM, HENRY (1817 - 1865)	800-3500	L
SUYDAM, JAMES AUGUSTUS (1819 - 1865)	2000-10000	L,M
SUZUKI, JAMES HIROSHI (1933 -)	500-3500	A
SVENDSEN, SVEND (1864 - 1934)	200-3000	L,F
SVOBODA, VINCENT A. (1877 - 1961)	*100-700	X (L,F)
SWAIN, C. (19TH - 20TH C)	*100-700	L,G
SWAN, EMMA LEVINIA (1853-1927)	100-1200	X(S)
SWAN, S.W. (19TH-20TH C)	*150-850	X(L)
SWANSON, GLORIA (1899 - 1983)	200-1200	L,F,S
SWANSON, JACK (1927 -)	400-3500	G,F
SWANSON, RAY (1937 -)	4500-30000	F,G
SWEENEY, S.C. (1876 -)	100-800	X (M)
SWEET, CHARLES A. (20TH C)	300-1500	X (L)
SWEET, F.H. (active 1880 - 1895)	100-600	X (L)
SWEET, GEORGE (1876 -)	300-1200	G,L

* Denotes watercolors, pastels, drawings, and/or mixed media

SWERINGEN, RON VAN (20TH C)	300-1800	F,G,L
SWETT, WILLIAM OTIS (JR) (1859 - 1939)	100-900	L,W
SWIFT, CLEMENT N. (19TH C)	300-3500	G,L
SWIFT, IVAN (1873 - 1945)	200-1200	L
SWINNERTON, JAMES GUILFORD (1875 - 1974)	400-10000	L
SWOPE, DAVID (18TH C)	*500-3500	F
SWOPE, KATE F. (19TH - 20TH C)	250-1500	X (L)
SWORD, JAMES BRADE (1839 - 1915)	600-18000	G,L,M,F
SWORDS, CRAMER (20TH C)	100-800	X (S)
SYARTO, RON (20TH C)	100-700	X
SYKES, ANNIE G. (20TH C)	*100-600	X (S)
SYLVESTER, FREDERICK OAKES (1869 - 1915)	300-3500	L
SYLVESTER, H. M. (19TH - 20TH C)	100-800	L,M
SYLVESTER, HARRY ELLIOTT (1860-1921)	100-900	L
SYMONS, GEORGE GARDNER (1863 - 1930)	500-42000	L
SYNDER, BLADEN TASKER (1864-1923)	150-3500	F,L
SZANTO, A. KAROLY L. (20TH C)	*300-1500	X (G)
SZYK, ARTHUR (1894 - 1951)	*500-4500	I

T

ARTIST	PRICE	SUBJECT
TABER, W. (19TH - 20TH C)	100-700	X (F,I)
TACK, AUGUSTUS VINCENT (1870 - 1949)	4000-220000	A,F
TAGGART, JOHN G. (active 1845-65)	150-1000	X (F)
TAHY, JANOS DE (1865 - 1928)	100-800	X (F)
TAIT, ARTHUR FITZWILLIAM (1819 - 1905)	1500-250000 +	F,G,W
TAL, ADAM (20TH C)	*200-1200	L,W
TALBOT, JESSE (1806 - 1879)	600-18000	F,L
TALCOTT, ALLEN BUTLER (1867 - 1908)	300-3000	X(L)
TALLANT, RICHARD H. (1853 - 1934)	300-2500	L
TANAKA, YASUSHI (1886 -)	400-3500	F,G,S
TANBERG, LILLIAN F. (20TH C)	100-700	X

 * Denotes watercolors, pastels, drawings, and/or mixed media

TANGUY, YVES	*600-50000	
TANGUY, YVES (1900 - 1955)	5000-300000	A
TANNER, HENRY OSSAWA (1859 - 1937)	2000-30000+	G,L,F,W
TANNING, DOROTHEA	*250-2500	
TANNING, DOROTHEA (1912 -)	1000-18000	A
TANT, CHARLES DU (20TH C)	300-2000	X (F)
TARBELL, EDMUND CHARLES	*250-6500	
TARBELL, EDMUND CHARLES (1862 - 1938)	4000-350000	F,G,S
TAUBES, FREDERICK (1900 - 1981)	350-3200	F,L,S
TAUSZKY, DAVID ANTHONY (1878 -)	300-1500	F
TAVE, DO (19TH - 20TH C)	300-1500	X (F)
TAVERNIER, JULES (1844 - 1899)	800-20000	L,S
TAYLOR, ANNA HEYWARD (1879 -)	*100-600	X (F)
TAYLOR, BERTHA FANNING (1883-)	*150-1200	F
TAYLOR, CHARLES JAY (1855 - 1929)	250-1800	I
TAYLOR, E. (19TH C)	100-700	L
TAYLOR, EDGAR J. (1862 -)	100-1000	I
TAYLOR, FAREWELL M. (20TH C)	*100-450	L
TAYLOR, FRANK H. (19TH - 20TH C)	*100-1800	L
TAYLOR, HENRY FITCH (1853 - 1925)	400-4000	X (L)
TAYLOR, JAY C. (19TH C)	100-750	L
TAYLOR, JOHN W. (1897-)	*100-600	L
TAYLOR, M.A. (early 19TH C)	500-3500	G,L
TAYLOR, RALPH (1896-)	1000-18000	F
TAYLOR, WALTER (20TH C)	*100-700	F
TAYLOR, WILLIAM FRANCIS (1883 - 1934)	300-1500	X (L,I)
TAYLOR, WILLIAM LADD (1854 - 1926)	*150-1800	I,M,L
TCHACBASOC, NAHUM (20TH C)	200-1000	X (F)
TCHELITCHEW, PAVEL	*200-20000	
TCHELITCHEW, PAVEL (1898 - 1957)	400-15000	A
TEAGUE, DONALD (1897 -)	*500-40000	I,F,L
TEATER, ARCHIE B. (20TH C)	100-650	X (L,G)
TEED, DOUGLAS ARTHUR (1864 - 1929)	250-4500	F,G,L,S
TEICHMAN, SABINA (1905 -)	300-5000	X (F)
TEPPER, SAUL (1899 -)	*200-1200	X (I)

* Denotes watercolors, pastels, drawings, and/or mixed media

TERAOKA, MASAMI (20TH C)	100-1000	X (L,F)
TERELAK, JOHN (20TH C)	400-3500	M
TERPNING, HOWARD A. (1927 -)	15000-150000	F,I
TERRY, JOSEPH ALFRED (1872-)	200-1800	G,L,S
TESAR, JOSEPH (19TH-20TH C)	200-1800	X(M)
TESTAGUZZA, GINO (20TH C)	100-700	X (F)
THAL, SAM	*100-600	
THAL, SAM (20TH C)	300-1000	X (F,M)
THALINGER, E. OSCAR (1885 -)	100-1200	L,M,S
THATCHER, EARL (19TH - 20TH C)	*100-500	X (F)
THAYER, ABBOTT HANDERSON (1849 - 1921)	500-12000	F,L,W
THAYER, ALBERT R. (19TH - 20TH C)	300-2500	L,F
THAYER, SANFORD (20TH C)	300-3000	X (L,F)
THAYER, W.G. (19TH-20TH C)	100-500	X
THEIL, E. DU (20TH C)	100-300	X (L)
THEIME, ANTHONY	*300-2500	
THEIME, ANTHONY (1888 - 1954)	600-12000	M,L
THEOBALD, ELISABETH STUTEVANT (1876-)	100-850	L
THEOBALD, SAMUEL (JR) (19HT - 20TH C)	300-1200	X (L)
THERIAT, CHARLES JAMES (1860 -)	400-3000	X (F)
THEUS, JEREMIAH (1719 - 1774)	2000-18000	P
THEVENAZ, PAUL (20TH C)	*100-600	X (S,F)
THIEBAUD, WAYNE	*1500-60000	
THIEBAUD, WAYNE (1920 -)	5000-150000	A
THOM, JAMES CRAWFORD (1835 - 1898)	450-6000	G,F,L
THOMAS, A. (19TH - 20TH C)	400-3500	X (L)
THOMAS, ALICE BLAIR (20TH C)	100-850	X(L)
THOMAS, BYRON (1902 -)	400-2000	X (L)
THOMAS, CHARLES H. (19TH C)	*800-7000	M,F
THOMAS, DANIEL (19TH C)	*100-450	M
THOMAS, GROSVENOR (20TH C)	100-600	L,F
THOMAS, PAUL K.M. (1875-)	150-1000	L
THOMAS, REYNOLDS (20TH C)	*100-600	X(F)
THOMAS, RICHARD D. (20TH C)	100-850	G,L
THOMAS, STEPHEN SEYMOUR (1868 - 1956)	300-3000	F,L

 * Denotes watercolors, pastels, drawings, and/or mixed media

THOMASON, FRED T. (20TH C)	200-1000	X (G)
THOMPSON, (ALFRED)WORDSWORTH (19TH C)	400-30000	M,G,F,L
THOMPSON, BOB	*400-2500	
THOMPSON, BOB (1937 - 1966)	1200-18000	A
THOMPSON, C.A. (19TH C)	700-6000	G,L
THOMPSON, CEPHAS GIOVANNI (1809 - 1888)	200-8500	G,F,L
THOMPSON, CHARLES A. (active 1850-60)	250-950	X (L,G)
THOMPSON, ELISE (19TH C)	100-750	X(G)
THOMPSON, ELOISE REID (20TH C)	*100-650	X (S)
THOMPSON, FREDERICK LOUIS (1868 -)	200-1800	M,L
THOMPSON, GEORGE ALBERT	*100-650	
THOMPSON, GEORGE ALBERT (1868 - 1938)	300-5500	L,M
THOMPSON, HARRY IVES (1840 -1906)	800-4500	F,L
THOMPSON, J. HARRY (19TH - 20TH C)	100-650	X (L)
THOMPSON, JEROME B. (1814 - 1886)	1500-70000	L,G,F
THOMPSON, LESLIE P. (1880-1963)	500-12000+	F,L,S
THOMPSON, RODNEY (1878 -)	*100-450	I
THOMPSON, WALTER W. (1881 - 1948)	200-1800	L
THOMPSON, WILLIAM JOHN (1771-1845)	500-8000	G,F
THOMPSON-PRITCHARD, E. (20TH C)	150-850	X (L)
THOMSON, TOM (1877 - 1917)	1000-32000	L,W
THON, WILLIAM	*100-750	
THON, WILLIAM (1906 -)	350-1800	L
THONY, EDUARD (1866 - 1950)	*300-1500	G,F,L
THONY, GUSTAV (1888 - 1949)	1000-8500	L
THORN, JAMES CRAWFORD (1835 - 1898)	350-1500	F,L
THORNE, ANNA LOUISE (1878 -)	*100-750	X (F)
THORNE, DIANA (1895 -)	250-1000	X (W)
THORNE, S.A. (early 19TH C)	*600-2000	L
THORTON, CHARLES H. (19TH C)	100-850	L
THOURON, HENRY J. (1851 - 1915)	600-6500	X (G)
THRASHER, LESLIE (1889-1936)	100-1500	F,I
THULSTRUP, THURE DE	*250-1800	
THULSTRUP, THURE DE (1849 - 1930)	700-6000	F.M.I
THURBER, JAMES (1894 - 1961)	*200-3500	X (I)

* Denotes watercolors, pastels, drawings, and/or mixed media

THURN, ERNEST (1889 -)	100-800	X (S)
THURSTON, JOHN K. (1865 - 1955)	*100-800	M
TICE, CHARLES WINFIELD (1810 - 1870)	1000-6500	L,F,S
TIETJANS, M.H. (20TH C)	150-900	X (F)
TIFFANY, LOUIS COMFORT	*800-7500	
TIFFANY, LOUIS COMFORT (1848 - 1933)	700-18000	F,L,M
TILTON, JOHN ROLLIN (1828 - 1888)	300-2500	L
TILYARD, PHILLIP (1785 - 1827)	500-2000	F
TIMMINS, HARRY LAVERNE (1887 - 1963)	200-1500	I
TIMMONS, EDWARD J. FINLEY (1882 -)	200-1000	L
TINDALL, KARL (1892 -)	*100-500	L
TING, WALASSE	*300-2000	
TING, WALASSE (1929 -)	600-5000	A
TINGLEY, FRANK FOSTER (20TH C)	*200-850	X
TINSLEY, F. (19TH - 20TH C)	100-600	X (F)
TIRELL, PAUL (20TH C)	200-800	F,L
TIRRELL, G. (19TH C)	2000-8500	M
TITCOMB, MARY BRADISH (1856 - 1927)	1000-18000	F,I
TITCOMBE, WILLIAM HENRY (1824 - 1888)	400-3000	L,F
TITLE, CHRISTIAN (20TH C)	100-950	X(L)
TITLOW, HARRIET WOODFIN (20TH C)	300-1500	X (F)
TITTLE, WALTER ERNEST (1883 - 1960)	*150-700	L,F,I
TOBEY, ALTON (20TH C)	*100-500	X
TOBEY, MARK	*300-18000	
TOBEY, MARK (1890 - 1976)	900-50000	A,F
TODD, CHARLES S. (1885 -)	*400-1000	X (W)
TODD, HENRY STANLEY (1871 -)	150-750	F
TOFT, P. (19TH C)	*150-850	L
TOJETTI, DOMENICO (1806-1892)	400-2500+	F
TOJETTI, EDUARDO (1852-1930)	100-800	W,F
TOJETTI, EDWARD (19TH C)	100-800	X (F)
TOJETTI, M. (19TH C)	100-700	X (F)
TOJETTI, VIRGILIO (1851 - 1901)	300-8500	F
TOLEGIAN, MANUEL J. (20TH C)	200-1200	F,L
TOLMAN, STACY (1860 - 1935)	200-4500	L,M

 * Denotes watercolors, pastels, drawings, and/or mixed media

TOMANECK, J. (19TH - 20TH C)	100-1000	F
TOMLIN, BRADLEY WALKER	*500-15000	
TOMLIN, BRADLEY WALKER (1899 - 1953)	2500-75000	A,I
TOMPKINS, FRANK HECTOR (1847 - 1922)	600-10000+	F
TONEY, ANTHONY (1913 -)	100-750	X
TONK, ERNEST (1889 -)	850-6500	X (G)
TOOKER, GEORGE	*3000-8000	
TOOKER, GEORGE (1920 -)	10000-85000	G,F
TOPCHEVSKY, MORRIS (1899-1947)	150-2000	L
TOPPAN, CHARLES (1796 - 1874)	200-900	X
TOPPING, JAMES (1879-1949)	150-5000	L
TORAN, ALPHONSE T. (1898-)	100-800	X(S,F)
TORLAKSON, JIM	*200-2800	
TORLAKSON, JIM (20TH C)	400-4500	X
TORREY, ELLIOT BOUTON (1867 - 1949)	300-2500	F,G,L
TORREY, GEORGE BURROUGHS (1863 - 1942)	100-1200	M,F
TOSSEY, VERNE (20TH C)	200-1000	I
TOUSSAINT, RAYMOND (1875 - 1939)	*100-400	X (F)
TOWNSEND, ERNEST (1893 - 1945)	350-5000	F,L,I
TOWNSEND, HARRY EVERETT (1879 - 1941)	250-2500	I
TOWNSEND, LEE (1895 -)	100-750	G,F
TOWNSHEND, A.A. (19TH C)	*100-400	X(S)
TOWNSHEND, H.R. (early 20TH C)	100-500	X (L)
TOWNSLEY, CHANNEL PICKERING (1867 - 1921)	1000-7500	L,F
TRACY, CHARLES (1881 - 1955)	*100-700	X
TRACY, JOHN M. (1844 - 1893)	700-8500+	G,W
TRATMAN, ROBERT (20TH C)	100-900	X(F,L)
TRAVER, GEORGE A.	*200-1500	
TRAVER, GEORGE A. (1864 - 1928)	350-4000	M,L,G
TRAVER, MARION GRAY (1892-)	100-1000	L
TRAVIS, PAUL BOUGH	*250-2000	
TRAVIS, PAUL BOUGH (1891 - 1975)	300-3500	A
TREAT, ASA (19TH C)	700-3000	X (S)
TREBILCOCK, PAUL (1902 -)	200-4000	F
TREDUPP, CHARLES (19TH - 20TH C)	100-700	M

TREDUPP, G. (19TH C)	200-1000	X(M)
TREIDLER, ADOLPH (1886 - 1981)	*100-850	I
TRENHOLM, WILLIAM CARPENTER (1856-1931)	500-5000	M
TRENT, VICTOR PEDRETTI (1891 -)	100-850	L
TREVILLE, DE (20TH C)	100-500	X (L)
TRIBE, GEORGE T. (19TH - 20TH C)	100-600	X (L)
TRIESTE, JOANSOVITCH (19TH C)	400-2500	M
TRIGGS, JAMES M. (20TH C)	100-400	M
TRISCOTT, SAMUEL PETER ROLT (1846 - 1925)	*150-1500	M,L
TROCCOLI, GIOVANNI B. (1882-1940)	400-5000	F
TRONE, NETTIE (20TH C)	100-400	X(L)
TROTT, BENJAMIN (1770-1843)	400-3500	F
TROTTER, NEWBOLD HOUGH (1827 - 1898)	350-7000+	W,L
TROUBETZKOY, PIERRE (1864 -)	300-1200	F
TROUSSER, L. (19TH C)	*500-3000	X
TROVA, ERNEST	*600-3000	
TROVA, ERNEST (1927 -)	1200-22000	A
TROYE, EDWARD (1808 - 1874)	2500-60000	W
TRUE, DOROTHY (20TH C)	400-2000	X(A)
TRUESDELL, GAYLORD S.(1850 - 1899)	200-2500	W,F,L
TRUEX, VAN DAY (20TH C)	*100-500	L
TRUITT, ANNE (1921 -)	600-5000	A
TRUMBULL, EDWARD (early 20TH C)	*150-700	X (I)
TRUMBULL, JOHN (1756 - 1843)	2500-100000+	F,L
TRYON, DWIGHT WILLIAM (1849 - 1925)	500-35000	L
TSCHACBASOV, NAHUM (1899 -)	100-900	X (F)
TSCHADY, HERBERT BOLIVAR (1874 - 1946)	100-1500	L,F,I
TSCHUDI, RUDOLF (1855 - 1923)	300-1500	X (F,G)
TUBBY, J.T. (20TH C)	*150-850	X
TUCKER, A.P. (19TH-20TH C)	*100-500	M
TUCKER, ALLEN (1866 - 1939)	600-12000	L,F
TUCKER, MARY B. (active 1838-48)	*700-6000	P(F)
TUDOR, ROBERT M. (19TH C)	800-6500+	G,F
TUPPER, ALEXANDER GARFIELD (1885 -)	100-900	L,M
TURNBULL, GRACE H. (1880 - 1976)	200-1000	L,F,S

 * Denotes watercolors, pastels, drawings, and/or mixed media

TURNBULL, JAMES B. (1909 - 1976)	400-3000	X (F)
TURNER, A.L. (19TH C)	100-700	X (L,M)
TURNER, CHARLES YARDLEY (1850 - 1918)	500-9500	G,F,L
TURNER, HARRIET FRENCH (1886 - 1967)	100-400	X
TURNER, HELEN MARIA (1858 - 1958)	700-8500	F,L
TURNER, ROSS STERLING (1847 - 1915)	*200-2000	M,L
TURNEY, WINTHROP D. (1884 -)	100-850	X
TUTTLE, RICHARD (1941 -)	*700-25000	A
TWACHTMAN, JOHN HENRY	*300-20000	
TWACHTMAN, JOHN HENRY (1853 - 1902)	5000-190000+	L
TWACHTMAN, JULIAN ALDEN (1935 -)	200-900	X (L)
TWARDOWICZ, STANLEY (1917 -)	300-1200	A
TWINING, YVONNE (1907-)	400-3200	L,G,F
TWOHY, JULIUS (20TH C)	100-500	X (F)
TWOMBLY, CY	*4500-185000	
TWOMBLY, CY (1929 -)	2500-200000	A
TWORKOV, JACK	*500-14000	
TWORKOV, JACK (1900 -)	5000-50000	A
TYLER, BAYARD HENRY (1855 - 1931)	300-6500	L,F
TYLER, HATTIE (20TH C)	150-950	X (W)
TYLER, JAMES GALE (1855 - 1931)	500-25000+	M,I
TYNG, GRISWOLD (1883 -)	100-800	X (I)
TYSON, CARROLL SARGENT (JR) (1878 - 1956)	300-5000	L

U

ARTIST	PRICE	SUBJECT
UFER, WALTER (1876 - 1936)	1000-375000	F,L
UHL, S. JEROME (1842 - 1916)	250-2500	L,F
UHLE, BERNHARD (1847 - 1930)	100-900	F
ULLMAN, EUGENE PAUL (1877 - 1953)	200-5000	F,L,M
ULLMAN, PAUL (1906-1944)	200-1500	X(L)
ULREICH, EDUARD (20TH C)	100-800	X

ULRICH, CHARLES FREDERIC (1858 - 1908)	2500-250000	F,L
UPJOHN, ANNA MILO (20TH C)	*100-500	F
URBAN, JOSEPH (1872 - 1933)	*200-2500	I
URSULESCU, MIHAI (1913 -)	100-900	X (F)
URWICK, WALTER C. (1864 -)	400-3000	F,L
USHER, RUBY W. (20TH C)	*100-450	X (F)
UTZ, THORNTON (1914 -)	300-3500	I

V

ARTIST	PRICE	SUBJECT
VAGO, SANDOR (1887-)	100-2500	F,L
VAIL, EUGENE LAURENT (1857 - 1934)	300-4000+	M,F
VALENCIA, MANUEL (1856 - 1935)	200-3000	L
VALENCIA, RAMONA (20TH C)	200-1200	X (L)
VALENKAMPH, THEODORE V.C.(1868-1924)	300-3500	M,L
VALENSTEIN, ALICE (1904-)	*100-600	X(L)
VALENTINE, ALBERT R. (1862 - 1925)	100-900	F,S
VALLEE, JEAN FRANCOIS DE (18TH - 19TH C)	2000-6500	F
VAN BEEST, ALBERT (1820 - 1860)	800-7500+	M
VAN BUREN, RAEBURN (1891 -)	*100-750	I
VAN ELTEN, HENDRICK D.K. (1829 - 1904)	500-11000	L
VAN INGEN, HENRY A. (1833 - 1898)	500-4800	L,W
VAN LAER, ALEXANDER T.	*150-1000	
VAN LAER, ALEXANDER T. (1857 - 1920)	300-2500	L,M
VAN MILLETT, GEORGE (1864-)	100-2500	F,G
VAN SCRIVEN, PEARL A. (1896 -)	100-850	X (S)
VAN SOELEN, THEODORE (1890 - 1964)	450-6500	L,F
VAN STAPPEN, BARBARA (20TH C)	100-500	X (L)
VAN VEEN, PIETER J.L. (1875 - 1961)	350-7000	F,L
VANARDEN, GEORGE (19TH C)	300-2500	X(W)
VARADY, FREDERIC (1908 -)	*100-750	I
VARGAS, ALBERTO (1896-)	4000-18000	I

 * Denotes watercolors, pastels, drawings, and/or mixed media

VARIAN, GEORGE EDMUND (1865 - 1923)	300-2000	I,F
VARRIALE, W. STELLA (1927-)	500-3000	X
VASILIEF, NICHOLAS IVANOVITCH (1892-1970)	200-3000	F,M,S
VAUGHAN, CHARLES A. (active 1845-60)	200-800	F
VAWTER, JOHN WILLIAM (1871 -)	100-900	L,I
VEDDER, ELIHU	*200-3500	
VEDDER, ELIHU (1836 - 1923)	600-35000	F,I
VEEN, PIETER J.L. VAN (1875 - 1961)	350-7000	F,L
VEENFLIET, RICHARD (19TH C)	*100-800	X(L,G)
VEER, MARY VAN DE (1865-)	*150-900	F,S
VER BECK, FRANK (1858 - 1933)	*200-1200	I
VERNER, ELIZABETH O'NEILL (1884 -)	*250-5000	X (F)
VERNON, ARTHUE G. (-1919)	*100-500	L
VERNON, W.H. (19TH C)	*100-500	X(W,L)
VETTER, CORNELIA COWLES (1881 -)	100-300	X (L,S)
VEZIN, CHARLES (1858 - 1942)	500-6500	L
VEZIN, FREDERICK (1859 -)	300-2000	X
VIANDEN, HEINRICH (1814 - 1899)	300-2000	L
VIAVANT, GEORGE L. (1872 - 1925)	*400-4000	W
VICENTE, ESTEBAN	*1000-5000	
VICENTE, ESTEBAN (1904 -)	1500-25000	A
VICKERY, ROBERT REMSEN (1926 -)	1000-18000	F
VIGIL, VELOY (20TH C)	400-3000	X (F)
VIGNARI, JOHN T. (20TH C)	100-600	X (M)
VILLA, HERNANDO GONZALLO (1881 - 1952)	200-3000	F,L
VILLA, THEODORE B. (20TH C)	*500-4500	X
VILLACRES, CESAR A. (20TH C)	1000-5500	F,L
VINCENT, HARRY AIKEN	*250-1800	
VINCENT, HARRY AIKEN (1864 - 1931)	250-9200	M,L,F
VINGOE, FRANK (19TH C)	100-700	L
VINTON, FREDERIC PORTER (1846 - 1911)	500-5000	L,F
VIVIAN, CALTHEA (20TH C)	100-500	X
VOELCKER, RUDOLPH A. (1873 -)	200-1000	X (L)
VOGT, ADOLF (1843 - 1871)	200-2500	L,F
VOGT, FRITZ G. (1842 - 1900)	*1200-8500	P

* Denotes watercolors, pastels, drawings, and/or mixed media

VOGT, LOUIS CHARLES	*100-1000+	
VOGT, LOUIS CHARLES (1864 -)	400-5000	L,M
VOLK, DOUGLAS (1856 - 1935)	400-9000	L,F
VOLKERT, EDWARD CHARLES (1871 - 1935)	500-5000	G,F,W
VOLKMAR, CHARLES (1809 - 1890/95)	250-3000	L,F
VOLL, F. USHER DE (1873-1941)	*100-800	L,F
VOLLMER, GRACE L. (1884 - 1977)	150-1200	X (S)
VOLLMERING, JOSEPH (1810-1887)	1000-18000	L
VON PERBANDT, CARL (1832 - 1911)	400-4500	L
VON SCHMIDT, HAROLD (1893 - 1982)	900-50000	I,G
VONDROUS, JOHN C. (1884 -)	100-900	X (I)
VONNOH, ROBERT WILLIAM (1858 - 1933)	1500-45000	L,F
VOORHEES, CLARK GREENWOOD (1871 - 1933)	400-3500	L
VOS, HUBERT	*300-1800	
VOS, HUBERT (1855 - 1935)	400-3500	S,F
VOS, IZAAK DE (20TH C)	100-600	L
VREELAND, ANDERSON (19TH - 20TH C)	300-2000	X (M)
VREELAND, FRANCIS VAN (1879 -)	*200-800	F,L
VREY, TOM (19TH C)	100-700	X(G)
VUKOVIC, MARKO (20TH C)	200-1000	X (S)
VYTLACIL, VACLAV	*300-1800	
VYTLACIL, VACLAV (1892 -)	700-5000	A,L

W

ARTIST	PRICE	SUBJECT
WACHTEL, ELMER (1864 - 1929)	500-5000	L
WACHTEL, MARION K.	*600-6400	
WACHTEL, MARION K. (1875 - 1954)	500-5000	F,L
WADE, C.T. (20TH C)	100-700	X (M)
WADHAM, W. JOSEPH (20TH C)	*150-900	L
WADLER, R.C. (20TH C)	150-700	L
WADSWORTH, ADELAIDE E. (1844 - 1928)	100-900	L,M

 * Denotes watercolors, pastels, drawings, and/or mixed media

WADSWORTH, FRANK RUSSELL (1874 - 1905)	300-2500	L,F
WADSWORTH, WEDWORTH (1846 - 1927)	*100-850	L,I
WAGNER, A.P. (20TH C)	100-600	L
WAGNER, BLANCHE COLLET (1873 - 1958)	300-1200	
WAGNER, EDWARD (19TH - 20TH C)	200-1200	X (L)
WAGNER, FRED	*100-800	
WAGNER, FRED (1864 - 1940)	250-5500	L
WAGNER, JACOB (1852 - 1898)	400-3000	L,F
WAGNER, JOSEF DE (20TH C)	100-500	X (F)
WAGONER, HARRY B. (1889 - 1950)	200-3500	L
WAGUE, J.R. (19TH C)	100-700	X (L)
WAITE, A.A. (19TH C)	150-850	X (F)
WAITE, EMILY BURLING (1887 -)	600-4500	
WAITT, MARION MARTHA P.(19TH C)	300-1500	L
WALDEGG, T. (20TH C)	100-700	L
WALDEN, LIONEL (1861 - 1933)	500-5000	M,G
WALDMAN, PAUL (1936 -)	600-5000	A
WALDO, HOWARD (19TH C)	*100-450	M,L
WALDO, J. FRANK (active 1870-80)	300-1200	L
WALDO, SAMUEL LOVETT (1783 - 1861)	400-5500+	F,M
WALES, GEORGE CANNING (1868 -)	*100-800	X (M)
WALES, J. (19TH C)	400-4500	X
WALES, NATHANIEL F. (active 1800-15)	2000-8500	F
WALES, ORLANDO G. (1865-1933)	300-2000	X(S)
WALES, SUSAN MAKEPIECE LARKIN (1839-1927)	*100-600	L,M
WALKER, CHARLES ALVAH (1848 - 1920)	300-3500	L
WALKER, DUGALD S. (1865 - 1937)	*100-800	I
WALKER, FRANCIS S. (1872 - 1916)	400-2500	L
WALKER, HAROLD (1890 -)	100-900	L
WALKER, HENRY OLIVER (1843 - 1929)	250-3000	F,L
WALKER, INEZ NATHANIEL (1911 -)	*400-1500	P
WALKER, J. EDWARD (20TH C)	100-850	L
WALKER, JAMES (1819 - 1889)	2000-35000	G,F,L
WALKER, JAMES S. (early 20TH C)	*100-300	L
WALKER, JESSE JENKINS (19TH C)	100-800	L

* Denotes watercolors, pastels, drawings, and/or mixed media

WALKER, WILLIAM AIKEN	*500-5000	
WALKER, WILLIAM AIKEN (1838 - 1921)	1500-60000	G,F,M,S
WALKLEY, DAVID BIRDSEY (1849 - 1934)	300-2800+	F,L
WALKOWITZ, ABRAHAM	*250-1500	
WALKOWITZ, ABRAHAM (1878 - 1965)	400-5500	A,F
WALL, A. BRYAN (1872 - 1937)	300-2000	X (F)
WALL, ALFRED S. (1809 - 1896)	350-4000+	L
WALL, HERMAN C. (1875 -)	300-1500	X (F)
WALL, WILLIAM ALLEN	*200-2800+	
WALL, WILLIAM ALLEN (1801 - 1885)	400-3000	F,L,M
WALL, WILLIAM ARCHIBALD (1828 - 1875)	300-1500	F,L
WALL, WILLIAM GUY (1792 - 1864)	600-18000	L
WALLACE, LILLIE T. (20TH C)	300-1500	X (M,L)
WALLER, FRANK (1842 - 1923)	200-5000	F,L,M
WALLINGER, CECIL A. (19TH C)	100-300	X (L)
WALLIS, FRANK (- 1934)	300-1000	X (L)
WALROND, E.M. (20TH C)	100-1000	L
WALSON, BONNIE (20TH C)	100-600	X(F)
WALTENSPERGER, CHARLES E. (1871 - 1931)	150-850	X (F)
WALTER, CHRISTIAN J. (1872 - 1938)	300-5000	L
WALTER, L. (19TH C)	300-1500	X (M)
WALTER, MARTHA (1875 - 1976)	600-30000	F,L
WALTER, WILLIAM FRANCIS (1904-)	100-800	L
WALTERS, EMILE (1893 -)	400-5000	L
WALTERS, H. (19TH C)	100-600	X (L)
WALTERS, JOSEPHINE (- 1883)	500-3000	L
WALTERS, RAY (20TH C)	100-500	L
WALTHER, CHARLES H. (1879-1938)	150-1800	L
WALTMAN, HARRY FRANKLIN (1871 - 1951)	200-1800	F,L
WALTON, HENRY (1804-1865)	*1500-10000	P
WALTON, WILLIAM (1843 - 1915)	200-1000	X (S)
WANDESFORDE, JAMES B. (1817 - 1872)	500-4800	G,L,F,I
WANSTREET, C. (20TH C)	100-500	M,L
WARD, CHARLES (1900 -)	200-1200	X (L)
WARD, CHARLES CALEB	*1000-7500	

 * Denotes watercolors, pastels, drawings, and/or mixed media

WARD, CHARLES CALEB (1831 - 1896)	1500-30000	G,F,L
WARD, EDGAR MELVILLE (1839 - 1915)	400-7500	G,L
WARD, EDMUND F. (1892 -)	800-6500	I
WARD, ELLEN (19TH C)	100-900	X (L)
WARD, H.M. (20TH C)	100-700	X(L)
WARE, THOMAS (19TH C)	800-3000	P
WARHOL, ANDY	*1000-100000	
WARHOL, ANDY (1928 -)	5000-300000 +	A
WARNER, EARL A. (1883-)	*100-500	M,L
WARNER, EVERETT LONGLEY (1877 - 1963)	200-4500	L,F
WARNER, NELL WALKER (1891-1970)	200-3500	M,S
WARREN, A. COOLIDGE (1819-1904)	400-2500	S
WARREN, ALONZO (19TH-20TH C)	200-1000	X(L)
WARREN, ANDREW W. (- 1873)	600-10000	M,L
WARREN, CONSTANCE WHITNEY (1888 - 1948)	*100-700	F
WARREN, EMILY (19TH C)	100-600	X(M,L)
WARREN, HAROLD BROADFIELD (1859 - 1934)	*100-700	L,M,F
WARREN, J. C. (19TH C)	300-1200	X (W)
WARREN, MELVIN CHARLES	*4000-24000	
WARREN, MELVIN CHARLES (1920 -)	15000-150000	F,G
WARREN, WESLEY (20TH C)	100-500	X (M)
WARSHAWSKY, ABEL GEORGE (1883 - 1962)	800-15000 +	L,F
WARSHAWSKY, ALEXANDER (1887 - 1962)	200-1500	L,F
WARTHEIN, LEE R. (20TH C)	100-800	X(F)
WASHBURN, CADWALLADER (- 1965)	200-1000	X (F)
WASHBURN, JESSIE M. (20TH C)	100-600	X (L)
WASHES, J. (19TH - 20TH C)	*100-500	X (S)
WASSON, GEORGE SAVARY (1855 - 1926)	100-850	M,L
WATERHOUSE, M.S. (19TH C)	150-1000	F
WATERMAN, MARCUS A. (1834 - 1914)	400-4800	F,L
WATERS, GEORGE W. (1832 - 1912)	300-3500	L,F
WATERS, SUSAN C. (1823 - 1900)	1500-45000 +	P,F,L,W
WATKINS, CATHERINE W. (20TH C)	250-1500	L
WATKINS, FRANKLIN CHENAULT (1894 - 1972)	300-3500	G,F,L
WATKINS, SUSAN (1875-1913)	200-2500	F

WATKINS, WILLIAM (19TH C)	400-2000	F
WATROUS, HARRY WILLSON (1857 - 1940)	500-45000	F,I,S
WATSON, A. FRANCIS (19TH C)	100-600	X (L)
WATSON, AMELIA MONTAGUE (1856 - 1934)	*200-950	L,I
WATSON, DAWSON (1864 - 1939)	200-2000	L
WATSON, EDITH SARAH (1861 -)	*100-300	X (L)
WATSON, ELIZABETH VILA T.(-1934)	100-850	F
WATSON, HENRY SUMNER (1868 - 1933)	300-2000	I,W
WATSON, HOMER RANSFORD (1855 - 1936)	400-7500	L
WATSON, NAN (19TH-20TH C)	200-1200	S
WATSON, ROBERT (20TH C)	100-800	F,G
WATSON, WALTER (19TH - 20TH C)	200-1800	L
WATSON, WILLIAM R. (19TH-20TH C)	100-600	L
WATTS, PETER (20TH C)	100-600	X
WATTS, WILLIAM CLOTHIER (1869-1961)	*100-900	L
WAUD, ALFRED R. (1828 - 1891)	*200-2500	I,M
WAUGH, COULTON	*100-450	
WAUGH, COULTON (1896 - 1973)	200-900	I
WAUGH, FREDERICK JUDD (1861 - 1940)	400-40000	M,F,S
WAUGH, IDA (- 1919)	300-2500	G,F
WAUGH, SAMUEL BELL (1814 - 1885)	350-4000	L,F
WAY, ANDREW JOHN HENRY (1826 - 1888)	500-12000+	S,L,F
WAY, EDNA (20TH C)	*100-700	M,L
WEAVER, JAY (20TH C)	450-2500	G,I
WEBB, A.C. (1888 -)	300-2000	F,I
WEBBER, CHARLES T. (1825 - 1911)	600-6500+	F,L
WEBBER, F. WILLIAM (19TH-20TH C)	150-1000	L
WEBBER, WESLEY (1839 - 1914)	250-5000	M,L,I
WEBER, C. PHILIP (1849 -)	400-8800	L
WEBER, CARL	*150-3200	
WEBER, CARL (1850 - 1921)	300-5000	L,W
WEBER, CARL T. (19TH - 20TH C)	100-500	X
WEBER, E.R. (20TH C)	100-700	X(S)
WEBER, F. WILLIAM (20TH C)	100-900	L,M
WEBER, FREDERICK (19TH C)	*300-1600	X (F)

* Denotes watercolors, pastels, drawings, and/or mixed media

WEBER, FREDERICK T. (1883 - 1956)	100-950	X (M)
WEBER, MAX	*300-15000	
WEBER, MAX (1881 - 1961)	500-65000	A,F
WEBER, OTIS S.	*100-600	
WEBER, OTIS S. (late 19TH C)	200-2500	M
WEBER, PHILIPP (1849 - 1921)	500-9500	L
WEBER,PAUL (1823-1916)	400-12000	L,F,W
WEBSTER, E. AMBROSE (1869-1935)	300-5000	X(F)
WEBSTER, W.M. (20TH C)	100-600	X(F)
WEDEPHOL, THEODOR (1863-1923)	*100-800	X(L,M)
WEEKES, A. (19TH C)	300-1800	X(G)
WEEKS, EDWIN LORD (1849 - 1903)	500-38000+	F,L
WEEKS, JAMES (1922 -)	3500-18000	A,L
WEGER, MARIE (1882 -)	100-600	X (S)
WEIGAND, GUSTAVE A.(1870 - 1957)	200-3200	L
WEINBERG, EMILIE SIEVERT (20TH C)	150-850	X (L)
WEINREICH, AGNES (early 20TH C)	200-900	X (L)
WEIR, JOHN FERGUSON (1841 - 1926)	600-25000	L,S,F
WEIR, JULIAN ALDEN	*500-18000	
WEIR, JULIAN ALDEN (1852 - 1919)	2500-440000	F,L,S
WEIR, ROBERT WALTER (1803 - 1889)	600-70000	G,F,L,I
WEIS, JOHN ELLSWORTH (1892-)	300-4200	X(F,L)
WEISER, MARY E. (19TH - 20TH C)	100-600	X (S)
WEISS, BERNARD J. (20TH C)	100-600	X (L)
WEISS, MARY L. (early 20TH C)	100-450	X (S)
WEISS, S.A. (early 20TH C)	100-750	X
WELBECK, G.A. (19TH - 20TH C)	150-950	X (L,F)
WELCH, JACK (1905 -)	*100-650	I
WELCH, LUDMILLA P. (19TH - 20TH C)	300-2500	L,W
WELCH, MABEL R. (- 1959)	150-1000	X (F)
WELCH, THADDEUS	*300-2000	
WELCH, THADDEUS (1844 - 1919)	400-7500	L,F
WELDON, CHARLES DATER (1844 - 1935)	1000-8500	I
WELDON, H.A. (19TH - 20TH C)	150-850	L
WELLER, CARL F. (1853 - 1920)	*100-500	X (L)

* Denotes watercolors, pastels, drawings, and/or mixed media

WELLINGTON, J.(19TH-20TH C)	100-900	L
WELLIVER, NEIL (1929 -)	3000-35000	A
WELLS, BENJAMIN B. (1856-1923)	400-3500	X(F)
WELLS, BETTY (20TH C)	*100-800	X
WELLS, C.H. (19TH C)	*150-600	L
WELLS, LYNTON (1940 -)	2000-20000	A
WELLS, NEWTON ALONZO (1852 -)	300-1500	L,S
WELLS, WILLIAM L. (1890 -)	*150-600	I
WELS, CHARLES (20TH C)	*100-500	X(F)
WELSH, WILLIAM P. (1889 -)	*200-1200	X (I,F)
WENBAN, SION LONGLEY (1848 - 1897)	300-2000	L
WENCK, PAUL (1892 -)	200-1500	L,I
WENDEL, THEODORE (1857 - 1932)	800-45000	L,M
WENDEROTH, AUGUSTUS (1825 -)	400-4500	F,W,L
WENDEROTH, FREDERICK A. (19TH - 20TH C)	300-1800	X (S)
WENDT, WILLIAM (1865 - 1946)	350-12000	L,F
WENGENROTH, STOW (1906 -)	300-1500	L,M
WENGER, JOHN	*100-600	
WENGER, JOHN (1887 -)	300-2000	X (F)
WENTWORTH, DANIEL F. (1850 - 1934)	400-2500	L
WENTWORTH, R. (19TH C)	300-1500	L
WENZELL, ALBERT BECK (1864 - 1917)	*100-3000	I
WERNER-BEHN, HANS (early 20TH C)	100-600	X
WERTINFIELD, JOSEPH (20TH C)	100-350	X (F)
WESCOTT, PAUL (1904 - 1970)	300-1500	X (L,M)
WESLEY, JOHN (1928 -)	300-2500	A
WESSEL, HERMAN H. (1878-1969)	400-5000	M,F
WESSELMANN, TOM	*1500-45000+	
WESSELMANN, TOM (1931 -)	2000-50000	A
WESSON, ROBERT (19TH C)	200-2800	L
WEST, BENJAMIN	*400-20000+	
WEST, BENJAMIN (1738 - 1820)	600-????	F,G,L
WEST, LEVON (1900 -)	*200-2000	F
WEST, PETER B. (1833 - 1913)	300-2000	G,W,L
WEST, RAPHAEL LAMARR (1769 - 1850)	*350-2500	F,I,L

 * Denotes watercolors, pastels, drawings, and/or mixed media

WEST, T. (19TH C)	100-600	X(L)
WEST, WILLIAM EDWARD (1788 - 1857)	400-2500	F,M
WESTERMANN, HORACE CLIFFORD (1922-)	*500-6000	A
WESTHCILOFF, CONSTANTIN (20TH C)	250-2500	X (L)
WESTON, MORRIS (19TH - 20TH C)	100-500	X (L)
WETHERBEE, GEORGE FAULKNER (1851 - 1920)	500-7500	F,L
WETHERBY, ISAAC AUGUSTUS (1819 - 1904)	800-6000	P
WETHERILL, ELISHA KENT KANE (1874 - 1925)	600-18000	M,W,L,F
WEYDEN, HARRY VAN DER (1868 -)	200-2800	L
WEYL, MAX (1837 - 1914)	450-5000+	L
WHEATON, FRANCISCO (19TH-20TH C)	*100-1400	L
WHEELER, CHARLES ARTHUR (1881 -)	150-750	X (F)
WHEELER, CLIFTON (1883 -)	300-3500	F
WHEELER, WILLLIAM R. (1832 - 1894)	250-950	F
WHEELOCK, MERRILL GREENE (1822 - 1866)	*200-1200	M,L
WHEELOCK, WALTER W. (early 19TH C)	250-950	F
WHEELOCK, WARREN (1880 - 1960)	150-1500	F,L
WHELAN, THOMAS (20TH C)	150-950	X (L)
WHISTLER, JAMES ABBOTT MCNEIL	*1500-90000+	
WHISTLER, JAMES ABBOTT MCNEIL (1834-1903)	5000-2600000	L,F
WHITAKER, CHARLES W. (20TH C)	150-800	X (L)
WHITAKER, GEORGE WILLIAM	*300-1500	
WHITAKER, GEORGE WILLIAM (1841 - 1916)	350-5000	M,S,L,F
WHITCOMB, JON	*200-800	
WHITCOMB, JON (1906 -)	200-4500	I
WHITE, CHARLES (1918 - 1980)	*800-6000	F
WHITE, CHARLES HENRY (1878 -)	600-3500	X (L,F)
WHITE, CLARENCE SCOTT (1872 -)	300-3000	L,M
WHITE, EDWIN D.(1817 - 1877)	200-10000	F,G
WHITE, H. WADE (20TH C)	100-750	L,I
WHITE, HENRY COOKE (1861 - 1952)	200-1000	L
WHITE, NONA L. (1859-)	*100-500	L
WHITE, ORRIN AUGUSTINE	*150-950	
WHITE, ORRIN AUGUSTINE (1883 - 1969)	400-3500	L
WHITE, THOMAS GILBERT (1877 - 1939)	100-3000	L,F

WHITEHEAD, WALTER (1874-1956)	300-1000	L
WHITEHORNE, JAMES A. (1803 - 1888)	300-1500	F
WHITEMAN, SAMUEL EDWIN (1860 - 1922)	200-1200	L
WHITESIDE, FRANK REED (1866 - 1929)	100-750	L,M
WHITING, HENRY W. (19TH C)	150-2500	L
WHITING, HENRY H. (19TH C)	400-4000	L
WHITING, LILLIAN V. (20TH C)	100-700	X
WHITMAN, A.M. (19TH - 20TH C)	*100-800	X (L)
WHITMAN, EDWIN (20TH C)	100-700	X (G)
WHITMORE, M. COBURN (1913 -)	500-8000	I
WHITON, H.W. (19TH C)	100-700	L
WHITTAKER, JOHN BARNARD (1836 - 1926)	400-4500	F,L
WHITTEKER, LILIAN (20TH C)	500-4500	L
WHITTEMORE, LILLIAN (19TH C)	*100-500	X (S)
WHITTEMORE, WILLIAM JOHN (1860 - 1955)	500-7000	F,M,L
WHITTREDGE, T. WORTHINGTON (1820-1910)	2000-150000+	L,M
WHORF, JOHN	*250-7200	
WHORF, JOHN (1903 - 1959)	500-23000	L,M,F
WICKEY, HARRY (1892 -)	*100-600	X (F)
WICKS, HEPPLE (19TH-20TH C)	100-600	L
WIDFORSS, GUNNAR MAURITZ (1879 - 1934)	*300-4500	L,F
WIDNER, G.O. (19TH C)	800-6000	L
WIEGAND, CHARMION VON (1899 -)	*300-1200	A
WIEGAND, GUSTAVE ADOLPH (1870 - 1957)	400-6200	L
WIEGHORST, OLAF CARL	*500-9000	
WIEGHORST, OLAF CARL (1899 -)	4000-80000	F,G,W
WIES, W. (19TH - 20TH C)	100-600	X (L)
WIESSLER, WILLIAM (1887 -)	100-900	X (S)
WIGGINS, (JOHN) CARLETON (1848 - 1932)	200-5000+	L
WIGGINS, GUY CARLETON (1883 - 1962)	500-48000	L
WIGGINS, SIDNEY MILLER (1883 - 1940)	150-950	X (L,M)
WIGHT, MOSES (1827 - 1895)	300-5000	G,F
WILATCH, MICHA (1910 -)	300-2000	X (L)
WILBUR, THEODORE E. (19TH C)	150-750	X (L)
WILCOX, FRANK NELSON (1887 -)	*250-4000	L,F

 * Denotes watercolors, pastels, drawings, and/or mixed media

WILCOX (WILLCOX), WILLIAM (1831 -)	200-800	L
WILDE, JOHN (1919 -)	2000-18000	F
WILDE (WILD), HAMILTON GIBBS (1827 - 1884)	200-1500	F,G,L
WILDER, ARTHUR B.	*150-750	
WILDER, ARTHUR B. (1857 - 1949)	300-3000	L
WILDER, F. H. (active 1845-50)	400-1500	F
WILDER, FRANKLIN (19TH C)	*2000-8500	P
WILES, IRVING RAMSAY	*500-6500 +	
WILES, IRVING RAMSAY (1861 - 1948)	700-15000	G,F,M,I
WILES, LEMUEL MAYNARD (1826 - 1905)	500-15000	L
WILES, M. (20TH C)	100-600	X (S)
WILEY, WILLIAM T.	*800-15000	
WILEY, WILLIAM T. (1937 -)	1000-20000	A
WILFORD, LORAN FREDERICK	*100-650	
WILFORD, LORAN FREDERICK (1893 - 1972)	250-2500	F,I
WILFRED, LEMUEL (20TH C)	300-800	X (L)
WILGUS, WILLIAM JOHN (1819-1853)	2000-25000 +	F
WILKIE, ROBERT D. (1828 - 1903)	500-12000	G,L,S,W
WILKINSON, J. WALTER (1892 -)	100-850	X (F)
WILL, JOHN M. AUGUST (1834 - 1910)	*100-650	F,L
WILLARD, ARCHIBALD M. (1836 - 1918)	300-???? +	F,L
WILLEY, PHILO "CHIEF" (1886 - 1980)	500-5000	P
WILLIAMS, CHARLES DAVID (1875 - 1954)	*200-1500	I
WILLIAMS, EDWARD K. (19TH-20TH C)	350-2000	L
WILLIAMS, FREDERICK BALLARD (1871 - 1956)	300-8000	F,G,L
WILLIAMS, FREDERICK DICKENSON (1829-1915)	250-3500 +	F,L
WILLIAMS, GEORGE ALFRED (1875 - 1932)	*100-1500	F
WILLIAMS, HENRY (1787 - 1830)	300-2800	F
WILLIAMS, ISAAC L. (1817 - 1895)	300-3000	F,L
WILLIAMS, J.F. (19TH C)	100-850	X(M)
WILLIAMS, JOHN SCOTT (1877 -)	*100-1000	L,I
WILLIAMS, M.C. (19TH C)	100-1000	G
WILLIAMS, MARY BELLE (1873 - 1943)	200-1500	L
WILLIAMS, MARY R. (1857 - 1907)	400-4500	F
WILLIAMS, MAY (20TH C)	*150-600	X(L,F)

* Denotes watercolors, pastels, drawings, and/or mixed media

WILLIAMS, MICAH	*1000-18000	
WILLIAMS, MICAH (active 1815-30)	1000-10000+	P
WILLIAMS, MILDRED EMERSON (1892-)	300-3200	X(F)
WILLIAMS, PAULINE BLISS (1888-)	300-3200	X(L)
WILLIAMS, ROBERT F. (20TH C)	150-1000	X (L)
WILLIAMS, VIRGIL (1830 - 1886)	300-3500	G,F,L
WILLIAMS, WILLIAM (c.1710 - 1790)	600-18000	F,L
WILLIAMS, WILLIAM JOSEPH (1759 - 1823)	500-4500	F
WILLIAMSON, CHARTERS (1856 -)	250-1200	L
WILLIAMSON, JOHN (1826 - 1885)	500-9000	L,F,S
WILLIS, ALBERT PAUL (1867-1944)	150-1500	L
WILLIS, EDMUND A.(VAN) (1808-1899)	300-4000	G,L,W
WILLIS, THOMAS (1850 - 1912)	*750-5000	M
WILLIS, W.L. (19TH-20TH C)	100-600	X(M)
WILLSON, B. (19TH C)	200-1200	L
WILLSON, JAMES MALLERY (1890 -)	100-900	X (L,M)
WILLSON, MARY ANN (active 1810-30)	*1000-7500	P
WILMARTH, CHRISTOPHER (1943-)	400-2000	X
WILMARTH, LEMUEL EVERETT (1835 - 1918)	700-18000	G,S
WILSON, ALEXANDER (1766-1818)	100-1000	X(S)
WILSON, CHARLES THELLER (1855-1920)	150-1000	L,F
WILSON, DONALD ROLLER (20TH C)	300-1500	X (F)
WILSON, DOUGLAS (19TH C)	200-1000	X
WILSON, GAHAN (20TH C)	*100-1000	X (F)
WILSON, H.M. (20TH C)	100-600	X (L)
WILSON, HARRIET (20TH C)	*100-600	X (S)
WILSON, JAMES (19TH C)	1000-6500	L
WILSON, JANE (1924 -)	2000-20000	A
WILSON, ROBERT BURNS (1851 - 1916)	*250-850	L
WILSON, SOL (1894-)	100-750	X (L,M)
WILSON, T. (19TH C)	100-650	L
WILTZ, ARNOLD (1889 - 1937)	200-1000	L
WIMAR, CHARLES (1828-1863)	5000-75000	F,M,W,L
WINGERT, EDWARD OSWALD (1864 - 1934)	100-650	X (L)
WINNER, WILLIAM E. (1815 - 1883)	500-10000+	G,F

 * Denotes watercolors, pastels, drawings, and/or mixed media

WINSLOW, HENRY (1874 -)	400-3500	X (L,M)
WINSOR, HELEN A. (19TH C)	300-1800	X
WINTER, ALICE BEACH (1877 -)	400-3500	F,I
WINTER, ANDREW (1893 - 1958)	400-9000+	M,L
WINTER, CHARLES ALLEN (1869 -1942)	200-8500	F,L,I
WISBY, JACK (1870-1940)	300-2000	L,M
WITHERSTINE, DONALD FREDERICK (1896-)	200-1200	L
WITHROW, EVELYN ALMOND (1858-1928)	200-3000	F,L
WITKOWSKI, KARL	*300-2500	
WITKOWSKI, KARL (1860 - 1910)	1000-18000	G
WITT, JOHN H. (1840 - 1901)	600-16000	F,L
WITTER, E.S. (20TH C)	100-850	L
WIX, O. (19TH-20TH C)	*150-950	L
WOELFLE, ARTHUR WILLIAM (1873 - 1936)	350-3500+	M,L,F,S
WOELFLE, WILLIAM (20TH C)	100-600	S
WOLCOTT, HAROLD (20TH C)	300-1200	X (F,L)
WOLCOTT, JOHN GILMORE (1891 -)	100-900	X (F)
WOLCOTT, ROGER A. (20TH C)	150-850	F
WOLCOTT, ROGER H. (20TH C)	150-800	X (L)
WOLF, BEN (20TH C)	100-450	X (F)
WOLF, CHAS. H. (early 19TH C)	10000-40000	P
WOLF, F.H. (20TH C)	200-800	X (S)
WOLF, GEORG (1882 - 1962)	500-7500	G,W,F,L
WOLF, GUSTAVE (1863-1935)	300-3500	X(M)
WOLF, HENRY (1852 - 1916)	150-650	L,F,S
WOLF, LONE	*600-3500	
WOLF, LONE (1882 - 1965)	1000-18000	X (F)
WOLF, WALLACE L. DE (1854 - 1930)	250-1800	L
WOLFE, BYRON (1904 - 1973)	*1000-8500	X (F)
WOLFE, JACK (20TH C)	200-1500	A
WOLFE, WAYNE (20TH C)	5000-30000	X (L)
WOLFF, B. (20TH C)	100-400	X (L)
WOLFF, GUSTAV (1863 - 1934)	300-3000	L,M
WOLLASTON, JOHN (active 1735-70)	2000-18000	F
WONNER, PAUL JOHN (1924 -)	*500-4000	X

* Denotes watercolors, pastels, drawings, and/or mixed media

WOOD, A.M. (19TH C)	100-500	X (L)
WOOD, ALEXANDER (19TH - 20TH C)	300-6500	F,L
WOOD, DOROTHY MACHADO (20TH C)	100-600	L
WOOD, GEORGE ALBERT (1845 - 1910)	300-3500	L
WOOD, GEORGE BACON JR (1832 - 1910)	300-3500	G,L
WOOD, GRANT	*1000-325000	
WOOD, GRANT (1891 - 1942)	1500-1375000	F,L,G,W
WOOD, HOWARD (1922 -)	150-850	A
WOOD, HUNTER (1908 -)	400-2500	M,F
WOOD, J. OGDEN (1851 - 1912)	150-1500	L,W
WOOD, JAMES LONGACRE (1863-1938)	1000-20000	F
WOOD, ROBERT (1889 - 1979)	700-15000	L,F
WOOD, ROBERT E. (1926 -)	600-8500+	L
WOOD, STANLEY L. (1860 - 1940)	500-5000	X (I,F)
WOOD, THOMAS WATERMAN	*2000-40000	
WOOD, THOMAS WATERMAN (1823 - 1903)	700-75000	G,F
WOOD, VIRGINIA HARGRAVES	*100-750	X (F)
WOOD, WILLIAM R.C. (1875 - 1915)	300-2600	L
WOOD, WORDEN	*250-1000	
WOOD, WORDEN (active 1910-1940)	500-3000	M,I
WOODBURN, STEPHEN (20TH C)	300-2000	X
WOODBURY, CHARLES HERBERT (1864 - 1940)	400-9500	F,M,L
WOODBURY, MARCIA OAKES (1865 - 1913)	250-2000	F
WOODCOCK, HARTWELL L. (1853 - 1929)	*100-600	M,L
WOODLEIGH, ALMA (19TH C)	100-850	L,F
WOODRACH, KARL L. (20TH C)	*100-350	X (M)
WOODRUFF, DANIEL F. (20TH C)	*500-2500	L
WOODRUFF, G.L. (19TH C)	300-1000	X (S)
WOODRUFF, JOHN KELLOGG (1879 - 1956)	*100-400	X(L)
WOODSIDE, JOHN ARCHIBALD (1781 - 1852)	1000-7500+	P
WOODSON, MAX R. (20TH C)	100-500	X (F,L)
WOODVILLE, RICHARD CATON (1825 - 1855)	2000-75000	G
WOODWARD, ELLSWORTH (1861 - 1939)	*500-3000	G,M,I
WOODWARD, LAURA (19TH C)	100-850	X (S)
WOODWARD, MABEL MAY (1877 - 1945)	600-20000	F,M,L,S

 * Denotes watercolors, pastels, drawings, and/or mixed media

WOODWARD, ROBERT STRONG (1885 - 1960)	400-3500	L
WOODWARD, STANLEY WINGATE (1890 - 1970)	100-3500	M,I
WOODWARD, WILLIAM	*300-3500	
WOODWARD, WILLIAM (1859-1934)	400-5000	G,F
WOOLF, SAMUEL JOHNSON (1880 - 1948)	100-1800	L,F
WOOLFE, MICHAEL A. (1837 - 1899)	*100-850	I
WOOLRYCH, F. HUMPHRY W. (1868 -)	100-800	F,L,S,I
WOOSTER, AUSTIN C. (19TH C)	350-16000	S,L
WORDEN, J. (20TH C)	100-300	X (F)
WORES, THEODORE (1860 - 1939)	450-5800+	F,M,I
WORTH, THOMAS	*200-1200	
WORTH, THOMAS (1834 - 1917)	500-4500	G,L
WRENN, CHARLES LEWIS (1880 - 1952)	100-1500	F,I
WRIGHT, CHARLES H. MONCRIEF (1870 - 1939)	500-6000	L,F,I
WRIGHT, CHARLES LENOX (1876 -)	400-3800	X (L,I)
WRIGHT, GEORGE FREDERICK (1828-1881)	100-1000	L,F
WRIGHT, GEORGE HAND	*300-3500	
WRIGHT, GEORGE HAND (1873 - 1951)	900-35000	I,G,F
WRIGHT, GEORGE W. (1834 - 1934)	1800-45000	G,F
WRIGHT, JAMES COOPER (1906-1969)	*100-850	S
WRIGHT, JAMES HENRY (1813 - 1883)	500-6500	L,M,F,S
WRIGHT, JAMES W. (20TH C)	100-650	X (L)
WRIGHT, RUFUS (1832 - 1895)	500-4500	F,L,S
WUERMER, CARL (1900 - 1982)	1500-18000+	L
WUERPEL, EDMUND HENRY (1866 - 1958)	200-1000	X (L)
WUIRT, WALTER (20TH C)	400-2000	A
WUST, ALEXANDER (1837 - 1876)	1000-14000	L,M,F
WUST, CHRISTOFFEL (1801 -)	600-4500	F
WYAND, D.E. (19TH - 20TH C)	*100-600	G,F
WYANT, ALEXANDER HELWIG	*400-5000	
WYANT, ALEXANDER HELWIG (1836 - 1892)	800-60000	L
WYCKOFF, H. (19TH C)	100-600	X
WYDEVELD, ARNOUD (19TH C)	200-1500	X (W,S)
WYETH, ANDREW	*2000-100000	
WYETH, ANDREW (1917 -)	20000-275000+	L,W,F

* Denotes watercolors, pastels, drawings, and/or mixed media

WYETH, JAMES (1946 -)	*1500-15000	L
WYETH, NEWELL CONVERS (1882 - 1945)	2000-66000+	I,L
WYLIE, ROBERT (1839-1877)	500-7500	G
WYMAN, F.A. (19TH C)	1000-7500+	L,F

X

ARTIST	PRICE	SUBJECT
XCERON, JEAN (1890 - 1967)	1000-8000	A

Y

ARTIST	PRICE	SUBJECT
YALE, LEROY (1841 - 1906)	200-1000	X
YARD, SYDNEY JANIS (1855 - 1909)	*200-2000	L
YARROW, WILLIAM HENRY KEMBLE (1891-)	*200-1200	L,M
YATES, CULLEN (1866 - 1945)	400-4500	M,L,S
YATES, ELIZABETH (1888 -)	150-900	X (S)
YATES, WILLIAM HENRY (1845 - 1934)	300-6000	F,L,S
YATRIDES, GEORGE (20TH C)	400-6000	G,F
YEATS, AGNES (20TH C)	*100-600	L
YECKLEY, NORMAN (19TH C - 20TH C)	100-700	X (L)
YELLAND, RAYMOND DABB (1848 - 1900)	400-25000	M,L
YENNAD, ADUASHA (20TH C)	100-600	X (M)
YENS, KARL (JULIUS HEINRICH) (1868 - 1945)	400-25000+	F,I,L
YEWELL, GEORGE HENRY (1830 - 1923)	500-15000	G,F
YOAKUM, JOSEPH E (1886-1973)	*400-6500	X
YOHN, FREDERICK COFFAY (1875 - 1933)	300-4500	I
YONG, JOE DE	*100-2500	
YONG, JOE DE (1894 - 1975)	500-5000	G,F
YORKE, MIGNON (20TH C)	*100-600	I

 * Denotes watercolors, pastels, drawings, and/or mixed media

YORKE, WILLIAM G. (1817 - 1883)	5000-25000	M
YORKE, WILLIAM H. (1847 - 1921)	5000-16000	M
YOUENS, CLEMEMT T. (19TH - 20TH C)	200-800	X (L)
YOUNG, AUGUST (1839 - 1913)	700-5000	G,F
YOUNG, B.S. (late 19TH C)	800-5000	X (M)
YOUNG, BARBARA (1920 -)	100-650	F
YOUNG, CHARLES MORRIS	*300-2500	
YOUNG, CHARLES MORRIS (1869 - 1964)	1000-7500	L
YOUNG, CLIFF (20TH C)	100-1500	F
YOUNG, EDWARD (1823-1882)	200-2000	L,M
YOUNG, FRED GRANT (19TH - 20TH C)	100-700	X (S)
YOUNG, HARVEY B.	*300-1800	
YOUNG, HARVEY B. (1840 - 1901)	400-8000	L,F,W
YOUNG, JAMES HARVEY (1830 - 1918)	400-3000	F
YOUNG, JOE DE (1894-1975)	200-1200	F
YOUNG, MABEL (20TH C)	350-1800	X (L)
YOUNG, MAHONRI MACKINTOSH	*100-700	
YOUNG, MAHONRI MACKINTOSH (1877 - 1957)	600-3000	F,L
YOUNG, OSCAR VAN (1906 -)	300-1500	X
YOUNG, PETER (20TH C)	800-15000	A
YOUNG, WILLIAM S. (active 1850-70)	300-4500	L
YOUNG-HUNTER, JOHN (1874-1955)	300-3500	L,F
YOUNGERMAN, JACK	*400-2000	
YOUNGERMAN, JACK (1926 -)	800-8500	A
YUTZLER, ARLINGTON (20TH C)	100-450	X (L)

Z

ARTIST	PRICE	SUBJECT
ZAJAC, JACK (1929 -)	400-2500	A
ZAKANITCH, ROBERT S. (1935 -)	4000-20000	A
ZAKHAROV, FEODOR (1882 - 1935)	200-1200	X (M)
ZANDT, THOMAS KIRBY VAN (active 1830-65)	400-4000	W
ZANDT, WILLIAM C. VAN (19TH - 20TH C)	300-2800	X (F,W)
ZANG, JOHN J. (19TH C)	600-5500	F,L
ZANTHO, DARIN (20TH C)	100-700	X
ZEIGLER, LEE W. (1868 -)	*200-1000	I
ZELDIS, MELCAH (1931 -)	500-7500	P
ZELLINSKY, C.L. (19TH C)	400-5000	W,F
ZELTNER, WILLIAM (19TH C)	*250-1200	X (F)
ZIEGLER, EUSTACE PAUL (1881 - 1941)	1000-25000	L,F,I
ZIMMELE, MARGARET SCULLY (1872 -)	150-950	L,I
ZIMMERMAN, FREDERICK A.(1886 - 1976)	150-1500	L
ZIMMERMAN, JOSEPH (1923 -)	100-1000	L
ZIMMERMAN, MASON W. (1861 -)	*150-900	X (L)
ZIMMERMAN, PAUL (1921 -)	100-600	X (F)
ZIMMERMAN, RENE (1904 -)	100-800	X (G,L)
ZIMMERMAN, WILLIAM (20TH C)	*150-650	X (W)
ZION, BEN (20TH C)	100-600	X (S)
ZIROLI, NICOLA VICTOR (1908 -)	300-3000	X (F)
ZISKIND, A. (20TH C)	200-1000	F
ZOGBAUM, RUFUS FAIRCHILD	*400-2500	
ZOGBAUM, RUFUS FAIRCHILD (1849 - 1925)	800-6500	I,F,M
ZOGBAUM, WILFRED M.(1915 - 1965)	900-6000	A
ZORACH, MARGUERITE T. (1888 - 1968)	400-6000	A,L,F,S
ZORACH, WILLIAM	*400-7000	
ZORACH, WILLIAM (1887 - 1966)	1000-70000	A,L
ZORNES, JAMES (1908 -)	200-1000	L
ZORNES, MILFORD (1908 -)	*200-1600	X (M,L)
ZORTHIAN, JIRAYR H. (1912 -)	*150-900	X (I)
ZOX, LARRY (1936 -)	800-8500	A
ZUANICH, FRANK (20TH C)	100-900	L
ZUBER, J. (19TH C)	500-2000	X (S)

 * Denotes watercolors, pastels, drawings, and/or mixed media

ZUCCARELLI, FRANK EDWARD (20TH C)	100-700	X (F)
ZUCKER, JOSEPH (1941 -)	*500-7000	A
ZUILL, ALICE E. (19TH C)	300-2500	S,L
ZWERLING, LISA (20TH C)	100-600	X

RECORD PRICES

The following prices are record *auction* prices realized - as of 1/15/88 - for each of the respective artists, and are isolated here because they are far above the "typical" price range for each artist. Within the alphabetical listing of artists, which make up the largest portion of this *Guide*, the price range for each of these artists will be followed by a "+" to indicate that you should refer to the list below for further information. [*note*: Most prices include a 10% buyers premium, and a "*" preceding a price indicates the work was a watercolor, pastel, or mixed media.]

ARTISTS	RECORD	SUBJ	DATE
ALBRIGHT, ADAM EMORY	18,700	G	9/87
ALLSTON, WASHINGTON	200,600	F	12/81
AMES, EZRA	99,000	F	1/86
ANSHUTZ, THOMAS POLLACK	*60,500	F	12/87
APPEL, CHARLES P.	9,350	L	3/86
BACON, FRANCIS	1,760,000	A	5/87
BADGER, S.F.M.	14,300	M	12/86
BASCOM, RUTH H.	(pair) *35,000	P(F)	12/86
BAUM, CHARLES	16,500	S	5/86
BEAL, GIFFORD	55,000	G	12/84
BEAL, REYNOLDS	40,700	M	5/87
BEEST, ALBERTUS VAN	18,000	M	8/87
BELKNAP, ZEBAKIAH	49,000	P(F)	4/81
BELL, EDWARD AUGUSTE	9,625	F	6/86
BENSON, EUGENE	20,900	G	11/85
BIERSTADT, ALBERT	792,000	L(W)	6/83
BIRNEY, WILLIAM VERPLANCK	27,500	G	5/86
BISTTRAM, EMILE J.	18,700	A	12/86

BLUEMNER, OSCAR	396,000	A	5/87
BLUM, ROBERT FREDERICK	473,000	F	6/82
BLUM, ROBERT FREDERICK	*104,000	F	12/82
BOUGUEREAU, E. J. G.	81,400	F	2/87
BREDIN, RAY SLOAN	35,200	F	5/86
BREWSTER Jr, JOHN	852,500	P(F)	1/88
BRICHER, ALFRED THOMPSON	*176,000	M	12/87
BRIDGES, FIDELIA	13,200	L	4/86
BROOKS, NICHOLAS ALDEN	26,400	S	12/84
BROWN, HARRISON B.	11,000	L	5/86
BROWN, JOHN APPLETON	28,600	L	3/85
BROWN, JOHN GEORGE	192,500	G	5/86
BROWN, WILLIAM MASON	50,600	L	5/86
BUEHR, KARL ALBERT	20,900	L	9/84
CADMUS, PAUL	99,000	G	12/86
CADY, HARRISON	6,325	I	11/86
CAHOON, RALPH	32,000	P	8/85
CALIFANO, JOHN	36,000	G	12/85
CARBEE, SCOTT CLIFTON	10,450	F	11/86
CARISS, HENRY T.	6,325	G	4/84
CARLSON, JOHN FABIAN	34,000	L	4/85
CASSATT, MARY S.	*1,045,000	F	12/87
CHAMBERS, THOMAS	88,000	P(M)	1/87
CHASE, WILLIAM MERRITT	*820,000	F	5/81
CHIARIACKA, ERNEST	11,000	L	12/86
CHITTENDEN, ALICE BROWN	27,500	S	10/87
CHRISTY, HOWARD CHANDLER	52,250	I	5/87
CHURCH, FREDERIC EDWIN	2,750,000	M	10/79
CLARK, WALTER APPLETON	11,500	L	12/87
COALE, GRIFFITH BAILAY	26,400	L	5/87
COATES, EDMUND C.	47,500	F	7/84
COLEMAN, CHARLES CARYL	170,500	S	10/84
COOPER, COLIN CAMPBELL	52,250	L	11/86
COUTTS, GORDON	8,800	F	6/81
CROPSEY, JASPER F.	660,000	L	4/81

CURRAN, CHARLES COURTNEY	88,000	S	6/84
DARRAH, ANN SOPHIA T.	6,600	S	10/84
DASBURG, ANDREW	115,500	A	12/87
DECKER, JOSEPH	220,000	S	12/83
DEHAAS, M. F. H.	16,060	M	9/86
DEMING, EDWARD WILLARD	33,000	G	4/82
DESSAR, LOUIS PAUL	12,650	F	1/80
DICKINSON, PRESTON	374,000	A(S)	12/87
DOLPH, JOHN HENRY	12,650	W	6/81
DOVE, ARTHUR G.	484,000	A	12/87
DUNNING, ROBERT SPEAR	286,000	S	12/85
EDWARDS, GEORGE WHARTON	11,550	L	10/86
ELDRED, LEMUEL D.	11,000	M	11/86
EMMET, LYDIA FIELD	50,600	F	4/87
ENNEKING, JOHN JOSEPH	121,000	L	6/83
ESTES, RICHARD	484,000	A	11/87
EVERGOOD, PHILIP	38,500	A(F)	12/87
FECHIN, NICOLAI	154,000	F	4/80
FERY, JOHN	8,167	L	10/85
FIELD, ERASTUS SALISBURY	66,000	P(F)	10/85
FOSTER, BEN	9,500	L	9/78
FRANKENSTEIN, GODFREY NICHOLAS	16,500	L	12/86
FRERICHS, WILHELM C. A.	22,000	L	11/85
FUERTES, LOUIS AGASSIZ	*16,500	W	1/84
GAUGENGIGL, IGNAZ MARCEL	77,000	F	5/87
GAY, EDWARD	18,700	L	5/87
GAY, WALTER	70,400	G	12/87
GENTH, LILLIAN MATILDE	12,500	F	11/80
GERRY, SAMUEL LANCASTER	16,500	L	7/82
GILCHRIST, WILLIAM WALLACE	33,000	F	5/85
GLACKENS, WILLIAM	715,000	L	12/87
GLARNER, FRITZ	154,000	A	11/87
GOODWIN, LABARRE	56,100	S	11/80
GRAHAM, JOHN D.	275,000	A	12/85
GRANT, FREDERIC M.	17,600	L(F)	12/86

GREACEN, EDMUND WILLIAM	88,000	F	12/87
GROOMS, RED	60,500	A	11/87
GWATHMEY, ROBERT	11,000	A	12/86
HABERLE, JOHN	517,000	S	5/87
HALE, PHILIP LESLIE	132,000	F	12/87
HALL, GEORGE HENRY	46,750	S	4/87
HALLETT, HENRICKS A.	7,700	M	12/86
HAMILTON, HAMILTON	18,150	L	8/83
HAMILTON, JAMES	21,500	M	12/79
HAMILTON, WILLIAM R.	12,650	F	5/86
HART, WILLIAM M.	38,500	L	12/84
HARVEY, GEORGE	185,000	L	5/87
HASSAM, CHILDE	308,000	L	12/86
HAVEN, FRANKLIN DE	7,150	L	4/85
HAWTHORNE, CHARLES W.	121,000	F	12/84
HAYS, WILLIAM JACOB (SR)	31,900	W	10/82
HEADE, MARTIN JOHNSON	341,000	L	4/81
HEALY, GEORGE P.A.	22,000	F	9/81
HENRI, ROBERT	462,000	L	5/87
HENRY, EDWARD LAMSON	275,000	G	7/80
HILL, JOHN WILLIAM	*55,000	L	11/80
HINCKLEY, THOMAS HEWES	20,900	W	5/87
HITCHCOCK, GEORGE	66,000	L	12/84
HOBART, CLARK	12,100	L	5/87
HOFFBAUER, CHARLES	*9,350	F	5/86
HOFFMAN, CHARLES	126,500	P(L)	1/86
HOFMANN, HANS	715,000	A	5/87
HOPPER, EDWARD	2,310,000	L	12/87
HORTER, EARL	18,150	S	11/87
HUTCHENS, FRANK T.	9,075	F	5/86
JACOBSEN, ANTONIO	60,984	M	6/85
JARVIS, JOHN WESLEY	71,500	F	1/87
JENSEN, ALFRED J.	66,550	A	5/85
JOHANSEN, JEAN MACLANE	26,400	F	12/86
JOHNS, JASPER	3,630,000	A	??/86

JOHNSON, DAVID	63,800	S	5/87
JOHNSON, JOSHUA	660,000	P(F)	1/88
KELLY, ELLSWORTH	319,000	A	11/87
KELPE, PAUL	38,500	A	12/87
KENDALL, WILLIAM SERGEANT	46,750	F	5/86
KENNEDY, WILLIAM W.	38,500	P	1/84
KENSETT, JOHN FREDERICK	616,000	M	12/87
KEY, JOHN ROSS	35,200	L	1/81
KING, CHARLES BIRD	49,500	F	5/79
KITAJ, RONALD B.	385,000	A	5/87
KNIGHT, LOUIS ASTON	21,900	L	5/86
KOONING, WILLIAM DE	*1,210,000	A	5/83
KOONING, WILLIAM DE	3,630,000	A	5/87
KRIMMEL, JOHN LEWIS	308,000	G	12/83
KROLL, LEON	41,800	F	3/86
KRONBERG, LOUIS	25,300	F	11/86
KUHN, WALT	143,000	A(F)	5/87
KUNIYOSKI, YASUO	616,000	S	12/87
LAWSON, ERNEST	220,000	L	5/87
LEE, DORIS EMRICK	24,750	G	11/86
LICHTENSTEIN, ROY	792,000	A	11/86
LITTLE, PHILIP	13,200	L	5/87
LOVERIDGE, CLINTON	18,700	L	5/87
LOW, MARY L. F. MacMONNIES	17,600	F	12/81
LOZOWICK, LOUIS	203,000	A	12/87
MAN-RAY	825,000	A	11/79
MARSH, REGINALD	165,000	G	12/87
MARTIN, HOMER DODGE	33,000	L	5/86
MASON, ALICE TRUMBULL	22,000	A	12/87
MEAKIN, LEWIS HENRY	10,175	M	12/84
MELROSE, ANDREW W.	37,500	M	10/73
MIGNOT, LOUIS REMY	82,500	L	7/87
MOORE, HARRY HUMPHREY	22,000	F	5/85
MORAN, EDWARD	66,000	M	5/86
MORLEY, MALCOLM	396,000	A	11/87

MULLER, HEINRICH E.	25,300	L	5/84
MURPHY, JOHN FRANCIS	19,800	L	9/81
McAULIFFE, JAMES J.	37,400	M	6/87
McCLOSKEY, WILLIAM JOHN	231,000	S	12/87
NEWELL, HUGH	27,500	G	5/81
NEWMAN, BARNETT	1,754,500	A	5/85
NIEMEYER, JOHN HENRY	14,300	F	12/86
NORDELL, CARL J.	11,000	F	6/82
NORTH, NOAH	39,600	P(F)	1/87
O'KEEFFE, GEORGIA	1,430,000	A	12/87
OCHTMAN, LEONARD	24,000	L	4/85
OLINSKY, IVAN G.	35,200	F	6/83
OWEN, ROBERT EMMETT	13,200	L	12/86
PAGE, WILLIAM	77,000	F	5/86
PALMER, WALTER LAUNT	39,600	L	12/87
PANSING, FRED	44,000	M	9/86
PARRISH, MAXFIELD	220,000	I	12/85
PASCIN, JULES	187,000	A	11/86
PASKELL, WILLIAM F.	2,500	L	2/85
PAXTON, WILLIAM M.	154,000	F	5/87
PAYNE, EDGAR A.	25,300	L	12/87
PEALE, CHARLES WILLSON	451,000	F	3/86
PEALE, REMBRANDT	4,070,000	F	12/85
PEARCE, CHARLES SPRAGUE	247,500	F	6/81
PERU, ALTO	28,600	F	5/81
PETERSON, JANE	*30,800	F	5/85
PETO, JOHN FREDERICK	506,000	S	6/84
PHILLIPS, AMMI	682,000	P (F)	1/85
PICKNELL, WILLIAM LAMB	30,800	F	12/87
PIERCE, WALDO	7,260	M	3/86
PIPPIN, HORACE	385,000	P	12/87
POLLACK, JACKSON	*1,210,000	A	11/87
POLLACK, JACKSON	2,750,000	A	11/87
POPE, ALEXANDER	187,000	S	11/81
PORTER, FAIRFEILD	280,500	L	12/86

PRENTICE, LEVI WELLS	50,600	S	5/87
PRIOR, WILLIAM MATTHEW	52,250	P(F)	10/85
PYLE, HOWARD	49,500	I	1/80
RANNEY, WILLIAM TYLEE	748,000	G	10/80
RAUSCHENBERG, ROBERT	*814,000	A	11/87
REAM, CARUCIUS PLANTAGENET	11,000	S	12/86
REDFIELD, EDWARD WILLIS	82,500	L	12/87
REDMOND, GRANVILLE	44,000	L	10/87
REHN, FRANK K.M.	4,950	M	11/84
REICHARDT (RICHARDT), FERINAND	17,050	L	12/86
REULANDT, LE GRAND de	26,400	M	5/86
REYNOLDS, W.S.	17,600	S	5/86
RICHARDS, WILLIAM TROST	187,000	L	5/84
RITCHELL, WILLIAM	18,700	M	9/86
ROBINSON, THEODORE	522,500	L(F)	12/86
ROCKWELL, CLEVELAND	52,500	M	11/87
ROCKWELL, NORMAN	253,000	I	4/81
ROESEN, SEVERIN	137,000	S	9/86
RONDEL, FREDERICK	22,000	L	4/87
ROSELAND, HARRY	66,000	G	12/86
ROSENQUIST, JAMES	2,090,000	A	11/86
ROTHKO, MARK	1,815,000	A	11/83
RYDER, CHAUNCEY FOSTER	35,200	L	6/83
SALLE, DAVID	*62,700	A	11/87
SARGENT, JOHN SINGER	1,430,000	F	5/86
SARGENT, JOHN SINGER	*192,000	F	8/86
SAYRE, FRED GRAYSON	11,000	L	5/86
SCHAMBERG, MORTON LIVINGSTON	63,800	A	3/86
SCOTT, JULIAN	33,000	F	6/83
SHAW, CHARLES GREEN	19,800	A	9/87
SHEELER, CHARLES	1,870,000	A (L)	6/83
SHEELER, CHARLES	*209,000	A	6/83
SHEPPARD, WARREN J.	12,100	M	3/85
SHINN, EVERETT	*242,000	F	12/85
SHIRLAW, WALTER	16,500	F	6/85

SIMMONS, EDWARD E.	52,800	F	5/87
SMITH, JOSEPH B.	32,000	M	11/83
SMITH, DAVID	990,000	A	5/87
SMITH, DECOST	14,300	G	12/86
SMITH, FRANCIS HOPKINSON	*34,100	L	5/87
SMITH, JACK WILKINSON	7,700	L	3/85
SONNTAG, WILLIAM LOUIS (Jr)	*9,900	M	12/87
SONNTAG, WILLIAM LOUIS (Sr)	41,800	L	12/87
SOYER, RAPHAEL	176,000	F	12/85
SPENCER, LILLY MARTIN	99,000	F	12/83
SPRINCHORN, CARL	*15,400	A	4/85
STEARNS, JULIUS BRUTUS	66,000	G	1/87
STEINBERG, SAUL	*154,000	A	11/83
STELLA, FRANK	418,000	A	5/87
STELLA, JOSEPH	2,200,000	A	12/86
STEVENS, WILLIAM LESTER	12,100	L	3/87
STEWART, JULIUS L.	170,500	F	12/84
STOCK, JOSEPH WHITING	77,000	P(F)	10/85
STRAUS, MEYER	15,400	L	12/86
STUART,GILBERT	990,000	F	1/86
STULL, HENRY	77,000	W	6/85
TAIT, ARTHUR F.	18,700	L	5/87
TANNER, HENRY OSSAWA	275,000	G	12/81
THOMPSON, LESLIE P.	26,400	F	5/86
TOJETTI, DOMENICO	16,500	F	1/88
TOMPKINS, FRANK HECTOR	16,500	F	12/86
TRACY, JOHN M.	50,600	G	9/83
TROTTER, NEWBOLD H.	17,050	W	1/82
TRUMBULL, JOHN	286,000	F	1/86
TUDOR, ROBERT M.	17,050	G	5/86
TWACHTMAN, JOHN HENRY	605,000	L	12/86
TWOMBLY, CY	418,000	A	11/85
TYLER, JAMES GALE	32,500	M	9/80
VAIL, EUGENE LAURENT	8,250	M	9/84
VOGT, LOUIS CHARLES	*4,950	L	12/86

WALDO, SAMUEL LOVETT	33,000	F	10/78
WALKLEY, DAVID B.	7,424	F	3/82
WALL, ALFRED S.	13,475	L	4/85
WARHOL, ANDY	660,000	A	5/87
WARSHAWSKY, ABEL GEORGE	26,000	L	4/86
WATERS, SUSAN C.	92,950	P(F)	9/81
WAY, ANDREW J.H.	20,900	S	5/86
WEBBER, CHARLES T.	13,200	F	11/86
WEEKS, EDWIN LORD	70,000	F	11/81
WESSELMANN, TOM	*93,500	A	10/87
WEST, BENJAMIN	*165,000	F	5/84
WEYL, MAX	9,900	L	3/86
WHISTLER, ABBOTT McNEIL	*154,000	F	12/85
WHITTREDGE, T. WORTHINGTON	280,000	L	9/81
WIGGINS, JOHN CARLETON	18,700	L	12/84
WILES, IRVING RAMSEY	*28,600	F	5/86
WILGUS, WILLIAM JOHN	143,000	F	12/86
WILLARD, ARCHIBALD M.	150,000	G	11/80
WILLIAMS, FREDERICK D.	6,050	L	5/85
WILLIAMS, MICAH	22,000	P	6/86
WINNER, WILLIAM E.	19,800	G	3/86
WINTER, ANDREW	18,700	M	5/87
WOELFLE, ARTHUR WILLIAM	9,350	L	12/80
WOOD, ROBERT E.	17,000	L	3/84
WOODSIDE, JOHN ARCHIBALD	286,000	P (L)	6/82
WORES, THEODORE	19,800	L	5/87
WUERMER, CARL	23,100	L	5/84
WYETH, ANDREW	462,000	W	12/81
WYETH, NEWELL CONVERS	135,000	I	?/83
WYMAN, F.A.	41,800	L	1/84
YENS, KARL	37,400	F	12/87

APPENDIX

RESOURCES FOR PRICING

Reference Books

Prices for books which are a compilation of the results of actual art auction sales can be very high - from $40 to $195. Unless you plan to buy and sell art regularly, you should check with a large public library, or art museum library for the titles you will need (see next page.)

For a complete list of the references available, write or call the following book dealers and request their catalog. You should become familiar with all of the art price guides and art reference books available to you, before you start buying art. One note: I do not believe these guides are available in any familiar chain bookstores.

Here is a list, first, of book dealers specializing in art whom I am familiar with and would recommend, and second, a list of those price guides which contain important listings of auction results of the sale of American paintings. You can look ahead, under Biographical Resources for a list of the important art dictionaries and specialized artists' biographies.

Art World Inter'nl
69 N. Federal Highway
Dania, FL 33004

(305) 923-3001

Dealer's Choice
6677 Tower Road
Land O'Lakes, FL 33539

(800) 238-8288 (toll free)
In Fla.:(813) 996-6599

Hacker Art Books
54 West 57th St.
New York, N.Y. 10019

Museum Gallery
Box 121
SouthPort, CT 06490

Ask for free catalog! (203) 259-7114

New England Gallery
R.F.D.2
Wolfeboro, N.H. 03894

(603) 569-3501 (NH)
(305) 733-9237 (FL)

The Reference Rack
73 Warba Drive, RD 8
Allentown, PA 18104

(215) 395-0004

Important Art Price Sources

(check each dealer - prices vary)

1. *Auction Prices of American Artists*, by Richard Hislop, Art Sales Index Ltd.,England.

   Four volumes available covering art sales from 1970 thru 1984. Prices from $40-$65. New!! Volume Five (1984-1986), @ $40 with most bookdealers.

2. *Jcaobsen's Eighth Painting and Bronze Price Guide*, by Anita Jacobsen.

   Lists the art sold at auction over a two year period - American and European. Some back volumes still available. Present volume is $50. Includes 2,635 American artists.

3. *Leonard's Annual Price Index of Art Auctions*, by Auction Index, Inc., 30 Valentine Park, West Newton, MA 02165

   Complete listing of sales results, American and European, during 1986-87. Past volumes available. Price $195.

4. *E. Mayer 1987 International Auction Records*, by Editions Publisol

A very thick (1,550 pages), well illustrated, international price guide to paintings, prints, drawings, and sculptures. Covers auction results for preceding year. Back copies available. Present price is generally over $180 (hardcover).

Note: My only complaint with "Mayer's" is that they never indicate in the entries, the nationality of the artist or his date of birth and/or death.

"On-Line" Database

For the serious art dealer,collector, appraiser, and auctioneer, the "on-line" database described below is essential. You go to your terminal, touch a few keys, and you quickly have access to the world's most complete coverage of international auction sales.

Artquest, a subcription computer service, was compiled by Richard Hislop, editor of Art Sales Index (ASI). This database contains the international sales results of the past 18 years. Presently on the database are results from the sale of over 40,000 American paintings, and over 875,000 works of art, worldwide.

You can retrieve information in innumerable ways: by artist, title, size, medium, nationality, price (i.e., descending or ascending order), most recent sales, and much more. *Artquest* can also give you an analysis of each artist's auction record during the past 15 years, year by year. Information can be accessed in seconds; important when you are paying between $1.50 - $2.00 per minute for "connect" time. It is worth the expense, though, because you can glean information in seconds from *Artquest*, which you could not gather from guide books, after weeks of investigation.

I subscribe to *Artquest*, and wholeheartedly recommend it to any active art dealer, collector, appraiser, or auctioneer. Any novice to computers can learn to use *Artquest* successfully in a very short time. For more information call or write:

Artquest
Art Sales Index, Ltd.
Pond House
Weybridge, Surrey KT13 8SP
England

TELEPHONE: Weybridge 56426
TELEX: 946240 CMEASY G

Note: Although the *Artquest* database is located in London, you can access it easily by using a local packet switching network. The literature you recieve from *Artquest* will explain it more thoroughly.

IMPORTANT AMERICAN ART AUCTION HOUSES

Here is a list, by state, of those auction houses which sell a large volume of artwork each year. A good number have in-house art specialists who do the research on each consignment and see that they are properly catalogued.

If you are considering consigning your art to auction, send a clear color photograph (the larger the better) with a description of the piece to several of the auction houses listed below. Make sure you tell them that: " I am interested in possibly consigning to you the enclosed work of art. Could you please send me an estimate of the price you feel my (painting, drawing, watercolor, or whatever) might realize at your auction, and please advise me if it would be suitable for one of your upcoming sales."

Please keep in mind, most *major* auction houses today will not accept a single consignment unless it is valued at over $500. Check the policies of each, when you initially contact them. In general, the commission rate charged the consignor will fall between 6% and 20%. The more valuable your piece, the lower the commission should be.

CALIFORNIA

Butterfield & Butterfield
220 San Bruno Avenue
San Francisco, CA 94103
(415) 673-1362

Sotheby's
308 North Rodeo Drive
Beverly Hills, CA 90210
(213) 274-0340

CONNECTICUT

Mystic Fine Arts
47 Holmes Street
Mystic, CT 06355
(203) 572-8873

DISTRICT OF COLUMBIA

Adam A. Weschler and Sons
905 E. Street NW
Washington, DC 20004
(202) 628-1281

ILLINOIS

Chicago Art Gallery
20 West Hubbard Street
Chicago, IL 60610
(312) 645-0686

MARYLAND

C.G. Sloan & Co.,Inc.
4950 Wyaconda Road
Rockville, MD 20852
(202) 468-4911

MASSACHUSETTS

Richard A. Bourne Co., Inc.
Box 141
Hyannisport, MA 02601
(617) 775-0797

Robert C. Eldred Co., Inc.
Box 796 1483 Route 6A
East Dennis, MA 02641
(617) 385-3116

Robert W. Skinner Inc.
Route 117
Bolton, MA 02116
(617) 779-5528

Philip C. Shute Gallery
50 Turnpike Street
West Bridgewater, MA 02379
(617) 588-0022

James R. Bakker
370 Broadway Street
Cambridge, MA 02139
(617) 864-7067

MAINE

Windjammer Gallery
128 Main Street
Bar Harbor, ME 04609
(207) 288-4247

Young Fine Art Gallery, Inc.
P.O. Box 313
North Berwick, ME 03906
(207) 676-3104

MICHIGAN

DuMouchelle's
409 East Jefferson Avenue
Detroit, MI 48226
(313) 963-6255

Frank Boos Gallery
420 Enterprise Court
Bloomfield Hills, MI 48013
(313) 332-1500

MISSOURI

Selkirk Galleries
4166 Olive Street
St. Louis, MO 63108
(314) 533-1700

NEW YORK CITY

Christie, Manson & Woods, International
502 Park Avenue
New York, NY 10022
(212) 546-1000

Sotheby's Parke Bernet Inc.
1334 York Avenue
New York, NY 10021
(212) 606-7000

Christie's East
219 East 67th Street
New York, NY 10021
(212) 570-4141

Phillips Son & Neale, Inc.
406 East 79th Street
New York, NY 10021
(212) 570-4830

William Doyle Galleries
175 East 87th Street
New York, NY 10028
(212) 427-2730

OHIO

Wolf's Auction Gallery
13015 Larchmere Boulevard
Shaker Heights, OH 44120
(216) 231- 3888

PENNSYLVANNIA

Fine Arts Co. of Philadelphia
2317 Chestnut Street
Philadelphia, PA 19103
(215) 564-3644

Samuel T. Freeman & Co.
1808 Chestnut Street
Philadelphia, PA 19103
(215) 563-9275

TEXAS

Texas Art Gallery
1400 Main Street
Dallas, TX 75202
(214) 747-8158

Western Heritage Sale
1416 Avenue K
Plano, TX 75074
(214) 423-1500

IMPORTANT AMERICAN ART DEALERS

The following is a short list of reputable art dealers with whom I am familiar. If you decide to sell or buy your artwork through a reputable dealer, at a fair price, consider contacting one, or more, of the following.

For a more comphrehensive list of other reputable art dealers, both here and abroad, please refer to *The 1986-1987 International Directory For Collectors* sold by *Art & Auction* magazine (paper, 232 pages, @ $10.00). Order through: *Art & Auction*, 250 West 57th St., Room 215, New York, NY 10019.

AMERICAN 18TH, 19TH AND 20TH CENTURY ART

WEST COAST

Petersen Galleries
332 N. Rodeo Dr.
Beverley Hills, CA 90210
(213) 274-6705

Goldfield Galleries
8400 Melrose Avenue
Los Angeles, CA 90069
(213) 651-1122

De Ville Galleries
8751 Melrose Avenue
Los Angeles, CA 90069
(213) 652-0525

MIDWEST

R.H. Love Gallery
100-108 East Ohio Street
Chicago, IL 60611
(312) 664-9620

Keny and Johnson Gallery
300 East Beck Street
Columbus, OH 43320
(614) 464-1228

EAST COAST

Henry B. Holt
21 Village Drive
Montville, NJ 07045
(201) 316-8883

Vose Galleries of Boston, Inc.
238 Newbury Street
Boston, MA 02116
(617) 536-6176

Hirschl & Adler Galleries,Inc.
21 East 70th Street
New York, NY 10021
(212) 535-8810

Kennedy Galleries
40 West 57th Street,5th Floor
New York, NY 10019
(212) 541-9600

Wunderlich & Co. Inc.
41 East 57th Street
New York, NY 10022
(212) 838-2555

Graham Gallery
1014 Madison Avenue
New York, NY 10021
(212) 535-5767

Alexander Gallery
996 Madison Avenue
New York, NY 10021
(212) 472-1636

Brown - Corbin Fine Art
115 Newbury Street Suite 404
Boston, MA 02116
(617) 267-5295

Currier's Fine Art
P.O. Box 2098
Brockton, MA 02403
(617) 588-4509

Coe Kerr Gallery
49 East 82nd Street
New York, NY 10028
(212) 628-1340

AMERICAN MARINE

Karl Gabosh
P.O. Box 142
Princeton, MA 01541
(617) 464-2093

AMERICAN ILLUSTRATORS

Judy Goffman Fine Art
18 East 77th Street
New York, NY 10021
(212) 744-5190

AMERICAN FOLK ART

Hirschl & Adler Folk
Director: Frank Miele
851 Madison Avenue
New York, NY 10021
(212) 988-3655

Marguerite Riordan
8 Pearl Street
Stonington, CT 06378
(203) 535-2511

Steven Score, Inc.
159 Main Street
Essex, MA 01929
(617) 768-6252

Olde Hope Antiques, Inc.
Edwin Hild
Box 209, Route 202
New Hope, PA 18938
(215) 862-5055

Frank & Barbara Pollock
1214 Green Bay Road
Highland Park, IL 60035
(312) 433-2213

Peter H. Tillou Fine Arts
Prospect Street
Litchfield, CT 06759
(203) 567-5706 (CT)
(813) 472-6794 (FL)

America Hurrah Antiques
766 Madison Avenue
New York, NY 10021
(212) 535-1930

Jay Johnson
America's Folk Heritage Gallery
1044 Madison Avenue
New York, NY 10021
(212) 628-7280

CONTEMPORARY ART

M. Knoedler & Co., Inc.
19 East 70th Street
New York, NY 10021
(212) 794-0050

Fischbach Gallery
24 West 57th street
New York, NY 10019
(212) 759-2345

The Pace Gallery
32 East 57th Street
New York, NY 10022
(212) 421-3292

Andre Emmerich Gallery
41 East 57th Street
New York, NY 10022
(212) 752-0124

Allan Frumkin Gallery
50 West 57th Street
New York, NY 10019
(212) 757-6655

Marlborough Gallery
40 West 57th Street
New York, NY 10019
(212) 541-4900

BIOGRAPHICAL RESOURCES

The following is a list of those references that deal specifically with American artists. The prices for these references may vary between $40 and $120.

- *Rediscovering Some New England Artists 1875-1900*, Rolf Kristiansen and John J. Leahy, Esq.
- *The Card Catalog of thr Manuscript Collections of the Archives of American Art*, Scholarly Resources Inc. (10 vol)
- *Dictionary of American Artists, Sculptors and Engravers*, Mantle Fielding, edited by Glenn B. Opitz
- *Dictionary of Women Artists*, Chris Pettey
- *Folk Artists Biographical Index*, George H. Meyer
- *Artists of the American West*
- *Who's Who in American Art*, Jaques Cattell Press
- *Dictionary of Contemporary American Artists*, Paul Cummings
- *Index of Artists*, Daniel Trowbridge Mallett (2 vol)
- *Dictionary of American Artists, Sculptors, and Engravers*, William Young
- *The New York Historical Society's Dictionary of Artists in America*, Groce and Wallace
- *Dictionary of American Artists of the 19th & 20th Century*, Alice Coe McGlauflin
- *Who Was Who in American Art*, Peter Hastings Falk
- *Concise Dictionary of Artists Signatures*, Jackson
- *Dictionary of Marine Artists*, E.R. Brewington
- *Women Artists in America*, Glenn B.Opitz
- *American Women Artists 1830-1930*, The National Museum of Women in the Arts
- *The Dictionary of Woman Artists (Born before 1900)*, Chris Petteys
- *American Women Artists From Early Indian Times To The Present*, Charlotte S. Rubinstein
- *Dictionary of American Artists*, F. Levy

- *The Boston Athenaeum Art Exhibition Record 1827-1874*, R. Perkins and W. Gavin III
- *National Academy of Design Exhibition Record 1861-1900*, Maria Naylor (2 vol)
- *Dictionary of American Artists*, Alice McGlauflin
- *American Art Analog*, Zellman
- *A Biographical Index of American Artists*, Smith
- *Olana's Guide to American Artists* (2 vol.), Olana
- *Encyclopedia of American Art*, Milton Rugoff
- *Index to Artistic Biography*, Patricia P. Havlice
- *Biographical Sketches of American Artists*, Helen R. Earle
- *The Concise Dictionary of Artists' Signatures*, Radway Jackson
- *The Classified Directory of Artists' Signatures, Symbols, & Monograms -American Artists*, H. H. Caplan
- *The Society of Independent Artists*, Clark S. Marlor
- *Painters of the Humble Truth - Masterpieces of American Still Life*, William H. Gerdts
- *American Impressionism*, William H. Gerdts
- *The Illustrator in America 1880-1980*, Walt and Roger Reed
- *Art and Artists of Indiana*, Mary Q. Burnet
- *19th Century Louisiana Painters and Paintings*, Martin and Margaret Wiesendanger
- *Artists of Early Michigan*, Arthur H. Gibson
- *New Hampshire Scenery - A Dictionary of 19th Century Artists of New Hampshire Mountain Landscapes*, Catherine Campbell
- *Provincetown Painters: 1890's to 1970's*, Everson Museum of Art
- *Artists in Virginia Before 1900*, R. Lewis Wright
- *The Boston Painters 1900-1930*, Ives Gammel
- *Artists In California 1786-1940*, Edan Milton Hughes
- *Artists of the American West*, Doris Ostrander Dawdy
- *Illustrated Biographical Encyclopedia of Artists of the American West*, Peggy and Harold Samuel
- *Publications in Southern California Art*, Nancy Moure (3 vol)
- *Plein Air Painters of California: The Southland*, Ruth Westphal
- *Plein Air Painters of California: The North*, Ruth Westphal
- *California Artists 1935-1956*, Dewitt Clinton McCall
- *Artists of the Old West*, Ewers
- *Masterworks of California Impressionism*, The Morton H. Fleisher collection
- *Contemporary Western Artists*, Harold Samuels

Agencies

The leading resource, nationally, for biographical information is the National Museum of American Art, Washington, D.C. (a division of the Smithsonian Institution). It offers comprehensive details on American Paintings executed before the year 1914. Researchers can visit in person or make inquires through the mail. I have reproduced below the information available from the Smithsonian with regards to the Museum.

The *Inventory of American Paintings Executed Before 1914* is a computerized index listing over 230,000 records of paintings in public as well as private collections throughout the nation. Information is indexed by artist, owner, location, and subject matter. Complementing the descriptive indexes is an Image File of approximately 45,000 photographs and reproductions which are available for study in the inventory office.

The *Peter A. Juley and Son Collection* of approximately 127,000 photographic negatives documents works of art and artists. located in New York City and specializing in photography of fine arts, the Juley firm which was active from 1896 to 1975 produced many negatives of art historical significance. They recorded works of art now lost, destroyed, or altered in appearance. Preliminary computer indexing of the collection has been completed. Negatives will be made available in the NMAA Slide and Photograph Archives.

The *Smithsonian Art Index* was initiated in 1976 by the National Museum of American Art to identify and to record works of art - drawings, prints, paintings and sculpture - in Smithsonian divisions which were not part of the museum collection. The Index was designed as a research tool or directory to a vast amount of material that had been overlooked by or was largely unknown to scholars and the public. A total of 9,565 records representing 207,208 objects in the Smithsonian Institution is indexed by artist, division, donor/source, and subject.

The *Slide and Photograph Archives*, a facility for the visual documentation of American art, consists of approximately 60,000 35mm color slide and 200,000 photographs and negatives. Slides and photographs are available for research on the premises and a smaller collection of 12,000 slides is available for borrowing by the public.

The *Pre-1877 Art Exhibition Catalogue Index* is a computerized project to index information from over 700 rare catalogues of exhibitions which were held between 1790 and 1876 at art unions, museums, state fairs, auctions, commercial galleries, and lotteries in the United States and Canada. When completed, the Index will provide valuable information on individual artists, patrons, art organizations, media, and subject matter as well as on the histories of specific works of art that my no longer be extant.

The *Permanent Collection Data Base*, a computerized listing, provides information on the over 30,000 objects in the museum's permanent collection. The object records in the data base are indexed by artists, title, medium, department and other classifications.

THE ARCHIVES OF AMERICAN ART

The Archives of American Art which have seven offices nationwide, are another very important source of biographical material on American artists. The following are their locations and telephone numbers.

Boston, Massachusetts	(617) 565-8444
Detroit, Michigan	(313) 226-5744
Houston, Texas	(713) 526-1361
New York City	(212) 826-5722
San Francisco, California	(415) 556-2530
San Marino, California	(818) 405-7849
Washington, D.C.	(202) 357-2781(Headqtrs)

If you live in New York City, a wealth of art resources can be found in *The Frick Art Reference Library*, located at:

10 East 71st Street
New York, NY 10021

(212) 288-8700

Last, but not least, are the fine arts departments around the country in our major public libraries and museums.

APPRAISAL ORGANIZATIONS

If you have need of an art appraiser, be sure he or she is a member in good standing of one of the respected appraisal organizations, nationally. Here are your leading sources for qualified appraisers. Always ask for references.

The Appraisers Assoc.
of America
541 Lexington Avenue
New York, NY 10022

(212) 867-9775

The American Society
of Appraisers
11800 Sunrise Valley Drive
Suite 400
Reston, VA 22070

(703) 620-3838

The Art Dealers Association
575 Madison Avenue
New York, NY 10022

(212) 940-8590

The New England
Appraisers Assoc.
104 Charles Street
Boston, MA 02114

(617) 523-6272

The Intr'nl Society
of Appraisers
Box 776
Hoffman Estates, IL 60195

(302) 882-0706

In addition to the list above, the *major* auction houses also have appraisal services.

AUTHENTICATION SERVICES:

The Art Dealers Association will be helpful when you need an expert to authenticate a valuable work of art.

The International Foundation for Art Research (IFAR) provides an authentication service for valuable works of art. For more information on all their services, write or call:

IFAR
Executive Director
46 East 70th Street
New York, NY 10021

(212) 879-1780

PAINTING CONSERVATORS

The following list of painting conservators was compiled with two important criterion in mind : that they either be members of *The American Institute for Conservation of Historic and Artistic Works (AIC)*, and/or that they come highly recommended by reliable professionals in the trade. Although *AIC* members agree to abide by *AIC's Code of Ethics and Standards of Practice*, the author and *AIC* cannot guarantee compliance with this code, and do not professionally endorse any member on the list which follows. Because of limitations of space, only a representative sample of conservators has been compiled from the United States and two foreign countries. Only telephone numbers are given. Please remember, the simplest and safest approach to take in finding a competent conservator is to get a referral from a reputable art gallery or museum. If you would like a complete list of *AIC* members, send for the *AIC Directory*(217 pages)($20 plus $1.75 postage). It also lists conservators of paper, textiles, photographs, furniture, and more - over 2000 members in all.

AIC
3545 Williamsburg Lane, N.W.
Washington, D.C. 20008

Telephone: 202-364-1036

CALIFORNIA

Greaves, James L.	(213) 857-6161
Lohnert, Andrej	(213) 436-1341
Lorenz, Richard	(415) 929-1240
Minguillon, Emilio	(619) 726-4665

CONNECTICUT

Goring, Ruth Walker	(203) 572-8873

DISTRICT OF COLUMBIA

Page, Arthur H. IV	(202) 333-6269

FLORIDA

Putnam, Harold	(305) 567-5870

INDIANA

Phegley, Monica Radecki	(219) 287-0266

LOUISIANA

Bessor, Louise C.	(504) 241-2587

MARYLAND

Archer-Shee, Audrey Z.	(301) 822-0703
Caraher, Josepha	(301) 435-7275
Dennis, Alexandra	(301) 986-1296
Jones, Sian B.	(301) 433-0038
Klatzo, Cornelia	(301) 530-0880

MASSACHUSETTS

Abrams, Linda M.	(617) 272-8391
Brink, Elise	(617) 566-5252
Coren, Simon	(617) 394-1416

MICHIGAN

Plaggemars, Howard O.	(616) 396-6607

MISSOURI

Larson, Sidney	(314) 445-2058

NEW JERSEY

Duff, Suzanne	(201) 228-9701
DeFlorio, Dante	(201) 744-2640

NEW MEXICO

Munzenrider, Claire	(505) 982-4300

NEW YORK

Bronold & Winnicke	(212) 982-3416
Farancz, Alan M.	(212) 563-5550
Katlan, Alexander	(718) 445-7458
Scott Jr., John C.	(212) 714-0620
Van Gelder, Mark E.	(607) 547-5585
VoorHees, Alan Lee	(607) 739-7898
West Lake Conservators, Ltd.	(315) 685-8534

RHODE ISLAND

Bosworth, David	(401) 789-1306

SOUTH CAROLINA

Dibble, Ginny Newell	(803) 254-1640

TEXAS

Kennedy, Ellen D.	(713) 520-1808
Rajer, Anton	(806) 655-7191
Van Slyke, Angelo	(713) 520-1808

VIRGINIA

Clover, Cecile	(804) 973-8126

WASHINGTON

Harrison, Alexander	(604) 732-5217

WISCONSIN

Rajer, Anton	(414) 457-3056

CANADA

Harrison, Alexander	(604) 732-5217

NEW ZEALAND

National Museum Library
Private Bag
Wellington, New Zealand

Additional References

PAINTING CONSERVATION:

- *The Care of Pictures*, George L. Stout
- *The Cleaning of Pictures*, Helmut Ruhemann
- *Conservation and Scientific Analysis of Paintings*, Madelaine Hours
- *The Restorer's Handbook of Easel Painting*, Gilberte Emile-Male
- *A Handbook on the Care of Paintings*, Caroline K. Keck

AID IN DATING PAINTINGS:

- *Antique Picture Frame Guide*, Richard A. Maryanski
- *Book of Picture Frames*, Grimm
- *Frames in America, 1700-1900: Survey of Fabrication, Technique and Style*, William Adair
- *American Costume 1840-1920*, Worrell
- *Two Centuries of Costume in America 1620-1820*, Alice M. Earle
- *Costume and Fashion: A Concise History*, James Laver
- *Treasury of American Design*, Clarence P. Hornung
- *American Artists' Material Suppliers Directory - 19th Century*, Alexander W. Katlan

Important Notes

Important Notes

Important Notes

Important Notes

Important Notes

Important Notes

Important Notes

Important Notes

Important Notes

Important Notes

Important Notes

Important Notes